AF608259

CONTESTED SPACES, COUNTER-NARRATIVES, AND CULTURE FROM BELOW IN CANADA AND QUÉBEC

Contested Spaces, Counter-narratives, and Culture from Below in Canada and Québec

EDITED AND INTRODUCED
BY ROXANNE RIMSTEAD
AND DOMENICO A. BENEVENTI

UNIVERSITY OF TORONTO PRESS
Toronto Buffalo London

Toronto Buffalo London
utorontopress.com

ISBN 978-1-4426-2990-5

Library and Archives Canada Cataloguing in Publication

Contested spaces, counter-narratives, and culture from below in Canada and Québec / edited and introduced by Roxanne Rimstead and Domenico A. Beneventi.

Includes bibliographical references and index.
ISBN 978-1-4426-2990-5 (hardcover)

1. Canadian literature (English) – 20th century – History and criticism.
2. Canadian literature (English) – 21st century – History and criticism.
3. Canadian literature (French) – 20th century – History and criticism.
4. Canadian literature (French) – 21st century – History and criticism.
5. Space in literature. I. Rimstead, Roxanne, 1953–, editor II. Beneventi, Domenic, 1970–, editor

PS8101.S63C63 2018 C810.9'38 C2018-903703-2

University of Toronto Press acknowledges the financial assistance to its publishing program of the Canada Council for the Arts and the Ontario Arts Council, an agency of the Government of Ontario.

Canada Council for the Arts Conseil des Arts du Canada

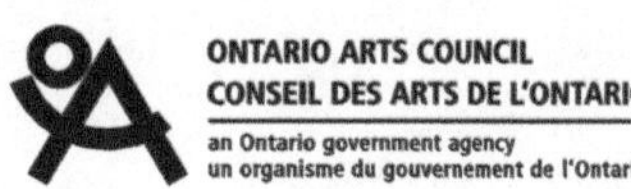

Funded by the Government of Canada Financé par le gouvernement du Canada

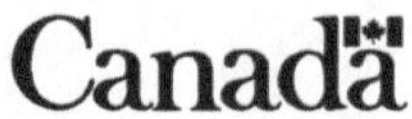

We dedicate this volume to Ben-Zion Shek (University of Toronto) and to Antoine Sirois (Université de Sherbrooke), pioneers in the study of social realism, urban space and fiction, and comparative Canadian literature.

Contents

Acknowledgments

The editors would like to thank all the contributors to this volume as well as all the scholars, academics, graduate students, and activist and community groups who participated in numerous conferences, speaking series, and research groups that originated this groundbreaking study. We would also like to acknowledge the Social Sciences and Humanities Research Council (SSHRC), FQRSC, the Université de Sherbrooke, and the CELAT (UQAM) for their financial assistance in organizing several conferences, speakers' series, and other collaborative projects, as well as manuscript preparation. Other essential forms of collaboration nourished this extended study on space, including that between literary scholars from across Canada and from abroad and local activists and community projects of recovery, cultural memory, and protest (ATSA, Action terroriste socialement acceptable; the CRIP, Centre de recherche en imagerie populaire / Research Centre in Popular Images at UQAM, and l'Autre Montréal). The importance of the contributions of community organizations cannot be emphasized enough, for such groups are at the front lines of making visible that which hegemonic social forces, neoliberal economic policies, and discourses of exclusion attempt to hide.

Special thanks go to our valued research collaborator Simon Harel, who coedited a linked volume with us in French (*La Lutte pour l'espace: Contre-récits et la culture d'en bas*, Laval University Press, 2017) and who invited us to join his FQRSC research group Zones de Tension: Expressions de la conflictualité dans les littératures canadiennes et québécois (2007–11). Previous versions of two articles by Rimstead and Beneventi were published in the online journal *Formules/Arcade* edited by Jean-Jacques Thomas in 2010 (NYU Buffalo). We would like to acknowledge Alain Régnier's diligent final proofreading of the manuscript.

CONTESTED SPACES, COUNTER-NARRATIVES, AND CULTURE FROM BELOW IN CANADA AND QUÉBEC

Introduction: Reading Space through Conflict

ROXANNE RIMSTEAD AND DOMENICO A. BENEVENTI

Reading contested spaces involves taking into account stories about who has the right to space; who wishes to contest those claims; how spatial conflict is lived and remembered; how space feels to those being contained, excluded, policed, or erased; and how space imprints future possibilities as well as past histories over time. Moreover, the same concrete, symbolic, and social spaces can be experienced differently by multiple subjects at various times, depending on social position, cultural roots, and perceptions. Indeed, space is not merely an empty place that can be claimed and occupied differently by each subject; it is itself produced differently by varying sets of practices, meanings, and social relations, enacted by diverse subjects or by the same subjects over time. Henri Lefebvre reminds us that "any space implies, contains and dissimulates social relationships – and this despite the fact that space is not a thing but rather a set of relations between things (objects and products)" (82–3). That space is a process, and a relational one at that, means that mobility is central to an analysis of how subjects occupy space over time. Arguably, however, our current obsession with mobility and fluidity (Bauman, Appadurai, Castells) as a mark of the complexity of space-time and urban flows within modernity and postmodernity masks the containment and lack of options experienced by many minority subjects. Often a lack of mobility indicates limited possibilities in the present or the past, but also the limited perception of future possibilities among people who have little spatial power within a given social system. Similarly, mobility may also, ironically, signal a lack of agency in the sense that for certain populations (such as homeless vagrants, street kids, prostitutes) conspicuous urban visibility may lead to endangerment, violence, or arrest.

According to David Harvey in *Spaces of Hope*, thinking about space and the possibility of producing alternative spaces or of using space otherwise in the present or the future is in part circumscribed by the repeated performance of older notions of space. The inability to find shared social projects and grounds for contestation is rooted in the limits on imagination, solidarity, political action, and conflict ingrained in our thoughts and practices as well as in concrete and embodied spaces (17). Harvey contends, "The inability to find 'an optimism of the intellect' with which to work through alternatives has now become one of the most serious barriers to progressive politics" (17). The essays in this collaborative collection are socially engaged to varying degrees and seek to inject a certain "optimism" in reading practices by focusing on conflicted and conflictual spaces that are often naturalized, forgotten, or unseen and unheard of within Canadian literary and cultural studies. This charge of a lack of academic attention to conflictual spaces may seem misleading since social historians and sociologists have dealt extensively with precisely these issues. Yet literary and cultural studies in North America are, however, generally behind the social sciences in the critique of social inequity based on economic privilege. Despite the "spatial turn" in theorization across the disciplines in the 1990s, a number of the spaces of poverty and dispossession have been neglected in literary analysis for over four or five decades now.

Our corpus in this collection comprises the spaces of representation in novels, short stories, autobiographies, and journalism, but also in other forms of performance that are not circumscribed by textuality, such as theatre history, popular memory, urban activism, housing, tramping, and slumming, as well as the articulation of a national or a global imaginary, thus highlighting spaces that are conceptual, imagined, built, embodied, performed, and lived rather than merely textual. Several articles are engaged efforts to reread material geographies of economic and class exclusion beside postcolonial, feminist, multicultural, and global concerns, while others are more focused on the analysis of spaces of representation *as* representation. Many of the articles also keenly analyse how embodied subjects inhere in physical spaces and their symbolic representation; indeed, if the populations under scrutiny in this collection are, in various ways, exposed to the elements and to the social discourse that seeks their erasure, their vulnerable positions as subjects from below are often marked upon their bodies. The analyses of contested spaces presented in this book take into account the way imagined spaces inflect material spaces such as bodies and built environments, and vice versa, in the tradition of pioneering work in human geography by Henri Lefebvre and more recently by David Harvey. Yet beyond the divisions between the imagined and the material world made early on in historical materialism, we are interested primarily in decoding spaces in terms of the new materialisms: for example, feminist materialism, cultural materialism (culture from below), discursive materialism (counter-narratives), and materialities of embodiment, of public art, and of social movements themselves.

Our claim to do materialist analysis, however, does not mean we are focusing uniquely or even primarily on "class, capital, and status" in every chapter since less than a quarter of the essays discuss capital or capitalism per se. This older and more traditional concept of historical materialism has been expanded in this collection by taking into account practices of embodied and personal space, practices of the space of memory and discourse, inner and human geographies as well as physical geography – in other words, both symbolic and material practices of space. Indeed, it is a strength of this collection that it does not isolate readings of class and capital from other forms of socially produced space and identities. In this collection, we consider how space and power are intricately intertwined in local landscapes, in individual lives, and on national and global scenes, often marking or defining embodied subjectivities of self and other, as well as both material and imagined spaces. We are also actively reaching across linguistic barriers, national borders, conceptual categories, communities, and silences to reread canonized texts and authors beside new voices and newly recognized or remembered performances of contested spaces. Pluralism in this respect is not idealized and harmonious but vexed and conflicted. Spaces of contestation imply disagreement, debate, dissent, and non-concurrence within and beyond the nation as opposed to the ideal of multicultural pluralism as harmonious diversity and celebratory difference (Mackey, *House*). Yet the negative connotation of words like "conflict," "dispute," "disagreement," "debate," "dissent," and "non-concurrence" cannot lock our study into notions of fragmentation as impasse, for these sites of contestation are places where differences are aired, negotiated, struggled over, performed, remembered, survived, and exposed in the hope that knowing conflict is a viable way of living conflict more progressively.

A number of recent studies of space in literature make a strong distinction between space and place, but one that testifies to widely shifting definitions. However, our focus in this collection is more concerned with the social production of meaning around space than the traditional notion of place as a fixed, identifiable, or mapped location. Timothy Cresswell explains in his authoritative overview of place that the pendulum continues to swing back and forth between different schools and trends in human and cultural geography, which prioritize one concept over the other as a category of analysis (*Place*). There is no longer any clear consensus on the distinction between the two shifting and porous concepts of space and place. In the late 1990s, for example, many geographers began favouring place over space as a category of analysis, but they expanded the notion of place to mean a process or a way of seeing rather than merely a fixed, named, or mapped location as it had often been identified previously. For some geographers and philosophers, the use of "place" replaced the entire concept of socially produced space as conceptualized by Lefebvre; and for others "place" reintroduced the local and concrete into readings of fluid, more abstract "space." However, in this book we are using both a traditional and restricted notion of place – as built, topographical, named, fixed, and/or "mapped" structures and locations – and place as symbolic and discursive meaning beyond mere location and place as internalized by individuals positioning themselves in identitary ways (Harvey, "Space"; Cresswell; Casey; Pile and Thrift). The discussion of place is most pertinent to an article on Indigenous space and the territorial imperative of remapping Indigenous space (Dagenais), and articles on specific neighbourhoods, streets, or parks in Montreal, Toronto, and Vancouver (Simon, Harel, Bentley, Smart, Rimstead). But, once again, we are more interested in the social production of these spaces/places alongside their concrete effect on human subjects as a region or neighbourhood than on their imprint as mapped places or regions. Space, and space-time (Massey, Harvey) in particular, are more often pertinent to our authors' inquiries into contested spaces as socially constructed, as our title suggests, while place tends to be more pertinent to the discussion of regionalism, *géopoétique*, and analyses which are largely phenomenological. In short, place is often the focus of analyses which highlight the influence of place on the human subject and the way the essence of the human subject is revealed through practices of place-making and of marking/mapping place (Casey). Contested spaces emerge as more fluid than places, as the process of competing social forces, often hidden, behind the designation of place, so that place becomes "a conditional form of 'permanence' in the flow of space and time" (Cresswell regarding Harvey, *Place* 57).

The reflections on contested spaces and culture from below in this volume are focused mostly on Canadian and Québécois literatures and cultures, with special emphasis on transnational and migrant subjects. Our task has been to decode the spatialization of power and the power of spatialization in literary and popular counter-narratives by and about working-class subjects, domestics, the homeless, displaced and declassed migrant subjects, poor or once-poor women, prostitutes, protestors, the unemployed, and activists, not to mention francophones adrift in an anglophone sea or First Nations subjects and communities contained by a settler nation. Of course, it is perhaps ironic that one of the largest countries in the world, with one of the lowest population densities, represents space as so contested in our literatures, and that certain conflicts are rendered invisible by naturalizing the spatialization of power. While postcolonial and Indigenous studies have succeeded in exposing the spatialized violence of settler-invader colonialism, there have been relatively few literary studies that expose class, status, and capital as underlying forms of spatialized power in Canada. And this is precisely why it is so important to learn to read otherwise, in order to revisit contested spaces and to make meaning out of these ongoing struggles.

Contestation does not always announce itself as such, nor is it always what it announces itself to be; it is often necessary to decode contested spaces as a means of making the terms and consequences of struggle more evident, rescuing contestation from organized forgetting, understanding its politics, and contextualizing the spatial issues at stake. Nor does contestation around the use of space always come from below, for it is part of an ongoing struggle between those with power over space, who wish to keep it or control it, and subalterns or emerging subcultures who wish to redefine space through counter-cultural practices. Contestation also occurs as a form of negotiation, appropriation, forgetting, hybridity, or co-optation of one's very own position and does not always imply a binary. Depending on the system of power controlling a particular space, the way one contests that control may entail complex and ambivalent struggles over racialized, gendered, or classed spaces; within urban, rural, or para-urban spaces; across symbolic, embodied, or concrete spaces; in relation to Indigenous or colonial spaces; and even within the interior space of one's own psyche.

Contested spaces are those spatial practices over which we struggle even while we construct and perform them. As implied in the notion of struggle, contestation comes from various positions, but it is not always revolutionary or progressive. For example, in Western society, municipal governments have, for quite some time now, declared war on the homeless in parks, shopping arcades, train stations, and other public spaces through the enactment of "Safe Street Acts" and other forms of repression and policing. As Rosalyn Deutsche notes in *Evictions: Art and Spatial Politics*, the hegemonic version of the correct use of public space as a park for recreational practices defines public good in the interests of propertied subjects who already own a place to lay their head but need a space for recreational use. Authorities often contest the claims of unpropertied and homeless subjects to use these public spaces as a haven, or place of rest, or a non-recreational campsite (as in tent cities). Government authorities often stage the harmonious use of public space by prohibiting and silencing alternative uses of public space, suppressing the spectacle and even the notion of conflict over space. Deutsche was a pioneer in arguing that conflict over public space is not simply a threat but a fundamental way of creating public space. Hegemonic practices define public space and the public good through contestation of the spatial practices of urban Others.

With this collection we unmask the power relations behind the social production and the cultural reproduction of space through the following vectors of shared meaning: contested urban space, counter-narratives and spaces of the nation/state, and culture from below. The stories and performances themselves represent space and conflict from these angles. We hope to emphasize that social hierarchies, discourses, and lived spaces are frequently intertwined and relational, and thus the contestation of one space very often leads to the contestation of another.

Part I: Contested Urban Spaces

The turn to examine the global city and the mobile, transnational subject may be premature if we are not yet able to recognize the logic of capital at closer range, not only in the social production of the city but also in the very psyche and the embodiment of the walker in the city. Vantage point and subjectivity shape the perception and practice of space as much as concrete structures. More importantly, however, concrete and symbolic spaces, capital included, shape each other in complex ways. In the first section of this collection, we analyse stories and counter-narratives about contested urban spaces in the form of contained spaces for the homeless, liminal spaces between linguistic communities, urban ghettos as alternative social spaces, the forced mobility of migrancy, iconic streets and markers that divide spaces, and locally contested spaces of globally orchestrated mega-events. In all of these stories of urban space, one finds the struggle to create new possibilities and new voices from below, despite containment by older forms of spatialized power.

We have come a long way towards the analysis of urban spaces since Justin D. Edwards and Douglas Ivison wrote in their collection *Downtown Canada* in 2005 that we needed to challenge dominant "stereotypes and prevalent myths which associate Canadian culture and identity with small towns, vast woodlands, and unruly terrains, in short, with the non-urban myths which persist" (12–13). Today, urban analyses dominate our literary readings of space. Increasingly, articles on contested urban space and culture from below have begun to emerge (see, for example, Kit Dobson on struggle work in Toronto and Glenn Deer on Asian mappings of Vancouver). In Québec, a new form of *géocritique littéraire* has emerged over the last decade, most notably in the work of Christiane Lahaie, which studies the relation between lived and imaginary spaces. Early works in Québécois literature read the city in materialist ways against a backdrop of both social realism and semiotic analysis. Two of the earliest materialist analyses of urban fiction in Québécois literature, Antoine Sirois's *Montréal dans le roman canadien* (1968) and Ben-Zion Shek's *Social Realism in the French-Canadian Novel* (1977), were seminal texts on urban space that were unparalleled in English Canada until decades later. A special issue of *Studies in Canadian Literature* called *Writing Canadian Space*, edited by John Ball, Robert Viau, and Linda Warley in 1998, ushered in a more theoretical analysis of space than studies of regionalism and urban literature had previously offered in English Canada. Lisa Chalycoff's contribution to that collection recommended drawing on Lefebvre's work for future, more nuanced studies of regionalism, and indeed, the study of urban fiction in English Canada first appeared under the rubric of regional literature, such as Toronto or Vancouver stories. The present collection is not in this tradition of regionalism with its focus on place more than space, or even in the important revival of that field in the last ten years (see works by Alison Calder in English and by Daniel Laforest in French, for example), although there is overlap in some cases where the importance of contestation emerges in regionalist analyses. The attention to space has mushroomed and sprouted hybrid experiments such as Doug Ivison's virtual online tour of literary Canada and his recent article on place in Lynn Coady's work; criticism by Tony Tremblay on place and space in Maritime fiction, especially in David Adams Richards's imagining of the Miramichi; and a number of important works on postcolonial and feminist approaches to space and place.

The turn towards the examination of space in Québécois and Canadian literary criticism since the 1990s is part of a generalized fascination with space and spatial theory internationally, influenced by the urban studies and human and social geographies of Henri Lefebvre, David Harvey, Michel Foucault, Michel de Certeau, Edward W. Soja, Doreen B. Massey, Nigel Thrift, Derek Gregory, David Sibley, Richard Sennett, and Saskia Sassen, among others. Equally important for the study of space in the literature of a settler nation are the rereadings of space, discovery, colonization, and indigeneity in the Americas that have rearticulated notions of territory and worldview (for example, see Mignolo, Coombes et al., Little Bear, McCall, McKegney, Roth, Bryant). In Canada and Québec thus far most of the recent literary and cultural inquiries have tried to strike a balance between materialist analysis and imagined space and communication flows as the locus of emerging urban identity (Straw and Boutros; Nepveu and Marcotte; Edwards and Ivison; Ball, Viau, and Warley; Simon). To varying degrees, critics have stressed discursive and semiotic analysis beside or above historical and materialist critique: for example, readings of regionalism and place (Riegel and Wyile; Ball et al.), of symbolic and inner space (Schaub), of cultural space (Cavell), and of transnational space (Kamboureli), as well as a plethora of works on postcolonial space and genre (New, Sugars, Moss). The impetus behind many of these contemporary studies of space has been the need for more inclusive practices of nation space that take into account the voices of excluded or devalued subjects, but there is still a need for greater attention to the capitalist reproduction of space in order to read culture from below in Canada.

Beyond any particular school of theory on space, it is the contestation of space that provides the common note among these chapters. At times the authors in this collection invoke established theories of the social production of space (Lefebvre, Harvey), the socio-dynamics of embodied space (Hall, Foucault, de Certeau, Grosz), and the undecidability, liminality, precarity, and porousness of space (Bhabha, Massey, Sibley). The contextualization of spatialized conflict is key to understanding the way space is won or lost, whether through historical materialism or the story of inner geographies and subjectivity or the exposure of the social politics involved in contested public spaces and public memory, especially when the cultural politics of capitalism remain unspoken. The recovery of minority voices and memory brings rigour and texture to these studies and shows how imaginary spaces and material spaces work in concert, producing new spaces or reinforcing and reproducing traditional ones. A groundbreaking aspect of this collection is the discussion and analysis of Canadian and Québécois spaces, side by side, across linguistic boundaries. Challenging the two solitudes of linguistic divides is as important as exposing other hidden spaces that have not been adequately examined in previous literary and cultural studies scholarship in Canada: flophouses and "slums," shantytowns and urban alleyways, underground spaces and peep shows, inner-city urban parks and hostels, bourgeois national memory and working-class subjectivity, and the idealized space of multicultural pluralism against the conflicted spaces created by Indigenous people, minority ethnics, women, the poor and the working class, and social activists.

Preparing the space of Vancouver for the global mega-event of the Olympics involved clearing away unwanted populations of the poor, the homeless, and urban activists in order to "embed Vancouver into global capital by using land and space as a raw exportable resource" (Derksen). Drawing upon the work of Henri Lefebvre, Michel Foucault, Guy Debord, and David Harvey, Jeff Derksen argues that a number of artists and activists enacted subversive forms of "publicness" that not only questioned the ways in which the Olympic Organizing Committee and city officials transformed large areas of Vancouver into a patchwork of secured zones but also interpellated the public in elaborating the possibilities of critique. The sense of possibility arising from such spatialized conflict draws attention to the dialectic between the possible and suppressed, according to Derksen. The marketing of Vancouver on the world stage demands the elision of its "still unsettled colonial past," as First Nations communities contest the appropriation and development of Indigenous lands for global spectacle. This smoothing out and erasure of urban conflict in official discourse is a form of silencing, and if the mega-event distorts public space, it also allows for the emergence of different forms of publics that critique gentrification, development, and governance. Departing from the work of Michael Warner, Derksen identifies the emergence of negative publics as "a series of acts rather than a community or tendency that fits into the existing fragmented and competitive public sphere[s]."

Constricted spaces can symbolize both protection and confinement, and Amaryll Chanady unpacks how these spaces operate within the dwellings, workplaces, and trajectories of immigrants in the city. In her discussion of the abject spaces that immigrants often occupy, she suggests the symbolic aspect of subterranean spaces in the city and how these represent immigrants' lowly status and restricted opportunities.

The city is symbolized as a body, with its privileged above-ground urban dwellers living and working in office towers while underground spaces are occupied by those who do the invisible work at the bottom of the socio-economic hierarchy. These "solidarities and exclusions" operate between different groups in intra-ethnic alliances and conflicts. She points out that space is not just a "contested commodity" but a complex process affected by "personal memory, group dynamics, class, and ethnicity, as well as concrete spatial configurations." Chanady examines both material and physical spaces as well as the symbolic or imaginary spaces of immigrant communities, suggesting that immigrant fiction often shows both the processual and experiential aspects of enclosed spaces; that is, the "lived experience" of embodied everyday life framed by the larger structural and historical dimensions of the spatial.

Montreal's iconic Boulevard Saint-Laurent, traditionally imagined as the dividing line between the English and French solitudes, is the street along which generations of immigrant communities were absorbed into the city's social, linguistic, and imaginary landscapes. Sherry Simon revisits one the most iconic streets in Canada to show how recent anglophone writing takes up the mythology of Boulevard Saint-Laurent while displacing its neat linguistic and cultural bifurcations, blurring and transgressing the borders between English and French languages and communities. If in the past traversing the divided spaces of the city "carried ... heavy ideological agendas" in terms of the cultural or linguistic tensions between English and French, seen, for instance, in the "crosstown journey," where marginal characters move within and outside of these linguistically coded spaces with their own different purposes – introducing new forms of contested meanings and practices tied to class identities, cultural memory of migrancy, linguistic mappings of the city, and sexuality.

Rawi Hage's *Cockroach* (2008) is a novel that traces the urban wanderings of an Iranian immigrant during a Montreal winter as he comes to terms with his traumatic past and his present economic insecurity. Rita Sakr focuses on liminality as a form of spatialized conflict by discussing how Hage's depiction of the underground of the declassed migrant comprises "implicit or explicit violence" – marked upon the traumatized bodies and psyches of the exiled community, in the violence of economic exploitation, and in the transnational violence of arms deals. The narrator's unpredictable – and at times unlawful – movements above and below the material and imagined city become a form of resistance to institutionalized spaces and identities, refiguring the city from the vantage point of disparate communities, rewriting "the unclean," as they are too often represented, back into "the structures of an exclusionary and tabooed modernity" (see p. 102).

Simon Harel rearticulates the condition of homelessness as a form of "*laisser-aller*": a lack of restraint or coming undone of the body and, more importantly, of the psychological and emotional matrix of the individual. Using the example of Place Émilie-Gamelin in Montreal, a space which has a history of charity and asylum for the "less fortunate," the excluded, and the socially undesirable, Harel argues that a complex and holistic understanding of homelessness is overlooked in contemporary urban theories of sociability and in urban planning. Drawing on the psychoanalytic theories of Jacques Lacan and D.W. Winnicott, who figure the unconscious as a "container," receptacle, and matrix, Harel shows how the meanderings of the homeless in novels by Kobo Abe and Robert Majzels foreground social habitus, whether depicting a lack of sympathetic habitus for the homeless in Montreal or its undoing or inversion in the figure of the "box man" in Tokyo. The cultural mobility that is evidenced in spaces of transit in the city of spectacle is mirrored by the physical, cultural, and class immobility of the unhomed. Harel reads particular forms of urban "laisser-aller," whether it be in a Montreal transformed into an "extraordinary encyclopedia," whose palimpsest layers evidence a "rarified public space" of passage, or in the metropolis of Tokyo, where "the constraints of the urban habitus" are called into question. The lack of a fixed address suggests the inability to inscribe one's identity upon the habitus of the city.

From open contestation in the streets to the phantasmagoric inner travels of homeless or migrant subjects, otherwise limited to constricted urban spaces, these readings of urban spaces reveal a continuum of possibilities for seeing the city otherwise; for example, in anger and in hope. Likewise, the challenging and remaking of public space and urban icons (such as Boulevard St Laurent, *le quartier* Saint-Henri, the cardboard box of a homeless man, or the junkyard) reveal not only the spatialization of conflict between city authorities and urban activists or street people, but also the way popular and literary imaginaries navigate lived spaces over time and hold them open to interrogation and to change.

Part II: Counter-narratives and Spaces of the Nation/State

It is impossible to pry apart discursive and material spaces since they construct each other reciprocally, but many contemporary discussions of discourse in Canadian literature have tended towards abstraction and the formal properties of discursive resistance such as irony, inversion, and deconstruction rather than the groundedness of discourse in historical, discursive, visual, feminist, or embodied materialities. Over several decades there has been an overarching and troubling tendency to avoid, if not erase, class conflict and economic hierarchy within the capitalist nation when analysing the spaces of Canadian counter-narratives. The essays in this section, focused on counter-narratives, attempt not to render counter-discourse as simply determined by material conditions, but to show how language and thought are shaped by, and in turn shape, spatialized conflict in the context of various forms of cultural hegemony. Counter-discourse is thus considered as a spatialized practice. Talking back or failing to talk back against linguistic, class, gender, and racial marginalization lead the subject into discursive struggle over space, but while the struggle itself is often waged over discursive space to testify or to be heard, the gestures and consequences of discursive contestation are profoundly rooted in embodied and concrete spaces. Although the term "counter-narrative" is frequently heard these days, it is actually undertheorized, with many critics simply giving a nod to Michel Foucault or Gilles Deleuze and Félix Guattari as a way of authorizing the concept.

Counter-narratives are essential for contesting and positioning the self and social movements, on both a micro and a macro level, as a complex form of relational resistance (versus a binary opposition) against master narratives, resistance that takes place within the space of social interaction (Bamberg). It is perhaps for this reason that much of the current theorization of counter-narrative as spatial practice is emerging in the social sciences rather than the humanities. Counter-narratives often function to externalize internalized oppression and, for women, this means a dual system of production under patriarchy and capitalism, which often includes unsayable knowledge of women's affective and embodied space (Marion Young, Godrej, Grosz). Youth also perform counter-narratives as a creative force to disrupt normative discourses and create spaces of protest (like the Occupy movement) against spatial and cultural exclusion (Walsh; Giroux). Migrant and displaced subjects also deploy counter-narratives as a way of resisting dislocation and finding a home or of protesting being "out of place" at home (Stanford Friedman 2004; Cresswell, *In Place*). Counter-narratives may also take the form of the visual (Rose, *Visual Methodologies*) or of performance or event (Bamberg; Harter et al.; Nicholls) as well as the verbal and textual, for example, in the case of counter-mapping and territorial claims made by Indigenous subjects (Roth). In the interdisciplinary tradition of cultural studies, we have considered these multiple notions of counter-narrative in this collection to include, alongside stories, other forms of narrative such as performance and public events like demonstrations and parades, ideological or embodied positioning, counter-memory and memory space, artistic interventions, and other cultural practices not always circumscribed by verbal or textual parameters.

Recalling Lefebvre's seminal thesis on the social production of space, for example, we note how the material interests that order space are often hidden from view to naturalize the hegemonic order they reproduce. Likewise, memory is a force behind the present and future ordering of space. Pierre Nora was right to speak of *lieux de mémoire* as complex sites of spatial practice rather than merely a symbolic or abstract mirror reflecting past uses of space. In a discussion of the triad of space in Lefebvre's work, Stuart Elden shows how lived space is a complex third space between the polarities of conceived space (representational and idealist) and perceived space (pure materialism). Memory acts are lived spaces that eschew the extremes of abstract and material and are reducible to neither because they are both at once. Memory intervenes in lived reality as much as it is shaped by that reality, and it is thus itself lived space rather than merely a mirror image of that space. Furthermore, as Elden suggests of Lefebvre's use of lived space, perceived and conceived spaces meet within lived space because the inner subjectivity of human subjects is as much a part of socially produced space as built environments are.

Counter-narratives (gestural, embodied, visual, event-based, and memory acts, as well as textual and verbal forms of stories) comprise different forms of contestation that are material as well as discursive, not only because they are rooted in socially produced spatial relations, but also because they affect and shape the social production of the world so powerfully (Laclau and Mouffe, Cloud, Bamberg). In particular, counter-narratives have the power to expose and unsettle the often hidden spatial order of the social world that divides subjects into above and below (Harvey, Sennett, Sibley, Lefebvre, Marion Young, Rose). Socially marginalized individuals and groups from below deploy counter-narratives to challenge hierarchies and reposition themselves within imagined and lived space as a way of understanding but also of acting on the world.

Alan Filewod argues that early interventionist political performances in Canada often took to the street or other public venues outside of the theatre, and these alternate spaces of performance – linked, for example, to labour parades, union outings, satiric lectures, and temperance meetings – need to be taken into account in order to revise Canadian theatre history. Filewod's work, itself a counter-narrative to previous tales of theatre history that focus on a narrower conception of theatre as institution, recovers memory and voices of alternative spaces in early Canadian theatre. These theatrical moments can themselves be read as contested spaces, invested not exclusively in dissent so much as in collective encounters from below, encounters in the form of aesthetic spectacles, traditional rituals, troubled politics, and even, at times, performances of ordered master narratives such as masculinity and Whiteness. Filewod rereads class in Canadian theatre history through the space of unruly performances outside of theatre houses: "Interventionist theatre has always been multiple, unruly, and for the most part unremarked, performing in a boundary zone where theatre as a social communication meets and refuses 'the theatre' as a disciplinary regime." Filewod goes on to examine how deep divisions and ambivalence characterized the very space of the theatre and the distribution of seats on the basis of race and status. He calls for and indeed inscribes a counter-history of theatre in Canada that follows theatricality from the stage to the box office to the street and back again in order to find unremarked spaces of unruly contestation through class and masculinity.

Contestation of gendered spaces for women has usually been a more interiorized practice than that of masculine cultural performance in response to the restrictions on women's movement and visibility in public space and in matters of the state. Mary Jean Green examines how women's experiences of being silenced tend to be lived out privately, in personal space, but nonetheless spaces permeated by anti-colonial, nationalist, and independence movements that too often leave women behind. The autobiographical novels of France Théoret and Assia Djebar stage the traumatic silencing of young women in terms of verbal and spatial interdictions in patriarchal societies. The striking depiction of two very similar suicide attempts in the life writing by women from Québec and Algeria, respectively, at moments of significant social and political change gives rise to the suspicion that this autobiographical parallel may indeed be more than coincidental. Indeed, shared near-death experiences of jumping from a moving streetcar and under one are read by Green as symbol and symptom of the silencing of women in emergent postcolonial and nationalist moments. They are the self-destructive forms of contestation, made possible within muted spaces. Emancipatory rhetoric often scapegoats women's roles, rights, and political voice in the push for a male-coded nationalist or religious agenda, be it in terms of "the limitations imposed on Algerian women by a rigid and unbending interpretation of their own Muslim tradition" or in terms of an anti-colonialism in Québec that provokes the rigidification of traditional religious and cultural values. In both Théoret's and Djebar's works, the public street serves as the stage upon which women express their extremely private distress. When the public display of violence is turned inwards to take the form of attempted suicide in the streets, the spatial interdictions against women circulating in public spaces and the social conventions that have bound them to silence in the domestic sphere stand accused. We will return to the theorization of feminist materialities later in this introduction when discussing culture from below, but at this point it is important to note that the interior geographies etched by gender are rooted in both micro and macro-politics of space, and thus intimately grounded in the spatial practices of colonial oppression and anti-colonial rebellion, as we shall see in Deena Rymhs's discussion of the nation-making exploitation of Indigenous masculinities during wartime in contrast to the lived sense of national (un)belonging among Native war veterans.

For Indigenous subjects, talking back as a form of counter-memory in relation to nation space has the potential to disrupt the dominant discourse of a settler state and its designations of space. Deena Rymhs's "For King and Country? War and Indigenous Masculinity" examines the agentive power of counter-narrative in respect to spatialized conflict over territory, national memory, and Indigenous identity. Rymhs shows how testimonies, interviews, poems, and other literary representations, most notably Joseph Boyden's prize-winning novel *Three Day Road* (2005), have unsettled the assumption that extraordinarily high rates of enlistment in active military service by Aboriginal men in Canada and the United States was primarily a result of loyalty to king and country. Rymhs's article on Boyden was submitted to this collection before the 2016–17 scandal around Boyden's right to speak for Indigenous subjects as a writer who may have exaggerated his Métis roots. Ironically, the novel itself has since become a contested space for the representation of Indigenous subjectivity and the experience of marginalization, forgetting, and appropriation in terms of the memory space of nation. As in several other essays in this collection, however, Rymhs is analysing a spatial configuration that presents itself in the form of fiction, historical fiction to be exact, rather than autobiographical or testimonial claims of authenticity. Whether or not the author is judged an authentic Métis speaker, the novel itself is a well-researched and strikingly beautiful rendition of male warrior spirit appropriated and deformed within the nation space of a White settler society. It will be interesting to see if future editions of the novel or Boyden himself alters this space of enunciation in view of disputes over appropriation and authenticity.

Racism among the ranks before, during, and after their military service left many Native subjects feeling as though they were fighting for an "enemy nation." Rymhs suggests that the construction of Aboriginal masculinity was a key element in Indigenous soldiers' complicated motivation for fighting in "foreign wars" and in their high rate of decoration for valour. The embodied space of battle and the effect that pressures of trauma had on the manliness of Indigenous soldiers, especially given the parallels between colonial and military rule, invite reflection on the contested space of Native masculinities, as Rymhs documents through her own critical counter-history: "Examining masculinity in the charged context of war illuminates the pressure that colonial, patriarchal models of male identity put on tribal notions of manhood." From this contested space of masculinity and national belonging, after the First World War in particular, arose highly activist Indigenous movements, spearheaded by Indigenous veterans who were effectively treated like throwaways because they did not receive the same recognition, veteran housing, or pensions as their non-Native counterparts.

While current readings of urban Indigenous identities carry us beyond the dichotomy of the Indigenous subject and the nation, we are becoming aware of more and more unfinished business between Natives and nation space in terms of redress, land claims, and border issues, not to mention Indigenous subjectivity. From the outset, critical readings of Indigenous space in Canadian literature tended to focus on the position of Indigenous subjects within colonial space, whether material or imagined, since both are reciprocal. Gradually, attention focused on how colonial space had mapped the settler nation over Native lands, and hence how Indigenous subjects and their relationship with the land were being displaced and forgotten. Increasingly, however, critics of Indigenous writing have begun to explore the different ways in which Indigenous subjects have inhabited space and place, both before and after colonization, according to Indigenous ways of knowing the land and Indigenous subjectivity. Locating oneself in respect to a sense of belonging and a custodial filiation towards the land (rather than ownership of the land as property), and thus knowing oneself through a symbiotic relationship with the land, may exceed the usual connection drawn between identities and a connection to place, not necessarily in intensity but in the nature of knowing involved and its spatial roots and consequences. For example, more recently work has emerged, both internationally and in Canada, on reading custodial versus proprietary representations of inhabiting the land (McCall; Roth); on pan-American sensibilities, border thinking, and spaces of hybridity and Métissage based on territory, kinship, and identity (Mignolo; Mignolo and Tlostanova; Anazaldua; Trudeau and McMorran); and on animistic and reciprocal notions of belonging to the land according to Indigenous cosmologies (Bryant; Little Bear). But Indigenous knowledge of the land is not to be idealized, for it is still often rooted in and circumscribed by settler imagination of entitlement, property, and settler structures of feeling (Mackey, *Unsettled Expectations*). Both essays on Indigenous writing in this collection address issues of Indigenous identities and space in terms of embodied memory and national (un)belonging.

As Rachel Bryant commented in her analysis of "cartographic dissonance," the contested spaces between Indigenous subjects and the settler nation arose fundamentally through a clash of geographies rooted deeply in opposing cosmologies: "Europeans refused to recognize the demands and cultural practices of Native space – or to respect the terms of another functioning geography – they threatened to collapse the system of sustenance that was so crucial to the physical and spiritual well-being of all" (Bryant 24). In "Jagged Worldviews Colliding," Leroy Little Bear concurs that while all collective world views are contested from within any given group, there are fundamental differences between non-Native and Native ways of inhabiting space based on different ways of knowing the land. Since European world views are based on objectivity and static views of the land, Little Bear observes, the more spiritual, holistic, and fluid way of knowing "Mother Earth" among Aboriginals is often misunderstood.

Little Bear suggests that, according to the Plains Indian philosophy of "flux," space-time is perceived and occupied differently by Aboriginals than by Europeans:

> The cosmos is observable and patterns are detected from a particular spatial location within the territory of a particular tribe. Tribal territory is important because Earth is our Mother (and this is not a metaphor: it is real) ... The Earth cannot be separated from the actual being of Indians. The

> Earth is where the continuous and/or repetitive process of creation occurs. It is on the Earth and from the Earth that cycles, phases, patterns, in other words, the constant motion or flux – can be observed. (78)

In contrast to the more materialistic, objectified, and linear visions of space-time according to European world views, Indigenous world views are "holistic and cyclical or repetitive, generalist, process-oriented, and firmly grounded in a particular place." Thus, time is dynamic and in motion, according to Little Bear, but goes nowhere. "Time just is."

Instead of mapping resource use and Indigenous territories according to Western abstractions of space, Robin Roth responds to the "challenges of mapping complex Indigenous spatiality" through a critique of abstract space that exposes its function in supporting nation states and proposes instead a counter-mapping in the form of dwelling space. (For our purposes, here, we can think of Roth's counter-mapping as a visual form of counter-narrative.) This alternative form of mapping would not be as invested in nation-building and the expansion of capital as abstract mapping, but rather in the "more-than-abstract" account of everyday dwelling space which would valorize Indigenous perspectives of space. Drawing on Timothy Ingold's discussion of the land as a place to be inhabited rather than a surface to be occupied and Henri Lefebvre's notion of space as a process that is both physical and mental, Roth proposes maps that emphasize space as multiple, subjective, and tied to spirituality: "Dwelling space is contingent on subjectivity, produced in relation (to social, political, economic processes) and through interaction (with the physical environment and with other people), and is thus material, dynamic, and multiple" (211).

Aspirational politics for Indigenous peoples spring from a geography of hope, informed not only by Indigenous knowledge and spirituality, but also by postcolonial critique (Coombes et al.). Instead of inscribing Indigenous people as heroes or victims, that is, champions of new political strategies or victims of colonial practices, more attention might be paid to the complex third spaces of enunciation (Bhabha) whereby the articulation of a sense of belonging is based on a sense of place but also takes into account that these places have been contested, occupied, and yet remain to be remade through geographies of hope (Coombes et al. 697).

A crucial element of the decolonization process, Indigenous testimonials speak a double-voiced discourse that interpolates both Native and non-Native communities in a geography of hope. In this collection, Natasha Dagenais explores the textual and discursive strategies of Aboriginal testimonial as territorial imperative in An Antane Kapesh's *Je suis une maudite Sauvagesse*, a life story which contests, in and through a bilingual text (Indigenous-French), the social, spatial, and cultural designations of the Innu of Québec. The manner in which this testimonial is laid out – with pages in the original Indigenous language, Montagnais, facing the French translation (often described as a text in parallel language or as side-by-side translation, or the dual page of translation) – challenges discursive space, disturbing the power of the colonizer's language over the Innu language. Refusing the space of minority language as object of knowledge, artefact, and trace, the testimonial allows the Indigenous subject to speak out and claim counter-narrative spaces that defy disappearance, thus suggesting the historical and political "urgency to communicate" (Beverley) to which the testimonial genre bears witness. Adding to this chain of witnessing, Dagenais provides her own translation of many excerpts hitherto unavailable in English. As this cultural testimony demonstrates, the story witnesses dispossession because, otherwise, there is no space from which to be heard. Moreover, the tropes and conventions of traditional Aboriginal storytelling are refigured as textual strategies of counter-narrative in Kapesh's testimony, characterized by circular time and orality, and providing a challenge to Western ideas of truth-telling and historical veracity. In addition to performing a counter-history through the form of retelling and making territorial claims, the testimony also performs a reappropriation of the land by remapping it and testifying to what it felt like to dwell there and to belong spiritually and bodily to that tribal territory. This aspect of the testimony constitutes a reimagining of both the territory and the community itself, a community that is "un-imagined" and silenced by the slow violence of colonization and nation space.

Perhaps the best way to understand why we are considering memory and, in particular, memory acts as contested "spaces" themselves, rather than merely symbolic representations of lived space, is to recognize how central the claims that memory makes are to spatialized conflict. Memories, whether in the form of life stories, public history, oral histories, icons, monuments, legends, or other *lieux de mémoire*, make spatial claims on the past, the present, and the future. These memory acts go beyond a representational or symbolic concern for authenticity or historical correctness; they are themselves spatial in the way they affect and colonize imaginary space and concrete territory: for example, land claims, national imaginaries, national heroes, war memorials, local identities, and exile and diaspora are both memory acts and spatial performances. Our authors address memory as materialist space rather than abstract space by considering memory's influence over the material world as well as the cultural politics of reordering spaces in the life world.

National memory tends to subsume or co-opt counter-narratives as a way of reducing the challenge posed to cultural and concrete space from the margins. Such is the fate of a radical left counter-narrative in the context of bourgeois national memory. The space of a national hero like the communist doctor Norman Bethune is subjected to a whitewashing of his contestatory politics by the bourgeois state. Candida Rifkind critiques the sanitization and co-optation of Bethune as left-wing icon of Canadian culture by first pointing out his status as "a contested signifier and an unstable sign in both liberal and leftist Canadian culture." She historicizes the contested space of his persona and his social contribution but notes that this contestation originated at least partly in his own propensity for drama and self-promotion as well as in his deeply contradictory lifestyle, divided "between his aristocratic demeanour and love of the good life versus his revolutionary politics and pragmatic self-sacrifice," contributing "to his instability as a signifier." The struggle over Bethune has re-emerged recently in former governor general Adrienne Clarkson's biography (one of three major biographies on the socially engaged doctor). Rifkind is able to decode the ideological nuances of Clarkson's recent celebration of Bethune's heroism, which inscribes him into a discourse of "global humanitarianism," while paradoxically downplaying "Bethune's revolutionary ideology as an ancillary rather than core feature of his medical practice, constructing his political commitment as a peripheral dimension of the person rather than the organizing drive." Most importantly, Rifkind observes that Clarkson's and John Ralston Saul's project to repatriate Bethune's heroism from China to Canada is "a temporal and spatial one that seeks a return to the past in order to remember the space of the nation differently."

In the late 1990s, during a period of heightened theoretical discourse on space across the humanities, human geographer Doreen Massey expressed concern that the concept of space was being emptied of its political potential, even among leading theorists, due to a tacit dichotomy between space and time. Massey's cornerstone essay on space-time (*Space*) argued that space was too often represented as static while time was conceived as the site of history and thus change. The epistemological shift suggested by Massey to address this underlying assumption (space/static versus time/active) was to begin to see space-time in terms of reciprocity rather than dichotomy. As scholars in this collection broach issues of cultural memory, body memory, historicized spatial conflict, and urban divides, the attention to space is more often than not linked to the usage and production of space over time and through time.

The struggle over concrete, discursive, and imagined space often engages the space of the legitimized state or the national imaginary, exposing and critiquing these seemingly ordered spaces of nation and the hegemonic narratives and mythologies. In the place of hegemonic nation space, counter-narratives usher in new, troubled, and disorderly alternative spaces of self- and collective representation. The capitalist settler state legitimates its ideologies through material strategies and practices in the aim of defining social discourse and those who may participate in its production. If the normalization and codification of public spaces produces the "proper" citizen who participates in the production and consumption of the marketplace, it also produces the obverse – the homeless, the criminal, the unemployed, the welfare recipient, the declassed migrant, the prisoner, the dispossessed Aboriginal, the racial and linguistic Other (Foucault). Reading culture from below, counter-discourse, and conflict does not mean essentializing new positions but rather problematizing the politics of spatialization further by reading unruly subjects and their challenge to spatialized power as ambivalent, shifting, and subversive.

Part III: Culture from Below

> (Social) space is not a thing among other things, nor a product among other products: rather, it subsumes things produced, and encompasses their interrelationships in their coexistence and simultaneity – their (relative) order and/or (relative) disorder. It is the outcome of a sequence and set of operations, and thus cannot be reduced to the rank of a simple object. At the same time there is nothing imagined, unreal or "ideal" about it as compared, for example with science, representations, ideas or dreams. Itself the outcome of past actions, social space is what permits fresh actions to occur, while suggesting others and prohibiting yet others.
>
> – Henri Lefebvre, *The Production of Space*, 73

When Henri Lefebvre first distinguished between representational spaces (lived spaces of architecture and infrastructure) as opposed to spaces of representation (written and performed notions of space), he insisted on the hegemonic role of the latter to reproduce the former. According to Lefebvre, lived and textual forms of space work in concert to produce visible space in both its concrete and symbolic forms, while also working hegemonically to mask the power structure behind relations of production; for example, by exposing bourgeois stories of space (say, recreational park space) while concealing the labour which produces them (say, the gardeners and landscapers who maintain and build the illusion of natural space and the park) or the alternative stories of using space (the homeless and their need to sleep on park benches or erect tent cities in the absence of an orderly or fair distribution of decent, affordable housing).

Stories of spatialized conflict often disclose a complex and historically contingent social logic, one that hides certain uses of space while making others publicly visible and valorized (Lefebvre). What is distinctive about this collection of essays on contested space in cultural performances is the visibility of the social logic of both class and poverty as important sets of practices in analysing who dominates space (whether, for example, housing, visual space, or the space of public memory) and how space is limited by thought as well as deed. For some time now, classed spaces and class identities have receded behind the analysis of other systems of power such as gendered, ethnic, and urban practices in literary discourse rather than appearing beside these practices as intertwined or reciprocal processes of producing space within a capitalist nation or the global market. When the dominant paradigm to explain spatial exclusion became "the margins" in the 1980s and 1990s, it usually displaced the social hierarchy of class as somehow too essentialist or too simplistic to be relevant in a "post-Marxist" age. The analysis of space in literary texts, even when focusing on minority subjects, has too often erased class dynamics and class exploitation as part of the process of social production. The normalization of class difference and spaces of capital within literary analysis and cultural studies in Canada has settled into hegemonic methods of analysing space in that the domination of space by capital seems invisible or normative even when racial or gendered domination is being critiqued.

Spaces of capital are discernable in the arrangement and imagining of bodies, houses, neighbourhoods, cities, and territories (Harvey, *Spaces*). Even our choices of how to inhabit, envision, and move through urban space tell a story of strategies and tactics of power, and these choices are delimited by an underlying story of above and below (de Certeau). Human subjects must compete for meaning and space when the flow of information, technology, and capital is prioritized by city planners and state officials in contemporary cities (Castells). Given that space is gendered and racialized as well as classed, it is the site, if not the process itself, of conflicts among bodies, hearts, and minds over public and private space (Massey, Sassen). Geographies of respect, hope, and exclusion are inscribed in both interior and exterior spaces so that they become part of our inner geographies and our inner struggles for meaning as well as material struggles with others (Sennett, New, Sibley). If we cast the net of meaning too wide in interpreting spatialized conflict, however, our questions will be too all-encompassing until they take in everything about life itself. For this reason, these essays focus on contested space and spatialized practices of contestation in selected contexts for specific subjects. Likewise, our authors have tended to select theorists who engage with issues of social justice for subjects from below, and in many cases this means engaging with theoretical paradigms based on the cultural reproduction of space (Lefebvre, Harvey, Sibley), rather than theories focused on deconstruction of dominant constructions or metaphysical notions of space. Furthermore, a number of our contributors do not base their readings in theories of space as such because their approach involves contextualizing and decoding the history and geopolitics of space as problematized in the narratives and performances themselves, rather than by theorists.

The present volume of essays practises new materialist strategies of reading space and conflict (feminist, cultural, visual, discursive, and new-historical materialism), to see beyond a pervasive cultural bias that locates the cultural in the discursive, that spurns reference to economic hierarchies, and that makes individualism and harmonious multiculturalism normative while undervaluing cultural reflection about conflict, class, and community. Evident from the past two decades of anthologies on multicultural literature and criticism in Canada is an operative meaning of pluralism grounded in ethnicity and race with a secondary glance, if any at all, to class identity and bourgeois hegemony – as if capitalism were normative and any attempt to analyse capitalist culture would be necessarily reductionist because it would be merely economist.

In attempting to understand culture from below as a complex space of marginalization, contestation, and hope, it is useful to consider multiple distinctions based on different types of spatial practices (for example, absolute, relative, relational, representational, experienced, lived, conceptualized, virtual, visual, discursive, textual, non-space, and so on), many of which are discussed by David Harvey in "Space as a Key Word." Harvey imagines what Raymond Williams could have written about "space" had he been writing his opus, *Keywords* (1976), in our time. Harvey begins with a tripartite conception of space as absolute ("a thing in itself" independent of matter), relative (existing as a relationship among objects), and relational (contained in objects that contain and represent relationships with other objects within themselves). A more concrete example of these practices of space is given by Harvey in the example of a house:

> When I look at a house, for example, I recognize it as a physical and legal entity that situates it in absolute space. I also recognize its position in relative space given its location with respect to employment, recreation, services, and the flows of people, electricity, water, and money that sustain it as a living habitat. But then I also understand its relationality to global property markets, changing interest rates, climatic change, the sense of what is or is not a historic building, and its significance as a place of personal and collective memories, sentimental attachments, and the like. What happens to the house over time can only be fully understood, I argue, by working through effects constituted through the three forms of spatio-temporality simultaneously. While this is hard to do in any easy empiricist or positivist sense, the insight that comes from such a dialectical approach are [*sic*] as exciting and innovative as they are often stunning. ("Space" 6)

To follow through with Harvey's illustration in terms of understanding the spatial practices of culture from below, we can look at the example of the slum and its objective, mapped, legal, and measured parameters as a fixed space. But this would be too flat to take into account the relative quality of the slum as a space that is positioned in relation to the city itself, its cultural centre, business, the suburb, roadways, flows of transient and second-generation inhabitants, street people, squatters, and affordable housing or lack thereof. The relationality of a slum would include practices that take into account relations themselves, such as class tourism, a sense of belonging, neighbourhood activism, urban renewal, gentrification, and a celebration of local history. Harvey then suggests that all these spatio-temporal levels analysed together compose a dialectical approach to space that is a place to begin analysis.

A number of the essays in this section on culture from below focus on the recovery of voices, memories, and figures from below (maids, "slum dwellers," neighbourhood activists, workers, prostitutes, migrants, poor families, street people, tramps, and the homeless), while all of the essays problematize the positioning of subjects in terms of above and below. This positioning of subjects is in respect to built environments, symbols of above and below, and class identities, but it is also often staged in terms of spectatorship and performance. Certain forms of knowing space and occupying space rely on this consciousness of being positioned beneath normative subjects or as lesser than dominant Others, as, for example, when we discuss class tourism and "slumming," archiving and retrieving suppressed memories from below, remembering growing up poor, selling sexual services to make a living, containment in closed spaces, and tramping.

The positioning of proper and improper bodies and spaces through the language of above and below is often determined by a discourse of slums or "slumming" that is rooted in the segregation and control of the built environment by an economic elite. The discourse of slumming has a historical genealogy that not only traces but also reproduces the distance between poor and non-poor subjects. Historically, poor-visiting and class tourism coexisted beside philanthropic and activist "descents" into urban spaces to save the poor, albeit more from themselves than from their condition. Roxanne Rimstead argues that residual forms of "slumming" haunt contemporary visits to poor neighbourhoods in Canada, whether through social realism in the slum novel or in journalistic accounts that continue to "rediscover" or unveil the poor as Other, and perhaps even in academic discourse itself when one eyes the urban Other from a distance. Ideologically, these contemporary representations of the "descent" into slums or abject spaces, such as domestic workers' lives, tend to reproduce the thrill and disdain of early class tourism, no matter how ironic or informed the slum observer claims to be about the ethical and epistemological implications of dressing up poor. Yet contemporary tenants' associations and other urban activists knowingly reappropriate the Victorian discourse of slumming in order to turn the world upside down and indict slum landlords and indifferent politicians. This essay argues for a more self-reflexive reading practice of slum novels (such as *Cabbagetown*) and reportage on poverty (such as Jan Wong's undercover Maid for a Month series in the *Globe and Mail*). Rimstead argues that the spaces of knowing we inherit and inhabit are never entirely new, but are marked by the palimpsest of time and ideologically residual; no descent into "the slums" is innocent of the past but is instead marked by previous performances, many of which the city and the nation may wish to forget as evidence of spatialized conflict.

Slumming and class tourism are often engaged in the reproduction of social hierarchies even as their practitioners momentarily enjoy a transgressive form of "passing" that positions them both inside and outside the communities they voyeuristically consume. This gaze also conflates the identities of marginalized populations with their sometimes difficult, unsafe, or even abject material living and working conditions; dirt, junk, disorder, and material residues taint slum areas and are in turn associated with those who live in them, manifesting as ascriptions of bodily disorder, a lack of discipline, potential criminality, and the taint of the morally suspect (Sibley). Recent scholarship in anthropology and human geography has examined the roles of dirt, waste, garbage, and refuse in various social and historical contexts (Douglas, Kristeva, Cohen and Johnson, Scanlan, Sennett, Ashenburg): for instance, in the ever-increasing spatial appropriations of capital as it seeks out spaces to deposit its refuse, in urban design technologies and policies that seek to evacuate waste from privileged areas of the city, in the management of material resources and residual populations in histories of colonialism, and in the racialized and classed discourses of the pure and the defiled within the modern nation state. Sibley, Ashenburg, and others have described how the logic of filth and dirt has historically been used to taint or discredit unwanted or troubling populations of racial and colonized Others, the poor and homeless, children, and women, while the fantasies of cleanliness, order, and purity are associated with Whiteness, social legitimacy, class privilege, and desirable citizenship.

Several essays in this volume approach culture from below through the representation or self-representation of female subjects who attempt to articulate what it feels like to inhabit or visit contested spaces of stigmatization and empathy, prostitution, and growing up female and poor in Montreal. The emotional (re)mapping of these gendered spaces in the city brings private and public spaces into relation, much as we see in other chapters of this collection (Green, Beneventi). But gendered spaces are about more than the social construction of the private sphere and its rootedness in public hegemonies. These contested spaces are also about new materialities – for example, embodiment, agency, mobility, gendered memories of space, the positioning of the self, and the everyday struggle to survive and redefine such spatial practices.

Feminist epistemologists have led discussions on positionality and standpoint theory in order to show how the subject's place of perception affects knowledge production and how power systems within patriarchy have traditionally undervalued ways of knowing usually attributed to women. In "The Implications of the New Materialisms for Feminist Epistemology," Samantha Frost observes, in 2011, that feminist epistemologists

> have wrested the insights of historical materialism from their basis in a critique of political economy and used them to generate a broader constructionist understanding of the creative and constraining force of human activity with respect to matter. Within this broader constructionist view, matter is more completely saturated with power: institutions, objects, and bodies themselves quite literally materialize or incorporate the imperatives that drive power relations. (73)

One of the outcomes of these new feminist materialist approaches to space is the focus on the particular versus generalized women's bodies, the micropolitics of everyday life, and the individual psyche and private, inner geographies as a basis for new forms of solidarity.

For Elizabeth A. Grosz in *Architecture from the Outside: Essays on Real and Virtual Space*, "embodiment means a multiplicity of bodies" (Eisenman xiii). "The limits of possible spaces are the limits of possible corporeality" (Grosz, *Architecture* 32). Using a Deleuzian framework, Grosz revisions architecture in terms of the bodies and subjectivities it has excluded or marginalized. Utopian projects in this sense depend upon complex and lived dissatisfaction with the past and the present rather than totalizing visions of the future. "After it is built, structure is still not a fixed entity. It moves and changes, depending on how it is used, what is done with and to it, and how open it is to even further change" (6). The "messiness" of feminist materialism lies partly in this willingness to take into account the diversity of bodies and the complexity of space, its temporality, and its transgressive potential. There is a reassuring concreteness to feminist materialism and feminist politics that will not forget lived lives and that question the omissions of abstractions.

At the nexus of classed and gendered experiences of embodied space are prostitutes as both subjects and objects. The iconization of the prostitute is key to decoding culture from below and to interrogating how we position certain bodies as abject or as vilified bodies expelled from socially acceptable space. Sherene Razack has argued that stories of prostitutes are often grounded in spatial journeys, wherein the White middle-class woman researcher journeys into the space of degeneracy and shame of the prostitute via storytelling, but that the latter remains unscathed by this movement from "good-girl" into "bad-girl" space and often defines it positively as a space of work and agency rather than a space of violence and exploitation where hierarchies of classed and racialized bodies rule through hegemonic masculinity (352–7). As Patricia Demers argues in our collection, a reconsideration of prostitutes' stories should take into account "their physical, social, and readerly locations" within red-light districts, whereby the everyday occupation of the immoral space of the city may constitute a form of agency that puts them at odds with the regulatory forces of patriarchy and capitalism but that also entraps them in a space of sexual violence. Demers offers a thoughtful overview of writings by and about female prostitutes in Canadian literature, while asking trenchant questions about the meaning of the space they occupy as bodies, as subjects, and even as entrepreneurs. Her essay offers a raw yet perceptive glimpse into the underworld through writing that "challeng[es] theories of victimization and complicity and spotlight[s] both critical intelligence and enacted, at times rationalized, naiveté." Through a reading of works by Maria Campbell, Evelyn Lau, Nelly Arcan, and others, Demers traces the itineraries of dirt and desire in the city, exposing the underground passages through which both circulate. She shows how these writers expose "the correlation between spatial containment and public vulnerability, perceived objectification and total exposure," and documents how the "annihilation of the inner self" required in this form of writing is often accompanied by brutal physical transformation, injury, and death.

Given the omnipresence of *Bonheur d'occasion* (1945) for generations of francophone readers, what more is there left to say about an iconic work of urban realist fiction that has come to epitomize the marginalized spaces of the poor in Montreal's Saint-Henri district? A leading critic of English-Canadian modernism, David Bentley offers a close reading of the spaces from below in the English translation of Roy's novel, *The Tin Flute* (1989), by uncovering new meanings in architectural space, city space, and the social production of space around homelessness. Bentley rereads the highs and lows of Roy's urban landscape through close reading techniques and uncovers the "dump home" as an important imaginary space radiating both abject and subversive meanings. Through comparison with contemporary texts on squatters' spaces and homelessness, this essay goes beyond the usual discussions of Roy's seminal urban novel in presenting the city dump as an alternate social space in the Canadian national imaginary – linking it to other academic work on Africville or Tent City in Toronto, for instance – and recovering a level of spatial conflict as class subversion and class solidarity. This revisioning of culture from below resonates with articles by Simon Harel, Domenico A. Beneventi, Patricia Smart, Roxanne Rimstead, Patricia Demers, and Rita Sakr as we map the spatialized conflict of homelessness and poverty in this collection.

Textual archives and self-portraits from below often inscribe space retrospectively and relationally as the memory of "growing up poor" in a particular place or neighbourhood. Patricia Smart examines the way four women from Québec – Lise Payette, Adèle Lauzon, Denise Bombardier, and France Théoret – use the language of self to situate memories of lived space, the affective and material space of poverty, the reproduction of social habitus within the family, the gendered experiences of poverty, and their own sojourns within the poorer quartiers of Montreal. As a pioneering scholar on the emergence of the feminine in Québécois literature, Smart compares and contrasts these contemporary autobiographic writings to Gabrielle Roy's iconic urban novel *Bonheur d'occasion*, because "the geographic and psychological landscapes" they describe were mediated by the experience of "young girls growing up in Montréal in the 1930s, 1940s, and 1950s." Smart shows how all four women reproduce stereotypes of ethnic and class identity in their depictions of Québécois girlhood from below. These autobiographical works also produce divergent spaces of poverty in that each subject lives material and imaginary spaces of the poor neighbourhood as complexly inflected by identity but experienced differently as shame, rebellion, struggle, and pride. While being a woman, being Québécoise, and being poor means occupying intertwined colonized spaces, once again it is the particular that mediates the more generalized positioning of these gendered subjects.

Spaces from below are characterized by both mobility and containment, but the essays collected here argue that these spaces are, above all, contested, complex, and ambivalent. In the same way contemporary demonstrators, prostitutes, and immigrants have increasingly become the focus of hysteria over culture from below, containment, and contestation under contemporary neoliberalism, the figure of the hobo or vagabond of the Great Depression worried the spatial, bodily, and sexual practices of an emerging nation intent on codifying domesticity, labour, (reproductive) sexuality, and the movement of bodies across spaces of production, consumption, leisure, and public life. As Jody Mason argues in her study of unemployment, the "placeless vagabond proved an unattractive figure" for historians and critics who "tended to privilege place-based, realist fiction" (18) in early nationalist canon formation. Domenico A. Beneventi examines how moral panic around the dirty, dishevelled bodies of hoboes – which "inscrib[ed] onto their very bodies a symbology of dirt, sin, and moral and social corruption" – solicited increasingly oppressive forms of regimentation through spatial practices of containment and banishment, through moral discourses of charity and rehabilitation, and through the physical and symbolic constriction of dwellings and bodies. In analysing Andrew Roddan's *Vancouver's Hoboes* (2004), J.B. Vaughn's *The Wandering Years* (1975), and Jean-Jules Richard's *Journal d'un hobo* (1965), Beneventi considers texts that witness homelessness from both insider and outsider positions so as to show the discrepancies between the mainstream constructions of homelessness which efface individuality and the more complex lived experiences of homelessness that include strategies of survival, endurance, self-sufficiency, community, counter-memory, trauma, escape, and adventure. Sexuality expressed outside of the heteronormative domestic sphere was seen as aberrant. Beneventi decodes this image of perverted sexuality as it extends to descriptions of homosexuality as the "doubled image of the hobo – as homosexual predator upon the social and economic resources of the nation, and as sexual predator feasting upon its robust youth – falls in line with historical constructions of homosexuality as deviance." In Jean-Jules Richard's *Journal d'un hobo*, gender performance becomes a strategy of survival for the vagabond who is an androgynous hermaphrodite undertaking a journey across Canada. These texts show the complexities involved in the lived experience of homelessness and show how discourses of the proper and improper citizen are inflected with assumptions about gender, sexuality, class, and the performativity of the body in both public and private space.

The various power relations that order and produce space often represent value in terms of above and below according to residual forms (Williams) and world views based on status and capital, hence habitual or entrenched forms of spatialized power. When we refer to culture from below or as seen from below, we are responding to the power of this spatialization of the lived and imagined world and the need to both expose and problematize these power relations rather than naturalize them as inherent or normative.

Contested spaces and spaces of contestation encounter more than erase difference, even when exploitation is at issue, and can, consequently, become a site of optimism rather than merely critique. While certain subjects analysed in this book contest ephemeral and symbolic spaces, such as discursive space or the space of memory, other subjects contest largely spaces of representation such as life writing, novels, or spectator events like parades or theatre. Still others recount contestation in the dialectic between spaces of representation and representational spaces or built environments like slums, enclosed spaces, hobo camps, and street corners. Consistently, however, these spaces are reread as if seen "from below," not by essentializing the space of outcast or minority subjects but by exploring the social cosmologies that position certain subjects below others in terms of power, status, and value. Both the function of contestation (whether towards reconciliation, negotiation, or reform) and the style of contestation (whether performative, private, imagined, confrontational, or material) are intertwined with these varied spatial practices and are thus infinitely variable and renewable. By seeking to know this complex spatial politics, we act on an optimism of the intellect that respects the power and promise of contestation.

WORKS CITED

Anazaldua, Gloria E. *Borderlands / La Frontera: The New Mestiza.* Aunt Lute Books, 1999.

Appadurai, Arjun. *Fear of Small Numbers: An Essay on the Geography of Anger.* Duke UP, 2006.

Ashenburg, K. *The Dirt on Clean: An Unsanitized History.* North Point Press, 2007.

Ball, John, Robert Viau, and Linda Warley, editors. *Writing Canadian Space / Écrire l'espace canadienne.* Special issue of *Studies in Canadian Literature / Études en littérature canadienne,* vol. 23, no. 1, 1998.

Bamberg, Michael. "Theorizing Master and Counter-Narratives." *Considering Counter-Narratives: Narrating, Resisting, Making Sense,* edited by Michael Bamberg and Molly Andrews, John Benjamins, 2004, pp. 351–72.

Bauman, Zygmunt. *Liquid Modernity.* Polity Press / Blackwell, 2000.

Beneventi, Domenico A. "Exposed to the Elements: Homelessness in Recent Canadian Fiction." *Canada Exposed / Le Canada à découvert,* edited by P. Anctil et al., Peter Lang Publishing, 2009, pp. 85–100.

Beverley, John. *Testimonio: On the Politics of Truth.* U of Minnesota P, 2004.

Bhabha, H.K. *Nation and Narration.* Routledge, 1990.

Bryant, Rachel. "Cartographic Dissonance: Between Geographies in Douglas Glover's *Elle.*" *Canadian Literature,* no. 220, Spring 2014, pp. 116–30.

Calder, Alison. "What Happened to Regionalism?" *50th Anniversary Interventions: Special Issue of Canadian Literature,* no. 204, Spring 2010, pp. 113–14.

Casey, Edward S. "Boundary, Place, and Event in the Spatiality of History." *Rethinking History,* vol. 11, no. 4, December 2007, pp. 507–12.

Castells, Manuel. *City, Class, and Power*. St. Martin's Press, 1978.
Cavell, Richard. *McLuhan in Space: A Cultural Geography*. U of Toronto P, 2002.
Chalycoff, Lisa. "Overcoming the Two Solitudes of Canadian Regionalism." Ball et al., pp. 160–77.
Cloud, Dana L. "The Materiality of Discourse as Oxymoron: A Challenge to Critical Rhetoric." *Western Journal of Communication*, vol. 58, no. 3, Summer 1994, pp. 141–63.
– "Rhetorical Criticism for Underdogs." *Purpose, Practice, and Pedagogy in Rhetorical Criticism*, edited by Jim A. Kuypers, Lexington Books, 2014, pp. 23–37.
Cohen, W.A., and R. Johnson. *Filth: Dirt, Disgust, and Modern Life*. U of Minnesota P, 2005.
Coombes, Brad, Jay T. Johnson, and Richard Howitt. "Indigenous Geographies II: The Aspirational Spaces in Postcolonial Politics – Reconciliation, Belonging and Social Provision." *Progress in Human Geography*, vol. 37, no. 5, 2013, pp. 691–700.
Cresswell, Timothy. *In Place / Out of Place: Geography, Ideology, and Transgression*. U of Minnesota P, 1996.
– *Place: A Short Introduction*. Blackwell Publishing, 2004.
de Certeau, Michel. *The Practice of Everyday Life*. Translated by Stephen Rendall, U of California P, 1984.
Deer, Glenn. "Remapping Vancouver: Composing Urban Spaces in Contemporary Asian-Canadian Writing." *Canadian Literature*, no. 199, Winter 2008, pp. 118–44.
Deutsche, Rosalyn. *Evictions: Art and Spatial Politics*. MIT P, 1996.
Dobson, Kit. "'Struggle Work': Global and Urban Citizenship in Dionne Brand's *What We All Long For*." *Studies in Canadian Literature / Études en littérature canadienne*, vol. 31, no. 2, 2006, pp. 88–104.
Douglas, Mary. *Purity and Danger: An Analysis of Concepts of Pollution and Taboo*. Routledge, 1966.
Edwards, Justin D., and Douglas Ivison. *Downtown Canada: Writing Canadian Cities*. U of Toronto P, 2005.
Eisenman, Peter. Foreword. *Architecture from the Outside: Essays on Real and Virtual Space*, by Elizabeth A. Grosz, Massachusetts Institute of Technology, 2001, pp. xi–xiv.
Elden, Stuart. *Understanding Lefebvre: Theory and the Possible*. Continuum, 2004.
Filewod, Alan. *Committing Theatre: Theatre Radicalism and Political Intervention in Canada*. Between the Lines, 2011.
Foucault, Michel. *Discipline and Punish: The Birth of the Prison*. Vintage Books, 1979.

– *The History of Sexuality*. Pantheon Books, 1978.
– *Madness and Civilization: A History of Insanity in the Age of Reason*. Pantheon Books, 1965.
– "Of Other Spaces: Utopias and Heterotopias." *Rethinking Architecture: A Reader in Cultural Theory*, edited by Neil Leach, Routledge, 1997, pp. 330–6.
Frost, Samantha. "The Implications of the New Materialisms for Feminist Epistemology." *Feminist Epistemology and Philosophy of Science: Power in Knowledge*, edited by H.E. Grasswick, Springer, 2011, pp. 69–83.
Giroux, Henry A. "Youth in a Suspect Society: Coming of Age in an Era of Disposability." *Truthout*, 5 May 2011, www.truth-out.org/news/item/923:youth-in-a-suspect-society-coming-of-age-in-an-era-of-disposability.
Godrej, Farah. "Spaces for Counter-Narratives: The Phenomenology of Reclamation." *Frontiers: A Journal of Women's Studies*, vol. 32, no. 3, 2011, pp. 111–33.
Gregory, Derek. *Geographical Imaginations*. Blackwell, 1994.
Grosz, Elizabeth A. *Architecture from the Outside: Essays on Real and Virtual Space*. MIT P, 2001.
– *Space, Time and Perversion: Essays on the Politics of Bodies*. Routledge, 1995.
– *Volatile Bodies: Toward a Corporeal Feminism*. Indiana UP, 1994.
Hall, E.T. *The Hidden Dimension*. Anchor Books, 1966.
Harter, L.M., J.A. Scott, D.R. Novak, M. Leeman, and J.F. Morris. "Freedom through Flight: Performing a Counter-narrative of Disability." *Journal of Applied Communication Research*, vol. 34, no. 1, 2006, pp. 3–29.
Harvey, David. "The Body as Referent." *Hedgehog Review*, Fall 1999, pp. 41–6.
– *Consciousness and the Urban Experience: Studies in the History and Theory of Capitalist Urbanization*. Johns Hopkins UP, 1985.
– *Social Justice and the City*. Johns Hopkins UP, 1973.
– "Space as a Key Word." Paper for Marx and Philosophy Conference, Institute of Education, London, 29 May 2004.
– *Spaces of Hope*. U of California P, 2000.
Ivison, Doug. "Canadian Literary Cities." With Marcel Barriault. *Canada: A Literary Tour*, Library and Archives Canada, 2009.
– "'It's No Different Than Anywhere Else': Regionalism, Place, and Popular Culture in Lynn Coady's Saints of Big Harbour." *Canadian Literature*, no. 208, Spring 2011, pp. 109–25.
Kamboureli, Smaro. *Scandalous Bodies: Diasporic Literature in English Canada*. Oxford UP Canada, 1999.
Kristeva, J. *Powers of Horror: An Essay on Abjection*. Columbia UP, 1982.
Laclau, Ernesto, and Chantal Mouffe. *Hegemony and Socialist Strategy: Towards a Radical Democratic Politics*. 2nd ed., Verso, 2014.

Laforest, Daniel. *Âge de plastique: Lire la ville contemporaine au Québec.* U of Montreal P, 2016.

Lahaie, Christiane. *Ces mondes brefs: Pour une géocritique de la nouvelle québécoise contemporaine.* With Marc Boyer, Camille Deslauriers, and Marie-Claude Lapalme, Instant même, 2004.

Lefebvre, Henri. *The Production of Space.* Translated by Donald Nicholson-Smith, Blackwell, 1991.

Little Bear, Leroy. "Jagged Worldviews Colliding." *Reclaiming Indigenous Voice and Vision,* edited by Marie Battiste, U of British Columbia P, 2000, pp. 77–85.

Mackey, Eva. *The House of Difference: Cultural Politics and National Identity in Canada.* U of Toronto P, 2002.

– *Unsettled Expectations: Uncertainty, Land and Settler Decolonization.* Fernwood, 2016.

Marion Young, Iris. *On Female Body Experience: "Throwing Like a Girl" and Other Essays.* Oxford UP, 2005.

Mason, Jody. *Writing Unemployment: Worklessness, Mobility, and Citizenship in Twentieth-Century Canadian Literatures.* U of Toronto P, 2013.

Massey, Doreen B. *For Space.* SAGE, 2005.

– *Space, Place, and Gender.* U of Minnesota P, 1994.

– *Spatial Divisions of Labour: Social Structures and the Geography of Production.* Macmillan Education, 1984.

McCall, Sophie. "'What the Map Cuts Up, the Story Cuts Across': Translating Oral Traditions and Aboriginal Land Title." *Cultural Memory and Social Identity,* edited by Roxanne Rimstead, special issue of *Essays on Canadian Writing* 80, Fall 2003.

McKegney, Sam. *Magic Weapons: Aboriginal Writers Remaking Community After Residential School.* Winnipeg: U of Manitoba P, 2007.

– "'pain, pleasure, shame. Shame': Masculine Embodiment, Kinship, and Indigenous Reterritorialization." *Canadian Literature,* vol. 216, 2013, pp. 12–33.

Mignolo, Walter D. "Geopolitics of Sensing and Knowing: On (De)Coloniality, Border Thinking, and Epistemic Disobedience." *European Institute for Progressive Cultural Politics,* Sept. 2011.

Mignolo, Walter D., and M.V. Tlostanova. "Theorizing from the Borders: Shifting to Geo- and Body-Politics of Knowledge." *European Journal of Social Theory,* vol. 9, no. 2, 2006, pp. 205–21.

Moss, Laura F.E. *Is Canada Postcolonial? Unsettling Canadian Literature.* Wilfrid Laurier UP, 2003.

Nepveu, Pierre, and Gilles Marcotte. *Montréal imaginaire: Ville et littérature.* Fides, 1992.

New, William H. *A History of Canadian Literature.* New Amsterdam Books, 1989.

– *Land Sliding: Imagining Space, Presence, and Power in Canadian Writing.* U of Toronto P, 1997.
Nicholls, Walter. "Place, Networks, Space: Theorising the Geographies of Social Movements." *Transactions of the British Institute of Geographers,* 2009, pp. 78–93.
Nora, Pierre. *Les lieux de mémoire.* 2nd ed., Gallimard, 1997. 3 vols.
Pile, Steve, and N.J. Thrift, editors. *Mapping the Subject: Geographies of Cultural Transformation.* Routledge, 1995.
Razack, Sherene. "Race, Space, and Prostitution: The Making of the Bourgeois Subject." *CJWL/RFD,* no. 10, 1998, pp. 338–76.
Riegel, Christian, and Herb Wyile, editors. *A Sense of Place: Re-evaluating Regionalism in Canadian and American Writing.* U of Alberta P, 1998. Textual Studies in Canada 9.
Rifkind, Candida. *Comrades and Critics: Women, Literature, and the Left in 1930s Canada.* U of Toronto P, 2009.
Rimstead, Roxanne. "'Knowable Communities' in Canadian Criticism." *Review: Literature and Arts of the Americas,* vol. 41, no. 1, 2008, pp. 43–53.
– *Remnants of Nation: On Poverty Narratives by Women.* U of Toronto P, 2001.
Rose, Gillian. *Feminism and Geography: The Limits of Geographical Knowledge.* U of Minnesota P, 1993.
– *Visual Methodologies: An Introduction to Researching with Visual Materials.* 3rd ed., SAGE, 2012.
Roth, Robin. "The Challenges of Mapping Complex Indigenous Spatiality: From Abstract Space to Dwelling Space." *Cultural Geographies,* no. 16, 2009, pp. 207–27.
Rymhs, Deena. *From the Iron House: Imprisonment in First Nations Writing.* Wilfrid Laurier UP, 2007.
Sassen, Saskia. *Globalization and Its Discontents.* New Press, 1998.
Scanlan, J. *On Garbage.* Reaktion Books, 2005.
Schaub, Danielle, editor. *Mapping Canadian Cultural Space: Essays on Canadian Literature.* Magnes Press, 2000.
Sennett, Richard. *The Conscience of the Eye: The Design and Social Life of Cities.* Knopf, 1990.
– *Flesh and Stone: The Body and the City in Western Civilization.* W.W. Norton, 1994.
Shek, Ben-Zion. *Social Realism in the French-Canadian Novel.* Harvest House, 1977.
Sibley, David. *Geographies of Exclusion: Society and Difference in the West.* Routledge, 1995.
– *Outsiders in Urban Societies.* B. Blackwell, 1981.
Simon, Sherry. *Cities in Translation: Intersections of Language and Memory.* Routledge, 2012.
– *Fictions de l'identitaire au Québec.* XYZ, 1991.

Sirois, Antoine. *Montréal dans le roman canadien.* Didier, 1968.
Smart, Patricia. *Écrire dans la maison du père.* XYZ, 2003.
Soja, Edward W. *Postmodern Geographies: The Reassertion of Space in Critical Social Theory.* Verso, 1989.
Stanford Friedman, Susan. "Bodies on the Move: A Poetics of Home and Diaspora." *Tulsa Studies in Women's Literature,* vol. 23, no. 2, Fall 2004, pp. 189–212.
Straw, Will, and Sandra Kathleen Boutros. *Circulation and the City: Essays on Urban Culture.* McGill-Queen's UP, 2010.
Sugars, Cynthia. *Unsettled Remains: Canadian Literature and the Postcolonial Gothic.* Wilfrid Laurier UP, 2009.
Thrift, Nigel. *Knowing Capitalism.* SAGE, 2005.
– *Spatial Formations.* SAGE, 1996.
Tremblay, Tony. *David Adams Richards of the Miramichi: A Biographical Introduction to His Work.* U of Toronto P, 2010.
Trudeau, Dan, and Chris McMorran. "The Geographies of Marginalization." *A Companion to Social and Cultural Geography,* edited by Vincent Del Casino et al., Blackwell Publishing, 2011, pp. 437–53.
Walsh, Christopher S. "Docile Citizens? Using Counter-narratives to Disrupt Normative and Dominant Discourses." *Transforming Practice: Critical Issues in Equity, Diversity, and Education,* edited by Janet Soler et al., Trentham Books, 2012, pp. 125–35.
Williams, Raymond. *The Country and the City.* Chatto and Windus, 1973.
– *Marxism and Literature.* Oxford UP, 1977.

PART I

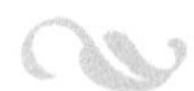

Contested Urban Spaces

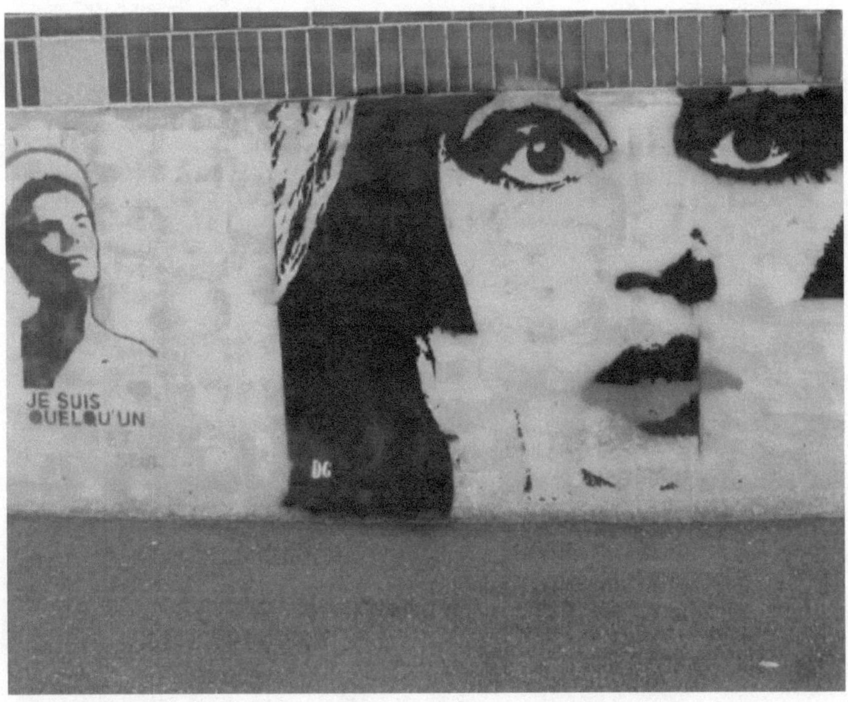

Je suis quelqu'un et seul.
Copyright Chris Erb, 2009.

1 Culture and Critique during Mega-Events: The 2010 Olympics and the Right to the City

JEFF DERKSEN

The sinuous energy of Henri Lefebvre's thought on cities is not just his understanding of space as a social practice, nor is it only his emphasis on the life and politics of the street as a defining counter-power to the "from above" urban planning that he saw impose functionality onto the city: Lefebvre also lays out a radical temporality of the city in which cities are always emerging and claiming the present, and can, through critique, grasp a future horizon. Like the Situationists, who drew their inspiration from and against him, Lefebvre argues that critique from the left specifically "attempts to open a path to the possible, to explore and delineate a landscape that is not merely part of the 'real,' the accomplished, occupied by existing social, political, and economic forces. It is a *utopian* critique because it steps back from the real without, however, losing sight of it" (*Urban* 6–7). Critique then becomes one powerful and lived aspect of the urban phenomenon and the imagining of a city.

Thought of in these terms, critique is not simply a stark or programmatic diagram that would help us understand how power functions in the city – for power is not nearly so diagrammatic despite it being grounded in places and structures. Nor is critique limited to the socially necessary act of pointing out whose voices are heard in city halls, or whose ideas are implemented, and how other, less convenient voices are pushed aside. Rather, critique is a process that is at the very heart of the urbanization of everyday life. In fact, pushed farther, critique can be proposed as a *return to life* through the attempt to "open a path to the possible" by an investigation of what negates the possible.

Critique, therefore, must be thought of broadly, as Michel Foucault does in his reworking of Trotsky's concept and Mao's slogan of "permanent revolution" into "permanent critique of our historical era" (Foucault,

"Enlightenment" 42).[1] As Judith Butler puts it, "[Foucault] maintains that the philosophical ethos of modernity involves sustaining a permanent critique of our historical era (a term that involves a transposition of the Maoist slogan of permanent revolution)" (787). And, by transposing Foucault's transposition, Butler raises the question: "Could it not be that critique is that revolution at the level of procedure without which we cannot secure rights of dissent and processes of legitimation?" (795). With critique elaborated as a permanent process aimed at securing dissent and the questioning of the solidification of legitimacy, this concept of critique intersects with Lefebvre's own permanent critique of modernity in general and modernist urban planning specifically. With this intersection of rights-based critique and a critique of modernity and governmentality as it manifests in its urban spatial regime (which itself can be seen in terms of *spatial justice*), critique shapes the relationships that we build throughout our lives *within* the city through its attention to the dialectic of the possible and the contained and of the real and the imagined. The role of critique is exactly what can make city life the most energizing and deeply affective. But critique must be turned towards affect as well when affect becomes naturalized and moves into governmentality, or as Foucault put it, "the techniques of government" ("Governmentality" 101).

In this spirit of critique, I took the event, or spectacle, of the 2010 Olympics as an opportunity to read the relationship of culture, neoliberalism, and urban development as it hit Vancouver and the everyday lives of those who live there. Over the months leading to the Olympics, and throughout the event itself, I wrote a series of columns that aimed at a theoretically informed reportage on how things unfolded, and I tried to theorize the tactics of neoliberalism as its zombie body again planted its feet in this "sustainable" and "creative" city. I sought to locate the ways in which activists, artists, and civil-society groups countered the coercion and force that produced "free-speech zones" (dubbed "protest pens"), a ban on signage that did not celebrate the Olympics, the enclosure of public spaces used by the poor and homeless, and a proposed bill that could put the homeless in shelters against their wishes (and against their rights). The effects of the Olympics on the city are still unfolding, but

1 For more information, see also Trotsky, and Raunig, "Critique."

the legacies of the forms of cultural and political resistance (or the imagination of critique) have agitated the smoother discursive surfaces of urban governmentality in Vancouver. The creative city has, perhaps unexpectedly, opened itself to wilder forms of creativity.

On the plywood cladding that encloses one of the many stalled construction sites in the city centre of Vancouver, British Columbia (BC), a spectral figure speaks from a block of posters bearing the familiar blue logo of Expo 86. This ghost from the recent past, identified as Premier Bill Bennett, addresses urbanites and tourists as citizens who have a pride of place and a civic duty: this address would be familiar only to those who recall the devastating days of British Columbia's period of neoliberalization in the 1980s. The land that the world fair was held on became the largest waterfront development in North America, yet the development miraculously produced no public profit for the city; instead, the land was passed off to developer Li Ka-shing to embed Vancouver into global capital by using land and space as a raw exportable resource.

One in a series of reproductions from the archive of Expo 86 and part of artist Jeremy Shaw's project "Something's Happening Here," this poster reiterates a government statement that coaxes citizens into the excitement of a world fair; but the address comes from the beleaguered position of a city that imagines itself on the edges of global capital, and a city that desperately wants to bring that capital in through this unmatched opportunity, a once-in-a-lifetime chance, to showcase our province to the world.

Ironically, this excited view of capitalist opportunity – which has its eyes set firmly on the present as the exceptional moment that cannot be missed, as a moment for which all stops must be pulled out – is exactly, and uncannily, the moment that the city, and its now more wary citizens, find themselves in as the 2010 Winter Olympics descend, literally, on Vancouver.

Shaw's public project is reinforced by the uncanny intersections of these two mega-event-fuelled moments in the globalization and neoliberalization of Vancouver. But these mega-events open the situated example of Vancouver beyond the global-local boosterism and city-to-city competition that neoliberalism breeds. More tellingly, these events spark Vancouver as a volatile node in the global-urban nexus in three ways. First, history and the present collide in an overdetermined manner: the still unsettled colonial past of Vancouver haunts the very notions of land and, crucially, of ownership (that bedrock of neoliberalism) through the

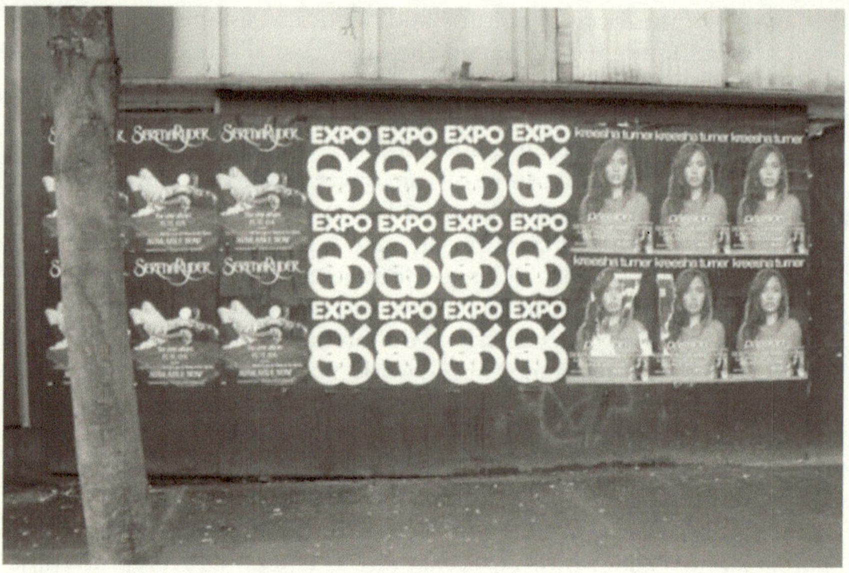

1.1 Jeremy Shaw, "Something's Happening Here."
Courtesy of Jeff Derksen.

land claims of the First Nations people. This legacy of dispossession also haunts the security of the Olympics, for the First Nations have a radical history of road blockages and standoffs, and they bear a powerful slogan, "No Olympics on Stolen Native Land." Second, the trajectory of neoliberalism raises crucial questions: what new shape of neoliberalism will be wielded by the local governments and the global players (from the International Olympic Committee to the financiers) now that neoliberalism itself is perceived to be powerful yet at the end of its long regime? How will this "dead, but dominant," as geographer Neil Smith describes it, or "zombie governance," as Jamie Peck recently called it, stumble forward? Third, there is the growing cultural question: What will be the role of culture, in this exceptional moment, in the transformation of the texture and possibilities of urban life, and in the possibilities producing a counter-discourse to the mega-event? Add areas of deep poverty and chronic homelessness; highly organized and wonderfully critical civil-society groups and activists; and a concentrated group of global elite players who have an intense engagement with real estate, urban development, and art; and Vancouver emerges as a ground zero for the conflicts on which neoliberalization thrives and for the crisis within it. The city is catalysing into a platform for new claims to that Lefebvrian rallying call "the right to the city."

The content of this series I would write could not be predicted beforehand, for this unsteady mix of actors and interests, of floating neoliberalism and grounded opposition, of activists and rights advocacy groups and the $900 million Integrated Security Unit created an event within the mega-event that could not be foreseen.

Public space in Vancouver, long since fragmented and policed and altered by the transformation of space into a speculative commodity, is now distorted by the Olympics and the push of the mega-event as a gentrifying force in the poorest working-class neighbourhood and as an acceleration of real estate as the economic engine throughout the city. While public space can be seen as a dead issue in this late neoliberal moment, with the public sphere evaporated into "3Ps" (public-private partnerships), it is this space – or this production of space – where possibilities brew. Yet the fate of the possibility and shape of particular spaces is not the key outcome; rather, it is a question of the kinds of publics (counter, neoliberal, activist, etc.) that will emerge through this struggle over space.

The political and cultural history of Vancouver is punctuated with what Michael Warner has called "counterpublics" and what Sven Lütticken has better described as the "secret publicities" of avant-gardist formations. These two acts – one that makes strange existing public space and the other more utopian in its radical futurity – are necessary at the present unsteady moment. But another form of a public is now effectively operating within the exceptional time of the mega-event. Spatializing Sianne Ngai's notion of "negative affect" that springs from a context of "obstructed agency," I think we can identify negative publics whose tactics are reactions to the clamp-down of critique and dissent and the restrictions on making space public. Negative publics can be thought of as a series of acts rather than a community or tendency that fits into the existing fragmented and competitive public sphere. Negative publicness does what counter-publics do – present oppositional discourses and refuse to be absorbed into a dominant common sense – but it also shows the limitations of existing public space and forms of publicness. As an act, negative publicness effectively tests these spatial, social, and political relations – and they have the possibility to produce space for unlikely allies and alliances.

Along with the many reactions to surveillance and enclosures in Vancouver, there have been acts of negative publicness on the cultural front. Countering the official Cultural Olympiad, "Fuck the Cultural Olympiad: Art & Anarchy" defined itself as "not an art show, but the opening of a cultural front" in direct opposition to the limits of institutionalized art. But this event also unleashed a dialectic with the possibilities of cultural critique that is social rather than institutional, a critique that has been, for the most part, soft in Vancouver. Over a four-part series of newspaper columns, I reported on the types of publics – and the cultural, social, and political acts – that emerged out of these contested, branded, penned-in, lived, and potential spaces.

The Olympics in Vancouver began by marking themselves as the "sustainable games," but more pressing social issues around housing, gentrification, and displacement quickly moved to the forefront through the push of civil-society groups and activists. Tied into an existing populist resentment towards the Olympics as a corporation and a supragovernmental organization, the pushback against the security force operating in the city and the new networks of surveillance shaped the resistance to the Games. Security felt like the dominant Olympic concern, and the urban terrain of Vancouver was fragmented, enclosed, and altered daily as blue fencing shrank the areas lived in by the city's impoverished population. At the same time, fresh surveillance cameras blossomed throughout the city, and streets were sealed as the International Olympic Committee (IOC) built a locked-down temporary city within this city. Combined with the 16,000-strong security force that was to come, the Olympics began taking on the feel of concentrated security occupation on "stolen Native land" and on urban space pulled out of daily life.

In this rapid and alienating production of space, struggles over the public sphere and public speech brewed as the types of negative public acts that I described earlier – acts that tested the boundaries of publicness – marked and contested the limitations on publicness in this time of mega-event exceptionalism. Speech acts were spatial acts in that moment, and even the rumour of an activist action caused the Olympic organizers to shift venues for events and announcements, to the point that the Olympics had little public contact. On the softer cultural front, the Cultural Olympiad produced space in ways different than the blue fencing barriers, the white tarps of temporary buildings for media, and the closed-off "red zones." Through an expansive public art program, the Cultural Olympiad was a process of "mapping and marking" the city in a rush to add more public art to "brand Vancouver." Compared to other cities, this was a belated program, but the cultural aspect of the

Olympics was not a temporary add-on designed to draw more tourists to the mega-event; instead, it signalled a highly localized programmatic shift driven by the migrating global policy of "the creative city."

The idea of the "creative city," shaped and promoted by Richard Florida, ties flawlessly into neoliberal urban governance as it caters to one class at the expense of others by proposing a cultural fix to social and economic problems.[2] This program – and Florida's heavy use of indexes of creativity – foregrounds culture in the neoliberal competition between cities and the race to brand cities around a dominating identity of creativity, identities often at odds with the city's history. With sustainability and eco-density as the new signifiers of a green consumptive lifestyle, Florida's brand of economic creativity laces human nature into Vancouver's famous and lavishly represented naturalized landscape. In this scenario, artists are not the blade of bulldozer gentrification – in fact, artists are not needed – but creativity as an economic engine becomes the rationale for gentrification. This marks a new role for culture in the new global stage of gentrification: culture is no longer only the accelerant – the starting fluid – of gentrification, leaving only a trace once its job is done, but culture is a spin-off of creativity refigured as an accumulation strategy.

Within this altered cultural landscape of the city, several new works of public art gained sharpened meaning from the Olympics context and disturbed the intention of art in the public sphere within the creative city. The public sphere has been fundamentally rearranged here, existing more as a private-public amalgam, but it was also tightly squeezed by the restriction on public speech and anti-Olympics signage that came from the IOC and the city. The IOC Charter bans any "demonstration or political, religious or racial propaganda in any Olympic sites, venues or other areas," and through clumsy city bylaws this seemed to extend to any statement negative to the Olympics, even if it was a sign in the window of this "city of glass."[3] A legal challenge to this closure of free speech was successful, but the threat remained potent. In a public artwork in the window of the new Audain Gallery in the Woodward's Building in the

2 For more information, see Peck, "Creativity Fix."

3 Even though the term "city of glass" is a relatively generic moniker, it is used for Vancouver and it also refers to Douglas Coupland's airport-bookstore-friendly book, *City of Glass* (Douglas and McIntyre, 2009).

heart of the Downtown Eastside – a site that is symbolic of the scale of transformation of the city – Ken Lum mounted a sly and effective textual work. "I Said No" was a powerful speech act of a negative public with twelve different exclamations of disagreement ranging from a simple "NO!" to "No Way Jose [*sic*]" and "No Bloody Way!" addressing the street. Contradicting the affirmative nature of most public art, "I Said No" amplified the right to say no, the very right which the IOC and the city had tried to erode. Cannily, this work relied on different public frames of meaning to give it a concrete address – it was a public work stripped of its referent, but it drew on the public to produce a particular meaning. At this site, and particularly during the Olympics, the possibilities of meaning were powerful and multiple, but I read it as a smart tactic that worked in three ways. First, it used public space to say "No!" to the erosion of the ability to say no, but, read within the dominant frame of public discourse, it was also a specific rejection of the Olympics (the very thing to which one cannot say "No!"). And third, it reflected the rejection of the many demands of housing, poverty reduction, and equity that civil-society groups and activists directed at the city and the IOC. "I Said No," with its multiple yet grounded address, is filled with public meaning.

In the courtyard directly behind this temporary work is Stan Douglas's massive photomural, "Abbott & Cordova, 7 August 1971." At a looming scale, Douglas's work is a superrealist reproduction of a riot that erupted on the adjacent street corner. Known as the Gastown Riot, this clash was really a police riot, complete with batons, helmets, and horses, as the police set upon hippies who had gathered for a "Smoke-In" to claim this area as the centre of the city's lingering sixties counterculture. Drawn from Vancouver's rich radical past of riots, the mural represents into the present *fear and expectation* of police action against anti-Olympics protesters. So, while the mural does the public-art work of cinematically commemorating a historical moment, it too was framed by the distortion of public space and the right to the city during the Olympic period.

Both of these works point to a creativity other than the narrowly defined form which the neoliberal policy of the creative city sells – and both of these works make a claim to city space. But perhaps the greatest and most creative claim to space, and the right to the city, however, came out of the restrictions on protest and speech as activists, in response to the clamp-down, devised smart and effective responses. The Olympic Resistance Network designed a series of posters that picked up on the contradictions between the Olympic Charter and the action of the IOC

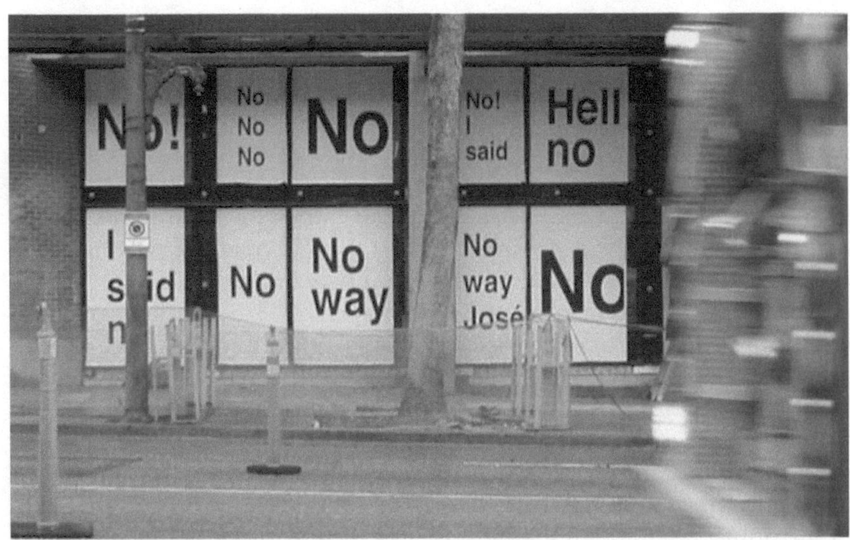

1.2 Ken Lum, "I Said No"; Audain Gallery window.
Courtesy of Sabine Bitter.

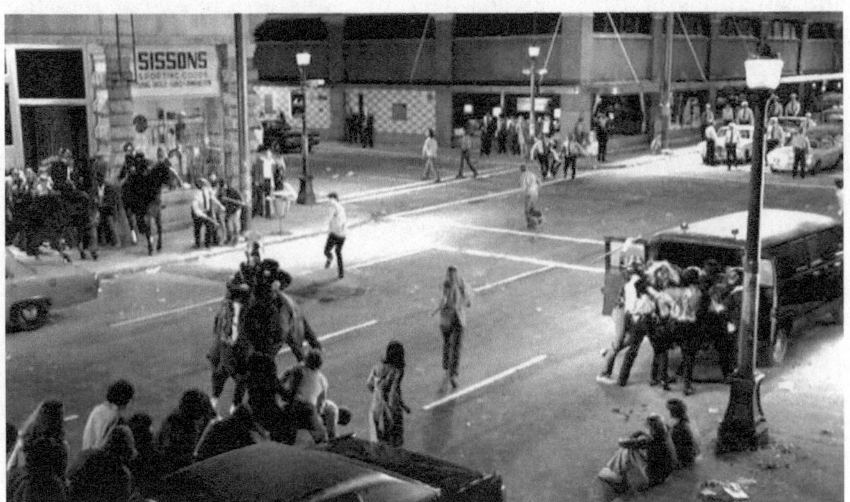

1.3 *Abbott & Cordova* by Stan Douglas and David Zwirner.
Courtesy of Douglas and Zwirner.

and its sponsors – each poster cited a contradiction and asked publicly of the IOC, "Do You Hate the Olympics?" In a semantic twist, these posters were pro–Olympic Charter, at least in the way the Charter trumpets universal human rights, but they were also sharp critiques of the actually lived Olympics. In its fanatical control of visual and textual language, the IOC alienated the Olympics from the city; on the other hand, activist groups were able to tie causes and communities together and to organize a five-day convergence timed to the Olympic opening. The expectation for those days was for a very different type of creative city.

Earlier, I reflected on the thick anticipation that the Games would occupy the city as a zombie force, clamping down and clogging up the streets with the $900 million Integrated Security Unit, the distrusted Olympic Organizing Committee (VANOC), and international tourists. Countering this, a convergence and coalition of artists, activists, civil-society groups, and social justice advocates formed a crest of opposition aiming to wrestle the city back, with all of its contradictions and possibilities, from the flat and affectless vision of the city as Brand Vancouver, a nature-drenched lure for those global citizens hoping to lay down capital in a green city vibrating with the post-Fordist pleasures of investment and tourism. But, as Henri Lefebvre opens his speculation on the events and situations of 1968, "Events belie forecasts: to the extent that the events are historical, they upset calculations" (*Explosion* 7). To rework Lefebvre for the situation of the Olympics and the explosive, affective, and annulled events throughout the city, what was forecast did not always materialize and the calculations of the opposing sides were less predictable than the lead-up promised.

But the Games hit the ground as a massive *situation* exactly in opposition to the Situationist International's sense: the situation of the Games was not meant to disrupt the familiar but to accelerate and exacerbate both the inequities and aspects of everyday life in the neoliberal city – from the enclosure of space *and* the controlled access to space, to "police presence" and the monopoly of violence, surveillance, and, most euphorically, consumption and cultural nationalism. These moments of urban disruption are not new, as Alan Filewod demonstrates in his discussion in this collection of the "gestic moments" of nineteenth-century spectatorship that strategically employed theatricality in order to enact and mobilize social critique in public and social space.

In the first week, the spectacle appeared to be heading for a disaster – the little snow for the alpine events (nature failing the natural city!), the low number of tourists, the callous reaction to the death of luger Nodar Kumaritashvili, the lack of street events without five-hour lineups, and the criticism of it all by (surprisingly!) the sports media sped up the limp boosterism based on speech acts ("It *will be* the greatest Games ever!") *and* made space for deeply moving mobilizations and effective actions. I'm tempted to build a marvellous catalogue of events that pry possibility from sleepy hegemony, but I will hold back and only highlight three before turning to the cultural scene.

The nineteenth Women's Memorial March for missing and murdered women wound through the contested areas of the city, growing to 5,000 people taking over the streets to arrive at the steps of the police station in order to call out the police on their shocking inaction. Although purposely separated from anti-Olympics marches, the event illuminated the unevenness of justice and access in the city and clashed against every official representation of Vancouver beamed globally. Also, the Vancouver Media Co-op (VMC) kicked into high gear as a space of representation of all anti-Olympics actions, from the planned to the spontaneous to the mercurial – such as the brief bridge blockage by the Salish Katzie First Nation. Generating the alternative news, VMC ignited the urgency of events and seized the representation of the present. Last, during a rally for housing, a community coalition set up the Olympic Tent Village on a lot used as a parking space for VANOC vehicles. The Tent Village ran as a highly visible symbol and as a self-managed site for several weeks – under police surveillance – and was a lever to negotiate housing for forty homeless folks who took shelter there. Unlike marches, the tactic was not disruption but *autogestion* or self-management, which as Lefebvre observes "is born and reborn at the heart of a contradictory society" (*State* 149).

The city, therefore, was not pressed down under the wet weight of surveillance, security, and mega-event euphoria, but the unevenness, the contradictions, and the possibilities of the city glowed red-hot. Within this clamour, varied cultural scenes emerged under the strategy of using the Olympics to *showcase* (a preferred verb of neoliberals) Vancouver as a localized *creative city* welcoming cosmopolitan capital. A range of tactics – from provocations and convergences to avoidances and capitulations – shaped up within the cultural scene. The capitulations were gestures of official culture that saw the Olympics as a populist opportunity – the most crunching example was spoken-word poet Shane Koyczan, performing during the truly unimaginative opening ceremony,

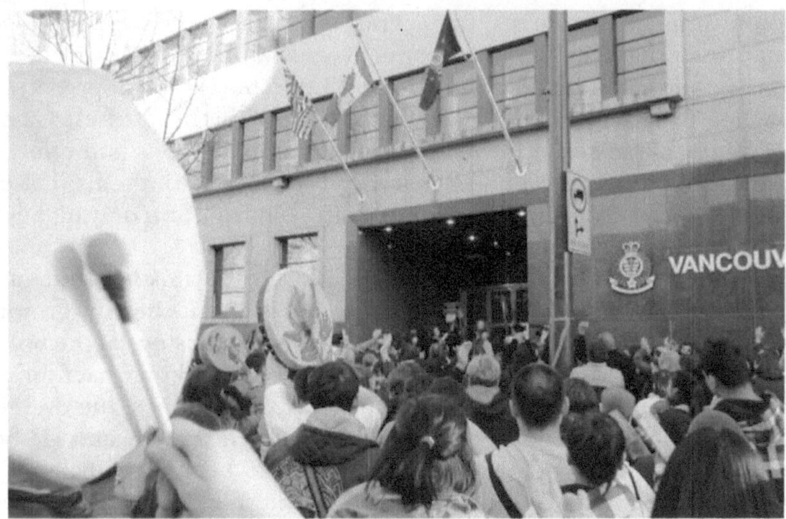

1.4 Missing Women's March, 14 February 2010.
Courtesy of Jeff Derksen.

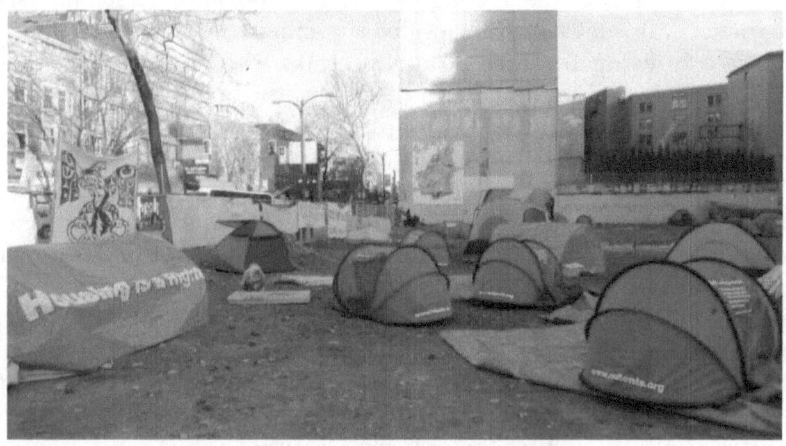

1.5 Tent Village on Hastings Street.
Courtesy of Sabine Bitter.

unloading every retrograde trope of Canadian identity.[4] In counterpoint to the forced inclusion to the situation, Artspeak Gallery mounted an effective refusal to participate with Lucy Pullen's "I Would Prefer Not To." The gallery windows were blanked out by reflective blinds that bounced light back at viewers but denied visual entry into the gallery space. For Pullen, this refusal illuminated "the blind spot in every spectacle," but the window also gained meaning within the urban landscape. Artspeak is on a gentrifying street where restaurant owners effectively blur the relationship of inside and outside by using glass facades: the neighbourhood people who use the street as part of their living space are now pressured to "move on" as they are seen to interfere with the "customers" inside. This "big window gentrification" is a recent tactic in the urban frontier of Vancouver.

The Candahar Bar, a project by Theo Sims and Presentation House Gallery, was a reconstruction of an Irish bar that hosted talks and performances which actively broke the contract of the Cultural Olympiad. Most sly was the exhilarating Cranfield and Slade performance of punk riot songs. On the last night of the Games, and at the same time that the city bubbled with the official euphoria of Canada winning the hockey gold medal, the band seized the situation, detoured it, and ignited an affective event which powerfully set the speech act of "Fuck You" (a song from the legendary Vancouver band the Stiffs) against the jargon of neoliberal populism. Cranfield and Slade harnessed the tension of the *deferred riot* (which never materialized en masse other than a clash between the police and the black bloc in the first week, the tactics that drew so much media attention) in a convergence with the now-invisible history of urban punk politics. It was a strong shout-along reminder – with "superior passional quality" as Guy Debord would say – that another city is possible.

The most transformative cultural events came through the artist-run centre Video In Video Out (VIVO) which staged, without Olympics funding,

4 A CBC report several days later described the poem as "referencing several clichés – And some say what defines us / Is something as simple as 'please' and 'thank you' – and made mention of No. 99 and saying 'zed' instead of 'zee,'" but added that it "contained a radiant pride" ("Olympic Ceremony Poet").

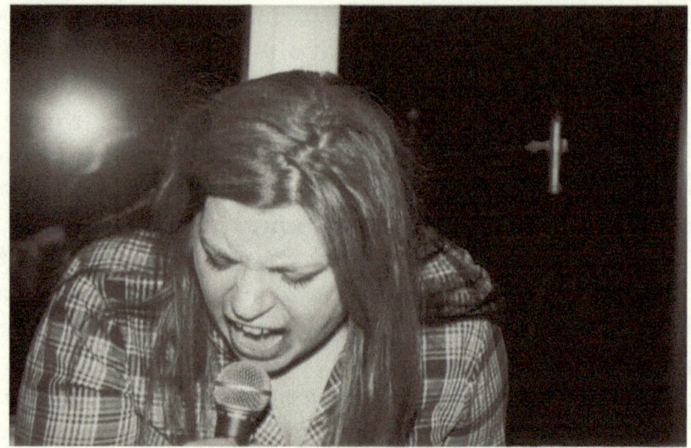

1.6 Cranfield and Slade, *Riot Songs*, at the Candahar Bar.
Photo by Brendan Hartley; appears courtesy of Kathy Slade.

a series of seminars, workshops, pirate radio broadcasts, and nightly events under the banner of "Safe Assembly." VIVO became the *transversal* site of artists, poets, intellectuals, and activists where the urgency for exactly such an alignment coincided with the necessity of assembly and transgression. During the "Nightly News" events, where VMC screened daily events, this urgency often boiled over into an intergenerational antagonism as the tactics of civil-society groups, cultural groups, and the black-bloc-tactic folks (an anarchist tactic in which an autonomous group, dressed in black with their faces covered, enact some property damage in the face of capitalism) clashed on the effectiveness of marches and policy pressure versus the eruptive *smashy-smashy* of symbolic store windows. The lines of solidarity short-circuited and broke the idea of the activist convergence as a consensual network; what was acted out was more transversal in the manner that Gerald Raunig defines it, as "lines that do not necessarily even cross, lines of flight, ruptures, which continuously elude the systems of points and their coordinates" (*Art* 205). Despite real moments where the convergence of art and action *were imagined as possible*, these lines revealed other faults – and ultimately raised the question of whether all tactics needed to be resolved with or within a coalition.

The language of mega-events is always the language of legacy and transformation. But, in Vancouver, the imagination of the legacy and the shift in the city display both the limits of the neoliberalization of cities and its sociospatial characteristics. In this sense, the specific imprint that the Olympics pressed on the city, despite the particular and dynamic political and cultural responses to the force of this mega-event, has also folded Vancouver deeper into a global model of urban governance. The stadiums and the transportation infrastructure, and the Olympic Village complex, are the visible aspects of this legacy, but the phantom force – shifts in governance and subtle rearrangements of the circulation of power – is the more calcified legacy. Even as neoliberalism fades and exists now as a machine that recirculates rusted and failed policies through different scales and places, it still is able to play off the global and the particular in a way that reshapes cities spatially, politically, and culturally.

Trying to track the way that the mega-event dropped down from above – like a long-lost modernist plan – and the mobilizations and counterproposals that sprung up from community organizations, I began this series of columns by speculating on the contestations of public space and on the forms of publicness that could emerge out of the intensification of policing and security measures that are now the Kevlar-dressed symbols of mega-events. But, in the Olympic moment, new forms of publicness based on rights to housing were ultimately overridden by an older form of cultural nationalism that took to the streets. This identity-based celebration blanketed the optimistic urban mobilizations that civil-society groups had set in motion long before the Games. Issues of sociospatial inequities in the city receded from the view of an imagined global public (and much of the politics contra the Olympics was based on bringing images to this public via the global media that used a visual programming of political space). The most visual, and visually compelling, protest – the Red Tent Campaign – which highlights the homeless crisis, was an act of publicness that has endured because it also extended itself nationally.

Other acts of publicness did not go unnoticed by the heavily financed surveillance. The massive Olympic security budget was recently trumped by the $1.2 billion spent on G20 security in Toronto: these two mega-events (for the G20 is a mega-event now as well) flowed into one extended security event. Community organizers who were highly public in anti-Olympics politics were targeted and snatched up by police in Toronto and slapped with conspiracy charges. The mass arrests in Toronto (up to 1,000 people) were the largest in Canadian history, larger even than the late-night sweeps of the War Measures Act in 1970 during the actions of the Front de libération du Québec. With this turn of deep antagonism to publicness, now towards both black-bloc tactics and milder democratic demands (and in Toronto the police put on more of a show of force to the "good" protesters), the terms *counter-publics, wild publics,* and *diverse publics* and other nuances lose the force of their argument. Sitting with wrists zip-tied, they tend to look the same. Acts of negative publicness, acts that demonstrate the limits of publicness, risk the danger of being an end-game of *struggles for publicness* itself in this atmosphere.

In the neoliberalized city, the idea of the public is off the streets. Publicness has been atomized and attached to ownership, and participation in "the public" is now based on property ownership. As a result, the public was told to stay home during the G20 – to be out was to invite arrest – and in Vancouver the public was invited to party on the city's streets, while to live on the street was to invite arrest.

Beyond claims to publicness that are met with huge security forces, what other spatial and cultural politics can emerge? Could a shift in the frame of such a politics be a legacy of this joined mega-event – the Olympics and the G20? Parallel to the anti-Olympics movement in Vancouver (a movement against the type of governance that brought the Olympics), a "right to the city" movement spearheaded by issues of housing, access, and democratic processes cohered. This program emphasized access to space, such as the right for the homeless to be in the street or to camp in parks, but it was also about the right to shape the politics of the city. The right to the city is, then, as Mustafa Dikeç argues, "not the right to urban space, but to a political space as well" so that the right to the city is "a way of actively and collectively relating to the political life of the city" (1790). A dramatic legacy of mega-events has been exactly the distortion of urban political life: the usual channels and guidelines of governmental process become even more subservient to private agencies and institutions, and democratic accountability becomes more and more difficult to locate. Mega-events therefore alter the processes that produce the city both spatially and politically. A call to the right to the city under these circumstances is made both more compelling and more troubled. But Dikeç extends this sense of the right to the city to a spatial justice that focuses "not on space per se, but on the processes that produce space, and at the same time, the implications of these produced spaces on the dynamic processes of social, economic, and political relations" (1793).

The Olympic Village in Vancouver, hunched on the post-industrial waterfront, is an aluminium-clad symbol of neoliberal governmentality and of a specific production of spatial injustice. From its ever-shrinking promise of social housing, to its post-crisis financial structure that had the city bail out hedge-fund-backed developers, to its web of private-public arrangements based on private profit and public risk, this new building also marks the long reterritorialization of the waterfront as an elite space, burying its working-class history deeper into the mud to have the waterfront transformation emerge as a real-estate gamble that hopes to shape the city's future yet again. The class anxiety around the complex, particularly who deserves to live in the subsidized housing, also marks the shift in the constitution of the public. And the nervousness around the "non-owners" who can live in the building (subsidized or renting at market) catches the antagonism that the sociospatial program of neoliberalism has built. So when people who did not want to buy a condo, but rather wanted to protest this string of broken social promises, tried to enter the open house set up to display the spaces on sale, the police erupted, roughed up some people, and then "locked down the area," which ended the event they were commissioned to guard – sales of condominiums. This minor event illustrates the spatial and class tension that the Olympics have accelerated in the city, and it marks the shift in the recognition of the public and acts of publicness. As neoliberalism's political legitimacy fades and as it tries to reshape itself during a crisis of its own making, a call for spatial justice is a strategic opposition that can also help characterize neoliberalism and show that it is never fully formed but is, instead, in process.[5]

Given the spatiality of neoliberalism and the transformation of the status of the public, what can public art orient itself towards? The Germany-based artists Köbberling and Kaltwasser were commissioned to create a public artwork on a fallow yet semiotically rich section of land near the Olympic Village. Opting for entropy rather than legacy, Köbberling and Kaltwasser have constructed a sculpture made out of temporary building material left over from the Village itself: the wheat-board architectural sculpture will decay with time and weather and transform into a plant nursery that will be "claimed and nurtured" by residents of the newly redeveloped waterfront area. The intention is that, once grown, the plants can be transplanted within the development by the residents. The tensions here between the community impulse, instigated by the artists, with

5 For more information, see Peck, Theodore, and Brenner.

its metaphors of reuse, decay, and renewal, and the production of a public of owners (always depicted as a community) pushed by the profit imperative that the building is defined by will no doubt be played out over time. As is common with mega-events, social contradictions and spatial production move from the streets to the waterfront.

The scale of this Olympic development represents the way that such megaprojects, "while being decidedly local, capture global trends, express new forms of national and local policies, and incorporate them in a particular localized setting." Laced into the competitive software of neoliberalism, "these projects," Eric Swyngedouw, Frank Moulaert, and Arantxa Rodriguez propose, "are the material expression of a developmental logic that views megaprojects and place-marketing as means for generating future growth and for waging a competitive struggle to attract investment capital" (546). Yet this Olympic project, and other projects of such a scale (like the Olympic Village in Athens or the DonauCity in Vienna), is both a product of and a shaping influence of the neoliberalizing of urban governmentality. This shift is described by Swyngedouw, Moulaert, and Rodriguez (in a collaborative study of twelve European large-scale urban development projects) as a "new choreography of elite power" that sees local democratic participation restricted or contained – not usually outright excluded, but brought in and consulted, even included on commissions in a "politics of recognition" that recognizes groups, or "stakeholders," yet grants them little power. The social returns on such megaprojects, in terms of Swyngedouw, Moulaert, and Rodriguez's analysis, are negative and harden an "institutionalization of public-private partnerships, [and] high-income groups as clientele of social democracy" (559). In Swyngedouw, Moulaert, and Rodriguez's description of this process, "the newly emerging regimes of governing urban revitalization involve the subordination of formal government structures to new institutions and agencies, often paralleled by a significant redistribution of policy-making powers, competencies, and responsibilities" (556). Following the neoliberal discourse of smaller government function but increased governmentality, these extragovernmental bodies are fractured and multiple and made up of the varied stakeholders driving or affected by the project. In reality, this model is implemented very unevenly and can override and transform the existing form of democratic accountability and may not operate with a clear set of guidelines. Thus the real Olympic legacy is often not a built environment of sports complexes, housing, and transportation but a refigured process of decision-making.

WORKS CITED

Butler, Judith. "Critique, Dissent, Disciplinarity." *Critical Inquiry*, vol. 35, no. 4, 2009, pp. 773–95.

Debord, Guy. "Report on the Construction of Situations and on the International Situationist Tendency's Conditions of Organization and Action." *Situationist International Anthology*, edited and translated by Ken Knabb, rev. and expanded ed., Bureau of Public Secrets, 2006. www.cddc.vt.edu/sionline/si/report.html. Accessed 24 June 2012.

Dikeç, Mustafa. "Justice and the Spatial Imagination." *Environment and Planning*, vol. 33, no. 10, 2001, pp. 1785–805.

Foucault, Michel. "Governmentality." *The Foucault Effect: Studies in Governmentality*, edited by Graham Burchell, Colin Gordon, and Peter Miller, U of Chicago P, 1991, pp. 87–104.

– "What Is Enlightenment?" *The Foucault Reader*, translated by Catherine Porter and edited by Paul Rabinow, Pantheon, 1984, pp. 32–50.

Lefebvre, Henri. *The Explosion: Marxism and the French Upheaval*. Translated by Alfred Ehrenfeld, Monthly Review, 1969.

– *State, Space, World: Selected Essays*. Translated by Gerald Moore, Neil Brenner, and Stuart Elden and edited by Neil Brenner and Stuart Elden, U of Minnesota P, 2009.

– *The Urban Revolution*. Translated by Robert Bonnono, U of Minnesota P, 2003.

Lütticken, Sven. *Secret Publicity*. NAi, 2005.

Ngai, Sianne. *Ugly Feeling*. Harvard UP, 2005.

"Olympic Ceremony Poet Bursts onto World Stage." *CBC.ca*, 14 Feb. 2010. www.cbc.ca/news/entertainment/olympic-ceremony-poet-bursts-onto-world-stage-1.902578. Accessed 24 June 2012.

Peck, Jamie. "The Creativity Fix." *Eurozine*, 28 June 2007. www.eurozine.com/the-creativity-fix/. Accessed 24 June 2012.

– "Zombie Governance and the Ambidextrous State." *Theoretical Criminology*, vol. 14, no. 1, 2010, pp. 104–10.

Peck, Jamie, Nik Theodore, and Neil Brenner. "Postneoliberalism and Its Discontents." *Antipode*, vol. 41, no. S1, 2009, pp. 94–116.

Raunig, Gerald. *Art and Revolution: Transversal Activism in the Long 20th Century*. Translated by Aileen Derieg, Semiotext(e), 2007.

– "What Is Critique? Suspension and Recomposition in Textual and Social Machines." Translated by Aileen Derieg, *EIPCP*, European Institute for Progressive Cultural Policies, Apr. 2008. eipcp.net/transversal/0808/raunig/en. Accessed 24 June 2012.

Smith, Neil. "Cities after Neoliberalism." June 2001. www.academia.edu/6424629/Cities_After_Neoliberalism. Accessed 24 June 2012.

Swyngedouw, Eric, Frank Moulaert, and Arantxa Rodriguez. "Neoliberal Urbanization in Europe: Large-Scale Urban Development Projects and the New Urban Policy." *Antipode*, vol. 34, no. 3, 2002, pp. 542–77.

Trotsky, Leon. *Permanent Revolution.* Translated by John G. Wright, Progress Publishers / Militant Publishing Association, 1931. *Marxist Internet Archive.* www.marxists.org/archive/trotsky/1931/tpr/pr-index.htm. Accessed 24 June 2012.

Warner, Michael. *Publics and Counterpublics.* Zone Books, 2002.

2 The Ambivalence of Enclosed Spaces in Immigrant Fiction: Between Refuge and Prison

AMARYLL CHANADY

The representation of enclosed spaces has often been ambivalent. On the one hand, enclosed dwellings such as huts and houses connote protection and intimacy, as Gaston Bachelard demonstrated in his study on the "poetics of space." On the other, they may symbolize imprisonment by poverty, an uncertain political status, social isolation, or personal trauma. In Canadian fiction, enclosed spaces have a particular resonance. Though they are absolutely necessary for survival in our northern climate, prolonged confinement in them can also lead to a sense of suffocation, such as the proverbial cabin fever. Immigrant fiction adds an additional dimension. Whereas the enclosed spaces of houses, bars, and cafes provide a sense of safety, familiarity, and comforting interaction with one's ethnic group, they may also involve ghettoization and isolation from the rest of society. Furthermore, they sometimes impede harmonious social interaction, or even exacerbate conflict, both within the group and between immigrants and residents. Conflict frequently arises in housing, the use of space in leisure activities, and the occupation of territory in the schoolyard, especially in limited spaces. Confined spaces may even trigger trauma through enforced proximity between people with a shared past.

Space is not merely an empty area in which events occur, a geometric entity defined by specific coordinates, or a contested commodity, but a built, structured, and occupied environment in which people interact according to complex factors related to personal memory, group dynamics, class, and ethnicity, as well as concrete spatial configurations. As Edward W. Soja points out, the spaces we live in are constructed by our thoughts and actions, while "human spatiality is the product of both human agency and environmental or contextual structuring" (6). Henri

Lefebvre had already emphasized the importance of human representation for the construction of space in his groundbreaking study, in which he argues that concretely lived space is indistinguishable from "mental space" on the one hand and from physical space on the other (27). Literature is particularly suited to the exploration of the personal perception of space, since it recreates what bell hooks calls the "passion of experience," linked especially to the suffering of particular groups (182). In the case of immigrant or minority writing, the portrayal of lived space often represents the experience of an entire community, as is also the case with Latin American testimonial narrative.

Lefebvre's category of "representational spaces," which he contrasts with the more abstract, rational, and hegemonic "representations of space," is especially relevant here, since it involves "complex symbolisms ... linked to the clandestine or underground side of social life, as also to art" (33). Contrary to the institutionalized space of dominant codes and practices, representational space is "alive": "It has an affective kernel or center: Ego, bed, bedroom, dwelling, house; or: square, church, graveyard" (42). It implies memory and is dynamic. Some of these examples echo Bachelard's protected spaces of the house, the hut, and the shell, discussed in his phenomenological study of the way in which protected spaces are perceived. Bachelard argues that the house anchors memory and gives it shape. Time is thus spatialized, in the sense of being situated in a particular space and formed by it in the imagination. Combining this concept of spatialization with Lefebvre's emphasis on social construction and the "underground side of life," I will discuss several literary texts written by immigrants that represent conflict through spatial figures, illustrating the effects of the built environment on various marginalized groups. At the same time, I will examine the symbolic significance of enclosed spaces, since many narratives emphasize both the characters' perception of and their interaction with space, as well as a self-conscious symbolic and allegorical dimension through which the authors reflect on the predicament of immigrants in broader terms. This may not be obvious to the represented immigrants themselves.

As Andy Merrifield points out, we can use metaphors to describe space either as "process," by which he means broader historical changes often linked to progress, or as "daily life," involving the everyday personal interaction with and perception of space. Whereas metaphors of process ignore the "richly textured everyday space," metaphors illustrating the "experiential world of daily life ... frequently portray a static and entity-based reality" (418). Contrasting abstract knowledge about historical processes with feeling and common sense, which often involve misconceptions and prejudice, he insists on the need to reconcile the two dimensions so that theory becomes an effective vehicle for transmitting the experiential through its translation into a new critical language. Although Merrifield is correct in his observation that people "can't be in two places at once" (419), fiction often creates several contradictory perspectives, usually associated with particular fictional characters, as M.M. Bakhtin argued in his reflections on polyphony and dialogism. Likewise, narratives can illustrate both processual and experiential dimensions, to use Merrifield's terms. This leads to a complex and ambivalent treatment of space in which the lived reality of characters, corresponding to hooks's "passion of experience," is simultaneously portrayed not just in juxtaposition to that of other characters but also from an outside analytical perspective that stresses the historical dimensions.

The depiction of enclosed spaces in immigrant writing frequently involves this double dimension. A short novel by the Egyptian-born Mona Latif-Ghattas, *Le double conte de l'exil*, is particularly interesting in this respect. Although it illustrates Tamara J. Palmer's analysis of the vertical mosaic, in which the literary critic links urban geography to the configurations of ethnic communities and class divisions, it specifically concentrates on an enclosed, ambiguous space that is conceptualized from several perspectives. Whereas Mordecai Richler's and Adele Wiseman's Jewish communities (discussed by Palmer) are surrounded by "invisible walls," the group of hospital employees in Latif-Ghattas's underground, windowless laundry are literally enclosed by walls; and whereas class boundaries for Richler and Wiseman are symbolized through the description of urban neighbourhoods located at different points on the north-south axis of the city map, or through the topographical distinction between hills and low-lying areas (Palmer 625–7), status in Latif-Ghattas's novel is symbolically linked to a location within a building. Contrast this with what David Sibley calls "geographies of exclusion," or forms of spatial organization in which certain groups are relegated to the margins of desirable locations or confined to undesirable spaces on a horizontal axis. The "social cosmology" created by the "persistent hierarchization of the cityscape into those above and those below" (as Roxanne Rimstead says in this volume, p. 247) moves indoors, thus acquiring the additional symbolic dimension of confinement and hopelessness. Contrary to spaces of resistance and social critique, as in Rawi Hage's novel (analysed by Rita Sakr in this volume), Latif-Ghattas's underground represents a "heterotopia of social control."

Her novel recounts the story of Madeleine, a Native woman who works in the laundry of a Montréal hospital and has a relationship with the illegal immigrant Fêve in her small apartment. While Fêve is deported to the Middle East at the end of the novel, Madeleine returns to her reservation, which Nathalie Prud'homme interprets as evidence of the refusal to accept immigrants and Native people as members of Québec society. The treatment of space, however, suggests a more complex reflection on social and historical dynamics. Whereas Madeleine's domestic space is generally depicted in positive terms, her place of work is the setting for problematic interactions between newcomers and long-term residents of various origins, not just francophone. The hospital laundry is a symbolically rich figure, since it represents a secure space for the long-term employees but also a hostile and alien space for newly hired workers such as the young East Asian man (the second important male character in the novel), who cannot pierce the tightly knit social group. Although Margaret Atwood's pronouncement that the "Canadian experience of immigrants seems programmed for failure" (158) does not apply to all foreign characters in this story, the following statement does, at least in the context of the laundry: "for the later immigrants, hostile cities replace hostile forests, and the place of the feared, unfriendly and treacherous natives has been taken by – of course – those earlier immigrants, the WASPs and the French" (Atwood 149). It becomes a contested space, which is portrayed mainly from the point of view of Madeleine, an outsider because of her Native status, but also, even if more indirectly, from that of the other employees, including the Asian man and representatives of the aforementioned WASPs and French, to which the story adds the Jews. Furthermore, the contrasting experiences of the employees are framed within a broader *processual* perspective of which they seem to be unaware, and which is created by a complex allegorical treatment of space.

Several key passages of the novel are set in the hospital laundry, in which the three White, middle-aged female employees see their jobs threatened by the arrival of a young, hard-working Asian employee and his mother. The tension between the overtly racist White employees and the young Asian worker is illustrated by the spatial configuration of the group. While the "three Claras" are always seated on the bench during their lunch break, the Asian man remains standing and is often joined by Madeleine, indicating their common status as racial outsiders. The two groups perceive this contested space differently. Although the Asian man sees a homogeneous White community of employees united in their hostility to the non-White newcomer and their refusal to make room for him on their bench (and in their work environment), the three Claras perceive his presence as an intrusion and a threat to their job security. They desperately join ranks to protect themselves from the model employee who is biding his time before he will symbolically take his place on the desired bench. The spatial figuration of conflict goes beyond the immediate lived experience of the groups involved, since the identity of the three Claras suggests a more complex symbolization of the sitting-standing binary that involves historical knowledge and a reflection on group formation and nation-building. In an obvious allegory of the founding of Canada, each Clara represents one of the main groups populating the nation: the francophone Clairette, the anglophone Clarence, and the Jewish Clara, whose family immigrated recently. Rather than simply symbolizing the conflict between White residents and non-White newcomers, as well as the uneasy inclusion of Native people, who are situated uncomfortably in between, the negotiation of space in the laundry illustrates the perpetual formation of solidarities and exclusions in society.

Contrary to dominant myths of nation-building, however, Latif-Ghattas's novel provides a perspective from below (in both the literal and the figurative sense), as well as a counter-narrative that deconstructs the optimistic stereotype of the hard-working immigrant who eventually becomes a respected and economically secure member of society. The construction of social space in the hospital building adds an additional dimension to the allegory of the laundry sitting arrangements. It is significant that the laundry is situated on the fourth level of the basement, and that the employees eat their lunch on a bench in the corridor instead of in the cafeteria situated one storey above. The underground location of the laundry and the lunch space highlights the position of all its workers at the bottom of the social ladder in their invisible contribution to the functioning of the hospital. Their status is even less prestigious than that of the more visible workers who eat on the third level. The bench in the corridor emphasizes not only marginalization with respect to the other workers but also the precarious nature of their jobs, threatened by professional injuries (the three Claras suffer from ailments caused by the repetitive nature of the movements required by their work) and younger, more productive workers. Although the main focalizer is Madeleine, the "passion of experience" of the three Claras is transmitted through their dialogue, as well as the narrator's emphasis on "their misery, their solitude and their boredom" ("leur misère, leur solitude et leur ennui" [Latif-Ghattas 21])[1] and their dreams of escape on a cruise ship.

Madeleine's perception of space is more detailed in its emphasis on visual and non-visual aspects, as well as the importance of personal imagination. Although she feels secure and comfortable in the secluded space of the laundry, she compares the sounds of the machinery to those of "trains entering a station, giving her the perpetual illusion of returning from a voyage" ("des trains qui entrent en gare, lui donnant l'illusion perpétuelle de rentrer de voyage" [16]). This ambivalent perception of space stresses her precarious status on the margins of the community of workers, a home associated with a stereotypical "non-space," to use Marc Augé's term for certain anonymous spaces of the contemporary world. Another description of the laundry as a "huge ship's hold, without a captain or a ship's boy" ("une vaste cale de bateau, sans capitaine et sans mousse" [73]), suggests the lowly status of the employees, their lack of a future, and their condition of being thrown together, without regard for personal affinities that might lead to warm personal relationships.

Place, moreover, as Doreen Massey has pointed out, is not bounded but inserted into a larger network. She describes places as "articulated moments in networks of social relations and understandings" that are larger than the "place itself, whether that be a street, or a region or even a continent," and that create a sense of locality involving a consciousness of links with the outside (28). The basement laundry in the novel is explicitly linked to the living space of the workers and their families through their daily commute and their conversations. These spaces reflect and intensify the marginal status of the three Claras and Madeleine, and they influence the relationship between the employees, whose perceptions of society are formed by the uneasy sharing of living space outside the laundry. Clarence lives in a poor neighbourhood in Montréal North; her niece shares a dilapidated apartment building with immigrants; Clairette's brother-in-law earns a low salary as a taxi driver with Haitian co-workers; and Madeleine shares her small, dark apartment with Fêve, an illegal immigrant who is a sewer maintenance worker, leaving home before daybreak and returning after dark. The sewer is both a

1 All translations are my own unless specified.

refuge from the authorities and an unwholesome space conveying human waste in an obvious allusion to illegal immigrants as unwanted.

The parallel between the basement laundry and Fêve's sewer and the allusion to living spaces shared by the laundry employees and immigrants, legal and illegal, illustrate an easily legible construction of urban space in which economically underprivileged people inhabit subterranean spaces and carry out cleaning operations (sewer and laundry) in the shadow of the visible city. Like a living organism, the city constantly renews its cells (the expendable workers in the basement corridor) and expels impurities or redundant elements (the Middle Eastern Fêve, who is deported, and the Native Madeleine, who returns to the reservation of her own accord after seeing that she has no place in the city). The spatialization of conflict from the point of view of marginalized subjects, for whom spaces are imbued with memories and emotions, represents a "culture from below" which stands in stark contrast to the utilitarian planning of the urban landscape, designed to ensure the smooth functioning of the modern city. The enclosed spaces of the novel, constructed differently through their bodily and imaginary appropriation by the various characters and their symbolic figuration in the novel, are all ambivalent. The warm, secluded, womb-like laundry in the bowels of the hospital is at the same time a trap for workers at the bottom of the social ladder and a contested space for those who cannot find other employment, while Madeleine's cramped, dark apartment is also a hiding place for the "undocumented people in the world" ("les sans-papiers du monde" [20]) in which warm human relations can emerge between those on the margins, but only temporarily, since it cannot keep out the immigration authorities. Both heterotopias are threatened havens, and this is symbolically indicated by their spatial configuration – the bench, the corridor, the laundry reverberating with train-like sounds, and the deformed doors of Madeleine's apartment, which cannot be closed properly to protect its occupants. The "passion of experience" of the characters is thus constantly contrasted with that of others in the story and with the frequent allegorical descriptions of social dynamics. In the case of the three Claras, the enclosed space illustrates both suffering and entrapment, as well as intolerance and narrow-mindedness – or, to use Merrifield's opposition, both everyday life and the more critical and analytical conceptualization of process from the outside.

Enclosed spaces may of course be described as primarily negative. In Austin Clarke's story "Canadian Experience," the unemployed Caribbean immigrant George struggles over the use of the bathroom with a poor aspiring actress in a dilapidated rooming house. In contrast to Latif-Ghattas's novel, it depicts domestic space, rather than the work environment, as contested territory. While the enclosed space of George's bedroom, with its dirty and inaccessible window, symbolizes his hopeless entrapment, the bathroom introduces the motif of interpersonal frictions and expulsion. It is linked symbolically to a network of places that connote filth and cleansing, such as the dirty underground transit system described as a rumbling intestine and the sewer conveying detritus to the lake. The equation of George with filth (indicated by his dirty clothes, his fixation on the mucus of the subway passengers, the contrast between himself and the cleanliness of several elements of the built environment as well as that of the elegant bank receptionist, and his suicide in the station among billboards alluding to filth and excrement) illustrates a construction of space in which antagonism between White residents and the Black immigrant is spatialized in a figure of the urban organism divided between the shiny office towers of visible wealth and prestige in the financial centre and the digestive mechanism below the surface that excretes filth and the unwanted immigrant. Batia Boe Stolar discusses the depiction of conflict in the West Indian ghetto of Clarke's stories. In her analysis of the sexual symbolization of the city, she describes the city in "Canadian Experience" as a "translucently white female character who deters, rejects, consumes, and ejects the black immigrant who seeks to enter her" (124). The built environment of the modern city, with its smoothly functioning transit system and impressive banking structures, is lived as a dysphoric space by the immigrant of colour. The most negative experiences occur in enclosed spaces such as the small bathroom, the crowded subway compartment, the elevator in the bank building, and the dark underground station. All these spaces illustrate not only entrapment but also the impossibility of warm human relations and the inevitability of conflict and eventual expulsion from the city.[2]

A more recent story by Clarke, "I'm Running for My Life," illustrates the Black-White conflict through a symbolic spatialization of the house, rather than the city, as figure of the body. Here, the conflict is situated within individuals, both Black and White, besides characterizing relations

2 For a detailed discussion of the story's emphasis on filth and expulsion in an inter-American context, see Chanady, "Trans-American Outcast."

between racial groups. May, Mr Moore's Black housemaid, initiates a sexual encounter with her White employer in the basement of the mansion after his wife has left him. Horrified by her act, she confides in her Black friend Gert, who describes the incident as rape and promises she will help May take revenge on him. Like the archetypal house described by Bachelard, Mr Moore's mansion has an upstairs that symbolizes reason and conscious action, whereas the basement connotes fear and instinct. While the book *The Joy of Sex* lies beside the bed in the upstairs room and is linked to the sterility of the married couple's programmed sex life ("for she wanted to do it by the book" [Clarke, "Running" 86]), the basement is the scene of a spontaneous and mutually satisfactory sexual encounter between May and the abandoned husband. Situated between these two levels of the house is the library, in which May throws an Indian blanket over her sleeping employer. When she enters the empty library to pick up and fold the blanket before the basement encounter, it feels to her "as if the animal from which it was made was still alive" (82). She later wonders whether the blanket drove her to commit the act of which she is later ashamed, and alludes to a dream in which she was a lion, thereby invoking a stereotypical binary in which White civilization is opposed to Native passion and animal instinct. The blanket, described as inhabited by Indian spirits, is found between the upstairs of reason and artificiality (and May's daydreams while trying on Mrs Moore's expensive clothes) and the basement of instinct and desire, and thus it serves as a bridge between the two. May is herself a site of conflicting emotions. As she confides to Gert, she feels dirty after her act, since she is a "Christian-minded person" (91) and regularly goes to church. The contested territory – that of the individual, torn between desire and decorum, instinct and reason – is symbolically illustrated by the functions of the various parts of the house.

This spatialized conflict, however, also involves a broader social and racial one between non-White workers and White employers. Again, the mediating element is the Indian blanket, which reminds May of the "men whom she saw standing at the corner of Bloor and Spadina, old men, some old before they are young; defeated warriors" (81). The blanket, which may at first appear to be a stereotypical symbol of "Indians" as close to nature and instinct, connects the house (site of an individual conflict) with the larger society marked by inequality and colonial history. This also explains May's feelings that Mr Moore "was assaulting her, in this silence, with the roar and violence of his eyes" (79), and her tears of frustration at his initial indifference towards her. The represented space of the house is a complex figuration of both individual and society, past and present, through the conflicting emotions of the Black maid. As Judith Misrahi-Barak points out with respect to one of Neil Bissoondath's short stories, "the house is clearly the metonymic expression of *the other*'s territory, all the more impossible to inhabit as it still reflects a master-slave relationship" (12). Elsewhere, she describes the houses in Caribbean-Canadian fiction as "a trap or even a grave, a sort of outgrowth of a city in which it has been impossible to make room for oneself" (13). She discusses claustrophobia and various images of entrapment such as basement apartments, Jonah and the whale, and bars that are both cocoons and prisons. What is particularly important, however, is the link between the representation of enclosed spaces and the complex depiction of problematic interpersonal relations, as well as the contradictory imaginary constructions of space. In "I'm Running for My Life," May's "passion of experience" is expressed with great empathy and linked to a broader social and historical context. At the same time, the sympathetic portrayal of Mr Moore's feelings and Gert's militant and hatred-inspired deformation of the sexual encounter as rape in order to destroy his life by bringing false accusations against him provide a more distanced reflection on race conflict. The symbolism of the enclosed space in the story emphasizes the difficulty of evading the past, the continuing presence of inequality and racial tensions, and the complex and ambiguous nature of "culture from below."

The gaze of the White man directed at the woman of colour, an inescapable aggression in the master's house in Clarke's story, is generalized to include immigrants of colour of both sexes and different races in the short story "Regarde, regarde les lions" by the Haitian Québécois writer Émile Ollivier. Rather than working in the darkness of the basement or the sewer, as in Latif-Ghattas's novel, the acrobats and other circus performers in this story are situated in the well-lit centre. Whereas the spectators are invisible in the darkness engulfing the bleachers, the performers ride in circles, teeter on tightropes, and frighten each other in lion costumes in full view. The two Haitian lion impersonators, driven by the foreign-looking tamer with a whip to attack each other like gladiators in a Roman coliseum, enact an allegory of conflict within immigrant communities. These, it is suggested, are separated from the dominant society as effectively as the visible performers are from the spectators, provoking fear in them as do the lions, which frighten the little boy at the circus. Again, the place of the circus is linked to a larger spatial network: Manès, the protagonist, remembers his home in Haiti, the perilous voyage to

Canada, and the box in which he had imprisoned a firefly as a child. The spatialization of conflict in the enclosed arena of the circus, linked to the box that imprisoned and killed the firefly, illustrates the lived space of the immigrant and deconstructs the neat construction of urban space with its heterotopias of entertainment and make-believe, isolated from spaces of work. For Manès, circular movement and enclosed spaces are central to his everyday experience, past and present, and exist both literally and symbolically.

While the circus also represents a place of refuge – from the cold and unemployment – it traps the immigrants in a ghetto of limited opportunity. The sense of suffocation in the stifling lion costume and the inability to leave a frightening space of coercion and humiliation illustrate the lived experience of the immigrant in a confined space, which is constructed not only by its material configuration and the users' movements within it but also by the emotional world of memories, internalized negative stereotypes, and dystopian interaction with other subjects sharing the same location. In spite of the shared predicament of other immigrants performing in the circus, no solidarity or warm human interaction emerges in the negatively charged space of the arena, except between the two Haitian lion impersonators, who leave the circus together. The ambivalence of the enclosed space is illustrated by the recurring memory of the firefly, whose light reflects the performers' brilliant world of illusion and whose imprisonment in the box, which quickly kills it, suggests the dehumanization of the immigrants, who must perform stereotypical and humiliating roles. Contrary to the box inhabited by the homeless man in Kobo Abe's novel (discussed by Simon Harel in this volume), the dominant affect triggered by objects enclosing the body in Ollivier's story (the box imprisoning the firefly, the constricting lion costume) is suffocation and claustrophobia. The immigrant protagonists cannot inhabit these dysphoric skins in an act of literal and emotional appropriation that would create a specific personal space and centre of perception "from below," since the costumes/boxes are simply imposed shackles that must be thrown off.

While both the house in Clarke's story "Running" and the circus in Ollivier's narrative about the Haitian lion impersonators are foreign spaces to the protagonists, even if they are central to their everyday lives, the bar in Bissoondath's story "On the Eve of Uncertain Tomorrows" is portrayed as a warm place of refuge, where outsiders can interact harmoniously and construct a sense of community. Decorated with objects and pictures from Latin America, it is a secluded haven for legal and illegal immigrants and political refugees, an artificial reconstruction of home, in which the owner helps compatriots hide from immigration authorities, provides free food when needed, and gives solace to the lonely and often desperate patrons. He even saves the life of a woman who tries to commit suicide in the washroom. The protagonist Joaquin, a political refugee from South America, feels "safer here than anywhere else" (435).

Its name (*La Barricada*), however, has a double meaning, since a barricade can protect and also entrap. The decrepit furniture transforms the place into a "closet for the soul" (435): its patrons thrive on dusty memories, exhibit a broken spirit, and harbour resentments from the past, without hope for a positive future. The bar is also an enclosed space that forces its users into close proximity with other patrons, who trigger painful memories of persecution and torture. The injured illegal immigrant Francisco reminds Joaquin of Jorge, his former torturer, reviving the trauma of his past and preventing him from noticing that the woman Tere, whose husband was killed by the dictatorship in her former Latin American home, has gone to the washroom to cut her wrists. The bar thus becomes a trap that prevents political exiles from leaving their painful past behind and interferes with positive human interaction. The caring community of immigrants and political exiles is not only a refuge but also a forced association of imagined (and possibly also real) enemies, since place is not bounded but anchored in a complex network of relationships and memories of other places, as in Ollivier's story and Latif-Ghattas's novel.

The sense of entrapment in the bar echoes that of the rooming house at the beginning of Bissoondath's story, where Joaquin contemplates his desolate surroundings: "withered buildings – garages, storerooms, walls of tin and brick – pressing in on the rear" (428). The desperate struggle of a pigeon to escape the "avian rape" on the balcony surrounded by chicken wire reminds him of his own situation: "And he is the one confined, by the chicken wire and by so much more" (428). What is particularly disturbing about this identification is that he feels no sympathy with the "unattractive birds, with panicky, red-rimmed eyes" suggesting "infection, physical corruption" (428). While the negative description of the birds points to his own perceived position as a permanently scarred torture victim arousing the disgust and horror of those who see his mutilated body, it also possibly suggests the difficulty of feeling sympathy for fellow sufferers whose plight reminds us of our own and prevents us from forgetting a traumatic past. His reaction to the kind interest shown by Amin in the rooming house illustrates a similar feeling. He "worries when Amin claims a communality of experience with him" (429), although he is also grateful for his companionship. The enclosed space of his room, which he describes as "three paces one way, three paces the other," brings back memories of the prison cell and torture suffered in his home country. He feels the "clasp of the blankets" and sees the shadows of household appliances as the "tyranny of shadowed things" (430), while the dripping faucet suggests Chinese water torture. The room is thus transformed into a prison by his past.

Joaquin's domestic "phobic space," to use Hamid Naficy's expression (which the critic applies to transnational films), ignores boundaries between past and present, here and there, and is probably similar to that of the other tenants, who are all immigrants waiting for the authorities to examine their status and decide on their future. The construction of phobic space through memory not only leads to a perpetual personal nightmare but also becomes an obstacle to shared human warmth in the rooming house. The tenants generally "keep to themselves," which Joaquin prefers, since "life has taught him that the friendliest smile may conceal the sharpest teeth" (430). The Vietnamese couple, with "eyes of a hounded intelligence" (431), glare at his intrusion in the communal kitchen, while he and the Sikh tenant sit at the table without speaking. Although he feels joy at the outbreak of spring, when people are "hungry for the sun like prisoners emerging into a prison-yard after a too-long, too-dark night" (433), the reference to the prison-yard indicates that liberation is only partial. Any new space can become a phobic reminder of the past and give rise to walls between people.

In the narratives discussed above, spatial figuration illustrates perceptions of society from below by emphasizing the lived space of immigrants, legal and illegal, poor and unemployed. These experiential spaces – characterized by painful memories, conflict, rejection, and negative self-perception – are at the centre of counter-narratives that deconstruct common literary themes such as the house, the place of work, and the circus in complex and ambiguous ways. They provide various reflections on social dynamics and historical processes that combine both the experiential, through passion and empathy, and the analytical, through rich spatial symbolization and the clash of divergent perspectives. Most of these enclosed spaces are sites of conflict, as well as havens of relative security and, sometimes, even human warmth. More importantly, however, they constitute a locus from which different voices give us critical insights on dominant culture and a deeper understanding of the experiences of those who remain invisible or are constructed as exotic Others by society's gaze.

WORKS CITED

Atwood, Margaret. *Survival: A Thematic Guide to Canadian Literature.* Anansi, 1972.

Augé, Marc. *Non-lieux.* Seuil, 1992.

Bachelard, Gaston. *The Poetics of Space.* Beacon Press, 1994.

Bakhtin, M.M. "Discourse in the Novel." *The Dialogic Imagination: Four Essays,* edited by Michael Holquist, and translated by Caryl Emerson and Michael Holquist, U of Texas P, 1981, pp. 259–422.

Bissoondath, Neil. "On the Eve of Uncertain Tomorrows." *Making a Difference: Canadian Multicultural Fictions,* edited by Smaro Kamboureli, Oxford UP, 1996, pp. 428–40.

Chanady, Amaryll. "The Trans-American Outcast and Figurations of Displacement." *Comparative Literature,* vol. 61, no. 3, Summer 2009, pp. 335–45.

Clarke, Austin. "Canadian Experience." *Other Solitudes: Canadian Multicultural Fictions,* edited by Linda Hutcheon and Marion Richmond, Oxford UP, 1990, pp. 49–63.

– "I'm Running for My Life." *In This City.* Exile Editions, 2008, pp. 74–95.

hooks, bell. "Essentialism and Experience." *American Literary History,* vol. 3, no. 1, 1991, pp. 172–83.

Latif-Ghattas, Mona. *Le double conte de l'exil.* Boréal, 1990.

Lefebvre, Henri. *The Production of Space.* 1974. Translated by Donald Nicholson-Smith, Blackwell, 2008.

Massey, Doreen. "A Global Sense of Place." *Marxism Today,* June 1991, pp. 24–9.

Merrifield, Andy. "Between Process and Individuation: Translating Metaphors and Narratives of Urban Space." *Antipode,* vol. 29, no. 4, 1997, pp. 417–36.

Misrahi-Barak, Judith. "The Cityscape in a Few Caribbean-Canadian Short Stories." *Journal of the Short Story in English,* vol. 31, 1998, pp. 9–22.

Naficy, Hamid. "Phobic Spaces and Liminal Panics: Independent Transnational Film Genre." *Global/Local: Cultural Production and the Transnational Imaginary,* edited by Rob Wilson and Wimal Dissanayake, Duke UP, 1996, pp. 119–44.

Ollivier, Émile. *Regarde, regarde les lions.* Albin Michel, 2001.

Palmer, Tamara J. "The Fictionalization of the Vertical Mosaic: The Immigrant, Success and National Mythology." *Canadian Review of Comparative Literature,* vol. 16, nos. 3–4, 1989, pp. 619–55.

Prud'homme, Nathalie. *La problématique identité collective et les littératures (im) migrantes au Québec: Mona Latif Ghattas, Antonio D'Alfonso, et Marco Micone.* Nota bene, 2002.

Sibley, David. *Geographies of Exclusion.* Routledge, 1995.

Soja, Edward W. *Postmetropolis: Critical Studies of Cities and Regions.* Blackwell, 2000.

Stolar, Batia Boe. "Building and Living the Immigrant City: Michael Ondaatje's and Austin Clarke's Toronto." *Downtown Canada: Writing Canadian Cities*, edited by Justin D. Edwards and Douglas Ivison, U of Toronto P, 2005, pp. 122–41.

3 Montréal Marginalities: Revisiting Boulevard Saint-Laurent

SHERRY SIMON

André Carpentier's *Ruelles, jours ouvrables* (2007) is a collection of observations written over the course of some five years of roaming the laneways of Montréal. His project is remarkable for the vigour and originality of its writing, and for the qualities of perseverance and discipline it shows – as the record of an author committed day after day, and year after year, to compiling writerly vignettes of passing time. The book is also significant in the context of Montréal history. Instead of constructing a narrative from the official perspective of boulevards, monuments, and city squares, Carpentier tracks the activities of city dwellers in the semiprivate, semipublic arena of the laneway. Using the passage of the seasons as his structuring principle, he tells his own story as a flâneur, observing a world normally hidden from view.

The transgressive aspects of this attention to what is not normally considered "on view" are signalled by the occasions when Carpentier is called upon – on one occasion by the police – to explain his motives. Carpentier's "strolling" could be interpreted as "lurking." Because he was not using the lanes for the purposes they usually serve, his gaze was interpreted as intrusive and possibly malevolent. But Carpentier was indeed following rules, injunctions that might have been devised by de Certeau or Alain Médam or Benjamin, to direct one's attention to the details of everyday life, to the sensuous surfaces of the city, to areas seemingly untouched by History – or rather where History presents itself in an unusual guise.

Carpentier discovers that beneath the surfaces of back lanes there are layers of history that have accumulated away from the spotlight of official chroniclers:

> Il y a un vaste passé sous le béton des villes, dont on a perdu conscience; tout ça, dont on a collectivement perdu la mémoire, parce que le présent, comme le moulin de la chanson, bat trop vite et trop fort ... Qu'en est-il de ces ruines et fragments de mémoires réunis sous le béton de cette *terra incognita* sous l'asphalte et sous les maisons, les hangars, les garages, sous le bois traité et le carrelage des terrasses? Toutes ces ruelles, ces coins dallés ont été des territoires de chasse, des lieux de fermes, des sentiers. (Carpentier 126–8)[1]

What Carpentier brings to light are fragments of unofficial memory, which he shapes into a kind of counter-narrative, a history from below, which proposes a scale of space and time different from conventional historical or travel literature. Rather than crossing vast expanses of space, he explores small spaces, in the manner of what Michael Cronin calls "endotic" travel (141–2) – that is, travel across small distances, and following itineraries that are not signposted by the expected markers. Such endotic narratives recall forms of memorialization which are similarly ironic in their take on History, counter-monuments like the marble disks that Gilbert Boyer placed on the paths of Montréal's Mount Royal. On these disks Boyer gathers wisps of language and gives them an ironic permanence in marble: "Not far from here Charles and I had an argument. I don't even remember why." The disks blend in with the surrounding ground, and you have to read carefully to make out the edges of the marble circles and then decipher the winding messages. In a previous project, Boyer had written fragments of poetry and inscribed them on plaques which were fixed to houses on residential streets of the Plateau and Little Burgundy, plaques that looked like the ones that say "Napoleon slept here" but instead talk of the wind or a passing whimsy.

Such forms of counter-narrative are particularly resonant in Montréal, where occupation of city space and the trajectory of narrative across the city have traditionally carried with them heavy ideological agendas. Carpentier and Boyer suggest ways of occupying the territory which dedramatize the traditional dividing lines of the city. In contrast to a long

1 "Beneath the asphalt of cities there is a vast history we have forgotten, because our present moves too fast and we have lost our collective memory ... What of the ruins and fragments of memory collecting under the *terra incognita* of asphalt and houses, of sheds and garages, of decks and terraces? All these laneways and paved surfaces were once farms, paths, hunting grounds" (my trans.).

tradition of Montréal narratives where trajectories carry loaded political meanings, these are ramblings on more casual terrain. They avoid the divides – the east-west language divide, the north-south class divide – which carry long-standing dramas of confrontation. And they speak of a moment in Montréal history when narrative topographies are being scrambled. Montréal literature has been dominated for decades by the narrative of east-west confrontation, and the geography of its imagination has been limited by a certain obsession with symbolic sites like the rich neighbourhoods of Westmount or the poor neighbourhoods of the east end. This is changing – and the city of fiction is opening up to new territories, both in English-language and French-language novels. For instance, *Côte-des-Nègres* (1998) by Mauricio Segura, *La brûlerie* (2004) by Émile Ollivier, and Pierre Nepveu's *Des mondes peu habités* (1992) for Côte-des-Neiges; Little Italy in Nicolas Dickner's *Nikolski* (2005); Montréal-Nord in Antonio D'Alfonso's *Avril ou l'anti-passion* (1990); Mile End in Lise Tremblay's *Danse juive* (1999) and also in Myriam Beaudouin's *Hadassa* (2006); or the suburbs in *Dée* (2002) by Michael Delisle. The novel in English also embraces a much broader range of locales. And by broadening the scope of geography, the novel can introduce stories of marginalities that were occluded by previous narratives, which were dictated by an often simple map of east-west Montréal. Changes in critical perspective invite the emergence of methodologies that allow Montréal to be exposed as a space of contradictions (see Harel in this volume), open to new interpretations. Spaces are revealed as "constructed," products of overlapping and conflicting discourses.

At the same time as new narrative spaces are being discovered, the old ones are being revisited. It is striking that several recent novels have chosen to fall back on the traditional symbols and icons of the city, and in particular Boulevard Saint-Laurent – the mythical dividing line that separates east and west. Mining the contradictory resonances of Saint-Laurent – its reality as both a dividing line and a contact zone – they continue to use the street for its dramatic potential and for its association with marginality. This is paradoxical since, as I will discuss, the street itself is changing very fast and is losing that very marginality. The three novels I will discuss are Heather O'Neill's *Lullabies for Little Criminals*, Zoe Whittall's *Bottle Rocket Hearts*, and Rawi Hage's *Cockroach* – each of which engages with one strong aspect of the historic symbolism of the street – O'Neill with the site of marginality, Whittall with the dividing line, Hage with the marketplace and battleground of immigrant life.

Chronotope and Heterotopia

The contradictory realities of Boulevard Saint-Laurent are constantly evoked in discussions of Montréal and continually re-analysed by historians and cultural critics. In addition to the authoritative book by Pierre Anctil, a 1998 article by Martin Allor synthesizes with particular acuity the heritage of the street as a singular space playing overlapping roles. Calling the street "Chronotope and Heterotopia" (terms by Mikhail Bakhtin and Michel Foucault respectively), Allor emphasizes the way the street has been a space of mediation, bringing together different temporalities and histories (the narratives of Mordecai Richler and of Michel Tremblay), levels of social relations (class, ethnic, and gender identities), and media productions (theatre, cinema, literature). The cultural geography of linguistic, ethnic, and class differences has intersected with the successive developments of leisure-cultural practices and cultural industry equipment – the first public projection of cinema in Canada took place on the Main in 1896. And the space of the Main has functioned (and continues to) as a hybrid space for cultural performances cutting across the distinctions of high and low (i.e., theatre and ztheatre and Yiddish theatre or Portuguese street festivals), and between public-sanctioned performance (*grands cinémas*) and illicit and policed activities (prostitution). These "present" pasts are sedimented into the current landscape of the Main, written into the architecture of the buildings on the street and into the practices of the various taste and cultural communities who walk its territory. More importantly, the history of this liminality is articulated and rearticulated across an ever-expanding archive of public texts which tell the stories of the Main and link them to versions of Québec identity (Allor 45).

Cinema, theatre, the heterogeneity of immigrant street life: all these have given an enhanced visibility to a street already enjoying an important symbolic identity. The street remains identified as a special site of cosmopolitanism in the city, a place of gathering and conviviality, of a generous overflowing of diversity, in the space between the two language-identified sectors of Montréal. Through its campaigns of promotion and nostalgia branding, the city continues to maintain the image of the street as a busy and warm space of mixing, an expression of the diversity of the city – even though these realities have changed drastically. The associations of the street with sexuality, and in particular with the red-light district of bars and all-night hot dog joints, are consonant with this idea of mixing and of liminality.

The street's strong identity as a cultural leisure-time site has been intensified by the recent renovation of the Monument-National, by the construction of Daniel Langlois's Ex-Centris multimedia complex, and more recently yet by the vast project of the Quartier des spectacles – involving a major renovation of the area at the south end of the boulevard around Montréal's traditional red-light district. Despite opposition from groups concerned to maintain the diversity of the street and its libertarian traditions, this huge initiative has seen the introduction of engineered change involving real estate and urban infrastructure. Most affected are the areas still associated with sexual licence, around the intersection of Saint-Laurent and Sainte-Catherine. Major change is also occurring a few kilometres farther north on the street, as deindustrialization is freeing up factory buildings just east of Saint-Laurent around Saint-Viateur in Mile End. This area, called "Saint-Viateur East," is becoming another flashpoint in the struggle by residents and artists to maintain the character of the neighbourhood around Saint-Laurent. A citizens' coalition has been active in proposing community-centred initiatives designed to prevent outright gentrification of these spaces.

These developments are hastening the disappearance of the few traces of the immigrant institutions which once defined the character of the street, as the shops, restaurants, and associations run and frequented by immigrants are replaced by those of a new business elite, *branché* and technologically savvy. Interventions by urban designers intended to enhance the "branding" of the street and recall its history seem only to have increased the blandness of the street, and long-term construction has caused serious damage to the businesses. The FRAG project introduced by the group known as ATSA (Action terroriste socialement acceptable, www.atsa.qc.ca/en/) highlights these many aspects of the street's past and present, while paradoxically drawing attention to the fact that this special character has almost completely disappeared.

The economic transformation of the street takes on a striking visual form in the case of the Peck Building at the corner of Saint-Viateur and Saint-Laurent. Built to accommodate the clothing industry in the early 1900s, the building was bought by the French video games giant Ubisoft. Paris-based Ubisoft is one of the world's top five producers of video games, with a Montréal staff of some 1,800. Today the techno-workers sit at their computer monitors at the same worksites where once there were sewing machines. The new world of globalized media has simply replicated the old sweatshop pattern, with computers taking the place of pedal-operated sewing machines. At the same time, Ubisoft consciously taps into the history and mythology of Saint-Laurent as a site of connectedness. The company cashes in on the immigrant history of Mile End by promoting its convivial neighbourhood as a perk to its workers, even – at one time – contributing to maintaining the fabric of the neighbourhood by organizing a yearly street festival. The encounter between immigration, media, and globalization takes on a complex interface in a traditional immigrant neighbourhood like Mile End, where Ubisoft taps into the history and mythology of the street and neighbourhood in order to enhance its cachet. Immigrants share with the new generation of mobile media workers a role as connectors of people and images across continents. In many cases, the same conditions of long hours and poor salaries prevail. What are dramatically different, however, are the processes and results of that labour.

Down and Out on Saint-Laurent

Lullabies for Little Criminals (*La ballade de Baby*) by Heather O'Neill is one of the most compelling novels of the last decades. It takes place in a Montréal identified by certain strongly resonant sites, such as Saint-Laurent, but at the same time where geographical and linguistic borders are blurred. It follows a twelve-year-old girl as she lurches through the end of childhood. Her mother has died and she is being brought up, so to speak, by a too-young father who is a child himself, a heroin addict who has not figured out how to take control of his life. The action begins somewhere around Saint-Laurent and Sainte-Catherine. But subsequent locales don't really make sense, there being a conflation of certain east-end locations with locations that seem to be more around the Lachine Canal or areas of Lower NDG (Notre-Dame-de-Grâce), where in fact Heather O'Neill did grow up. So there is a blurriness of locale that introduces a haze into a narration that is otherwise cruelly lucid. The voice of the narrator is compelling as she tells the story of her father's failures and the various substitutes she attempts to create for him.

The young girl is called Baby, her father is called Jules. But – is that Jules (as in English with the "s" pronounced) or Jules (as in French with a silent "s")? He is from a village called Val-des-Loups, and at one point Baby quotes from *L'avalée des avalés* (1966) by Réjean Ducharme, citing it as a favourite novel. This linguistic undecidability is echoed by the use of Saint-Laurent as an in-between geographical space, but it is made even more evident in a strange linguistic slip at the start of the novel. The novel begins with Baby and her father moving into yet another dilapidated downtown hotel, which she calls the Hotel Austriche (2). This is neither *Autriche* (Austria) nor ostrich, but a strange unidentifiable amalgam – “Austriche” – which perhaps belies carelessness, a carelessness that could have gotten past the copy editors of the book, but also perhaps attempts to underline the in-between space of the city where language separations have melted into shapelessness. Other expressions in the novel seem to betray this decay of language, such as Jules saying, “We’re localized here” (5). Some of the characters have French names, like the pimp Alphonse or Baby’s friend Xavier.

By using the corner of Saint-Laurent and Sainte-Catherine as her starting point, O’Neill taps into the mythology of the city – exploiting the symbolic resonance of Saint-Laurent as the dividing line, and of course the legendary red-light district. The pre-adolescent Baby thinks this neighbourhood is the “the most beautiful in town,” with its bright lights and prostitutes in gorgeous high-heeled boots. Part of the impact of the novel is obviously the reversals in perspective you get from a twelve-year-old who expresses no conventional judgmentalism, and who captures moments of wonder in what the dust jacket calls the “urban jungle.” But it is precisely her “street smarts” that get her by. After Baby moves with her father to what they call the Ostrich Hotel, Jules walks her to school in the morning to make sure she knows her way. But Baby has no need of help, knowing the neighbourhood backwards and forwards because of their many moves from one hotel room or apartment to another. “I wish I could get lost,” she says. But she knows only too well how to get around (6).

As Domenico Beneventi has shown, the power of O’Neill’s novel stems from its

> restaging of contemporary Montréal in a strikingly new and audacious way; by articulating the embodied experiences of the city “from below,” that is, from the vantage point of the dispossessed, the poor, the excluded, the exploited, and the *sans-papiers* forever caught in the *non-lieux* of government agencies, child protection services, welfare lines, immigration offices, and the street itself. (265)

This is a power that O’Neill’s novel shares with Rawi Hage’s *Cockroach,* both novels that have been abundantly analysed in recent years. Before turning to *Cockroach,* however, I might mention here a lesser-known novel, yet one that restages the cultural geography of Montréal in contrasting ways.

Old-New Stories

O'Neill's perspective from below contrasts quite starkly with *Bottle Rocket Hearts* by Zoe Whittall, published in 2007, which displays a more recognizable geography, one that replays the old stories of the east-west divide. The protagonist is a student who moves from her parents' house in the west end (Dorval) to an apartment on Esplanade facing Mount Royal (Mile End) – a trajectory that has become quite conventional for anglophone students in Montréal. The heroine in fact is studying fine arts at Concordia. The new twist is that the heroine has a girlfriend, Della, who lives in the "east end of the city, where Papineau and Ontario Street intersect, a part of the city I'd only ever been to go to gay bars and once to get my tongue pierced" (12–13). Della "lives in the extreme present": she is French Canadian, impossibly cool, and very emphatically politicized. On the night of the referendum, October 1995, our heroine travels by bike to a bar on the east side and is very conscious of being the only anglo in the place. While the drama of that night is taking place (the extremely close vote, the explosive and self-destructive remarks by Jacques Parizeau), the heroine is preoccupied by her embarrassment and her jealousy in relation to Della and her friends. And so the commentary on the referendum is a playful one, the personal winning out over the political.

This is at once a new and a very old story, echoing many elements of the crosstown journey that has marked Montréal narratives since at least the 1960s (Simon). Yet there are some indications in the novel of the new Montréal. Della's former girlfriend "flows between French and English seamlessly, like it's all one language" (Whittall 23). Remarkably, however, the novel in its printed version shows a complete disregard for French, allowing egregious mistakes to appear. "Vien ici, je te manques [*sic*!]," says Della (62).

The book is a happy and tragic collage of personal and collective politics, jealousy and love, in-between spaces of emotion – "a portrait of Montréal in the mid-nineties that successfully recreates its hedonistic, Salvation Army band, gender-bending glory," according to Heather O'Neill on the book's dust jacket. It conveys the experiences of a new generation of Anglos, somewhat more at ease with the city yet still caught in the dramas of its divides. The novel gives a new spin to an old story – one that sees the protagonist cross the city in search of excitement, sexual and political.

Rawi Hage's novel *Cockroach* also replays an old story – giving Saint-Laurent an important role as a street of immigrants – of cheap bars and poets holding forth, and desperate newcomers trying to steal from one another. The main character returns over and over to the cafe on Saint-Laurent (the cafe Artista), where he either devises schemes to exact a return of money he has loaned or steals from fellow immigrants. The novel is strong in its evocation of a new generation of immigrants scarred from former war zones, troubled by past histories, longing to break through the layers of cold that isolate them from the life of the city. For Simon Harel, Hage's character enacts the psychic suffering of the refugee, a person defined more than anything by his non-status, by the fact that his words do not count; and for Smaro Kamboureli, Hage is above all a figure of the immigrant whose story will not turn out well, who will remain an alien body in the city. The narrator's impotent rage leads him to imagine himself as a giant cockroach, the only living creature that will survive after humanity perishes in the apocalypse. He breaks into people's houses and moves among their possessions, crawling along their walls and their drains. He is driven by a thirst for revenge and a desire to wreak havoc on the favoured classes. The immigrant is an outsider, doomed to reliving his old stories of hatred and without any cushion of solidarity. Hage's immigrant is a solitary person, whose dramas are far less light-hearted than more ironic immigrant tales of conflict, such as Dany Laferrière's *How to Make Love to a Negro* (*Comment faire l'amour avec un nègre sans se fatiguer*, 1985). Anger, not irony, is Hage's primary emotion.

Hage's novel shares with contemporary anglo literature a sense of linguistic undecidability. Like O'Neill, like Whittall, Hage evokes a French city. The English is alternately crude and poetic, the language itself carrying a charge of violence, speaking of the anger of the character, who is still in the grip of the dramas that have driven him from his home. There is also a strong presence of French in the novel – this time quite correct and matter-of-fact. Hage evokes a community of polyglot immigrants: Iranians, Algerians, Lebanese, speaking a mixture of French and English, Arabic and Farsi.

The cruelty and rage of Hage's novel are reminders that the immigrant contact zones of Montréal have not always been treated as pure conviviality. Michel Tremblay has been known largely for the way he brings out the carnivalesque, transgressive, and liminal spaces of sexuality on the street in his novels and plays, but he has also suggested some of the less savoury aspects of this liminality. In the 1978 *La grosse femme d'à côté est enceinte*, he describes an expedition of housewives from the Plateau taking a tram down Saint-Laurent to go shopping downtown. As long as they were on Mount Royal, says the narrator, all was well, but as soon as they turned onto Saint-Laurent going south, they all became nervous, because all of them owed money to the Jewish shopkeepers. They take their revenge on a Jewish woman who gets on the tram with her sack of provisions – pretending to block their noses and making fun of what she has in her bags. "Y paraît qu'y gardent leurs transferts pour se faire du papier de toilette!" laughs Madame Jodoin. And when one of her friends is worried that the old Jewish woman might understand French, Madame Jodoin laughs, "A' comprend pas le français, al'a rien à nous vendre" (22–3).[2]

This cruel exhibition of racism defines the street as a barrier, separating one group from another. Tremblay's story, like the novels we have discussed, reinforces Allor's characterization of Saint-Laurent as a sedimentation of sometimes contradictory meanings. In contrast to André Carpentier, who, as I mentioned at the outset, looks for trajectories through the city that avoid the overcharged trajectories of the past, these novels exploit the historical resonance of Montréal geography. All three novels draw on the continued power of the myth of Saint-Laurent as a liminal space of contradictions – just as they focus attention to the increasing linguistic porosity of the city, the seepage of French into English-language writing and by extension the decreased power of the dividing line to hold divisions fast. All three also introduce zones of marginality – the underclass of the drug world in O'Neill, the marginality of lesbian and gay communities in Whittall, the unsituatedness of the immigrant in Hage. For O'Neill and Hage in particular, the city is divided against those who have no entitlement.

By portraying Saint-Laurent as a space of marginality, these writers are faithful to the history and collective memory of the street. What they are not providing, however, is an accurate contemporary representation of the street in Montréal's changing urban landscape. In this they are perhaps also being faithful to a certain tradition of Montréal writing. The collective imagination always seems to lag behind – and can in fact simply ignore – sociodemographic and economic realities. This "disconnect" becomes particularly apparent at certain turning points in the history of the city. The urban identity of Québec was not fully integrated into Québec literature, for instance, until well after the interwar period.

2 "She doesn't understand French, she has nothing to sell us" (my trans.).

And yet statistics show that the population was significantly urban by the end of the Second World War. In the same way, the sectarian divides of Montréal long prevented representation of the cosmopolitan nature of the city. The sense of urban citizenship does not necessarily coincide with the simple presence of populations within the city but requires a process of cultural maturation.

Where these novels do become interesting indicators of their time is in the way they use the mixed language of Montréal. The presence of French in all three novels is significant. All three acknowledge Montréal as a French-language city and integrate a sense of its language environment. O'Neill's hazy invocation of geographical and language borders is a particularly original contribution to the aesthetic of the Montréal novel.

The turn of the new century may perhaps become another of the important moments of change in the self-perception of Montréal. It is possible that the cultural engineering projects undertaken by the city will irrevocably change the character of Boulevard Saint-Laurent – reducing the number of roles it has played and smoothing over the many disparities which have been a source of both the wealth and the poverty of Montréal life. Perhaps the street will resist these efforts and see the invention of yet new forms of liminality and transgression.

WORKS CITED

Allor, Martin. "Locating Cultural Activity: The 'Main' as Chronotope and Heterotopia." *Topia*, vol. 1, no. 1, 1998, pp. 42–54.

Anctil, Pierre. *Saint-Laurent: La Main de Montréal.* Éditions Septentrion, 2002.

Beneventi, Domenico. "Montréal Underground." *Journal of Canadian Studies / Revue d'études canadiennes*, vol. 46, no. 3, Fall 2012, pp. 263–86.

Boyer, Gilbert. *La montagne des jours.* Montreal, Centre international d'art contemporain, 1992, 36 pp.

Carpentier, André. *Ruelles, jours ouvrables: Flâneries en ruelles montréalaises.* Boréal, 2007.

Cronin, Michael. "The Advent of Micro-Modernity." *Irish Journal of French Studies* 9, 2009, pp. 137–55. www.ingentaconnect.com/content/irjofs/ijfs/2009/00000009/00000001/art00008.

Hage, Rawi. *Cockroach.* Anansi, 2008.

Harel, Simon. "Langue monosémique, récit pluriel: La traduction de la souffrance psychique en langage de la Cité." 2014. www.academia.edu/

6933111/Langue_monosémique_récit_pluriel_la_traduction_de_la_souffrance_psychique_en_langage_de_la_Cité.

Kamboureli, Smaro. "Forgetting, Remembering, and Unforgetting: Collective Memory and the Nation-State in Rawi Hage's *Cockroach*." *Towards Critical Multiculturalism: Dialogues between/among Canadian Diasporas*, edited by Ewelina Bujnowska, Marcin Gabryś, and Tomasz Sikora, Agencja Artystyczna PARA, 2011, pp. 134–53.

O'Neill, Heather. *Lullabies for Little Criminals*. Harper Perennial, 2006.

Simon, Sherry. *Translating Montréal: Episodes in the Life of a Divided City*. McGill-Queen's UP, 2006.

Tremblay, Michel. *La grosse femme d'à côté est enceinte*. Éditions Leméac, 1978.

Whittall, Zoe. *Bottle Rocket Hearts*. Cormorant, 2007.

4 Heterotopia and Its Discontents: Exploring Spatial, Social, and Textual Liminality in Rawi Hage's *Cockroach*

RITA SAKR

In a brilliant passage near the end of Rawi Hage's novel *Cockroach*, the narrator reflects on the deceptive homogeneity and peacefulness of the Montréal snow that conceals a physical and metaphorical underground:

> The snow covered everything and I walked above cotton, on silent carpets, on beach sand. Softness is temporary and deceiving. It gently receives you and gently expels you. I saw no one, no one ... I thought: I will tell every tourist I encounter, every sister who has ever received a postcard, that nothing here exists; there is no queen, there are no seals, no dancing bears, moose, cabins, high trees, bonfires. Descriptions of these are all a ploy, an illusion, a conspiracy. There is nothing but that which freezes, and the only way to escape it is to dig deep holes, dig and sail under it ... All that exists, all that will ever exist, shall pass through this passageway under the ice, the dead corpses when they turn to dust, the big happy meals, the wine, the tears, ... all that is killed, beaten, misused, abused, all that have legs, all that crawl, all that is erected, all that climbs, flies, sits, wears glasses, laughs, dances, and smokes, all shall disappear into the underground like a broken cloud. (*Cockroach* 249–50)

The narrator in Hage's novel imaginatively escapes to the underground, which he sometimes delusionally, sometimes lucidly perceives as a space where illusions about social justice and peace vanish. This underground welcomes the marginalized, the unclean, and the oppressed and inverts society's falling economic and political towers: the "big happy meals" that leave millions hungry and unhappy, and the monuments that are "erected" on the "dead corpses" of "all that is killed, beaten, misused, [and] abused."

In "Of Other Spaces," Michel Foucault introduces his conception of heterotopias as "counter-sites ... in which the real sites, all the other real sites that can be found within the culture are simultaneously represented, contested, and inverted" (24). Foucault mentions "heterotopias of deviation: those in which individuals whose behavior is deviant in relation to the required mean or norm are placed," and he cites "psychiatric hospitals, and of course prisons" (25). It is possible to expand this category further to include the heterotopic spaces of the unemployed, the welfare recipient, the refugee, the declassed migrant, and the petty criminal, all of which figure prominently in Rawi Hage's novel *Cockroach*. Hage's characters enter these heterotopic spaces according to what Foucault describes as the "system of opening and closing that both isolates and makes them penetrable" (26) – a system of exclusion that "gently receives you and gently expels you" (*Cockroach* 249). These are marginalized or "othered" spaces that refract and magnify the inadequacies in the ideological and socio-economic structures of the neoliberal state.

Developing Foucault's theorization of heterotopia, Kevin Hetherington's book-length study *The Badlands of Modernity: Heterotopia and Social Ordering* outlines six ways in which the term "heterotopia" has been employed: to refer to "paradoxical" sites; "ambivalent" sites; sites that have "an aura of mystery, danger, or transgression"; sites of "absolute perfection"; sites "that are marginalized"; and "incongruous forms of writing and text that challenge and make impossible discursive statements" (41). As this chapter will show, *Cockroach* unfolds spaces that are marked by sociocultural paradox or ambivalence as well as sites that are dangerous because they comprise implicit or explicit violence. Furthermore, *Cockroach* reveals how sites of "absolute perfection" like monumental spaces are contested by what I will explain later as "heterotopias of resistance," which, in this novel, are the underground and the filth that tentatively defy social ordering and undermine the "clean" city. Finally, as a counter-narrative that examines marginalized spaces, Hage's novel may be read also as a discursive heterotopia in the sense that it forms a narrative space for the exploration of the blind spots and drawbacks in the structures of the neoliberal state. The novel is hence part of an expansive literature of human rights that traces the multiple "other spaces" disrupting the smooth surface of Western democracies.[1] From this

1 See my forthcoming essay, "Expanding the Space of Human Rights in Literature, Reclaiming Literature as a Human Right."

perspective, heterotopia can form a useful conceptual groundwork to approach the contested spaces of Rawi Hage's *Cockroach*. However, as I will show, heterotopia faces methodological and epistemological challenges in *Cockroach* since this text and its various contexts defy categorization as straightforwardly "other spaces" and, instead, present a spatialization process that is fissured, composite, and ultimately liminal. Traversing discursive and material heterotopias, my chapter is therefore a critical journey into the liminal spaces and voices that are embodied and articulated in *Cockroach*, the second novel by Rawi Hage – who was born in Lebanon, immigrated to Canada, and is now living in Montréal.

The fissured and liminal texture of *Cockroach* allows for a reading of this novel as a schizophrenic text in two respects. First, as the subsequent close readings will show, Hage's novel dramatizes a constructive yet pessimistic vision of histories of violence (civil war, physical and sexual abuse, arms trade) that are situated across spatially and temporally double axes (Lebanon, Iran, Algeria/Québec, and past/present).[2] Punctuating this schizophrenic text are the many traumatized characters raving in search of a stable identity. Second, *Cockroach* is also a schizophrenic novel because it invites a critical and ethical "schizoanalysis" according to, but also beyond, Gilles Deleuze and Félix Guattari's theorization of this term. In contrast to certain strands of psychoanalysis, Deleuze and Guattari argue that schizoanalysis "treats the unconscious as an acentered system, in other words, as a machinic network of finite automata (a rhizome), and thus arrives at an entirely different state of the unconscious" (19). I will show that *Cockroach* operates rhizomatically on textual and narrative levels and thus invites a schizoanalysis that unravels the unconscious of history, individuals, material space, and discourse generally as acentred and pluricentred discontinuities colluding and clashing in what Deleuze and Guattari call multiple "lines of flight" (208). The significance of this rhizomatic dynamic is twofold. On spatial and social levels, the narrator's movements across urban space are random, his itineraries unpredictable, and his relations to law and order elusive. He breaks into apartments and steals without being seen, defiantly observes

2 Although the war-torn country that the narrator comes from remains unnamed in the text, there are several indications throughout the novel (and in its critical reception) that this most probably refers to Lebanon, which is the setting of Hage's earlier novel, *De Niro's Game*.

people eating in restaurants "behind thick glass" (*Cockroach* 86), and urinates on car wheels then disappears. The "multiple lines of flight" that represent this "improper" urban resident's movements are threatening since they disturb the stability of established spaces and identities, thus subversively proclaiming his right to social and spatial justice (see Soja). His invisibility is feared while his visibility is unwanted, just like a cockroach underground. Yet it is precisely through this social invisibility expressed in solitary anonymity that the situation of the non-citizen or "improper" citizen – the cockroach underground – is potentially resistant.

The description of *Cockroach*'s underground seems to coincide with Marc Augé's definition of "non-place" ("*non-lieu*"): "The community of human destinies is experienced in the anonymity of non-place, and in solitude" (120). However, in Hage's novel, the "improper" citizen has no sense of belonging to an urban community "in transit" (Augé 120) despite the purportedly common experience of anonymity and basic humanity. The narrator's anonymity is paradoxical because it is a symptom of both his exclusion from and his resistance to a clearly designated community of "proper" citizens, and hence of "proper" human beings, whose social identities are anchored to a system of values that distributes its "others" across distinct heterotopias. The narrator remains "in transit," and thus in liminal status, among these various heterotopias and disrupts the deceptive "softness" (*Cockroach* 249) of the "proper" citizens' spaces with his rhizomatic movements.[3]

On a textual level, the rhizomatic texture of the narrative and the schizoanalysis that it invites are highly political engagements with the possibilities and impossibilities of articulating liminal spaces for the displaced, on the macropolitical level of migrating or immigrating communities as well as on the more intimate and concrete level of the individual whose displacement and exilic relations are not only geopolitical but also socio-economic, existential, psychological, and intrinsically human.

Reflecting on exile, Edward W. Said notes that for the displaced individual "both the new and the old environments are vivid, actual, occurring together contrapuntally" (186). The first-person narrator of

3 See Simon Harel's related discussion, in this volume, of literary representations of "homelessness and contained space" (suggesting a link between heterotopia and the space of the homeless).

Cockroach is constantly negotiating two spaces – Beirut and Montréal – that occur not as binary oppositions belonging to the separate domains of memory and actuality. Rather, the old and new spaces are simultaneously present in the narrator's consciousness, imaginatively and actually, contrapuntally orchestrating the voices of trauma: Beirut and Montréal, or rather Beirut-in-Montréal. The place names in Beirut are silenced in the double act of forgetfulness and textual erasure, while particular Montréal sites that presumably reflect, in various ways, cultural hybridity and in-betweenness are named with a remarkable insistence – especially McGill University, St-Laurent Boulevard, and Ste-Catherine Street. A similar process occurs in Régine Robin's *La Québécoite* that presents Montréal as a discursive site where place naming is unrelenting and trauma is negotiated through the dynamics of evocation, erasure, and in-betweenness with respect to other spaces and other times: "Le ghetto – la guerre – les sirènes, c'est la reine du sabbat mais il n'y a plus de sabbat. La parole immigrante traverse les mots – la voix d'ailleurs – la voix des morts ... Désormais le temps de l'entre-deux. Entre deux villes, entre deux langues, entre deux villes, deux villes dans une ville" (63).[4]

In *Cockroach*, both Beirut and Montréal are articulated as trauma because both are marked by histories of violence. These are the history of civil war and its interpersonal repercussions in Lebanon and the seemingly less spectacular histories of Montréal's rich and poor in their dangerous flirtations with implicit and explicit violence, ranging from class conflict on a local level to arms trading on an international level. The narrator experiences a psychological liminality between these two spaces and histories: the first space and history have left an indelible, damaging mark on his unconscious while the second bombard his consciousness with continuous shocks. For instance, the history of the Lebanese war is reawakened when the traumatized narrator delusionally imagines his cockroach alter ego reminding him of the time "when you [the narrator] collected bullets, and when you followed Abou-Roro down to the place of the massacre and watched him pull golden teeth from cadavers"

4 "The ghetto – the war – the sirens; it is the queen of the Sabbath but there is no more Sabbath. Immigrant speech traverses words – the voice of elsewhere – the voice of the dead ... Now is the time of the in-between. Between two cities, between two languages, between two cities, two cities in one" (my trans.).

(*Cockroach* 202).[5] In *Cockroach*'s Montréal, the narrator realizes that the sound of bullets may be muffled but the weapons are present, hidden in the closets of rich young men or stored in secret places to be sold to Third World dictatorships.

These histories, though significantly different in geopolitical sense and scale, seem to conspire against not only the narrator but also the novel's other characters, whose personal stories are entangled in vicious cycles of violence from which immigration, asylum, and legal residency and citizenship in Western states offer no respite. Interspersed throughout *Cockroach* are the stories of the exiled Algerian professor who is caught between the grips of mythomania and welfare cheques; and of Shohreh, Farhoud, and the other Iranian refugees whose traumatic personal experiences of oppression and sexual exploitation by their former jailers in Iran get their final turn of the screw in the act of vengeance at the end of the novel. There, Shohreh attacks her former jailer and rapist, whose presence in Montréal signals a presumable arms deal between Canada and Iran.[6] This evokes another contemporary history of violence beyond the binary opposition of a violent Islamic Republic and a peaceful multicultural Western nation. In an interview with CBC, Hage reveals this awareness of underlying violence in sanitized urban environments: "I'm not naïve about cities, I'm not naïve about nations ... Just because a city has some culture and looks nice, doesn't mean it hasn't got an undercurrent of violence. Montréal is a large military industrial complex. Under all that beauty there is something very ugly." In portraying interconnected networks of corporate capitalism, wars, and human rights abuses, *Cockroach* harks back to the political geography that *De Niro's Game* traces and that extends from Western fallen empires to Eastern former colonies and failed democracies, thus unravelling the paradoxes of post-imperial history and its trajectories of violence. As Mark Libin affirms, "Hage's narratives refuse to distinguish between the idea of the West as hospitable host for the refugee and the idea of the West as the colonial aggressor that initiated the wars and turmoil and created

---

5 For a discussion of the Sabra and Shatila massacre, the traumatic memory of which occupies several pages of *De Niro's Game* and is elliptically evoked here, see Najat Rahman's article and my essay "'War Is Surrealism without Art.'"

6 André Forget offers an in-depth analysis of the agency of refugees in Hage's works in his MA thesis.

the refugee situations it now strives to alleviate" (82). Instead of radical dystopian visions, Hage presents heterotopia as the constitutive paradoxical or ambivalent space of the Western democracy.

Cockroach not only tells the traumatic stories of refugees and exiles in Montréal but also peeks at the traces of personal dissatisfaction, escapist fantasies, and psychological inadequacies in the apparently stable lives of Montréal's rich – the sons and daughters of its powerful professionals and industrialists – whom the narrator grudgingly describes as "corrupt, empty, selfish, self-absorbed, capable only of seeing themselves in the reflection from the tinted glass in their fancy cars" (185). The novel reveals psychological and emotional shortcomings even in the life of Genevieve, the government-appointed therapist whose journey into the narrator's unconscious ends with his intrusion into the secret corners of her ordered mind and ordered apartment.

The multiple spatialities and temporalities that *Cockroach* traverses in its rhizomatic historical meanderings among the lives of nations, communities, and individuals complicate the categorization of this novel. *Cockroach* is part of an emergent literature that, in unravelling multiple histories across geopolitical borders, cannot be placed in a clear-cut framework that would set it distinctly apart from Middle Eastern, Arab, and various migrant literatures in comparative Québécois and Canadian spaces. This novel also schizophrenically displays a submerged post-war identity since it is haunted by its literary and historical unconscious; by this I mean Rawi Hage's first novel *De Niro's Game* and the Lebanese civil war that it rewrites.[7] In this context, the narrator's fragmented memories of war, massacre, and urban conflict mark *Cockroach* with a raw memorial dimension that represents different spaces of political and cultural memory. As such, Hage's novel contributes to the dialogue becoming increasingly complex yet productively nuanced in Canadian and Québécois literary spaces under the influence of emerging migrant voices from nations that have been scarred by civil strife. Second, what Hage's novel reveals is the

7 Rahman comments on the displacement and discontinuities in the novel's textual, contextual, and intertextual referents: "Written in English by an Arab francophone Montréal visual artist who lived through the war in Beirut in 1982, the novel unveils linguistic, spatial, and temporal disjunctures in its transposition of Beirut's war via mythical and historical stopovers in Rome and Paris. Another form this kind of transposition and dislocation takes is that of intertextuality, for the novel evokes the famous scene in the film *The Deer Hunter* (1978)" (807).

inextricability of personal history and national history, as the dynamic interplay of several micro-histories prevents a macro-historical stasis at the centre of the novel. Third, this inextricability is the symptom of a major characteristic of trauma, which Cathy Caruth astutely sifts from Freud's late work. In her introduction to *Trauma*, Caruth argues that "what trauma has to tell us – the historical and personal truth it transmits – is intricately bound up with its refusal of historical boundaries; that its truth is bound up with its crisis of truth" (8). *Cockroach* intensifies this crisis in relation to historical and personal truth particularly by blurring the boundaries between the narrator's real experiences, memories, fantasies, and hallucinations as he painfully grapples with past and present wounds and as he seeks an identity, a space, and a life at the border of physical and psychological death – the death of his sister and of numerous others in his war-torn country and his attempted suicide and deterioration in Montréal.[8] Accordingly, a mentally and existentially schizophrenic and almost fatalistic perspective marks the textual and contextual spaces of the novel:

> And I panicked, thinking I was the only naked one in the battle. I somehow managed to cover myself with a towel and clung to the bathroom door, but then the door shifted back and forth in front of me. All I wanted was to cross it, to get to the other side and throw my carcass on the sheets of the wounded and the dead. And a part of me felt thin, as if I were on top of a spear and fretting like a banner in the wind. I watched myself, conscious that another me was escaping ... I was split between two planes and aware of two existences, and they were both mine. I belong to two spaces, I thought, and I am wrapped in one sheet. I looked at the ceiling. I felt it shifting for a very brief moment, sideways, then down and up. And then that terrible sadness came back into the world like an omnipotent blinding cloud, and tears dropped from my eyes for no reason, as if I was crying for someone else. (*Cockroach* 119)

8 For an exploration of trauma and violence in *De Niro's Game* and *Cockroach*, see especially Syrine Hout's work, as well as Dalia Said Mostafa's "Journeying through a Discourse of Violence" and Julia Borossa's "Violence, Trauma, and Subjectivity." For a discussion of the contested spaces of suicide, in a postcolonial context, see, in this volume, Mary Jean Green's chapter, "Women's Space in Postcolonial Perspective."

This passage exemplifies the expression of personal and collective trauma through the motifs of doubling and in-betweenness. Like numerous other instances in the novel, this excerpt traces the hallucinatory edges of the real and metaphorically marks the conflicts within the narrator's multiply hyphenated identity as he strives to forge a liminal space for himself. Syrine Hout also suggests that "this existential self-perception provides the protagonist with a liminal space as one of possibility, not for becoming a culturally hybridised person … but for coping, emotionally and materially, with life in exile" (161).

Cockroach begins with an account of the narrator's attempted suicide and the subsequent therapy he receives, and it ends with the narrator killing the man who formerly tormented and raped his beloved Shohreh in her Iranian jail. Near the middle of the novel, the narrator says, "All those who leave immigrate to better their lives, but I wanted to better my death. Maybe it is the ending that matters, not the life … Maybe we, like elephants, walk far towards our chosen burials" (160). The narrator's statement implicitly negotiates an existential liminality that operates on two levels. On one level, this longing for a better death, merging the human and non-human, expresses the narrator's absurdist attitude towards existence. This is the result of his experience of war which dictates an abnormal system of values whereby an individual's hopes revolve around the quality of death rather than life. In an interview with Eddie Taylor on *De Niro's Game,* Hage says, "I emphasized absurdity in my writing. Absurdity is one of those indefinable ambiguities that lingers between violence, humor, apathy, loss, and even sympathy and hope. War is certainly an ultimate act of absurdity" (15). In *Cockroach,* absurdity is paradoxically an apathetic affirmation of a tragic past that marks the present psychologically and materially. On another level, the pessimistic vision permeating the novel is not merely a dispassionate, abstract glance at the immigrant's fate, nor is it just a pathetic elegy of hopeful migrants and hospitable nations. Instead, this vision also diagnoses, with almost clinical precision and genuine compassion, specific manifestations of a particular immigrant's – the narrator's – disempowerment, collapse, and extreme imaginative liveliness that acquire universal significance.

The narrator's fanciful reconstructions of reality are a nexus of traumatic hallucinations and lucid insights on the life of Montréal's underprivileged, who suffer the consequences of poverty, unemployment, crime, improper housing, and occasional hunger. As he sits in a restaurant sipping the Coke that he can hardly afford, the narrator wishes he were a cockroach so that he could "crawl under the swinging door and hide under the stove, licking the mildew, the dripping juice from the roast lamb, even the hardened yogurt drops on the side of the garbage bin" (*Cockroach* 67). He then imagines "all the crumbs, all the loose bits of food that had jumped during the evening from the cook's knives and tilted plates" as these "fell into underwaged fists and made ... [him] sob" (68). After he is hired at that same restaurant, he reflects sarcastically on the value of work, which he describes as "that place were [*sic*] humans and insects are equally fed" (211). Hunger also re-emerges in Hage's most recent novel, *Carnival*, in which the main character Fly describes how he "was reminded that famine is no laughing matter. No city masquerade, no costume, smile, or acrobatic act can appease the vacuity of hunger" (208). Even in the heterotopic site of the carnivalesque, hunger signals the inadequacies in the social justice provisions of the welfare state.

Cockroach's narrator's bold sarcasm emerges in another instance when his half-visionary, half-hallucinatory immersion in the life of a cockroach allows him to make incisive social criticism. Raving against a man who tries to sell him religious salvation and good citizenship, the narrator deconstructs humanity through the eyes of his alter ego: "Look at you, human, all dressed up ... You can't be handsome without ... stealing the wool from the backs of sheep, without making the poor work like mules in long factories with cruel whistles and punch-in cards" (284). This is an uncompromising critique of the duplicity of both capitalist and socialist representations of the space of labour as the worker's heterotopia. Theorizing a socio-economically resistant space for "the people," Margaret Kohn warns against unrealistic readings of heterotopic space since it often maintains forms of hegemonic control and socio-economic disadvantage. She writes,

> Heterotopias can be the bases of guerilla struggles against normalization but they can also perfect more nuanced forms of social control. Thus, we need a more precise concept: the heterotopia of resistance. The heterotopia of resistance is a real counter-site that inverts and contests existing economic or social hierarchies. Its function is social transformation rather than escapism, containment, or denial. By challenging the conventions of the dominant society, it can be an important locus of struggle against normalization. (508)

Cockroach unravels the space of work – the Iranian restaurant in which the narrator is employed – as a space where social transformation fails because existing socio-economic hierarchies are highly pronounced among the imaginary community of immigrants in the land of social justice. Moreover, in the French restaurant where he works for a while as a dishwasher, all positive heterotopic possibilities are negated in the mind of the narrator, who obsessively identifies patterns of implicit intercultural conflict and discrimination in the behaviours of "the Frenchies laughing behind swinging doors, making fun of the cowboys who gave a compliment to the chef" (28). The narrator describes the chef, Maître Pierre, as xenophobic towards linguistic and racial others – based on the fact that he speaks English with an "exaggerated" French accent and refuses to promote the narrator to a waiter because of his dark complexion (29). Later in the novel, the narrator extends his interpretations of socio-economic and cultural gaps in Montréal as he gloomily reflects on a rich woman's comment that "St-Laurent Street is becoming too noisy and crowded with all kinds of people" (88). Assertively claiming that he "knew what the bitch meant by noisy and all kinds of people," the narrator refracts the reputedly multicultural St-Laurent Boulevard, which loses its quality as a hybrid cultural heterotopia to become a space of danger and exclusion. In a world where he reads signs of socio-economic containment rather than fulfilment, and cultural tension rather than harmony, the narrator is alienated from all heterotopias except those rare heterotopias of resistance that emerge phantasmically in his mind or punctuate the material spaces of his daily life – the underground and filth.

Disillusioned by humanity and neurotically impaired by failed attempts at communication and love, the narrator expresses an anguish that is both personal and universal. He raves against his compatriots, his family members and friends who drowned themselves in violence and intercommunal strife; against immigrants from the Middle East, Eastern Europe, and elsewhere who have flooded Montréal with their misery and mutual distrust; against newcomers who enter poor clinics to "say 'Ahh' with an accent, [and] expose the whites of their droopy, malarial eyes" (*Cockroach* 79); against Montréal's affluent and corrupt youth to whom the narrator provides overpriced, low-quality drugs; against Montréal's winter, which he imagines as telling him "with tight lips and a cold tone ... to go back where ... [he] came from if ... [he does] not like it here" (193); and even against his therapist Genevieve, who approaches his violent past, personal losses, attempted suicide, and dependence on theft on the basis of impersonal psychiatric paradigms and her duties to taxpayers, while she addictively savours his stories of distant, violent lands.

Among these men and women, these imagined communities, the narrator frantically asks "how to exist and not to belong?" (*Cockroach* 210). This question recalls, with a difference, a line from *Les métamorphoses d'Ishtar* by the Lebanese Québécois poet Nadine Ltaif, who writes, "Voilà comment est mon exil / ... À peine suis-je née / que je n'éxiste déjà plus" (10).[9] Ltaif's poetic response to the double condition of war and exile is refracted in *Cockroach*'s narrative kaleidoscope, in the narrator's traumatized journeys through internal and external spaces and through real and imagined experiences. The question of exile, belonging, and existence afflicts the traumatized psyche of *Cockroach*'s narrator as he engages in hallucinatory dialogues with the cockroaches that invade his filthy apartment. In this psychodrama induced by drugs, childhood memories, and identity crisis, the cockroaches evoke his liminal position between the human and non-human conditions: "You are one of us. You are part cockroach. But the worst part of it is that you are also human ... Just keep your eyes on what is going on down in the underground" (203).

In Hage's *Cockroach*, the narrative of the "underground" complicates the implications of a cultural heterotopia of resistance while revealing its dark historical implications. After helping the Russian wife of the Macedonian/Greek janitor to steal an old lady's trunk filled with objects that the latter's husband, a deceased British officer, had stolen "from the Indians, or the Chinese," the narrator refuses any payment in return for this "favour":

> Oh nothing, I said. I am just doing it for history's sake.
> You mean to see things go from one culture to another?
> No, to watch the loot of war buried, the stolen treasure put back where it belongs, in the underground. I laughed loudly. The underground!
> The basement! The janitor's wife laughed with me. History is coming back to the basement, she laughed. (42)

In this bleak meditation on colonial conquests and wars, the "underground" is a space that unravels moments of cultural contact as instances of cultural theft rather than exchange. In this instance, *Cockroach*'s

9 "This is my exile / ... No sooner was I born / that I no longer existed" (my trans.).

underground also recalls the skeleton-covered Bosphorus seabed in the episode titled "When the Bosphorus Dries Up" of Orhan Pamuk's novel *The Black Book.* The surreal vision of the Bosphorus drying up reveals "the long-lost skeletons of Orthodox priests, still clutching their staffs and crosses, their ankles still weighed down by balls and chains," and "the armoured Crusaders, mounted on horses whose magnificent skeletons are still stubbornly standing" (19, 20). This is the imagined invisible underworld of Istanbul. Exposing a violent history, this underground is a counter-monumental space that contests and inverts the Istanbul urban fabric, which is punctuated with monuments celebrating the Turkish Republic and its founder Atatürk.[10] Similarly, the underground that *Cockroach*'s narrator imagines is a heterotopic space inverting and contesting a sanitized historical and cultural landscape punctuated by the statues that are "erected" to celebrate the nation's designated heroes and forget "the killed, beaten, misused, abused" (*Cockroach* 250). In this apocalyptic heterotopia, "all that is killed, beaten, misused, abused, all that have legs, all that crawl, all that is erected, all that climbs, flies, sits, wears glasses, laughs, dances, and smokes, all shall disappear" (250).

In *Cockroach,* the heterotopia of the underground harbours not only the historical relics of past cultural conflict but also the evidence of present socio-economic and cultural disadvantage in the lives of the disempowered among immigrant groups – as in the case of the janitor and his wife. In his study of "place" in Italian Canadian writing, Domenico A. Beneventi underlines the significance of the underground in the experience of immigrant communities. Beneventi notes that "seeking out economic prosperity in a new country … voiceless labourers occupy a confined, subterranean space in the city [Toronto], for the basement apartments to which they are confined [signal] their social status as well as their cultural isolation" (227). For *Cockroach*'s narrator, the underground is particularly a phantasmical heterotopia since he is alienated from all real spaces that he physically crosses and inhabits, including the ethnic heterotopias and the labourers' ghettoes that punctuate Montréal. It is in this imagined heterotopia of resistance, an imagined

10 For a more detailed study of the historical, political, and sociocultural meanings of monumental space in literature – and of the significance of the concept of heterotopia in this respect – see Rita Sakr, *Monumental Space in the Post-imperial Novel.*

underground, where the process of "normalization" is defied and social inequalities temporarily nullified.[11]

In imagining a man's hallucinatory fall into the underground life of a cockroach, Hage may have been indirectly inspired by Franz Kafka's *Metamorphosis* and Fyodor Dostoyevsky's *Notes from the Underground* – as some critics have noted. Like the ordeals of Kafka's and Dostoyevsky's protagonists, the crisis of *Cockroach*'s narrator is a product of personal and historical traumas crippling a successful process of identity formation and cognitive mapping.[12] A psychoanalytical reading of the narrator's contradictory feelings towards cockroaches and the underground may lead us from Lebanon to Montréal, from the traumatic loss of his sister with whom he played underground – under the quilt – to his underground life as a thief, and from the cockroaches that frightened him as a child to those that overtake his apartment and his mind as a grown-up. Yet, if we move from this straightforward psychoanalytical reading to a more complex schizoanalysis, we unravel the unconscious of the narrator and the unconscious of the text as pluricentred matrices anchored to multiple spatialities, temporalities, and experiences.

For example, near the beginning of the novel, the narrator tells his lover Shohreh, "I can live in filth and hunger ... My mother lives far away, and if we ever get married, no one has to clean because I can tolerate filth, cockroaches, and mountains of dishes that would tower above

---

11 In this volume, Amaryll Chanady's "The Ambivalence of Enclosed Spaces in Immigrant Fiction" offers an incisive analysis of the relationship of the migrant's marginalized and underground spaces to questions of trauma, ethnic conflict, exclusion, and the concept of heterotopia as "threatened havens."

12 My understanding of "cognitive mapping" synthesizes Kevin Lynch's notion of city "legibility" as "the ease with which its parts can be recognized and can be organized into a coherent pattern" (2–3) and Fredric Jameson's Althusserian conception of "cognitive mapping" as "a pedagogical political culture which seeks to endow the individual subject with some new heightened sense of its place in the global system" in order to "regain a capacity to act and struggle which is at present neutralized by our spatial as well as our social confusion" (54). Yet I am also referring to a general notion of the ability of the urban resident/citizen to mentally and imaginatively accommodate the details and connections in his/her city in a way that enables a sense of belonging. This ability seems to be tragically impaired in the case of *Cockroach*'s narrator, except if we read the latter's mental journeys into the contested spaces (including the underground) of Montréal and Beirut as an ultimately successful, though troubled realization of multiple cognitive maps that challenge spatial and ideological boundaries.

our heads like monumental statues, like trophies" (*Cockroach* 52). In his study titled *On Garbage*, John Scanlan contends that "where the reality of excremental waste is a feature of daily life this can quite accurately indicate the absence of structures and beliefs common to modernity" (124). During the fifteen-year war that devastated Lebanon and especially its capital, Beirut, garbage became an ordinary part of Beirutis' lives. Instead of being drawn to such paradoxical emblems of modernity as monuments, Beirutis moved around immense piles of garbage that, in this case, became signs of anti-modernity precisely because of their unusual position in the spatial and social fabric of the city. By emphasizing the narrator's half-ironic, half-tragic monumentalization of such conventionally unwanted and unworthy objects as "filth, cockroaches, and mountains of dishes," Hage's novel conveys the effects of the traumatic war that disfigured Lebanese space and the consciousnesses of the Lebanese people. In this, *Cockroach* seems to extend the vision of such post-war Lebanese novels as Rashid al-Daif's *Taqaniyyatu l'Bu's* (*Techniques of Misery*) wherein monumental – in the sense of gigantic – piles of garbage occupy a conspicuous location in Beirut and are interpreted by the narrator as worthy of attention and analysis. While the spatialization of piles of garbage in war-torn Beirut indicates the deconstructive impact of violence on the structures of modernity, the monumentalization of filth in *Cockroach* suggests a heterotopia of resistance that reaffirms the centrality of the unclean in the structures of an exclusionary and tabooed modernity.[13] In *Cockroach*'s schizophrenic psychosocial spatiality, there is no strict opposition between an official, sanitized monumental space and a marginal, unclean heterotopia where the "improper" citizen may dwell. Rather, *Cockroach* blasts these binaries in its iconoclastically subversive vision of monumental filth. What is striking in this extreme image of festive figuration of sensory violence is its almost Brechtian alienating

13 My analysis here indirectly engages with ideas in Mary Douglas's *Purity and Danger* where she states that "our idea of dirt is compounded of two things, care for hygiene and respect for conventions" (8) and that "if uncleanness is matter out of place, we must approach it through order. Uncleanness or dirt is that which must not be included if a pattern is to be maintained ... it involves no special distinction between primitives and moderns" (50). My approach to the spatial and social dynamics of filth in *Cockroach* emphasizes the subversive result of including dirt within "a pattern" that is distinctly modern. Interestingly, the covers of both Douglas's and Hage's books (the cloth-bound Anansi edition) are illustrated with pictures of a drain.

effect in the sense that it shocks to awaken social consciousness and highlight ideological violence and also serves as an urgent call to "tolerate."[14] In this reimagining of the liminal spaces of citizenship, *Cockroach* marks its important place in an international literature of human rights. Hage's literary-political contribution in this respect culminates in *Carnival*, a novel that exposes the oppressive effects of neoliberal practices of surveillance and discipline to assure "clean citizenship." These practices occasionally include physical violence as in the case of the beatings to which the activist Otto is subjected at the hands of officers "for dirtying [his] shoes" (*Carnival* 108). In *Carnival*, while the main character Fly embodies a relatively optimistic image of the cosmopolitan reader who is able to potentially secure an advantageous status as citizen, worker, traveller, and reader by asserting the right to literature as a basic human right, Hage's works, particularly *Cockroach*, reveal patterns of exclusion that prevent the realization of full citizenship, freedom of movement, labour, and cultural literacy in terms of equal human rights. In this context, *Cockroach*'s "mountain of dishes" heterotopically refracts Fly's "towers of books" (45).

In *Cockroach*, it is also possible to read the monumentalization of filth as a strikingly parodic image of a sanitized monumental space if we juxtapose it with the narrator's sarcastic comment on the war-hero statue during a meeting with his therapist: "Genevieve, I said. Well, if you give me some time for a long walk, maybe in the park across the street, among the trees, I will light a cigarillo somewhere around the war-hero statue, and consult with the pigeons and the begging squirrels. I might be inspired and be able to get back to you next time with wonderful stories" (48). This is one of the most poignantly suggestive moments of the text, as it deflates the relevance of an idyllic and "clean" monumental-natural space that accommodates "wonderful stories" to the narrator's war-scarred psychological and cognitive maps. It also implicitly traces the gap between the unmarked heterotopia of the unmemorialized martyrs of

14 I am referring particularly to Bertolt Brecht's work on the concept of the alienation effect and its social functions, which he explains in such essays as "On the Experimental Theatre." He defines alienation as such: "To alienate an event or a character is simply to take what to the event or character is obvious, known, evident and produce surprise and curiosity out of it" (14).

the Lebanese war and the imposing monumental space of the Québécois war hero.[15]

Cockroach carries the smell of the suffocating dust and dirt that fill the pages of Hage's *De Niro's Game*, which narrates a young man's journey through the Lebanese war and ends with his venture into the promised land of immigration. The land which *Cockroach*'s narrator traverses is disillusioning and threatening, for its physical and metaphorical heterotopias are marked by the cockroaches that follow the poor, the displaced, and the traumatized across the seas. *Cockroach* is thus a discursive heterotopia that explores liminality on historical, spatial, social, and psychological levels while revealing the discontents of many heterotopic imaginings with respect to social and spatial justice, peace, and intercultural relations. At the same time, through its various literary transactions, *Cockroach* articulates its own textual liminality and multiple literary citizenship in a literature of human rights that relates to Lebanese, Middle Eastern, Canadian, and Québécois spatialities and temporalities, as well as its complex identity that is post-war, migrant, emergent, minority, but also uniquely plural.

WORKS CITED

al-Daif, Rashid. *Taqaniyyatu l'Bu's* [Techniques of misery]. 2nd ed., Riyad el-Rayyes, 2001.

Augé, Marc. *Non-Places: Introduction to an Anthropology of Supermodernity.* Translated by John Howe, Verso, 1995.

Beneventi, Domenico A. "Ethnic Heterotopias: The Construction of 'Place' in Italian-Canadian Writing." *Adjacencies: Minority Writing in Canada*, edited by Domenico A. Beneventi, Licia Canton, and Lianne Moyes, Guernica, 2004, pp. 216–34. Essay Series 49.

Borossa, Julia. "Violence, Trauma, and Subjectivity: Compromise Formations of Survival in the Novels of Rawi Hage and Mischa Hiller." *The Ethics of Representation in Literature, Art and Journalism: Transnational Responses to the*

15 It is useful to note here that the Beirut Martyrs' Statue, which was erected to commemorate the Arab activists executed by the Ottomans in 1915 to 1916, was heavily damaged during the fifteen-year war in Lebanon (1975–90). While there have been individual commemorative efforts, no official, national war memorial was built after the war mainly because there is still no overall consensus as to how to historicize the conflict and its victims.

Siege of Beirut, edited by Caroline Rooney and Rita Sakr, Routledge, 2013, pp. 119–34.

Brecht, Bertolt. "On the Experimental Theatre." Translated by Carl Richard Mueller. *The Tulane Drama Review*, vol. 6, no. 1, Sept. 1961, pp. 3–17.

Caruth, Cathy. "Introduction: Trauma and Experience." *Trauma: Explorations in Memory*, edited by Cathy Caruth, Johns Hopkins UP, 1995, pp. 3–12.

Deleuze, Gilles, and Félix Guattari. *A Thousand Plateaus: Capitalism and Schizophrenia*. Translated by Brian Massumi, Athlone, 1988.

Dostoyevsky, Fyodor. *Notes from the Underground*. Translated by Jessie Coulson, Penguin, 1972.

Douglas, Mary. *Purity and Danger: An Analysis of Concepts of Pollution and Taboo*. 1966. Routledge, 2002.

Forget, André. *Cockroaches: Refugee Justice in the Novels of Rawi Hage*. 2013. Dalhousie U, MA thesis.

Foucault, Michel. "Of Other Spaces." Translated by Jay Miskowiec. *Diacritics*, vol. 16, no. 1, 1986, pp. 22–7.

Hage, Rawi. *Carnival*. Norton, 2013.

– *Cockroach*. Anansi, 2008.

– *De Niro's Game*. Anansi, 2006.

– Interview with CBC Q. "Hage's Cockroach Crawls through Montréal's Underbelly." CBC, 30 Oct. 2008. www.cbc.ca/news/entertainment/hage-s-cockroach-crawls-through-montreal-s-underbelly-1.733334.

– Interview with Eddie Taylor. *Nox*, Feb. 2007. Rpt. in Rawi Hage, *De Niro's Game*. Harper Perennial, 2008, pp. 7–16.

Hetherington, Kevin. *The Badlands of Modernity: Heterotopia and Social Ordering*. Routledge, 1997.

Hout, Syrine. *Post-war Anglophone Lebanese Fiction: Home Matters in the Diaspora*. Edinburgh UP, 2012.

Jameson, Fredric. *Postmodernism, or, the Cultural Logic of Late Capitalism*. Duke UP, 1991. Post-Contemporary Interventions.

Kafka, Franz. *The Metamorphosis*. Translated and edited by Stanley Corngold, Bantam, 1986.

Kohn, Margaret. "The Power of Place: The House of the People as Counterpublic." *Polity*, vol. 33, no. 4, 2001, pp. 503–26.

Libin, Mark. "Marking Territory: Rawi Hage's Novels and the Challenge to Postcolonial Ethics." *ESC: English Studies in Canada*, vol. 39, no. 4, 2013, pp. 71–90.

Ltaif, Nadine. *Les métamorphoses d'Ishtar*. Guernica, 1987.

Lynch, Kevin. *The Image of the City*. MIT P, 1960.

Pamuk, Orhan. *The Black Book*. Translated by Maureen Freely, Faber, 2006.

Rahman, Najat. “Apocalyptic Narrative Recalls and the Human: Rawi Hage’s *De Niro’s Game.*” *University of Toronto Quarterly*, vol. 78, no. 2, 2009, pp. 800–14.
Robin, Régine. *La Québécoite.* XYZ, 1993.
Said, Edward W. “Reflections on Exile.” *Reflections on Exile and Other Essays*, by Edward W. Said, Harvard UP, 2000, pp. 173–86. Convergences: Inventories of the Present.
Said Mostafa, Dalia. “Journeying through a Discourse of Violence: Elias Khoury’s *Yalo* and Rawi Hage’s *De Niro’s Game.*” *Middle East Critique*, vol. 20, no. 1, 2011, pp. 21–45.
Sakr, Rita. *Monumental Space in the Post-Imperial Novel: An Interdisciplinary Study.* Bloomsbury, 2013.
– “‘War Is Surrealism without Art’: Representing the Unrepresentable in Mahmoud Darwish, Rawi Hage and Robert Fisk.” *The Ethics of Representation in Literature, Art and Journalism: Transnational Responses to the Siege of Beirut*, edited by Caroline Rooney and Rita Sakr, Routledge, 2013, pp. 23–36.
Scanlan, John. *On Garbage.* Reaktion, 2005.
Soja, Edward. *Seeking Spatial Justice.* U of Minnesota P, 2010. Globalization and Community Series.

5 *"Laisser-aller"*: Homelessness and Contained Space in Kobo Abe's *The Box Man* and Robert Majzels's *City of Forgetting*

SIMON HAREL

Any discussion of homelessness, in the world of signs, requires taking seriously what I call an affect of the psychic apparatus. The expression refers to the unconscious subject (used by Lacan) as bearing a close resemblance to a container, a receptacle, and a matrix. Indeed, if one applies to the letter the remarks of psychoanalysts as different as Didier Anzieu and Wilfred Bion, this psychic apparatus describes the necessity of being oneself, a sense of primal identity, about which D.W. Winnicott (*Paediatrics*), another important psychoanalyst who worked on issues that relate to this chapter, was both its clinician and theorist.

To control one's emotions, to be in control of oneself, to act as a subject in a world that is not disturbed (by expressions of anger or rage, or by an out-of-place attitude): this is an additional rational exercise. My intention here is to lead the reader onto other paths. *Laisser-aller* is a complex and multifaceted term that can be described at the outset to mean to let go or to let oneself go. It can also refer to a lack of containment or restraint, a type of *laissez-faire*, or perhaps even more, a coming undone.

Homelessness is in fact a type of *laisser-aller*, a letting go connected to this lack of containment or restraint – in other words a type of *laissez-faire*, or perhaps even more, a coming undone.[1]

This chapter was translated by Natasha Dagenais, Université de Sherbrooke.

1 In his contribution to this collection, Domenico A. Beneventi discusses the "messiness" of the homeless body in terms of its physical appearance, but also how such a body is equated with a narrative of failure, pollution, and danger to public order that often occludes moments of agency in the strategic uses of space. D.M.R. Bentley also discusses the homeless and, specifically, the shantytown as a space that is heterotopic, "deliberate," and adjacent to an imagined national space.

It is important to note that homelessness is different from other issues, as reflected in the example of Émilie-Gamelin Square in the eastern part of downtown Montréal. The public space officially opened in 1992 amidst a varied urban universe including institutional buildings, commercial buildings, and residential buildings. In the heart of the neighbourhood one may find cultural, social, and ethnic diversity. Although eclecticism characterizes the architectural makeup of the space, the cultural mobility of the heterogeneous population (from students at UQAM and the Cégep du Vieux Montréal to spectators at the Théâtre Saint-Denis, as well as the film enthusiasts who go to the Cinémathèque québécoise) contributes to making this space an ideal place for interactions and conflicts of all kinds. As I write these lines, the conception and implementation of the Quartier des spectacles, as well as the plans for the Centre hospitalier de l'Université de Montréal (CHUM) and numerous residential and private business projects, have created significant changes in the neighbourhood's population.

In this regard, the scenography of Émilie-Gamelin Square represented a considerable undertaking. The architect responsible for the layout of the Square viewed himself as a potential observer who, once settled in the Square, could contemplate the urban landscape of Sainte-Catherine and Saint-Hubert Streets. Still, these lofty ideas cannot compete with how space is used pragmatically in the city! For those who have the opportunity to walk in Émilie-Gamelin Square or in the neighbouring streets, it is the urban landscape outside of the Square that possesses a true vitality. However, there are some people considered "undesirable." These undesirable passers-by who are denied passage in this place live in the surrounding areas and observe from a distance the gardens, the now-defective fountain – in other words, a dead space. In reality, these are the people who look at a space that has become an architectural object of little scope, even though the project designers of Émilie-Gamelin Square had originally envisioned a plan that would dictate how to look at the city. The Émilie-Gamelin Square project is part of the thinking of the time, also present in the project for the urban revitalization of Bryant Park in New York; that project aimed to rethink the urban landscape in terms of targeting its uses based on a strategy called "domestication by cappuccino" (Zukin). Indeed, these projects could be viewed as a strategy created to distance the population of "undesirables" from urban public space. Thus, the homeless and former psychiatric patients, who are displaced with violence, are at the margins of cities and places.

Within the layout of Émilie-Gamelin Square are metal sculptures by architect Melvin Charney, which portray an image of the urban landscape found in the southern part of downtown Montréal. Nonetheless, this place, which seems to have been made up "from scratch to finish," is not as new as it first appears. Émilie-Gamelin Square was once Berri Park. There was no hesitation then in referring to Montigny Park by the first name of the subway station Berri de Montigny, which changed in 1987 to Berri-UQAM. Today, near the public washrooms of the Berri-UQAM station, at the intersection of Sainte-Catherine and Saint-Denis, there is a sculpture, a gift by the Sisters of Providence, the community of Mother Gamelin. This is significant. After all, the intersection of Sainte-Catherine and Saint-Hubert is where Providence Asylum originally stood, having been built there between 1841 and 1843. It is impossible to disregard the presence of this asylum in the heart of the city, an asylum that offered soup and lodging and stood for community work. It is impossible to forget that the asylum played a role in the setting of Montréal East for more than a century. It is impossible to ignore the fact that the asylum was a place where people were constantly coming and going, including travellers and the displaced, and the many workers present during the rapid industrialization of the Port of Montréal, located 700 metres from the place now called Émilie-Gamelin Square. Therefore, the displaced, the homeless, and the rejected of Émilie-Gamelin Square are not ghosts or lunatics in the middle of a city in steady motion. All these subjects that mill around and stamp about in the margins of an "uninhabited" place represent the underside of this grandiose scenography embodied today by Émilie-Gamelin Square.

The preceding details about certain little-known facts of the representation of Émilie-Gamelin Square in the heart of Montréal reveal more clearly how homelessness is a social practice that continues to be debated. Furthermore, there are legal prohibitions against homelessness. The homeless are not neutral subjects who live innocently in the downtown areas of North American urban centres. Homeless people are perceived as undesirable, to be integrated or reformed according to the rules and habitus of good behaviour. Yet homelessness represents the blind spot in any theory on urban progress, of this togetherness that resembles, in the Montréal context, a festive cohort. The exhilaration reflected in the culture of *laisser-aller* in the Montréal context often evokes a normative habitus. In the past, there was much interest in migrant writing – from the contestatory tone of Métis writing to the cultural disjunctions that alterity produces; these types of discourse that appear to please, at least on the surface, force the reader to tread carefully.

The problem with homelessness, supposing that it is in fact a problem, is that it is based on a political construct. Earlier I emphasized how there is a certain discontent underlying the consensus of togetherness in the republic of Montréal (an imaginary space), and this reality will be examined in this chapter. The world of Montréal aims to be a brilliant space: from the years of the *Vice Versa* cultural journal to the social and poetic mission of the founder and CEO of the Cirque du Soleil, Guy Laliberté, who went into space in a Soyuz TM-16 on 30 September 2009 (with spokespersons Yann Martel, U2, and Al Gore as part of the global charity event that aired on 9 October on his One Drop Foundation website).

However, the area of Montréal is a minor *terra incognita*, a space for the creation of a heterogeneous identity. From the outset, I would like to point out a disturbing phenomenon: the euphoric affirmation of cultural mobility confirms the immobility of the homeless. Instead of addressing the problem of homelessness as a flaw in the representation of, or an example of asymmetry in, urban practices, it is critical to cope with this reality and act without delay. The subjectivation of homelessness (in short, its enunciative composition) is an imperative task to undertake because it allows for a redefinition of the sometimes grandiloquent expressions that reflect the culture of alterity.

In his novel *City of Forgetting*, Robert Majzels paints an original portrait of the world of Montréal. He describes the types of *laisser-aller*, the erratic journeys of the homeless protagonists who have appropriated the Montréal landscape. Some of the characters in the novel include Che Guevara, Le Corbusier, Lady Macbeth, Clytaemnestra, and Lord Paul de Maisonneuve.

> Back in the camp, Clytaemnestra slips her arm free without so much as a smile of thanks (and yet, just before the moment of separation, wasn't that an ever-so-slight pressure Suzy felt against her breast?) and walks straight-backed and proud to her bed, a makeshift shelter patched together from scraps of wood and tin and branches.
>
> ...
>
> The other inhabitants of the camp have not begun to stir. Only Lady Macbeth is busy cooking something. (13)

City of Forgetting incorporates numerous cultural references, which turn the novel into an extraordinary encyclopedia, a fictitious world in which Montréal has the main role. Indeed, the narrative creates a rarefied public space: the streets are the site of transmigrations which are both ridiculous and assertive. Le Corbusier promotes the revolutionary side of his Modulor, which he attempts to sell to one of the Rockefellers, whose office is located in Place Ville-Marie. Lord de Maisonneuve tries to stem the rising waters in a Montréal that is pious yet savage. Che, for his part, continues his battle, at the cost of a heightened mental confusion. The reader should keep in mind that Mount Royal is perceived as the Andes. Moreover, the least transgression is reason enough to trigger an investigation that is steeped in paranoia; for example, Che is hounded by double agents, mercenaries, and counter-revolutionary agents who live in the city.

In a different context (*Le voleur*), I examined the figurative plasticity of Montréal in the novel *Le piano-trompette* by Jean Basile. In that study I focused on the absence of a clear separation between identity and alterity, sameness and self-referentiality, the self and the other. *City of Forgetting* seems to echo Basile's intention, except that Majzels here addresses the problem of homelessness. Montréal is a fable (a space favourable to the questioning of the narrative), a Don Quixotesque work of fiction that borders on the grotesque. While Basile, in *Le piano-trompette*, carefully reconstructs a caricature of the Montréal counterculture of the 1970s, Majzels uses a tone that dissects the old and new mythology of foundation stories, and this is how Majzels is able to counter their effectiveness.

It is no doubt unusual to find in the same passage and, particularly, in the same space, the characters Lady Macbeth, Clytaemnestra, and Le Corbusier speaking about the area of Montréal, suddenly rarefied, as if it were the root of a troubling narrative. However, this is not the only fascinating quality characteristic of Majzels's work. Still more remarkable in *City of Forgetting* is the author's focus on the problem of homelessness, which is in the foreground of the novel. What does it mean, in fact, to be homeless in a city where its authorities play a part in the legal and administrative habitus in the *laisser-aller* of that same city? In Émilie-Gamelin Square, for example, subjects are forced to control their emotions and pretend that the homeless are merely passing through as temporary subjects who are not allowed to walk around freely, as spectators or visitors in the heart of the city. Majzels's novel would seem to suggest that there is a certain impurity associated with the city, seen as wastage. The title of the work, *City of Forgetting*, foreshadows the story about forgetfulness and anamnesis, loss of memory and hypermnesia. Yet another contradiction?

Is Majzels pointing out that homelessness is the shameful secret of all urban displacements? As in the heterotopias described by Michel Foucault (from the asylum to the cemetery), could it not be said that homelessness is a disturbing symptom found in the absence of a proper space/place?

For the reader of *City of Forgetting*, it is clear that the characters' ruminations are key to the story. The characters clash and oppose one another while they are confronted with their various interpretations of the surrounding space:

> Le Corbusier steps out of the elevator and onto the plush carpet of the outer office. Ah, this is more like it. Of course, there are no signs to indicate the identity of the establishment, but the carpet, the dark mahogany desk, the upholstered chairs – the scent of Rockefeller is everywhere ... The military man, who may be wounded or at least having difficulty with his breathing, rises and, wincing imperceptibly, tries the door to the right. The door being clearly locked, the man turns to address Le Corbusier.
>
> "If it's El Líder Maximo you've come for, he's not seeing anyone."
>
> Le Corbusier smiles indulgently. "I'll just wait for the receptionist."
>
> "Suit yourself." The man in fatigues shrugs and returns a wryer version of Le Corbusier's smile. "If he won't see us, I doubt he has time for you."
>
> "I am expected," Le Corbusier announces.
>
> "I was with him from the start, in Mexico. On the Granma."
>
> "We have been corresponding," exclaims the architect, brandishing a handmade copy of his letter addressed to Mr. Rockefeller. (90)

Unlike displacement, rumination is the prime example of what makes things worse for the homeless. Whereas displacement reveals a spatial interaction between two markers in space, as well as the movement of subjects who can be moved from one point to another, rumination is the decisive step in the act of repetition, or the denotative link to space where the expression of sameness prevails. Displacement as a motif signals the mobility of the subject in space, but rumination confirms cultural immobility. In his novel, though Majzels seems to focus at first on the creation of identity as a palimpsest (in the sense that each character represents the fluid form of an identity to be redefined), he also pinpoints key ideas, or freezes specific images, thus making known the characters' stubbornness on a fixed space.

I mentioned earlier that Majzels's novel evokes the work of another writer, Jean Basile, the author of *Le piano-trompette*. In this novel, Basile describes a multitude of Montréalers whose distress increases following a catastrophic event of unknown origin. Basile was referring to the Big Freeze, a sudden and severe global cooling that was clearly apocalyptic. As depicted in Basile's novel, this event confined the shock of Montréal society, like a cooling and regression, as if the individual (and collective) subject were caught in an endless displacement. Thus, in Jean Basile's novels, including *La jument des Mongols*, the characters lead nomadic lives as they travel and circulate, but *Le piano-trompette* is the exception to the rule. This novel describes in a soft yet acerbic tone a new vision of the Montréal of the 1970s, all the while exposing an erratic displacement. Although the theme of flight is at the forefront of *Le piano-trompette*, which is a type of fable on human beings just after a final Big Bang, there are still a few remaining accomplishments central to the urban setting.

This explanation also applies to Robert Majzels's *City of Forgetting*. Indeed, the two novels display the same intertextual appetite. Containing detailed descriptions of the city, *Le piano-trompette* and *City of Forgetting* each evoke a narrative space that is both dense and distended. In Basile's text, the subject is inscribed in a space that takes on the appearance of concentric circles. The subject of the enunciation favours the liminal and peripheral forms of a travelling identity within Montréal. I defended this perspective in *Le voleur de parcours*, in which I drew on the sociological reflections of Georg Simmel to clarify the principle of spatial interaction (the transition from here to there, or from what is near to what is far). I surmised that a commonplace (the existence of Mr Barnabé in *Le piano-trompette*) could represent an exemplum, an inductive reasoning based on an exaggerated condition of the urban subject. Mr Barnabé is the everyday man portrayed by Michel de Certeau, who alludes to the ordinary link to everyday life, to the vagaries of life. The exemplum, or credible formula of the commonplace, is built upon the persuasive power of a truncated syllogism that still reflects its own space (*espace propre*), an expression favoured by de Certeau in *L'invention du quotidien*.

The connection of the subject to space, therefore, is not seriously challenged. Intertextuality in *Le piano-trompette* can be found through a number of transmigrations (Rasputin living in the hold of a cargo ship grounded in the Old Port of Montréal) that echo a syncopated breath, rhythm, and technique. Through a narrative voice that focuses on the character of Mr Barnabé, *Le piano-trompette* takes the shape of a saga, a credible story. Because the intertextuality is not out of place, nor are the transmigrations (the sudden shift from one era to another), the euphoric pulse that is heightened (the possibility of travelling, of changing identities, without this being a catastrophic act) remains a probable alternative.

This is where to be in control of oneself (a concept important to psychoanalysts) mirrors – paradoxically? – the concept of *laisser-aller.* Still, does this concept not imply agreeing to break all links with the self, or the wish to remove the constraints of expression – what it contains, what it embodies? I suggest that homelessness calls into question those constraints that represent an urban habitus. The primary issue for homeless subjects, also called hoboes, transients, or vagrants, is one of inscription. In their clearest guise, homeless subjects have no fixed address. They do not have a real home; they do not rent from a hospitable matrix, which could provide, for a brief period, a right to the city. Not to inscribe oneself is a drawback because inscription is in fact the condition for the symbolic representation of a habitus. In short, it symbolizes the necessity to forge a permanent state, a length of time that takes on the status of a place. Human beings situate themselves where they live. They represent the places where they live. Their thinking is shaped by the walls, ceilings, and floors, as well as by the furniture where they are staying.

This is what contradicts the idea, otherwise presented completely naturally, that human beings escape the idiocy of places, the idiosyncrasy that a form of place gives rise to secrecy (or secretly) in them. Is *laisser-aller,* letting go or letting oneself go, about accepting failure, which gives concrete expression to the fact that places, instead of being opponents in the quest for the self (the concern for the self), represent a palimpsest? If that is the case, then places are not neutral but matrices of a secret affectivity. As homelessness involves a shortage of normative representations of place, this means that it is an agonizing form of the dissolution of identity. And yet, as in Jean Basile's *Le piano-trompette,* one notices that personal identity, owing to a proliferating intertextuality and to the fragmented world of urban Montréal, reveals that there still remains a principle of unity. The *laisser-aller* that is associated with the representation of homelessness is, however, isolated, contained in a narrative: a Montréal saga. As for *City of Forgetting,* Robert Majzels adopts that same principle of intertextuality which highlights an unrestrained cosmopolitanism (substantiated by a territorial base, a city, which is victim to the transmigrations of identity):

> On the staircase leading down from Sainte-Catherine, Clytaemnestra bends carefully to gather up another abandoned transfer. She works her way systematically through all the trash containers in the corridor, but they offer only odd newspaper sections and crumpled tissue. The corridors leading

> to the bus terminal and the university are lined with knickknack stores, five-and-ten-cent joints, snack bars, pinball parlours, but she prefers to work the métro. (29)

The situation is different for the Box Man, the title character of the novel of the same name by Kobo Abe. In this work, the Japanese author focuses on the status of the homeless subject in the heart of the city. A sometimes uproarious narrative, *The Box Man* (1974) is both a detective novel and a manifestation of phenomenology. Abe's story unfolds in Tokyo, but it begins more precisely in a port area where, among the enormous scaffoldings for cranes, containers, and railroads, an ordinary man decides one day to become a box man, as is shown at the beginning of the novel: "This is the record of a box man. I am beginning this account in a box. A cardboard box that reaches just to my hips when I put it on over my head. That is to say, at this juncture the box man is me. A box man, in his box, is recording the chronicle of a box man" (3). The tone is clearly set. The first pages of the narrative are dedicated to describing the structure of the box, which must be adapted to the peculiarity of the human being who will be inside this new dwelling place: "The greatest care must be taken when making the observation window. First decide on its size and location; since there will be individual variations, the following figures are purely for the sake of reference" (5).

It becomes apparent that nudity, the absence of protection (in the sense that clothes provide protection), is highlighted. On account of his nudity and the fact that the box barely protects him, the subject feels vulnerable and distraught. He is forced to question his sense of orientation. At first glance, the novel – is it because of Abe's construction of the story (the detailed directions for the future homeless subject on how to dress or what to wear)? – arouses astonishment. *The Box Man* is neither a fable on the tragic circumstances of the homeless subject nor a prescriptive judgment on the motives that should allow the homeless subject to abandon his precarious position. It is not even a narrative about the hardships of a stigmatized identity subjected to the stereotypes and prejudices of the sedentary characters that inhabit the surrounding space. Instead of working within these representations of homelessness, Abe describes the complex forms of *laisser-aller*. It should be noted that it is not at all unusual to associate homelessness with desertion or wanderlust. In fact, many people forget that homelessness is a *laisser-aller* circumscribed by markers representing a repetitive walk in the heart of the city.

In his novel, Abe reveals that the precariousness of the box man comes from the vulnerability of his dwelling place – in other words, the box which covers him:

> Any empty box a yard long by a yard wide and about four feet deep will do. However, in practice, one of the standard forms commonly called a "quarto" is desirable. Standard items are easy to find, and most commercial articles that use standard-sized boxes are generally of irregular shape – various types of foodstuffs precisely adaptable to the container – so that the construction is sturdier than others. (4)

The precariousness of the box man is also heightened by his invisibility in the eyes of others:

> For example, in your case, I'm sure you've not yet heard of a box man. Though there can't be any statistics, there is evidence that a rather large number of them are living in concealment throughout the country. But I've never heard that box men are being talked about anywhere. Evidently the world intends to keep its mouth tightly shut about them. Have you ever actually seen one? (8)

Whereas for Abe, Tokyo represents a space without a future, for Majzels, Montréal is turned into a mythic space enabling the reconstruction of a fluid identity (exploiting, as in Basile's *Le piano-trompette*, transmigrating identities). *The Box Man* draws the portrait of a portable identity. There are no cultural references in Abe's work. At best, there is mention of the news in brief found in popular newspapers. Furthermore, there are no literary allusions (such as quotations embedded in the text, as in Majzels's *City of Forgetting*) but only the dreary description of a port world strewn with impurities. In connecting Abe with the issues that pertain to the goal of this chapter, namely, self-containment or self-control, it is important to point out that Abe speaks from an unusual viewpoint. The character of *The Box Man* (which the reader notes can be duplicated) finds great pleasure in not coming out of his shell. Everything leads to the box man slowly becoming the shape of the object which, in turn, objectifies and reifies him. Abe promotes neither a return to a natural state nor the reconquest of an identity (under the guise of the subject assuming more responsibility in a lived space, as is so often the case in discussions and debates on homelessness in the heart of cities). Rather, the character takes pleasure in melting into his dwelling place, in order to become something – an object, an opaque shape – imperceptible in the eyes of others. The following quotation reflects this idea: "Instead of leaving the box, I shall enclose the world within it. Now the world must have closed its eyes. Things will definitely go the way I wish. In the building articles such as matches, candles, lighters, to say nothing of my flashlight, anything that creates shadows or forms, has been disposed of " (176). Here, it is a question of an inward-looking identity, as if the subject, safe in his dwelling place, were recreating a primary habitation fit to live in (similar to the primary creativity emphasized by Winnicott ["Creativity"], a feeling of transience and poignant affectivity that makes up personal identity). In addition to the ideas of "letting go" and being in control, or rather not being in control, *laisser-aller* refers to taking flight, to moving far off, to experiencing exile and banishment, all of which can easily be associated with trauma. However, this is not the case for Abe's box man. As revealed in the Japanese novelist's description of the homeless subject and in J.M. Coetzee's description of disgrace, to let oneself go, or to let go of the ordinary catastrophes of everyday life, means to accept the inevitability of death and the concrete nature of the limits of human beings' willingness to give an orthopaedic presentation of the body.

Discourses that insist on the mobile forms of travel and displacement imply a relationship steeped in contrasts that link the subject to a distant alterity. This last idea is fixed in space as an unattainable target – Simmel viewed it as such in his portrayal of the inhabitants of Sirius, a portrayal that is both near and far, as in the portrayal of the stranger in the community that claims to integrate him. However, there is no Sirius constellation in *The Box Man* by Kobo Abe. It is important to forget these ideas of the world that insist on the representation, albeit seductive, of another place invoking the promise of all utopias, of all desires that we as human beings would like to see fulfilled. Contrary to the preceding statement, homelessness is shown in Abe's box man as a precarious state, as a throng of easily duplicated identities, suggesting a power struggle that will lead to crime.

In the discourse that I have just touched on, a type of inhuman ethology, or a power struggle that ends with homicide, becomes obvious. This discourse alludes to everyday life in the heart of big cities, where there is constant tension. A prime example taken from real life is the case involving former Ontario attorney general Michael Bryant, who was charged with criminal negligence and reckless driving during a "classic" case of road rage concerning a cyclist.[2] This incident depicts the uncontrollable tension in the heart of cities, as if there were too many homeless people.

Abe's novel is original in terms of its approach. Here there is no obvious ideological stance or sociological reflection. Moreover, it is even less of a meditation on homelessness. In fact, Abe's tone is dry, incisive, and sharp – as if the book were an adventure novel set in the heart of Tokyo – and *The Box Man* becomes a reflection, not unlike that of Jorge Luis Borges and Samuel Beckett, on the laughable wanderings of human beings in the heart of cities: "In His Dream the Box Man Takes His Box Off. Is This the Dream He Had Before He Began Living in a Box or Is It the Dream of His Life After He Left It ... ?" (162). In other words, did the narrator dream up a fictional story that enabled the creation of a possible world, or is it through the homeless subject that the fictional story itself gave birth to the narrator? Kobo Abe does not advocate that homelessness is a state of inertia or an absence of movement through cities. Indeed, homelessness here is the framework for a dreamlike wandering in the novel, a way of perceiving the world that forces individuals to part with any unnecessarily cumbersome dwelling place. With regard to this idea, the conclusion of the novel is enlightening:

> Oh yes, before I forget, one more important addition. In processing the box the most important thing in all events is to ensure leaving plenty of blank space for scribbling. No, there'll always be plenty of blank space. No matter how assiduous one is in scribbling, one can never cover all the blank space. It always surprises me, but scribbling of a certain type is blank itself. At least there'll always remain enough space to write one's name in. But if you don't wish to believe even that, it doesn't make the slightest difference. (177–8)

This excerpt of *The Box Man* points to the dwelling place as not being a formal container. The dwelling place is not an envelope whose artificial characteristics protect the subject from the climatic animosity of the outside world, of the incisive look of the crowd that ignores yet covets the homeless, who must be figured out at all costs. The box is an emotional

2 See Rosie DiManno, "DiManno: The 28 Seconds That Changed Michael Bryant's Life," *Toronto Star*, 26 May 2010, www.thestar.com/news/crime/2010/05/26/dimanno_the_28_seconds_that_changed_michael_bryants_life.html.

container, a scriptural matrix (to borrow de Certeau's idea from *L'invention du quotidien*). Finally, the box is, to use the Freudian idea of the mystic writing pad, the dream matrix, the inscription of signifiers whose permanence is similar to a dreamlike representation.

At the outset, the box, which corresponds to the signifier of separation, allows for the defining of what is inside and what is outside, interiority and exteriority, an intimacy, all of course relative, and a visibility in a public space, and this, in turn, often results in a feeling of general discomfort regarding the homeless subject. For lack of a private space, the box man in Abe's narrative lives on the streets; he dresses and undresses himself, performs his ablutions, and eats as if the outside world did not exist. He does not act this way because he is uncivil. Rather, he acts this way simply because he has no place of his own. In addition to the radioscopic drive that forges a place of separation (thus enabling individuals to reclaim a semblance of their own private space), it is necessary to underscore what I have called, in the context of my study of V.S. Naipaul's work, "the sniper-outlook" (*Humanités jetables*). This symbolizes an incisive radioscopic drive whose role is to annihilate the perception, deemed undesirable, of a fragment of the real world, a world that individuals wish to annihilate through frustration and intolerance (Harel, *Lieux*). This can be seen in the following excerpt: "Place of shooting: The mountainside end of the long black wall of the soy-sauce factory (the shadow of the wall cuts diagonally across the foreground of the picture)" (Abe 23). Such a perspective alludes to the act of photography. In *The Box Man* the homeless unnamed narrator is, in fact, a photographer, who, from inside his dwelling, continually films the real world, as if he could thus give coherence to a world otherwise depersonalized: "First conjecture concerning the true character of the sniper. I should like you to refer to the 'Case of A.' When someone is infected by the idea of a box man and tries himself to become one, there is a general tendency to overreact by shooting him with an air rifle. Thus I did not cry out for help or make any attempt at pursuit" (24). At first glance, the "film-shooting" (the act of targeting others) appears to irritate neighbours and the militia whose sole purpose is to eliminate the homeless from this urban space. However, this is not the case. In fact, the reader is faced with a territorial war without mercy, a war based on the principle of the fight/flight alternative. This is what gives Abe's novel a certain narrative style that highlights contained space and conflictual space. As a result, the reader notices that the homeless themselves are the ones who refuse, as a rule, to share this space:

> As I pressed down on the wound, my fingers became sticky and covered with blood. Suddenly I was uneasy. It may be all right in one of the busier quarters of Tokyo, but in this commercial section of T City, there isn't room for two box men. If he insists on becoming a box man, it necessarily follows that a territorial dispute will be unavoidable. When he realizes he can't drive me out with an air rifle, it doesn't mean that he won't come for me next time with a shotgun. (25)

There are two perceptions of the urban world in Abe's novel. The first involves the protective nature of the dwelling place, in spite of poverty, and the feeling of abandonment. In this context, the outlook is interiorized, as in the scriptural matrix I mentioned earlier. The second perception shows the dwelling place as a target (from the sniper's outlook) of an attacker or aggressor, who seems, to the reader's surprise, to be doubled. This is not a negligible issue. Indeed, Abe's *The Box Man* constructs a power struggle, which may be viewed as a goal to conquer an identity that will put an end to the succession, or duplication, of artificial identities. The narrator of *The Box Man* often makes references to the "Case of A" and the "Case of B," which are ways to enumerate – as if referring to a medical or asylum file – subjects who no longer have a personal identity (no last name, no first name). At best, this identification process helps to protect a secret, the confidentiality of a medical file. However, there is no perennial identity in Abe's work. As previously explained, the dwelling place in *The Box Man* is inscribed superficially. This becomes increasingly obvious as the story unfolds and reaches its conclusion. It is important therefore to remind the reader of the conclusion I quoted earlier about the box man's advice to make sure to provide enough blank space for "scribbling." Significantly, the excerpt alludes to the narrator's inscription on the *surface* of his dwelling place.

The dwelling place (or abode) is thus the place for receiving signifiers, notes, reminders (as is the case in an organizer), and indications as to addresses to remember. Is the dwelling place then, against all expectations, the new shape of a novel – a space where its matrix, although often seen as caricatured, still remains the altar of a constantly evolving identity? This is part of the complexity of *The Box Man* by Abe, whose work is halfway between Kafka and Beckett. In this novel, the author tells the story of an incarcerated man in an existential matrix, in what I call an ecumene, in other words a signifier of habitability. While Robert Majzels suggests that Montréal is the historical, mythological, and sometimes incongruous sedimentation of characters who have acquired, in the heart of the city, a right to (re)presentation (from Le Corbusier to Paul de Maisonneuve), Kobo Abe presents ordinary characters who live in an ordinary world.

In his novel, Abe portrays a tense world, a tormented space. Here, the homeless subject is limited to a small sensory window that enables him to see the world:

> Next comes the installation of the frosted vinyl curtain over the window. There's a little trick here too. That is, the upper edge is taped to the outside of the opening and the rest left to hang free, but please do not forget to anticipate a lengthwise slit. This simple device is useful beyond all expectations. The slit should be in the center, and the two flaps should overlap a fraction of an inch. As long as the box is held vertical, they will serve as screens, and no one will be able to see in. When the box is tilted slightly, an opening appears, permitting you to see out. (6)

The construction of the dwelling place includes a small opening that allows the homeless subject to see without being seen. This may be surprising to the reader because the man in the box never stops being seen as an undesirable person in a community of inscribed habitus built to last. From this perspective, walking and wandering find expression in regulated movements in a universe where living permanently in public space is seen as an unacceptable act. Therefore, the homeless subject described by Abe provides a new point of view of the world because he lives in a box which he manipulates skilfully, and this box conceals him. As a result, he believes himself invisible in the eyes of others. The inside of the box, his abode, gives him, for a time, the illusion that he is able to avoid the demands of the normative world, which imposes on everyone a public space and a private space, according to a sanitary ecology that promotes the idea that one is at home in a private space but with others in a public space.

How does this relate to the expression "*laisser-aller*" that I used at the beginning of this chapter? The expression can also be translated, in somewhat academic terms, as a lack of narcissistic containment, as a deficiency in the somatopsychic coherence of the Self. I discussed at the beginning of this chapter Émilie-Gamelin Square and the homeless of Montréal, who represent contrasting choreographies in the heart of the city. If the homeless disturb, then it is because they evoke the idea of *laisser-aller* by letting go of their bodies, their voices, without apparent fear or reserve. This flaw in self-containment makes people in the normative world feel ill at ease; it means a fluidity or liquefaction of the subject (to borrow the idea of the liquefaction of contemporary society described by the British sociologist of Polish origin Zygmunt Bauman).

In other respects, this fluidity of identity implies a deep pain because the homeless are condemned to wander for life. *Laisser-aller* (which alludes to an urban drift, or ruination in the heart of the city) indicates profound changes to the habitability of the centre of contemporary metropolitan areas. *Laisser-aller* represents another connection with housing conditions because the actual houses no longer just refer to the private space of property ownership. It is important to take into account research undertaken in anthropology (e.g., work in the style of François Laplantine) on the microproperties of identity, as well as on the disjunctions of cultural space that enable us to avoid all the traps that consist in scripting space as if it were a place that belonged to us, over which we have hold. In this matter, the following excerpt from *The Box Man* is revealing:

> When anyone comes into contact with the scenery around him, he tends to see selectively only those elements necessary. For example, though one remembers a bus stop, one can have absolutely no recollection of a large willow tree nearby. One's attention is caught willy-nilly by the hundred-yen piece dropped on the road, but the bent and rusty nail and the weeds by the wayside may just as well not be there. On the average road one usually manages not to go astray. However, as soon as one looks out of the box's observation window, things appear to be quite different. The various details of the scenery become homogeneous, have equal significance. Cigarette butts ... the sticky secretion in a dog's eyes ... the windows of a two-storey house with the curtains waving ... the creases in a flattened drum ... rings biting into flabby fingers ... railroad tracks leading into the distance ... sacks of cement hardened because of moisture ... dirt under the fingernails ... loose manhole covers. (41–2)

In this description of Tokyo "from below," the formation of horizontalness corresponds to a traditional definition of habitability. Whereas Robert Majzels's *City of Forgetting* aims to transcend, Kobo Abe's *The Box Man* highlights a point of view that must be put into perspective, as if the field of perception had to be narrowed and subjected to a minimalist exercise. Certain details must be reiterated concerning these issues in *The Box Man*. Specifically, Abe's narrative is presented as a phenomenological fable told from the viewpoint of the homeless subject, and the dwelling place is joined to the body of the homeless subject: "Despite all of that I shook my box and continued doggedly walking. But the box could not make time along the road. Since the ventilation was bad, I broke out in a sweat. Even the insides of my ears itched with the dampness. As I leaned forward, the box tilted, and there was the sound of it striking my hips. The very fragile sound of something made of paper" (42). The dwelling place represents the body of the subject. The small opening in the cardboard box symbolizes the watchful eye of the homeless subject, in other words, the box man's eyes. Thoughts, notes, and addresses are scribbled on the interior of the surface area of the box, and this surface, to borrow Anzieu's expression, is the second skin of the creator, the secret dermis. Consequently, physical and psychic space is laid out according to the principle of containment or confinement, which may nonetheless turn out to be the promise of *laisser-aller*. To see without being seen, to flee the oppression of urban life, to live happily in a world where anonymity is acceptable – these examples of freedom are the promise of "portable privacy." The expression may seem strange. In fact, it may seem like an inappropriate remark. Yet, in *The Box Man*, the reader is informed of the homeless subject's living conditions:

> Now should I bid goodbye to the box? But my underwear and my shirt for some reason were taking a long time to dry. The rain had lifted, but because of the moisture-laden, low clouds they were long in drying. Fortunately I felt fine there naked in the box. Perhaps it was because I had carefully cleaned off the dirt, but the various parts of my body felt strangely fresh, and I even experienced an actual longing to embrace myself. But I did not intend to stay like this forever. I hoped the morning calm would end soon. (69)

Through the promise of a narcissistic reconciliation ("embrace myself"), the dream of an intensely close connection with a self that is separated from the external world (the streets, the daily activities of the homeless wandering in the heart of the city), I have attempted to describe *laisser-aller*, to let go or to let oneself go, as an example of what urban drift entails. Contrary to discourses that emphasize the animated forms of wandering (a goal, a movement, a will, a project), the type of *laisser-aller* that I have focused on concerns itself with mobility and immobility, displacement and stagnation, perception and blindness.

WORKS CITED

Abe, Kobo. *The Box Man.* Translated by E. Dale Saunders, Vintage, 1974.
Anzieu, Didier. *Le moi-peau.* Dunod, 1995.
Basile, Jean. *La jument des Mongols.* Typo, 1991.
– *Le piano-trompette.* VLB Éditeur, 1983.
Bauman, Zygmunt. *Liquid Modernity.* Blackwell, 2000.
Bion, Wilfred. *Elements of Psycho-Analysis.* 1963. Karnac, 1989.
Coetzee, J.M. *Disgrace.* Penguin, 2000.
De Certeau, Michel. *L'invention du quotidien: Arts de faire 1.* Gallimard, 1990.
Harel, Simon. *Espaces en perdition, tome I: Les lieux précaires de la vie quotidienne.* Laval UP, 2007.
– *Espaces en perdition, tome II: Humanités jetables.* Laval UP, 2008.
– *Le voleur de parcours.* XYZ, 1999.
Laplantine, François. *De tout petits liens.* Mille et une nuits, 2003.
Majzels, Robert. *City of Forgetting.* Mercury Press, 1997.
Simmel, Georg. "Digressions sur l'étranger." *L'école de Chicago: Naissance de l'écologie urbaine,* edited by Yves Grafmeyer and Isaac Joseph, Aubier, 1984, pp. 53–9.
Winnicott, D.W. "Creativity and Its Origins." *Playing and Reality.* 1971. Routledge, 2005, pp. 87–114.
– *Through Paediatrics to Psycho-Analysis: Collected Papers.* 1975. Brunner-Routledge, 1992.
Zukin, Sharon. *The Cultures of Cities.* 1995. Blackwell, 2004.

PART II

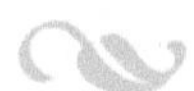

Counter-narratives and Spaces of the Nation/State

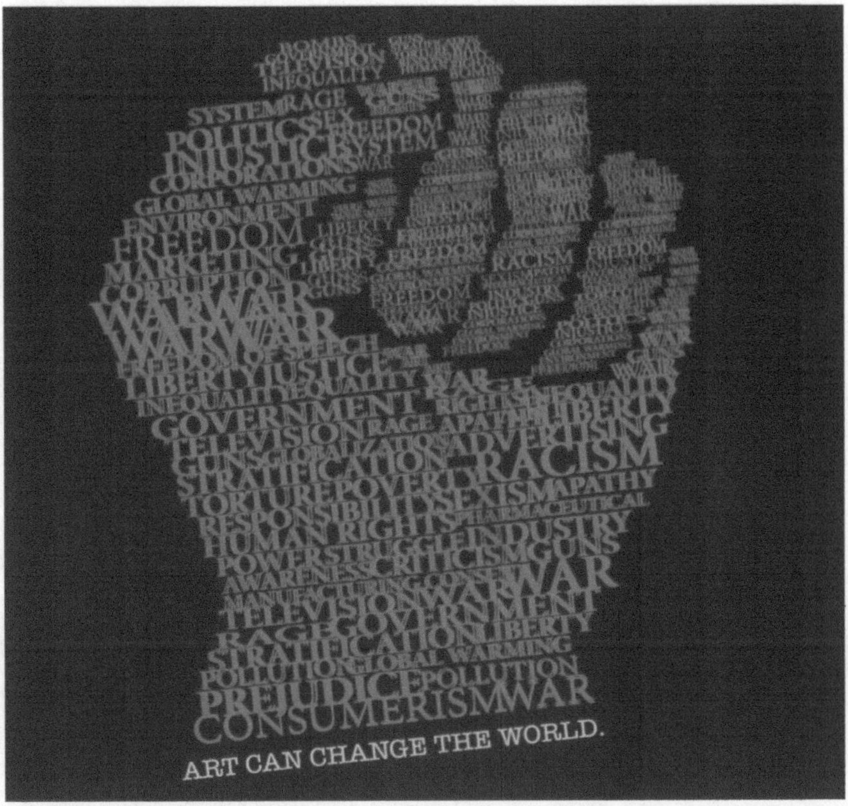

"Art Can Change the World" (66 cm x 45.5 cm lithograph).
Copyright Jason Milan, 2004.

6 Unruly and Unremarked: Theatrical Spectatorship from Below in Nineteenth-century Canada

ALAN FILEWOD

In 1919, there appeared this brief story in the Vancouver *Province*:

> PROTESTS BY WAY OF A LIVING BOUQUET
>
> Mayor Gayle's secretary, Mr. Charles Read, was presented with a bouquet on Friday afternoon. The central effect of the bouquet consisted of green tips cut from vacant property bushes in some part of the city. The green tips, however, were almost entirely smothered by huge bunches of tent caterpillars at the young agile age when they hang to the tree by their tail and wriggle the rest of their body lustily in the air, anxious to migrate to greener pastures.
>
> The bouquet was presented by a determined looking citizen, who said his object was to show the city how wealthy corporations look after their property – to the detriment of the small man trying to raise fruit and vegetables in his garden plot. The wriggling mass had been cut, he said, from some vacant railroad property adjoining his own.
>
> Not able to tender his living protest to the mayor in person, the determined citizen left in search of Ald. Owen, who has charge of caterpillar extermination energies. (7 June 1919)

Behind the scrim of journalistic bombast we can discern an unremarkable event. A man (I imagine him as my grandfather, a stern working-class gardener) strides into City Hall and thrusts a bouquet of caterpillars at a bureaucrat. He doesn't get past the secretary, so he leaves. As an act of political protest, this is about as local and ordinary as it can get. But something else is happening in this event. The unnamed "determined citizen" didn't just enter and throw down a cutting covered with caterpillars. By presenting it as a bouquet, in a parody of courtly formality, he chose to turn it into what Brecht would call a *gest*, a theatricalized action that embodies, enacts, and watches a social critique.

This gestic moment, with its use of performance to confront power and compel spectatorship, was a deliberately theatrical act, even if it lacked aesthetic intent and none of the participants recognized it as theatre. With this example, I suggest that political intervention theatre has always operated in this way, outside of the disciplinary frames of the theatre. Interventionist theatre has always been multiple, unruly, and for the most part unremarked, performing in a boundary zone where theatre as a social communication meets and refuses "the theatre" as a disciplinary regime and industry.

"Political theatre" is a weighted term that embraces a range of understandings and practices. For many, it describes the engaged dramaturgies of playwrights who use the stage as a platform for political analysis or advocacy; for others, it refers to the use of theatre as a process of community activism. It opens up a loose cluster of related terms: theatre from below, working-class theatre, dissent theatre, radical theatre, theatre of protest, *théâtre engagé*: all of these take on different meanings as they pass through time and discourse. My interest is in the use of theatre in political action, not just as a platform of representation and reflection but as an instrument of change, in which popular activism is enacted in demonstrative theatricality. This is my attempt to reverse the fundamental method of tracing the development of radical and political theatre in Canadian theatre cultures. It relocates attention away from forms to practices, away from the archive to the unremarked, and away from the attempt to locate historical working-class culture to an understanding of instances where class politics manifest as performances.

The relation of theatre and dissent was a major preoccupation in the twentieth century, when on the one hand mass political movements exploited theatre for propaganda, and on the other engaged artists sought ways to use their art for their activism. But in the very different culture of the nineteenth century, the relation of theatre, politics, and dissent is much less clear.

When we survey the history of theatre in Canada, we chart our way through absences that force us to reconsider the discursive structures and epistemes that frame the search. In theatre history, our inquiries impose contemporary understandings of disciplinarity onto past practices. To even speak of theatre history compounds the problem because the phrase stages assumptions about the nature of theatre, of artistic practice and disciplinarity. The foundational concepts, including the very idea of "the theatre," are subject to major historical reconstitutions. We look at the nineteenth-century theatre from the far side of an epistemological rupture brought about by the modernist proposition of theatre art and the disciplinarity of the theatre profession that developed in the century in response to the transformation of popular spectatorial practices (and spaces) with the invention of cinema. In theatre culture, it has long been understood that film "killed" theatre in the early twentieth century. In actual fact, film supplanted theatre. The audiences and playhouses remained but theatre migrated, spatially, socially, and discursively.

Theatrical Ambivalence

> DISTILLER. Good morning, Mr. Conscience; though I know you to be one of the earliest risers, especially of late, I hardly expected to meet you here at day-dawn.
>
> CONSCIENCE. I am none too early, it seems to, to find you at your vocation. But how are you going to dispose of this great black building?
>
> DISTILLER. Why, I do not understand you.
>
> CONSCIENCE. What are you doing with these boiling craters, and that hideous worm there?
>
> DISTILLER. Pray explain yourself.
>
> CONSCIENCE. Whose grain is that? and what is bread called in the Bible?
>
> DISTILLER. More enigmatical still.
>
> CONSCIENCE. To what markets do you mean to send that long row of casks? And how many of them will it take upon an average to dig a drunkard's grave? ("Debates" 54)

A number of conditions sunder our understanding of what theatre "is" today from what it was and how it was seen (and by whom) in nineteenth-century Canada, a society that was intensely theatrical but at the same time indignantly anti-theatrical. When we speak of theatre today we generally and loosely refer to the acted performances of plays on stage, mindful that all of these terms ("acted," "performance," "plays," and "stage") are unstable and variant. But we have a general consensus that recognizes boundaries, no matter how porous, between theatre and related arts, such as dance and opera. As anyone who has tried to glean the difference between opera and musical theatre, or theatre and performance art, comes to appreciate, these are historical categories of disciplinarity and reception.

On the busy stages of the nineteenth century, audiences saw an even greater variety of performance forms. In a single week in any North American city (in, say, the 1880s), a spectator might choose to take in a visiting Shakespearean actor, a medicine show, a circus parade, a minstrel show, a music hall variety show, a pantomime, a ballet, a comic hypnotist, a scientific phrenologist, a satiric dialect lecturer, a military re-enactment spectacle, a temperance melodrama, and a chalk-talk lecture. (Today many of these forms still exist, having migrated to television studios.) Balloon ascensions, firework extravaganzas, Uncle Tom shows (big and small) – all appealed to the appetite for spectacle and sensation. Where crowds had money to spend, entertainers were there to collect it. Even the respectable "moral" entertainments, such as mock parliaments, temperance dialogues, and chatauquas, revelled in the public delight in theatricality and show. Legitimate theatre, especially when it featured touring actors from Britain, gave the middle and upper classes occasion for social display. Theatre, like alcohol, was pervasive across all social strata, deeply loved and widely condemned. It was a place of pleasure and an opportunity for sin, and for much of the century it appealed to mainly male audiences from the employee classes. It was invariably eroticized, whether only by nuance and implication or by salacious teasing.

In the middle of the nineteenth century, when theatre troupes used railroads to spread out across the continent, theatrical performances were popular culture, characterized by vulgar populism, urban rowdyism, and mainly working-class male audiences. But the theatre business became institutionalized and gentrified over the second half of the century, when corporate centralization by New York booking syndicates bought up and tamed the playhouses, trafficked in the celebrity of star actors and the prestige of European modernism, and appealed to middle-class women. As Richard Butsch has pointed out in his history of American audiences, "By the 1890s, legitimate theater was a woman's entertainment" (78). This was particularly true of the large eastern cities; on the frontiers though, theatre continued to share social (and often physical) space with gambling dens, saloons, and brothels.

The emerging middle-class culture was stressed by its love of theatrical performance and its disapproval of the unruly theatre industry and the vulgar populism of melodrama. Mark Blagrave, in his work on temperance soiree performances in nineteenth-century Nova Scotia, makes note of the opening address of the musical *Cadets of Temperance*, in which we are told, "Our entertainment is not intended to affect you like a show, which excites momentary pleasure and is then forgotten" (26). This was the ambivalent dilemma of the nineteenth-century spectator: if theatre could be moral and instructive, then it could also be – and usually was – immoral and harmful, not least because it brought young men into the ambit of alcohol, prostitution, and gambling. Even as late as 1891, the Ministerial Association of Toronto declared theatre evil and theatre-going a sin. The *Labor Advocate* took offence:

> Verily we should be grateful to our censors for settling this momentous question for us, but matters of such moment demand of serious consideration. It is a pity that their time is so occupied with such serious things, as it would be nice to be told what to do to prevent girls being driven to lives of shame by two and three dollars a week salaries; to get a little information on the question "Have one part of humanity a right to own the planet and charge the rest of us for the use of it"; to be shown some remedy other than charity, for a state of things under which able-bodied men search in vain for work to enable them to provide for the wants of their loved ones. (10 April 1891)

Theatre was a sin for some, but theatricality was pervasive. As made clear in a report in the *Guelph Herald*, describing in detail a visiting temperance lecturer in 1850, theatrical pleasure was understood to be an important part of effective proselytizing:

> It were vain to attempt to give an idea of Mr. Gough's peculiar style and manner of address. We have listened with long-remembered delight while a Kemble and a Kean embodied in appropriate tone, and look, and gesture, the immortal conceptions and sublime language of Shakespeare, and have laughed till our sides ached under the wonderful powers of mimicry possessed by a Matthews, a Mackay, and a Weeks, but Gough, while unlike any of these, possesses some of the highest qualities of each, while moreover he is the author of his sentiments he utters and not merely the representative of the conceptions of another mind. (5 November 1850)

The language of performance adapted to fit moral boundaries. On the side of respectability and morality, theatre wasn't "theatre" but rather entertainments, soirees, concerts, recitals, even theatricals. (Home theatricals, mixing tableaux and charades, were common in middle-class families.) Schools, temperance societies, and churches produced instructive dramas, usually offered as "dialogues" to distance them from the disrepute of the popular stage. Here too we find the unperformed literary dramas of the day, the versified historical romances of the Mason and Orangeman Charles Mair and of the bourgeois feminist Sarah Anne Curzon, and the polemical dramas that staged imaginary theatres in newspaper editorial columns and pamphlets, such as *The Female Consistory of Brockville,* an 1856 dramatic rant about local church politics (Candidus), or the dramatic satires on local politics that Mary Ellen Smith has traced in New Brunswick newspapers. Drama was respectable, the more so the further it was removed from the stage. But "theatre" remained a place of deception and temptation. Language marked social place, which is why so many nineteenth-century playhouses, whether standing alone, or built into the upstairs of a hotel or a town hall, were called "opera" houses. The theatre industry was quick to capitalize on these distinctions. On a poster for a touring *Uncle Tom's Cabin* show (one of the hundreds that criss-crossed the continent for fifty years), we read,

> Little Miss Ethel, Smallest Child Actress as EVA will appear in each performance with the Newest Song Specialties.
>
> Our Uncle Tom is nine feet high, the tallest on earth.
>
> Every Christian mother should see that her children do not miss the opportunity to see this grand production of the greatest of moral dramas. (*Ogden's*)

In 1883, the *Labor Union* offers an insight into the problematic social positioning of theatre as an adaptive business practice in a sarcastic review of P.T. Barnum's book *The Art of Money Getting*:

> Get up some kind of show likely to tickle children: – get a few Canadians, bleach their hair, call them Albinos from the African kingdom at Muskatingo; get a very fat woman – tattoo or paint her arms, call her a cannibal ... who has been raised on roasted children; get an elephant that England has got tired of, publish 10,000 lies about him; get a happy family and drug it well; get some spotted horses which will canter around in a ring, and a few low and painted women who can ride on them naked.
>
> Call this a *Great Moral Show,* send free tickets to the clergy, plaster every wall with gaudy pictures, blow a steam calliope about the town, have the schools all adjourn: – do this and keep doing it, and you can get every half dollar in a town, so that the inhabitants can't pay the grocer's bills for months to come. (19 February 1883)

The robust and religion-bound Canada of the nineteenth century had a vast, diverse, and plural theatre culture, but it oriented towards artisanship, especially of the actor, and the sensation of spectacle. The emergent theatre profession produced templates and performance tropes that were reproduced locally across North America but only when absorbed into the idea of the amateur, domesticated and legitimized as social practice. Theatre was a useful, pleasurable mode of social being, of homosocial organization and fellowship; performance offered structure, sequence, and order. When operated as a business, theatre gave that power of creating fellowship and spectatorial pleasure to outsiders, and thus stood as a potential threat not just to morality but to the very social order that it generated. At the mid-century, the theatre was suspect because of its rough working-class masculinism; by the end of the century, it was less unruly but even more suspect because of its entrepreneurial opportunism, its American republicanism, and its racial influences. Vincent Massey, one of the major cultural theorists who advocated an art-theatre profession in Canada, expressed his wariness of the New York syndicates run by "New York gentlemen with Old Testament names" (197). The introduction of modernist theatre, brought by New York syndicates and endorsed by educated critics like Hector Charlesworth (who was one of the first Canadian advocates of Ibsen), introduced the new idea that theatre was a fine art but increasingly linked it to the idea of the nation. For the generation of early twentieth-century theatre intellectuals like Charlesworth, Sandwell, and Vincent Massey, theatre was both a fine art and a condition of nationhood, in which theatre work and dramatic canon would consolidate in the disciplinary regime of "the profession."

The idea of an artistic political theatre would emerge out of this statist concept as theatre artists took positions in the ideological wars of the twentieth century. For the nineteenth-century spectator, it was not the practice or the content of theatre that expressed political meaning but the place and context. When we seek political theatrical performance in the nineteenth century we find four clusters of practices: literary polemical dramas, pedagogical paratheatre (temperance dialogues, mock parliaments), staged political burlesques (most famously, William Fuller's musical satire *HMS Parliament*), and in the last decades of the century, ornate craft union parades. What we do not appear to see is theatrical performance as an expression of dissent or an occasion of intervention. In the extremely busy theatre culture in Canada, particularly after the building of the railroads, the burgeoning disciplinarity and aesthetics of the theatre business, emerging – however subjunctively – as "the" theatre, was clearly a property of the entrepreneurial middle class, even as it drew on the working classes for its labour and its audiences.

Spectating Performers

> In place of the usual address and discussion at the weekly meeting of the Single Tax Association on Friday evening there was a literary, musical and artistic entertainment, entitled "An Evening with Tom Hood." The leading participants were Mr. Samuel Jones, Miss Craggs, Mr. Keith Smith, Mr. AF Chamberlin and Mr. AE Phillips. The presentation of Hood's whimsical and pathetic creations was greatly appreciated by the audience.
>
> – *Labor Advocate*, 23 January 1891

Mindful that the absence of the past speaks to an anxiety of absence in the present, when we might expect to see traces of interventionist theatre in the nineteenth century, in which the free address and spectatorial politics of theatrical performance might offer the occasion of performance as dissent, we see something else altogether. For example, in 1883, at the climax of the failed strike by telegraph operators that shut down wireless communications across North America, we find this notice in the *Palladium of Labor*: "A benefit concert in aid of striking telegraphers was held at the camp pavilion in Toronto on Wednesday evening. Mr. F. Jenkins, of this city, was present and sang a couple of solos" (18 August 1883).

We find countless examples of such events, of celebratory dinners, concerts, smokers, picnics, all of which have a performance element, all of which express and produce ideological or political community in spectatorial pleasure, and all of which contribute to a sphere of class-porous political domesticity. A "splendid banquet" held by the Regina local of the Bricklayers' and Masons' International Union in 1910, at the tail end of that very long century, followed a "sumptuous repast" with a program that included the chairman's address and various toasts, three speeches, a recitation, and twenty-six songs and duets by members present. That the ambivalence of these performance events at once mirrored and countered the equally homosocial and ornate banquet-and-toasts culture of the upper classes is understandable when we consider Michael Bamberg's observation that "looking at narratives-in-interaction, we may be better off to see how complicity and countering are activities that go hand-in-hand, making it difficult to specify a *tout court* distinction between them" (353). Bamberg continues to make the point that "counter ... and master narratives emerge in co-presence."

These cultural narratives were homosocially exclusive, but as the century advanced, women's groups adapted these performative socializations to their own ends. The most famous of these were the temperance entertainments and fetes of the Woman's Christian Temperance Union and the mock parliaments of the women's enfranchisement movement at the end of the century that have been examined in detail by Kym Bird. But even less polemic performances drew upon a parodic simulation of the public life to frame theatrical pleasure. An example is "The Spinsters' Convention," performed in 1908 by the young ladies of Macdonald Hall, the women's domestic science college affiliated with the Ontario Agricultural College in Guelph. As described by the *OAC Journal*,

> Fri. Feb. 21st, there was held in the College gymnasium, a short entertainment on behalf of the Y.W.C.A. of Macdonald Hall ... Eighteen of the oldest maids imaginable, having banded themselves together as the Young Ladies Single Blessedness Debating Society, are doing their utmost to secure for themselves all those blissful joys attended upon the possession of a husband. The scene produced was one of the regular meetings of the society, and it certainly gave a fairly thorough knowledge of the methods employed by these damsels in the pursuit of their desires. Perhaps the most useful piece of information provided was the exact state of the matrimonial market up to date. As the Secretary read her report, each Spinster took down carefully such items as seemed particularly fitted to her special need.
>
> Toward the close of the Session, Professor Make-over entered, bringing his marvelous remodeloscope, with the aid of which he undertook to transform each member of the Society, in turn, into their heart's desire. The only obstacle was the fact that before entering the machine each maiden was required to give her exact age. In the first two instances this was reluctantly, but more or less successfully done; and the results fully justified our expectations: but the third candidate for beautification was so hopelessly ancient that she came out unaffected, while the fourth so completely forgot her dignity as to insist that her fleeting blushes arose out of her timid inexperience of twenty years of sheltered youth. Alas! In spite of the Professor's protests, she rushed madly to her doom, her innocent frame was ground limb from limb, and the precious remodeloscope utterly destroyed.

> This put an effectual stop to any further effort, and the ensuing consternation and frenzied panic may better be imagined than described. ("College Life: The Spinster's Convention" 173–5)

When the ladies of the Macdonald Institute performed their satiric skit on beauty and marriage, they did so in the context of a parodic meeting, while in that same week the men of the Agricultural College across the green amused themselves with a mock parliament where they debated an act "to provide legislation for the restocking of the Speed River with trilobites," "an act respecting the enfranchisement of women," and "a bill to amend the regulations governing pie-makers and home-seekers at Macdonald Hall" ("College Life: The Mock Parliament" 131–47).

At dinners, recitals, parodies, and concerts, the performance of the public self, even when satiric, legitimized the entertainments as something other than theatre, but at the same time the popular stage and the assembled, collaborative anthology performances of the minstrel show and its vaudeville successors gave them performance templates. The *Labor Advocate* carried an advertisement of a series of books that suggest the reach of these forms: *Wilford's Original Dialogues and Speeches for Young Folks, Ritter's Book of Mock Trials, Rowton's Complete Debater, Burdett's Dutch Dialect Recitations and Readings* ("selected gems of Humorous German dialect pieces"), *Brudder Gardner's Stump Speeches and Comic Lectures* ("The newest and best book of Negro comicalities") (10 April 1891).

I want to probe the problem of distance between the ambivalent theatre and the circulation of social practices it produced in terms of two constants that can frame an understanding of the subsequent development of working-class theatre in Canada: mobility and spectating performance. To approach that, I want to follow a typifying theatricalized subject, say a striking telegrapher, from the cosy performative enclosure of public-life fellowship to two other spaces of performance.

The first has been examined in detail by labour historians: the craft union parades that began in the 1880s and served as predecessors and models for the later Labour Day parades. As shown by historians such as Craig Heron and Steven Penfold, in their history of Labour Day in Canada, and Susan Davis, in her groundbreaking history of working-class parades in Philadelphia, these craft union events mobilized the growing civic power of skilled labour in the industrial cities and superimposed class interests on already established sectarian and ethnic identities. Heron and Penfold look at craft union parades and Labour Day parades as street performance, arguing that "the 'art' involved in these events was simple, sometimes crude, but always colourful and engaging. While borrowing heavily from many familiar forms of public celebration, it created the most visible, persistent, and widespread form of collectively produced working-class cultural production that Canada has ever seen" (xv). The claim to public space variously followed on, referred to, or continued celebratory processional performance traditions of civic festivals and military parades. The craft union parades mobilized working-class presence on streets and parade routes that hosted numerous parades of different kinds. In Toronto, the annual Orange parade was a major event for close to a hundred years. King Billy on his white horse may be the longest-running role in Canadian political theatre. These processions of power manifested claims to the "right of the city," in what Jeff Derksen, in his chapter on the Vancouver Olympics in this volume, describes as the "struggles for publicness" (p. 56).

The craft union parades were notable for their inclusion of civic and military authority, as overlapping spheres of male social organization. As described by the *Globe*, the Toronto parade of 1882 numbered "between 3 and 4000 men" marching in union formations with distinctive props and costumes, some with allegorical or illustrative floats, including the Shoemaker's traditional King Crispin (24 July 1882). With them marched four regimental bands (the Grenadiers, the Governor General's Horse Guard, the Queen's Own Rifles, and the Garrison Battery), the band of Loyal Orange Lodge, representing Protestant civic power, and the Emerald Band, representing Irish labour. We can see this as a public display of the convergence of power blocs and at the same time as a performance of the overlapping spheres of masculinist and ethnic participatory hegemony.

As Heron and Penfold demonstrate in their detailed account of the craft union parades, working women were generally excluded, and racial minorities were locked out entirely except in parody and surrogation. The regimental and cultural society bands did not just represent power blocs in civic society; they were also the spheres between which performing men passed on a daily basis. Our typographer may also be a sergeant in the militia; he may be an Orangeman; he is likely a Knight of Labour; and he may be a Mason, an Oddfellow, a Forester, and Knight of Temperance.

This leads to the second space of performance, not on the street but hidden from it, in the highly theatrical world of fraternal societies in which millions of men in North America worked their way through a manifold of degrees, rituals, and ceremonies, to the point that, as Mark

Carnes has noted, "the writing of rituals was a major growth industry" (144). The spawn of fraternal ritual societies reproduced the template formula of Freemasonry, which itself saw a massive proliferation of subsects and affiliated rites; the 1907 *Cyclopaedia of Fraternities* lists more than 600 such societies in North America (Stevens). The template of costumed ritualists, secret signs, ornate levels of achievement, binding oaths, and initiation into mysteries was a performance practice that covered the immense cultural range between Masonic Lodges, the Ku Klux Klan, the Mormon Church, the Knights of Labor, and the temperance movement. The Knights of Labor in particular come into the frame of discussion because they were instrumental in the formation of the craft unions and their claim to public space.

The fraternal societies can be understood in many ways, from many disciplinary positions: as emergent middle-class homosocialization, as the negotiation of class transformation in modernism, as the interpellation of aspirant middle-class subjectivity into imperial discourse, or as a theatricalized way of getting away from the women. They were a form of theatre – not just *theatrical* but theatre, as much as J.W. Bengough's Single Tax chalk talks or a temperance mock parliament, discernible along an axis of performance and spectating. They can also be understood as the first real multiplayer role-play games, in which progress through a virtual world offers prestige and the somatic satisfaction of meaningful work. Observers noted often that the main business of fraternal lodges was writing, staging, and participating in initiation ceremonies for constantly proliferating rites and degrees – or, in the language of gamers, levelling up.

At the same time, the rituals and offices were serious business. The Knights of Labor's ritual manual, *Adelphon Kruptos,* consists of forty-two pages of descriptions of offices, rules, rituals, secret signs, and oaths (Wagar). The Knights had a political advocacy platform for workers' rights, the eight-hour day, graduated income tax, arbitration, and equal pay for equal work for women, but this work was to some extent impeded by the amount of time spent on what seemed to some to be meaningless ceremony. But as the Masons had firmly established, the ceremonies were indeed meaningful, if not in their content, then in their social dimension as performance that shaped the field of reception.

Fraternal associations enveloped social life in masculinist performance. Take, for example, the career of Henry Robertson of Collingwood, Ontario. In his entry in a historical register of Supreme Grand Masters of the Knights Templar, which office he held in 1891 to 1892, we see the range of civic fraternal and political associations that marked male success and literally staged the persona of power. He was in public life variously a lawyer, QC, chairman of the high school board in Collingwood, chairman of the public library board, president of the Collingwood golf and curling clubs, reeve of Collingwood, president of the West Simcoe Reform Association of the Liberal Party, and a member of a provincial Royal Commission on law reform. He joined the Masons at the age of twenty-one and rapidly ascended as Worshipful Master, Deputy District Grand Master, Grand Steward Junior Warden, Deputy Grand Master, and Grand Master of the Grand Lodge of Ontario. He was exalted in the York rite. In Capitular Masonry, he was a founder member of the Manitoba chapter and Grand First Principal of the Grand Chapter of Royal Arch Masons in Ontario. In Knights Templary, he was a charter member and Presiding Preceptor of the Ontario Preceptory in Collingwood. He was elected as Provincial Grand Prior for the Toronto district in 1890 and elected Supreme Grand Master of the Sovereign Great Priory of Canada in 1891. He was also a 33° Scottish Rite Mason and a Grand Master Oddfellow (Jenkyns 118–20).

This is a typical profile of a high-ranking Mason of the time, in which virtual identity is sustained in a network – indeed a kind of web – of affiliations and alliances that cross civic, family, and recreational boundaries. Robertson's career shows the particular network of the political elite – all that is missing is a militia commission – and may mark the consolidation of civic power by the professional middle class, but its structure is essentially the same as the wage-earning typographer who moves between his class-specific identities. For both men, performance and spectatorship, and the reciprocal constitutive relation of the two that we call theatre, were instrumental in the creation of social and political identity. This has a disconcerting implication for those who turn to the labour parades to seek evidence of a working-class cultural movement. What they find is the working-class instance of a masculinist performance culture that serves to unlock social strata. In her detailed examination of social life in nineteenth-century Petrolia, Christina Burr argues that "the fraternal order was an ideal way of responding to class differences while at the same time making possible a limited degree of class action and class expression" (131).

Moving between these theatricalized locations, of concert fellowship, public parades, and fraternal virtuality, the nineteenth-century man was in effect using performance to construct systems of order and attainment. We can see in these locations how performance expresses emergent power by activating its capacity to transform public space and to invoke spectatorship. Public performances manifest power as they give evidence of processes of organization and mobilization. Hegemonic power has a wider field of resources: in fact, the state itself is the largest and most public of these performance organizations, renewed and made known through its manifold performances on all levels of social life. As we see with Grand Master Robertson, hegemonic power and performance meet at the point where they both become a practice of the body.

The parading craftworkers and the fraternal ritualists participated in overlapping performances. Regardless of their degree of social affinity (a Mason might be a mason, or he might be an employer of masons), their performances shared a significant feature: they were both performer and spectator. Spectatorship situated within performance, the audience looking out through the performance: to perform the public self in a theatricalization of social space meant that the physical geography of the performance situated each participant as the chief spectator of his fellows, and it reflected one's own self-performance. In the *Adelphon Kruptos*, we read the instructions for opening a service, with the specific spots assigned to various officers:

> Precisely at the hour for opening, allowing five minutes for difference in time pieces, the Master Workman, standing at the Capital. [*sic*] Shall give one rap and say; "All persons not entitled to sit with us will please retire." The Worthy Inspector then takes the Globe and Lance and proceeds to mark the Inner and Outer Veils with them. Previous to that time all persons were at liberty to enter the room, but the Veils are then closed and none can enter without giving the Password. When the Worthy Inspector goes to the Outer Veil to put the Globe in its place, the Outside Esquire takes position in the anteroom, and when the Worthy Inspector enters the Inner Veil, the Inside Esquire takes position at the Inner Veil. Once the Veils are "secured," "The Master Workman will give three raps. Officers and members will form a circle around the centre, Officers in front of their stations as near as possible." (Wagar 5)

All are fixed within the gaze of the performing members; each is given the best seat in the house. Masonic rituals, with their dramatic scenarios and backdrops, placed members within a theatrical narrative of which they were both actor and secret audience. In this spectating performance, I see an unwillingness to submit to the division of performance and reception that became increasingly stratified, controlled, and aestheticized in the legitimate theatre of the later nineteenth century. Electric light, modernist dramaturgy, and changing decorum in a regendered theatre culture calmed the participatory unruliness of the old playhouse culture; outside the playhouse, theatrical culture continued to depend on the simultaneity and convergence of performance and spectatorship. The public performances of the self were commonly organized around mobile occupation of public space, the most common forms being the procession and the parade. When we examine the relationship of mobility and dissent, we follow a vector that moves towards the decomposition of hierarchy and organization in mobile performance. The great craft union parades, the Orange 12 July processions, and the ceremonial movements of the fraternal societies were performances devised to generate order, organization, and power.

Unruly Performance

> On Wednesday of last week two or 300 unemployed laborers assembled in St. Andrew Square and formed a procession, carrying a black flag with the legend, "Work or Bread." They marched by West King Street to the City Hall where a large crowd had gathered.
>
> – *Labor Advocate,* 20 February 1891

If we look for a tradition of organized, aestheticized political theatre in nineteenth-century Canada, we will find very few examples; perhaps the most obvious is Les amateurs typographes, formed by members the Union typographique de Québec in the 1830s, with its repertoire of nationalist and republican plays. If we widen our scope and look at organized theatricality, then we see a rich culture of politically and socially assertive performance as the working class marched into its place in hegemonic civic life and middle-class women staged themselves into political discourse. But even these – the craft union parades, the fraternal orders, the social reform theatricals – were the performances of hegemonic negotiation in the class positions in industrial democracy, and their pervasive masculinism reinforced a deeper gender hegemony. The issue then is not just one of disciplinarity, nor is the binary at play here a simple one of enclosed playhouse and public street. Both stage and street performed to promote a social order in which working-class aspirations wore middle-class garb and striking telegraphers drank tea at concert recitals.

To seek traces of theatricalized dissent, we need to look past the record, into the unrecorded, the unremarked, and what I have been referring to as the unruly, in the sense of standing beyond the reach of discipline and disciplinarity. The paradox for the theatre historian is that most human performance is unrecorded and leaves few traces. The performances of the knockabout farce on a makeshift stage, of the market-square busker and the street-corner comedian, may not be art – they are unruly, beyond discipline – but they are the most common forms of theatrical performance, and it is here that we can suppose theatrical dissent appears and escapes. In Canada, instances of the unruly are many; they can be discerned whenever nineteenth-century masculinity erupted into performance. The crowded history of charivaris (or shivarees), callithumpian parades, and mumming often expressed working-class anger in costumed licence, although that anger was more often incited by religion and ethnicity than by class conflict.

Following the path of the theatre discipline, we can trace unruly dissent from the playhouse to the street, where it disappears from view. Ironically, theatrical spectatorship from below was most commonly from above, in the highest and cheapest tiers of the playhouse, known still as "the gods." As playhouses increased in size to meet popular demand for sensationalist performance, they became focal points of urban politics and factionalism. Nineteenth-century theatre history in Europe and the United States is filled with stories of theatre riots. In Canada, riotous behaviour took place on a smaller scale. One of the earliest records of theatre in York, Upper Canada, is an 1825 legislative select committee hearing into the transgressive rowdyism of an all-male audience of parliamentarians at the performance of a touring American troupe of players on New Year's Eve (Firth 312). As theatres increased in size, so did the riots. In a typical example, a mob armed with clubs stormed a theatre in Saint John in 1845 to disrupt the premiere of Thomas Hill's local political satire *The Provincial Association* (Mullaly). The playhouse was a meeting place in which social and cultural boundaries were tested, often violently. In his history of theatre on the Western frontiers, Chad Evans includes an account of a violent race riot in the Colonial Theatre in Victoria in 1860, when American miners protested the presence of Black spectators in better seats (62). A year later, a Black family in gallery seats was showered with flour and vegetables from above (64). The theatre in Victoria was a convergence zone of very different spectating communities: naval officers and ratings from the British fleet, American miners, immigrant prospectors, English settlers, and, relegated to the cheapest seats, the Indigenous audience. In mid-century Victoria, the Colonial Theatre may have been the most politically volatile space in town.

Evans also gives us a detailed account of the box-house theatres of the mining towns of the Kootenay, such as the Theatre Comique in Kaslo, which was a variety theatre and a saloon with two bars and a staff of eighty "box rustler" bar girls. Evans describes the box-house theatre as a "perfectly designed trap" (and the predecessor of today's casinos) (77). In the box-house theatre, spectatorship spills into the brothel rooms and out into the street. The actual theatrical performance is incidental; it functions as an occasion of spectating and a place of public display because it is axiomatic that a theatre audience watches the show and each other. If we close the show, we still have the theatricality and spectacle of the place itself, at which point the audience becomes the show.

Perhaps the most notorious of such places was Joe Beef's Canteen in Montréal. Joe Beef, whose real name was Charles McKiernan, is one of the most notorious folk heroes in Québec history. An Irish veteran of the British army, his canteen was a four-storey waterfront tavern, hostel, soup kitchen, zoo, and theatre. Beef became famous for providing free meals and support for striking canal and mill workers. He was himself a self-created persona, who advertised that

> Joe Beef, the Son of the People.
> He cares not for Pope, Priest, Parson, or King
> William of the Boyne; all Joe wants is the Coin.
> He trusts in God in the summer to keep him
> from all harm; when he sees the first frost and
> snow poor old Joe trusts to the Almighty Dollar
> and good old maple wood to keep his belly warm. (DeLottinville 195)

His canteen was a must-see stop for out-of-town visitors, for whom it was evidence of a dissipation that only Montréal could achieve. According to one writer in an 1881 *New York Times*,

> I was introduced to Beef, and he showed me some of his curiosities, as a special mark of his favor. Most of them were too disgusting to look at, too indecent to describe. He had snakes done up in glass jars, and toads, and a variety of other articles. In a small dark room, just back of the bar-room, an enormous black bear was chained, and by his side were fastened a score or

> more of ferocious dogs. The next room was the "theatre," where, on Sundays, religious services are held. A half-drunken clown and a black monkey were performing on the stage for the edification of half a dozen tramps, who were stretched on the benches. ("Canadian Voyageur")

Similarly *Montréal by Gaslight,* a muckraking pamphlet from 1889 (after McKiernan's death) – which ostensibly documents the perfidy of Montréal's nightlife but in so doing provides a detailed catalogue of brothels, their locations, identifying features, and specialties – offers a lurid description of the canteen, dwelling in detail on its filth but concluding, "But let one thing be remembered – many a tired head has here found rest; many a hungry mouth has here been filled" (116). And many found entertainment. If there was any place in Canada that could be described as a dissenting, insurgent working-class theatre, this was it. It was an intensely performative space, and Joe Beef himself was a theatricalized character. Peter DeLottinville makes the point that McKiernan "eagerly debated topics of the day, or amused patrons with humorous poems of his own composition. He had a remarkable ability to ramble on for hours in rhyming couplets" (193). But to the middle classes, the canteen was only spoken of as a space of disruption, filth, and danger. We can only imagine the performances that erupted there, but the presence of striking workers, performing bears, parrots, a rhyming landlord, indigent tramps, petty criminals, and a "half-drunken clown" opens the possibility of a politicized theatre that was so unruly as to be inconceivable to anyone not present.

If the box-house theatres are theatres that move away from the decorum of "the" theatre, and if Joe Beef's Canteen is in effect a box-house theatre with only the sketchiest of stages, what are we left with if we move out of the premises altogether, onto the street – without form, without discipline, with nothing but unruly performance in public space? We are left with mummers and their equivalents, however named. Here basic elements of disguise and grotesquerie exist to license unruly behaviours, often but not exclusively on festive occasions. Mummers are most commonly associated with Newfoundland, where the (much-changed) tradition continues to the present day, but mumming also continues elsewhere, on Hallowe'en, on festive holidays, and in the public disguised performances of sports fans. And as with sports fans today, it could often turn violent. In Newfoundland, disguised mumming was banned in 1860 after the death of a Protestant mummer in a religious riot in Bay Roberts. In

St John's, as one witness later recalled, rival Irish gangs of mummers slugged it out in costumes, and as one witness later recalled, "men were often beaten badly for old grievances by the fools. I remember, as a boy, how proud I used to be to shake hands with the fool ... Each company had one or more hobby horses, with gaping jaws snapping at people" (Story 177–8). Scholarly historical accounts of mumming have tended to examine performance traits and characteristics to establish typologies, because most of them have been written by folklorists and anthropologists. They seek to identify the patterned activity – evidence of order and a kind of disciplinarity – with the result that mumming is understood to manifest in structure (like the mummers' plays or ritualized house visiting) and decompose in riot. But the heart of mumming is a delight in unruly public disorder.

The determined gardener who presented his caterpillar bouquet in City Hall was in his own way a mummer, masked in gesture, whose unruliness was his activism. For the most part, such unruliness was unremarked, because it could only be seen as disorder and disruption. This more than anything explains the apparent but deceptive absence of "working-class political theatre" in the nineteenth century. That deceptive absence forces us to ask whether we have been looking at the question from the wrong end. Seeking performance of dissent and political theatre in the nineteenth century, we find less than we expect, and our genealogical mechanism, which seeks antecedents for the agitprop and interventionist theatre of the twentieth century, is disrupted (until we realize that their sources are mass communication, not theatre). Joe Beef reminds us that we have the question inside out, because it assumes that the theatre culture of his time was framed in artistic disciplinarity and sanitized from political activism and dissent. But if we start with the hypothesis that all theatre in the nineteenth century was "political," tending to the unruly in location, in spectatorship, or in the simulations of the public self, the question then becomes an exploration of how theatrical modernism became disciplined and socially calmed.

WORKS CITED

Bamberg, Michael. "Considering Counter-Narratives." *Considering Counter-Narratives: Narrating, Resisting, Making Sense*, edited by Michael Bamberg and Molly Andrews, John Benjamin, 2004, pp. 351–71.

Bengough, J.W. *Bengough's Chalk-Talks: A Series of Platform Addresses on Various Topics, with Reproductions of the Impromptu Drawings with Which They Were Illustrated.* Musson, 1922.

Bird, Kym. *Redressing the Past: The Politics of Early English-Canadian Women's Drama, 1880–1920.* McGill-Queen's UP, 2004.

Blagrave, Mark. "Temperance and the Theatre in the Nineteenth Century Maritimes." *Theatre History in Canada / Histoire du théâtrè au Canada,* vol. 7, no. 1, 1986, pp. 23–32.

Burr, Christina. *Canada's Victorian Oil Town: The Transformation of Petrolia from a Resource Town into a Victorian Community.* McGill-Queen's UP, 2006.

Butsch, Richard. *The Making of American Audiences: From Stage to Television, 1750–1990.* Cambridge UP, 2000.

"The Canadian Voyageur: Continuing the Descent of the St. Lawrence. Some Information. Montréal. Joe Beef's Canteen. Bound for Québec." *New York Times,* 20 Aug. 1881.

Candidus, Caroli. *The Female Consistory of Brockville: A Melo-Drama in Three Acts.* Brockville, ON, 1856.

Carnes, Mark. *Secret Ritual and Manhood in Victorian America.* Yale UP, 1989.

"College Life: The Mock Parliament." *OAC Review,* vol. 20, no. 7, Apr. 1908, pp. 131–47. archive.org/details/oacreviewvol20iss7.

"College Life: The Spinster's Convention." *OAC Review,* vol. 20, no. 7, Apr. 1908, pp. 173–5. archive.org/details/oacreviewvol20iss7.

Davis, Susan. *Parades and Power: Street Theatre in Nineteenth-century Philadelphia.* U of California P, 1986.

"Debates of Conscience with a Distiller, a Wholesaler Dealer, and a Retailer." *A Collection of Temperance Dialogues for Divisions of Sons, Good Templar Lodges, Sections of Cadets, Band of Hope, and Other Temperance Societies,* edited by S.T. Hammond, Hunter, Ross, and Co., 1869, pp. 1–17.

DeLottinville, Peter. "Joe Beef of Montréal: Working-Class Culture and the Tavern, 1869–1889." *Canadian Working-Class History,* edited by Laurel MacDowell and Ian Radforth, Canadian Scholars' Press, pp. 190–214.

Evans, Chad. *Frontier Theatre: A History of Nineteenth-century Theatrical Entertainment in the Canadian Far West and Alaska.* Sono Nis, 1983.

Firth, Edith. *The Town of York, 1814–1834: A Further Collection of Documents of Early Toronto.* Champlain Society, 1966.

Heron, Craig, and Steven Penfold. *The Workers' Festival: A History of Labour Day in Canada.* U of Toronto P, 2005.

Jenkyns, Michael. *The Sovereign Great Priory of Canada of the United Orders of Malta and of the Temple, 1855–2002: The Supreme Grand Masters.* Gryphon Jenkyns Enterprises, 2003.

Massey, Vincent. "The Prospects of a Canadian Drama." *Queen's Quarterly*, vol. 30, 1922, pp. 194–212.

Montréal by Gaslight. Montréal, 1889. CIHM microfiche 11210.

Mullaly, Edward. "The Saint John Theatre Riot of 1845." *Theatre History in Canada / Histoire du théâtre au Canada*, vol. 6, no. 1, 1985, pp. 44–55.

Ogden's Big Spectacular Uncle Tom's Cabin Company. ca. 1900. Poster.

Smith, Mary Ellen. "Three Political Dramas from New Brunswick." *Canadian Drama / L'art dramatique canadien*, vol. 12, no. 1, 1986, pp. 144–7.

Stevens, Albert. *The Cyclopaedia of Fraternities: A Compilation of Existing Authentic Information and the Results of Original Investigation As to the Origin, Derivation, Founders, Development, Aims, Emblems, Character and Personnel of More than Six Hundred Secret Societies in the United States*. 1907. Gale Research, 1966.

Story, G.M. "Mummers in Newfoundland History: A Survey of the Printed Record." *Christmas Mumming in Newfoundland: Essays in Anthropology, Folklore, and History*, edited by Herbert Halpert and George Story, U of Toronto P, 1968, pp. 165–85.

Wagar, Samuel, editor. *Adelphon Kruptos: The Secret Ritual of the Knights of Labor*. 1886. Rpt. 2003. www.gompers.umd.edu/KOL%20ritual.pdf.

7 Women's Space in Postcolonial Perspective: France Théoret's *Une belle éducation* and Assia Djebar's *Nulle part dans la maison de mon père*

MARY JEAN GREEN

The relationship of women and space, particularly the space of the city, has been the subject of much discussion at least since the 1980s, when a new generation of women geographers, building on the work of women anthropologists, added their voices to the pioneering work of male theorizsts like historian Michel Foucault. Somewhat surprisingly, from our current perspective, Foucault's pioneering essay, "Of Other Spaces," failed to mention differences determined by gender. He went on to lead his readers to the work of Gaston Bachelard without remarking that this poetic analysis of *la maison* (in French, both the *house* and the *home*) makes no reference to the special role of women within it, as *house*wife and *home*maker.

As might be expected, women anthropologists were among the first to study space as experienced by women in cultures across the world, as represented by Shirley Ardener's 1981 essay collection entitled *Women and Space.* Mildred Mortimer has noted how Ardener observed that "societies generate social boundaries by establishing culturally determined 'ground rules' and 'social maps' that affect men and women differently ... patriarchal societies establish rules that affect women's movement, physically and psychologically" (4). Not long after this pioneering work by anthropologists, women geographers began to detect evidence of spatial differentiation based on gender even in Western urban settings. A well-known example is based on Walter Benjamin's study of the nineteenth-century Parisian poet Charles Baudelaire, whose essays and poems often reflect his own position as a flâneur, a man who spends his time walking around the city observing the activity of others. As some feminist scholars quickly noted, there exists a representation of the flâneur but not of his female counterpart the *flâneuse* (or at least as represented by Baudelaire; the women who walked the streets of Paris by themselves were often exactly that: in English, the term "streetwalker" has long been synonymous with "prostitute"). But, as Deborah L. Parsons points out in *Streetwalking the Metropolis*, this observation of a gendered division of urban space has been hotly debated by feminist scholars. Studies of nineteenth-century women painters like Berthe Morisot revealed that in their work Parisian life is frequently observed from a balcony or set in the privacy of the home, while other scholars succeeded in locating the presence of a *flâneuse* in the work of twentieth-century women writers like Virginia Woolf.

The confinement of women to the home may often be seen as a relic of the historical Middle Eastern harem. Nonetheless, it is a practice that, rather surprisingly, has deeply affected the lives of well-known contemporary women writers in various francophone cultures, at least in their childhood years. The freedom to walk around in the city is a recurring problem for women in the work of Algerian francophone writer Assia Djebar and, perhaps more surprisingly, in the writing of Québécoise francophone France Théoret.

In their autobiographical writing, both these writers describe teenaged girls who, in the mid-1950s, make a desperate bid for freedom, in an apparent attempt to end their lives. In two works she has recognized as autobiographical, France Théoret, through her narrator, represents her younger self throwing herself from a moving streetcar in May 1957 in Montréal after experiencing, as she writes in her 1982 narrative *Nous parlerons comme on écrit* (*We Will Speak the Way One Writes*), "le désir d'aller me conjoindre au soleil un matin de mai" ("the desire to join myself to the sun one morning in May"; 12). The adolescent girl survives, but the blow to her head as it strikes the pavement leaves her with a persistent stutter, inhibiting her ability to speak. Théoret elaborates this first enigmatic account of the episode in 2006 in *Une belle éducation* (*Such a Good Education*), which the writer has identified as autobiographical despite the fact that the central character is named Evelyne rather than France. Here, Théoret stresses the fact that this unpremeditated suicidal act was a reaction to her father's condemnation of her attempt to study Latin, a subject he viewed as unnecessary and inappropriate to his conception of her limited future as a traditional wife and mother.

The young woman who would adopt the pen name Assia Djebar relates in her 2007 autobiography, *Nulle part dans la maison de mon père* (*Nowhere in My Father's House*), that she had attempted to throw herself under an approaching streetcar in the city of Algiers in October 1953.

She did this, as she explains, "dans l'exaltation de me dissoudre aux quatre coins de l'immense espace de la baie d'Alger" ("in the exaltation of dissolving myself in the four corners of the immense space of the Bay of Algiers"; 367). She too survives, saved by the quick action of the driver, but the shock of her brush with death effectively silences her throughout the ensuing twenty-one years of a marriage with the man whose overbearing presence she had attempted to flee.

Like Théoret, Djebar had first mentioned her near-death experience briefly and enigmatically in an early novel, her 1985 *L'amour, la fantasia,* a text that, like Théoret's *Nous parlerons comme on écrit,* has been recognized as an exemplary feminist autobiography of the early 1980s. In each text, the writer embeds the events of her own life in the larger experience of other women of her culture, past and present, a plural women's experience emphasized in the assertive plural *Nous* of Théoret's title. Years later, each writer returns to a suicidal moment that had apparently remained as enigmatic for the writer as for her readers. In both cases, the writers' later work, published in the first decade of the twenty-first century, seems to connect this moment of suicidal rebellion against paternal authority with historical events in her own society. Djebar's *Nulle part dans la maison de mon père,* the last work published before the writer's death in February 2015, is clearly a deeply personal meditation on the childhood and adolescence that led up to the near-fatal moment of rebellion in October 1953. This date, as Djebar pointedly reminds her readers, is almost exactly one year before the collective insurrection that launched the Algerian Revolution in November 1954. Similarly, Théoret's *Une belle éducation* embodies in the symbolically named character of Evelyne (daughter of Eve) the experience surrounding this evidently autobiographical episode in 1957, shortly before the beginning of Québec's Quiet Revolution of the 1960s. To one who follows the writing of francophone women, the textual coincidence is striking.

Throughout the postcolonial francophone world, the 1980s was a time for celebration by women writers who, calling themselves feminists or not, were eager to celebrate the role of women in a collective experience of liberation and independence. The early autobiographies of Djebar and Théoret have served as crucial markers of this perhaps momentary conflation of feminism with a national independence movement, as have autobiographical texts by many other women, like the Senegalese Mariama Bâ. Assia Djebar, the first Maghrebian to be elected to the Académie française, has been widely recognized as an important spokesperson for Algerian intellectuals in the wake of independence and the Islamist violence of the 1990s. In Québec, France Théoret has played an important role in the feminist literary movement of the 1970s and 1980s, broadly known as "writing in the feminine."[1] In my own history of Québec women's writing, *Women and Narrative Identity*, I have seen Théoret – particularly in her *Nous parlerons comme on écrit* – as an important voice in the integration of feminism with Québec nationalism, as in that work she boldly proclaimed herself "Écrivaine et Québécoise" ("woman writer and woman of Québec").[2]

Because the Algerian Revolution has served as a model for the anti-colonial struggle throughout the world, it is relatively easy to place the rebellious gesture of Assia Djebar's adolescent in the context of a struggle against a dual oppression: both the literal state of colonization imposed on Algerians by the French and the limitations imposed on Algerian women by a rigid and unbending interpretation of their own Muslim tradition. As has been described by both Frantz Fanon and Albert Memmi,[3] this religious heritage had, in their analysis, been rigidified by the cultural stagnation fostered by colonial domination.

Interestingly, Memmi also extended this analysis of colonial cultural stagnation to the situation of francophones in Québec, whose long repression by anglophones had reproduced, in his view, two aspects of the colonial experience that had been central to his earlier analysis of the French North African colonies: the suppression of a native language by another in a situation of "colonial diglossia" and the rigidifying of traditional religious and cultural values, as they became what he called the "refuge-values" of a dominated people ("Canadiens-français"). These "refuge-values," in the case of Québec, included the role played by women in producing unlimited numbers of French-speaking children. In his article "Les Canadiens-français sont-ils des colonisés?" ("Are French Canadians Colonized People?"), Memmi was able to situate Québec among postcolonial cultures, as many Québec writers of the Quiet Revolution had also attempted to do. As I have argued elsewhere, Memmi's analysis has been useful in opening the study of Québec literature to postcolonial theory ("Locating").

---

1 For an analysis of Théoret's position within this movement, see Karen Gould's *Writing in the Feminine.*

2 These words of Théoret serve as the epigraph for the chapter entitled "Rewriting the Narratives of Identity" in my book *Women and Narrative Identity*, 103.

3 See especially Fanon's "L'Algérie se dévoile" and Memmi's *Portrait du colonisé.*

Seen in this postcolonial context, the relationship between the two cultures and two sets of women's autobiographies, Algerian and Québécois, comes into focus. Both Théoret and Djebar return, after a hiatus of more than two decades, to the once-told story of their childhood in order to trace the effects of a socially embedded repression of women that had driven them to attempt violence against their own lives. In both cases, the daughter's desperate act is portrayed as a response to a paternal interdiction: in Algeria, a father's refusal to let his daughter circulate freely on her own; in Québec, the refusal of a father to allow his daughter to enjoy another form of freedom in pursuing her dream of higher education.

In Algeria, as we know, violence against women and intellectuals has, in recent decades, engendered mass killings that have threatened the stability of the entire society: they were also the cause of Djebar's decision to live away from her homeland, in France or the United States. This state of exile is certainly reflected in the title chosen for her final autobiographical text, where she represents herself as "nowhere in my father's house." In this late-life autobiographical writing, the scene in which she attempts to throw herself under a streetcar, recounted only briefly in the earlier *L'amour, la fantasia*, becomes the focus of the book. It is the concluding event in a long process of rebellion against her father's traditional attitudes towards women's freedom to circulate in public, a position that stands in unexpected contrast to his support for the education of his eldest daughter. Her father was, in some sense, the hero of *L'amour, la fantasia*, Djebar's first autobiographical text. There he is represented as bravely challenging traditional taboos of Algerian culture by accompanying his daughter to school: as the text begins, she walks hand in hand with her father ("main dans la main du père" [11]). The later rewriting of her life in *Nulle part*, however, begins with the little girl walking with her veiled mother, while the father, despite still being a supporter of education, is often relegated to a more negative role. Although he sends his daughter out to school and lives with his family in the French teachers' quarters, he reacts with surprising condemnation when he finds the small girl trying to ride a neighbour's bicycle. His words of interdiction – "je ne veux pas que ma fille montre ses jambes en montant à bicyclette" ("I don't want my daughter to show her bare legs while riding a bicycle"; 49) – are incomprehensible to the child, seeming to separate her legs from the rest of her body. The episode has such a traumatic effect that it prevents her from ever again getting on a bicycle.

As Djebar's narrator becomes an adolescent, however, a second tradition-based paternal interdiction inspires not trauma but rebellion. When her father tears up the letter she receives from the young man who will later become her husband, she reassembles the pieces and enters into a forbidden correspondence with him. Later, he will take her on long walks through the city of Algiers as she escapes from the limitations placed on her by her family. It is in the course of one of these walks, when her fiancé himself surprisingly assumes a patriarchal tone, that the narrator attempts to run off towards the open space of the glistening Bay of Algiers, in the process suddenly throwing herself in front of an oncoming streetcar. The instantaneous transformation of an escape to freedom into a desire for death is hard for the older narrator to fully comprehend, but she comes to see that it was a response not to her fiancé but to her father, an expression of her guilt for disobeying a paternal interdiction. As she walks through the streets of the city with her forbidden male escort, she repeats to herself as a mantra, "Si mon père le sait, je me tue!" ("If my father finds out, I'm killing myself"; 354); in the space of a moment, this phrase transforms itself into the thought, "Mon père ... me tue!" ("my father is killing me"; 354). In Djebar's more recent meditation on moments of childhood trauma, she realizes that she had been traumatized by a series of repeated paternal interdictions, grounded in a traditional culture he had in other ways left behind. And it is from that October day in 1953, when she had attempted to end her life, that she dates her real exile from her father and her homeland, summed up in the image of the "father's house" appearing in her title: "Je n'ai plus de maison de mon père. Je suis sans lieu là-bas depuis ce jour d'octobre" ("I no longer have my father's house. I am without a home over there since that October day"; 386).

As Patricia Smart has reminded us in *Écrire dans la maison du père* (*Writing in the Father's House*), the "father's house," in Québec as well as Algeria, is an apt and far-reaching description of a traditional culture in which women have struggled to find a place and a voice. Québec's "quiet" liberation from a "domination" imposed from without and within has involved far less physical violence than the armed fight for Algerian independence, but the struggle of Québec women for individual independence has often been debilitating, as we are reminded by Théoret's account of a daughter's failed suicide and a mother's failed revolt, the story of a symbolically named Eva (Eve) and her daughter Evelyne. The struggle between two models of culture, portrayed in this text as two different theories of education, provides a new history of Québec's Quiet Revolution as it affected women and modes of thought. To read the autobiographical writing and rewriting of France Théoret in a comparative and postcolonial context is to gain a deeper understanding of the importance of her work and of the relationship of Québec to contemporary francophone cultures in other areas of the world.

The cover of Théoret's *Une belle éducation*, with its painting of a sunny winter urban scene, offers statements that soon prove ironic, not unlike the apparently high-minded but outmoded traditional ideology that governs the protagonist's experience at home and school, an ideology rooted in rural poverty but rigidly preserved and imposed by what is revealed to be a poverty of spirit. In the cover painting, entitled *Après-midi d'hiver, place Ste-Famille* (*Winter Afternoon in Holy Family Square*), artist Louis Muhlstock has transformed the cold of an urban winter into a scene of light and warmth, the curves of bare branches softening the geometric lines of buildings whose brick is warmed by the winter sun. By its title, the scene is allied to the warmth of the holy family, the traditional Québec family whose life illuminates the interior of these brick buildings as the sun brightens their exterior walls. But the first words of the text awaken the reader from this lovely vision: "Dès notre arrivée, je remarque la nudité de la rue et l'absence des arbres" ("The moment we arrive I notice how bare the street is and that there are no trees"; 9; von Flotow 3). Even the light that inundates the homes is absent from Théoret's verbal picture: Evelyne's family inhabits a dark cellar infested with rats, from which all light is consciously banned. The only door that opens directly to the street is closed off by the mother in the interests of security. A fitting residence for the Québec family of the 1950s, the house is shut off from the world, and the children are forced to enter through the back by way of a muddy courtyard, enclosed by blank walls. The constant tracking of mud into the kitchen condemns Evelyne and her sister to endless washing of the linoleum floor, as it is immediately dirtied once again. In their dark cellar, family meals are a repetitive round of boiled potatoes, canned vegetables, and chopped meat, filling plates that the father hurls against the enclosing walls in protest of his fate, occasioning yet another mopping of the floor.

Although *Une belle éducation* is formally identified as a novel, the events it recounts are autobiographical, which we know because Théoret acknowledged their autobiographical nature after their initial appearance in *Nous parlerons comme on écrit* in 1982. The adolescent attempt at suicide is evoked in that early novel in the words, "Ma tête a frappé sec le pavé rue Notre-Dame un matin de mai" ("My head smashed into the pavement on Notre-Dame one morning in May"; 22), which are twice again reiterated in similar form (19, 45). But the act itself remains largely unexplained. In her 1993 writer's diary, *Journal pour mémoire,* Théoret incorporates the same events into a series of first-person reflections on her own life (although, strangely, the streetcar incident is absent from this somewhat rambling text). But in 2006, in *Une belle éducation,* it reappears at the very centre of the text.

In a sense, *Une belle éducation* is the realization of the project Théoret had outlined in *Journal pour mémoire,* the history of the origin and evolution of her desire for knowledge. In approaching this subject in *Journal pour mémoire,* the writer had lamented the fragmented, disjointed nature of her writing and her life, her inability to arrange events in terms of cause and effect, seeing her intellectual awakening as a series of isolated "moments privilégiés" ("privileged moments"; 112), a description that would seem to apply to *Nous parlerons comme on écrit.* In *Une belle éducation,* however, she submits these adolescent moments to a strict chronology and also, I would suggest, to the ordering imposed by novelistic form – in this case, the characteristically upward trajectory of the Bildungsroman or *novel of development,* as it is generally known in English. In its French formulation, as the *roman d'apprentissage,* the genre is much more closely associated with the idea of apprenticeship or education, as suggested by the great nineteenth-century model of what has been called a negative education, Flaubert's *Éducation sentimentale.* In its classic form, however, the Bildungsroman is a novel of the development of its protagonist through apprenticeship to mastery,[4] and this is indeed the trajectory followed by the protagonist of *Une belle éducation,* as, through the education of which she had begun to dream as an adolescent, she ascends from her family's dark, rat-infested basement to her own home, filled with light and air.

In the novel this developmental trajectory is launched by a single choice, presented to Evelyne by the assistant director of the convent school in which her mother enrols her in apparent support of Evelyne's educational goals. In this symbolic meeting, the daughter is offered the opportunity to enter the "special" section, which is distinguished from the "general" curriculum by the addition of Latin and geometry. It is the

4 For a perceptive analysis of women and the Bildungsroman, see Susan Fraiman, *Unbecoming Women.*

study of Latin that will change her life, as the hours spent translating from Latin to French open her to the nuances of language, the complex resonances of words. The few moments she has to spend with her homework in the family's crowded basement kitchen offer a rare experience of personal pleasure, and she silently but stubbornly defends them against her father's repeated demands for her presence in the family store. In the "special" section as well, Friday afternoons are devoted to individual composition, an exercise in which the adolescent not only learns to express herself but begins to exchange her drafts with a friend, initiating a first experience of feminine literary communication.

A turning point in the life of Evelyne, as in the life of France Théoret herself, the institution in 1950 of the "special" section for women in public educational institutions in Québec was a crucial step forward in women's education, which was finally made equal to the education of men in the sweeping educational reforms of the 1960s (Dumont and Fahmy-Eid 60). Formal education for women in Québec had existed since the French settlement, but it had always been differentiated from that of men, who alone were encouraged to study classical languages and mathematics (Thivierge 120). These subjects, prerequisites for university study, weren't made available to Québec women until the early decades of the twentieth century, although this curriculum was taught only in a handful of elite convent schools (Dumont and Fahmy-Eid 106–12). For the daughters of families like Evelyne's, access to subjects like Latin and geometry became widely available only in the 1950s – and even then, as Théoret's scene makes clear, only to those with exceptional grades. Nonetheless, for at least one girl from a working-class district of Montréal, the access to Latin creates a desire for greater knowledge and opens the door to higher education. Although the mature Evelyne is not identified as a writer, it is clear that the study of Latin marks the beginning as well of her apprenticeship with language. The moments of pleasure Evelyne experiences with Latin translation and French composition give rise to what is called an "interior voice," whose repeated message – "je sais que je ne sais pas" – supports the inner resolve that keeps her going through what, in the novel's second half, is represented as years of silent resistance to the traditional feminine itinerary mapped by her parents.

In fact, the single event that seems to precipitate the streetcar scene, or at least the event that immediately precedes it in the development of the narrative, is the father's attempted interdiction of Evelyne's study of Latin. Seemingly oblivious to his daughter's education until this point, he suddenly comes upon her with her Latin homework and stings her with a thrice-repeated condemnation: "le latin, ce n'est pas pour toi, ce n'est pas pour nous ... Nous n'avons pas besoin de ça, le latin" ("Latin isn't for you, it's not for us ... We don't need that! Latin!"; 54–5; von Flotow 47). In this version of the scene, Evelyne is incapable of responding but evades her father's attempted blow and retreats into a religiously inspired self-examination in which she has no choice but to condemn herself: "Je me suis perçue à travers son regard, je me suis jugée déraisonnable. Je bats ma coulpe, au bord de la déraison" ("I see myself through his eyes, as unreasonable. I beat my breast, on the verge of losing my mind"; 54; von Flotow 47). "Les phrases de mon père m'ont bouleversée" ("My father's words have shattered me"; 54; von Flotow 47), she concludes, and in the next paragraph she is shown waking up on the morning of her suicide attempt. As in the case of Djebar, a paternal interdiction is closely tied to the adolescent wish for death, which is described by Théoret as an overwhelming desire for freedom: "Je suis émue, extasiée devant ma propre liberté, j'imagine qu'un pareil moment ne reviendra pas. Ce qui est là me comble, il m'est impossible de poursuivre pareils instants. Je désire mourir" ("I was overcome, ecstatic at my own freedom, I imagined such a moment would never come again. I am fulfilled by what is, it is impossible to have the same feeling ever again. I feel I want to die"; 57; von Flotow 50).

In the penultimate section of *Une belle éducation*, tellingly dated June 1968, the narrator is able to sum up the success of what she refers to as an "apprentissage existentiel long et laborieux" ("a slow and laborious existential learning"; 134; von Flotow 129). Yet, as feminist critics have reminded us, the novel of education as written and experienced by women is rarely this simple. Elizabeth Abel, Marianne Hirsch, and Elizabeth Langland have argued in *The Voyage In* that the female Bildungsroman asserts its difference from the classic literary model of male development: "The heroine's developmental course is more conflicted, less direct" (11). The developmental progress of the genre's woman protagonist is often complicated by what Susan Fraiman calls "counternarratives" (10–11), alternative paths of development that offer themselves to the heroine and place themselves in her way. This concept is certainly relevant to the destinies of Evelyne's only friends, *la blonde* and *la brune*, both of whom leave the "special" course after the first year, one to get married and the other to become a nun – perhaps not coincidentally, the two paths offered to women in 1950s Québec.

But here, as in the women's novels of development studied by Abel, Hirsch, and Langland, the major source of conflict for the woman protagonist is the pull of relationships within the family, particularly with the mother: "separation tugs against the longing for fusion and the heroine encounters the conviction that identity resides in intimate relationships especially those of early childhood" (11). Like Gabrielle Roy's Florentine Lacasse, whose childhood experience also takes place in the Montréal working-class district of Saint-Henri, Théoret's Evelyne has great empathy with a mother overburdened by responsibility: "Je suis semblable à ma mère, mieux que son double, je vois son destin funeste et noir" ("I am like my mother, I am more than her double; I can see her dark fate looming"; 43; von Flotow 37). The unhappiness of the older woman, trapped in the dark basement in her seemingly hopeless life, at times driven to apparent madness, resonates with Evelyne, and the daughter often blames herself for failing to protect her mother.

Thus, her mother Eva offers Evelyne not only a different model of life but also a conflicting model of education. It is, in fact, in connection with the mother that the term "une belle éducation" is first used in the text, in a context that casts an ironic shadow on the meaning of the title.[5] The annual New Year's visit to the paternal grandparents, the only social event that marks this family's bleak social calendar, becomes the occasion for displaying the good manners the children have been taught by their mother, the "belle éducation" with which she is providing them.

The phrase Théoret has chosen for the title is used twice in the text, both times by the mother, to describe the education she gives her children. In both instances, it refers to table manners, which consist, in this household, of the children's silence at meals, where only the parents are entitled to speak. And appropriately the mother speaks again in this context of "la belle éducation qu'elle nous donne" ("she is providing us with a good education"; 19; von Flotow 13), a style of education contrasted to that of the father, who is "un homme sans principes, forcément sans éducation" ("a man without principles, and of course, without education"; 20; von Flotow 13). This statement is corroborated a few pages later when the father flings his plate of uneaten food on the kitchen floor.

The *belle éducation* served up daily by the mother is, in large part, reaffirmed by the teaching nuns at the local school, who drive home the message that the feminine vocation is one of respect for authority and

5 The English translation of the novel renders the title as *Such a Good Education,* a phrase that does not quite capture the refinement and elegance implied by the French term, *une belle éducation.*

sacrifice of self for others, warning the students against speaking of themselves and their accomplishments. In a scene that seems to recall the experience of Québec's first woman university student, Marie Gérin-Lajoie, the director of Evelyne's school tells her that she has obtained the highest score in the class on the academic aptitude tests, but she makes clear that Evelyne should not take pride in this accomplishment, nor should she speak of her success. In the case of Marie Gérin-Lajoie, who had obtained the highest score in the baccalaureate exams in 1916, her success was concealed and the top place publicly awarded to a man: as the Collectif Clio describes it in *L'histoire des femmes au Québec*, "il ne semble pas convenable qu'une jeune fille se soit classée devant les garçons" ("It does not seem right for a girl to be classified above the boys"; 322). This traditional view of women's education is summed up by Marie-Paule Malouin and Micheline Dumont: "toutes ces jeune filles qui poursuivaient leurs études au-delà du seuil atteint par la majorité des jeunes Québécoises devaient éviter que leur savoir acquiert une visibilité qui court-circuiterait les rôles féminins prévus pour elles selon les normes sociales de l'époque" ("all the girls who continued their studies beyond the level attained by the majority of girls in Québec had to avoid making their knowledge visible in a way that would short-circuit the feminine roles for which they were destined according to the social norms of the time"; 111).

In fact, the education offered by the mother and reiterated by the nuns consists largely of a repeated interdiction of speech. The mother's philosophy, as represented in the text, is based on the proverb "Trop parler nuit" (30) (an English equivalent might be "Least said, soonest mended," but the French seems somewhat more sinister). The message is general, but it is also personalized, as the narrator comments, apparently repeating the words of her mother, "Sa parole à elle a le pouvoir de ruiner sa vie" ("Her own words have the power to ruin her life"; 31; von Flotow 22). The mother's second proverbial teaching is similar to the first: "Toute vérité n'est pas bonne à dire" ("not every truth should be told"; 30; von Flotow 23) – a phrase that ominously seems to inscribe in Théoret's text, even before the concluding chapter, an implied censorship of the novel's project of baring the truth of an oppressive childhood.

Unexpectedly, however, in the final section of the text, dated October 1985, Evelyne has an intimate conversation with her aging mother in her own home in Montréal, warmed by the autumn sunlight that enters through the French doors. If the mother's definition of "une belle éducation" has cast an ironic shadow on the meaning of Théoret's title, the mother's reappearance in the text's concluding section casts a similarly ironic shadow on the heroine's developmental accomplishment. Strangely, the conclusion of this new version of Théoret's autobiography stands in sharp contrast to the much-analysed final chapter of *Nous parlerons comme on écrit*, in which the protagonist walks boldly alone through the streets of Montréal. Yet, in Théoret's own summary of that early novel for my students in 1990, she took care to note that her conclusion gave "a place to the mother."[6] In this case, the mother is not the protagonist's own but a generic Québec mother, most often referred to in the text as "les mères" ("mothers").

In the last scene of *Une belle éducation*, Evelyne makes a final attempt to break the silence that has separated her from her mother, daring to ask about Eva's own adolescent act of rebellion against a repressive father – or, as symbolically expressed in the text, her abrupt departure from "la terre paternelle" ("the paternal land").[7] As the daughter evokes this episode, which had been told to her by an aunt, her mother not only remains strangely silent but literally cuts off the daughter's words: "Elle me coupe la parole" ("she cuts me off"; 144; von Flotow 142). And she enjoins her daughter never again to speak of an act of rebellion that, for her, remains unsayable, "une image indicible et monstrueuse" ("an unspeakable monstrous image"; 145; von Flotow 143). As the novel ends, the mother once again betrays a strange disarray as she attempts to reassert a traditional authority over a daughter from whom she sets herself forever apart.

I began this study by comparing two rewritten autobiographies by women that appeared at the same historical moment, in 2006 and 2007. In both, the authors turn back to a youthful suicide attempt made in apparent response to a paternal interdiction. It is easy for us, as North Americans, to understand and condemn a traditional Islamic claustration of women that made even Assia Djebar's loving father appear

6 Interview with France Théoret, 27 Feb. 1990, Dartmouth College, Hanover, New Hampshire.

7 This is not only a reference to a much-used term in nineteenth-century Québec, but also to a well-known nineteenth-century novel entitled *La terre paternelle*, which, like many *romans de la terre*, exhorts the rural francophone population of Québec to remain on the land rather than leave for the anglophone-dominated cities.

repressive to the daughter whose education he had otherwise encouraged. It is perhaps more difficult to place this Algerian repression in parallel with a situation much closer to our own lives, a repression that sought to limit women's intellectual development and thus, in another setting, impose the veil of religion or confine them to the home.

WORKS CITED

Abel, Elizabeth, Marianne Hirsch, and Elizabeth Langland, editors. *The Voyage In: Fictions of Female Development.* UP of New England, 1983.

Ardener, Shirley, editor. *Women and Space: Ground Rules and Social Maps.* 1981. Berg, 1993.

Bachelard, Gaston. *The Poetics of Space.* 1958. Translated by Maria Jolas, Beacon Press, 1994.

Benjamin, Walter. *Charles Baudelaire: A Lyric Poet in the Era of High Capitalism.* Verso, 1983.

Collectif Clio. *L'histoire des femmes au Québec depuis quatre siècles.* Quinze, 1982.

Djebar, Assia. *L'amour, la fantasia.* Éditions Jean-Claude Lattès, 1985.

– *Nulle part dans la maison de mon père.* Fayard, 2007.

Dumont, Micheline, and Nadia Fahmy-Eid. *Les Couventines.* Boréal, 1986.

Fanon, Frantz. "L'Algérie se dévoile." *Sociologie d'une révolution: L'an V de la révolution algérienne.* Maspero, 1982.

Foucault, Michel. "Of Other Spaces." *Diacritics,* vol. 16, no. 1, Spring 1986, pp. 22–7.

Fraiman, Susan. *Unbecoming Women: British Women Writers and the Novel of Development.* Columbia UP, 1993.

Gould, Karen. *Writing in the Feminine: Feminism and Experimental Writing in Québec.* Southern Illinois UP, 1990.

Green, Mary Jean. "Locating Québec on the Postcolonial Map." *Postcolonial Thought in the French-Speaking World,* edited by Charles Forsdick and David Murphy, Liverpool UP, 2009, pp. 248–57.

– *Women and Narrative Identity: Rewriting the Québec National Text.* McGill-Queen's UP, 2002.

Malouin, Marie-Paule, and Micheline Dumont. "L'évolution des programmes d'études (1850–1960)." *Les Couventines,* edited by Micheline Dumont and Nadia Fahmy-Eid, Boréal, 1986, pp. 83–112.

Memmi, Albert. "Les Canadiens-français sont-ils des colonisés?" *L'homme dominé,* Gallimard, 1968, pp. 86–95.

– *Portrait du colonisé.* Gallimard, 1985.

Mortimer, Mildred. *Writing from the Hearth: Public, Domestic and Imaginative Space in Francophone Women's Fiction of Africa and the Caribbean.* Lexington Books, 2007.

Parsons, Deborah L. *Streetwalking the Metropolis: Women, the City and Modernity.* Oxford UP, 2000.

Roy, Gabrielle. *Bonheur d'occasion: Roman.* Boréal, 2009.

Smart, Patricia. *Écrire dans la maison du père: L'émergence du féminin dans la tradition littéraire du Québec.* Québec/Amérique, 1988.

Théoret, France. *Une belle éducation.* Boréal, 2006.

– *Journal pour mémoire.* L'Hexagone, 1993.

– *Nous parlerons comme on écrit.* Les Herbes Rouges, 1982.

Thivierge, Nicole. "L'enseignement ménager, 1880–1970." *Maîtresses de maison, maîtresses d'école,* edited by Nadia Fahmy-Eid and Micheline Dumont, Boréal, 1983, pp. 119–42.

von Flotow, Luise, translator. *Such a Good Education,* by France Théoret. Cormorant Books, 2009.

8 For King and Country? War and Indigenous Masculinity

DEENA RYMHS

I think the best thing about Canada's military [is] it doesn't matter if you're purple, green or orange, whether you're sixteen, seventeen, or fifteen, you're all soldiers, you're all soldiers, you're all one ... We were all equals, all sharing the same heartaches, the same laughter, and the same joys. And that was what was important.

– Ed Borchert, Métis veteran

Wars are interesting experiences so long as you live through them.

– Horace Kelly, Haida veteran

Indigenous men have served in numerous conflicts ranging from the American Revolutionary War to the peacekeeping mission in Afghanistan, yet their motivations for doing so remain complex and often difficult to isolate. Just as challenging to unravel are the models of masculinity engendered by war. This chapter explores the complicated subject positions of Indigenous men serving the state in global warfare[1] – roles that would simultaneously enhance and undermine their status as "men" and "civilized" persons in the eyes of White powers. Drawing on Joseph Boyden's[2] novel *Three Day Road* and Garry Gottfriedson's poem "Forgotten

1 By "global warfare," I am referring to large-scale world conflicts of the twentieth century and after.

2 The recent controversy surrounding Boyden's biographical claim to Indigenous identity marks an important development in Canadian literature and discussions of voice appropriation in particular. I do not wish, in the short span of this essay, to make a pronouncement on Boyden's "Indigenousness," nor do I think it my place to do so.

Soldiers," I examine how Indigenous soldiers redefined their war service in seemingly totalizing colonial contexts. While many motivating factors – tribal and family tradition, commitment to treaties, spiritual sacrifice, and a steady paycheque – prompted Indigenous men's military service, Indigenous men's voluntary enlistment was not always a gesture of loyalty to the larger nations for which they served. Arthur N. Gilbert's perspicacious observation that "Indian affairs are in the grey area between domestic and foreign" (240) provides a cue for re-examining the distinct reasons that Indigenous men joined the war effort at rates often higher than any other segment of the population in Canada and the United States. As Janice Summerby observes, this response nearly depleted reserves of their young men in the First World War:

> Only three men of the Algonquin of Golden Lake Band who were fit and who were of age to serve remained on their reserve. Roughly half of the eligible Mi'kmaq and Maliseet men of New Brunswick and Nova Scotia signed up, and, although small, Saskatchewan's File Hills community offered practically all of its eligible men. In British Columbia, the Head of the Lake Band saw every single man between the ages of 20 and 35 volunteer. (6)

The same was true of the Second World War. In 1942 John Diefenbaker remarked in the House of Commons, "In Western Canada the reserves have been depleted of almost all the physically fit men" (qtd. in Summerby 22). Like the wars themselves, which were constructed in myriad ways to weld together the nation,[3] the war service of Indigenous men was constructed as proof of their loyalty to Canada. Boyden's and Gottfriedson's literary works, which participate in this construction of social memory, unsettle this assumption that Indigenous men's war service was a gesture of loyalty to the Canadian state.

Three Day Road elicited a tremendous response from popular and critical readerships in Canada. Nominated for the 2005 Governor General's

---

Up until now, *Three Day Road* has been one of the most widely known historical novels on Indigenous soldiers in the First World War and on the cultural politics of their recruitment, their contribution, and their marginalization in the space of the nation.

3 Jonathan F. Vance's *Death So Noble*, which examines the construction of the First World War in popular memory and the historical archive, offers an illuminating discussion of the relationship between narrative invention and national identity formation.

Award for Fiction and trumpeted by filmmaker Nelofer Pazira on CBC Radio's Canada Reads in 2006, Boyden's novel became so popular with Canadian readerships that its counter-narrative has arguably become incorporated into a national consciousness of the First World War.[4] Like Candida Rifkind's chapter in this collection, which highlights "the contested spaces of commemoration and the politics of recovering a radical past," my discussion is interested in the complex reckonings generated by Boyden's novel and Gottfriedson's poem. Both texts resist the grammars of national commemoration by emphasizing the political contexts of Indigenous military involvement, contexts often overlooked by a Canadian public eager to incorporate Indigenous military service within a national rhetoric. *Three Day Road* revisits the First World War through the experiences of two Cree soldiers from northern Ontario, but Boyden's text is more than a war narrative. Setting up a continuum between the trauma of war and the trauma of colonization, this novel asks what it meant for Indigenous soldiers to be fighting for the same country whose policies were hostile to the survival of their cultural communities back home. In the process of exploring this question, *Three Day Road* offers a razor-sharp criticism of racism in the military and on the home front – a racism that would persist, rather than dissolve, with the war's end.

"Forgotten Soldiers" similarly explores, while also never fully resolving, Indigenous men's motivations for serving in Canada's military. This lesser-known poem by Secwepemc author Garry Gottfriedson was commissioned by filmmaker Loretta Todd for her documentary *Forgotten Warriors*; Gottfriedson later republished the poem in his first collection of poetry, *Glass Tepee.* While Boyden's narrative incorporates many familiar temporal and geographical signposts of the First World War, as well as a commemorated sniper from that war, Francis Pegahmagabow, Gottfriedson's poem is spoken by an unnamed "forgotten soldier" from the Second World War. Considerations of genre might account for the different reception of "Forgotten Soldiers" compared to *Three Day Road.* Novels are one of those literary forms that easily cross over to popular readerships. That same popularity can create a tendency, as I noted

4 Consider the following customer review of *Three Day Road* posted on the Amazon.ca website: "Everyone interested in First World War history, particularly from a Canadian perspective [,] should read this book" (Kitay). See also Anouk Lang's "A Book That All Canadians Should Be Proud to Read."

earlier, for their narratives to be incorporated within national narratives even when they attempt to challenge readers' conceptions of national history. Since the Canada Reads competition began in 2002, all the winning titles in English have been works of prose and predominantly prose fiction. No work of poetry has emerged as the winner, leading one to wonder if poetry is something that "Canada Reads." Receiving far less exposure than *Three Day Road*, "Forgotten Soldiers" differs from Boyden's novel in more ways than just genre and critical reception. The poem takes the form of an oral address to "Canada" by an unnamed veteran who returns home haunted by violent images of a war and "sentenced ... to live on skid row among rats" (84). Besieged by traumatic images that intrude on the speaker's consciousness and conflate his pre- and post-war existence, "Forgotten Soldiers" offers a crescendoing indictment of Canada's treatment of Indigenous communities not unlike that of *Three Day Road*. In contrast to *Three Day Road*, however, "Forgotten Soldiers" places Indigenous sovereignty more at the centre of its reflection by reclaiming "Canada" as the speaker's land to defend.

The conflicted position of Indigenous soldiers fighting for what Elizabeth Cook-Lynn, quoting her veteran father, calls an "enemy nation" has been frequently noted in the literature on Indigenous veterans.[5] As James Dempsey observes in a Canadian context, the ardent response of Plains Indigenous communities to the First World War surprised the Canadian mainstream public: "It was thought that Indians, who had suffered poverty and privation at the hands of the government and White society in general, would have no reason to fight in a 'foreign' war" (1). I wish to push beyond the implications of Indigenous soldiers sacrificing themselves for the very countries that were often inimical to their cultures' survival to consider the relationship between war and masculinity and the different ways that Indigenous men regarded their war service. In many instances, the model of masculinity that Indigenous men saw themselves achieving through their military service fulfilled both a spiritual and political purpose. Masculinity studies have become increasingly aware of their own epistemological foundations, yet even as critics gesture towards the need for understandings of masculinity that address cultural differences, there remains much more work to be done on

5 Cook-Lynn writes that her father served as a private in the US Army "a decade before he was made a citizen of what he always called an enemy nation" (63).

appreciating diverse expressions of manhood across various locations.[6] Even this chapter's focus on "Indigenous masculinities" begins with a deficit: as Māori scholar Brendan Hokowhitu notes, examining masculinity from a comparative Indigenous approach can lose sight of particular contexts, local experiences, and the micro-histories of place (in McKegney, *Masculindians* 99).

This chapter proceeds from an understanding of masculinity not as a unitary concept (as the word itself might suggest) but as shorthand for culturally situated, historical processes of subjectivity formation – processes inflected by ideology and power relationships. In using a term like "masculinity," I am mindful of the dangers of a biological determinism that aligns gender identity with biological sex. I am also aware of the impossible task of defining masculinity in any concrete and stable terms. However, these challenges do not make the exercise of theorizing masculinity any less important. "Although we seem to have a difficult time defining masculinity," notes Judith Halberstam, "as a society we have little trouble in recognizing it" (1), and indeed we invest materially and affectively in the very gender structures that hurt us. The elusiveness of defining masculinity necessitates, rather than obviates, interrogating the very categories that become naturalized to the point of becoming unnameable.

---

6 Some recent works in the field of Indigenous masculinity include Sam McKegney's collection of interviews, *Masculindians: Conversations about Indigenous Manhood*; Kim Anderson, Robert Alexander Innes, and John Swift's "Indigenous Masculinities: Carrying the Bones of the Ancestors"; Ty P. Kāwika Tengan's *Native Men Remade: Gender and Nation in Contemporary Hawai'i*; Brendan Hokowhitu's "Tackling Māori Masculinity: A Colonial Genealogy of Savagery and Sport"; and Peter L. Bayers's "Charles Alexander Eastman's *From the Deep Woods to Civilization* and the Shaping of Native Manhood," as well as a special issue of *GLQ: A Journal of Lesbian and Gay Studies* devoted to sexuality, nationality, and indigeneity (guest-edited by Daniel Heath Justice, Mark Rifkin, and Bethany Schneider). Other salutary examples are Taiaiake Alfred's *Wasáse: Indigenous Pathways of Action and Freedom*; Philip J. Deloria's "'I Am of the Body': My Grandfather, Culture, and Sports"; and Brian Klopotek's "'I Guess Your Warrior Look Doesn't Work Every Time': Challenging Indian Masculinity in the Cinema." See also Karen Anderson and Katherine M.B. Osborne for local, historical examinations of Indigenous masculinity. While there remains much more work to be done on theorizing Indigenous masculinities, critical race theorists like Robert Reid-Pharr, bell hooks, Robert Staples, Mark Anthony Neal, David Marriott, Michele Wallace, Devon Carbado, David Eng, José Esteban Muñoz, José Limón, Carl Guttierez-Jones, Harry Stecopoulos, Michael Uebel, and Patricia Hill Collins have also made foundational contributions to the writing on race and masculinity.

In settler-colonial historical contexts, masculinity – and gender more broadly – operated as a technology of colonialism. This insight is not my own but the critical consensus of scholars working in the field of Indigenous LGBTQ studies and Euro-American discourses of sexuality.[7] Arguing that "gender reifies colonial power" (31), Chris Finley notes that heteronormative ideas about gender and sexuality not only served to maintain colonial institutions but also became internalized as traditional within Indigenous communities. As Paul Gilroy points out in his discussion of homophobia and misogyny in Black cultural contexts, "In a situation where racial identity appears suddenly impossible to know or reliably maintain with ease, the naturalness of gender can supply the modality in which race is lived and symbolized" (7). Examining masculinity in the charged context of war illuminates the pressure that colonial, patriarchal models of male identity put on tribal notions of manhood (a pressure nowhere more evident than in the requirement that "status Indians" in Canada become enfranchised – and therefore lose their status rights – if they served in the First and Second World Wars). At the same time, the relationship between Indigenous warrior traditions and the voluntary service of Indigenous men also points to cultural differences in how Indigenous soldiers approached war.

Before getting deeper into these cultural differences, I wish to insert space as an important critical frame for analysing gender. To think critically about masculinity is to acknowledge the constitutive role of space in producing and disciplining gender identities. The residential school, the battlefield, and the barracks, in different historical contexts, generated gender expectations in ways that corresponded to the larger ideological projects of which they were a part. My insistence on the critical usefulness of space for unpacking constructions of gender extends a foundational insight that has accompanied the "spatial turn" in the humanities and social sciences. Seeing the social and spatial as deeply interfused, this critical sensibility recognizes how the social order produces space and vice versa. Domenico A. Beneventi compellingly illustrates this point in his chapter on homelessness in this collection. As Beneventi observes, the state of being homeless – of living in public space while also being place*less* – overdetermines one's identity to such an extent that particularities of age, race, and gender are often elided. Through this

7 See, for instance, Driskill; Morgensen; Justice; Rifkin; and Smith.

example, Beneventi exposes a social logic (in this case, a capitalist ontology centred on private property) that cements identity to place.

Three Day Road's narrative opens up onto a number of charged spaces overlaid with colonial power. Xavier's and Elijah's childhoods are rent by traumatic experiences in residential school, where racial, gender, and sexual shaming were routine institutional practice. These institutions – which instilled heteropatriarchal norms, punished expressions of gender diversity, and disrupted Indigenous kinship structures – also did the larger political work of severing intergenerational relationships, eroding Indigenous systems of governance, and setting the foundation for settler-colonial expropriation of Indigenous land bases. As Sam McKegney puts it,

> gender segregation and the derogation of both the feminine and the body that occurred systematically within residential schools were not merely by-products of Euro-Christian patriarchy; they were not just collateral damage from aggressive evangelization by decidedly patriarchal religious bodies. Rather, this nexus of coercive alienations lay at the very core of the Canadian nation-building project that motivated the residential school system. ("pain, pleasure, shame. Shame" 13)

The imposition of a patriarchal gender system and the disavowals that accompanied this system – disavowals of the body, of tribal kinship structures, and of non-binary gender systems – operated as part of a larger colonial project of dispossession, political reorganization, and resource distribution.

Niska's narrative in *Three Day Road* pulls into focus some of these broader forces of colonial space-making and shifting balances of power in early twentieth-century northern Ontario. Her life story bears witness to colonial reorderings of space in which the bush and the village figure on opposite ends, spaces analogized in the irreconcilable figures of the "bush Indian" and "home guard Indian." (The reserve, a colonially engineered space, has yet to become part of Niska's geography.) In this emerging spatial order, place correlates to ideology – a threshold acutely felt by Niska when she enters the town and perceives her difference even in relation to the other Oji-Cree people there. But how do these settler-colonial geographies, and the dynamics of power mapped on to them, relate to the war setting of Europe that Elijah and Xavier enter? In Boyden's novel, this is a war where frontiers similarly are being redrawn, where contests over territory are fought with high stakes. The First World

War was motivated by imperial and economic interests. In this sense, the two spaces – northern Ontario and the European battlefield – mirror each other, spanning the orbit of empire and revealing their shared importance to Western imperial geopolitics.

Xavier and Elijah, of course, do not escape colonial power once they leave northern Ontario and enlist in the war. Colonial structures infuse the social order of the military in ways that continue to subject them to the politics of race and gender even while they are fighting for its mission. For Xavier and Elijah, the military is not a suspension of the social order but an extension of it. However, even in this setting where the military has total authority over them, the two soldiers are eventually granted a degree of autonomy from the rest of their unit to carry out their sniping. This decision to allow Xavier and Elijah to accomplish their work by their own methods comes out of the recognition of their exceptional abilities as marksmen. Their spatial autonomy correlates to a masculine autonomy, to the military's esteem (whatever its exploitative potential) for their superior ability as Indigenous hunters. In this regard, Xavier and Elijah resist full enclosure in the symbolic and social space of the military.

While Boyden and Gottfriedson depict Indigenous soldiers who retain their distinct cultural identities even in the totalizing environments of the military, they also chart the struggle to maintain this cultural ethos in the grip of a barbaric war. In *Three Day Road*, Xavier grapples with the idea of sacred sacrifice in the midst of unrelenting violence and psychological trauma. Initially, he is struck by how well his hunting skills translate in the context of war, where everyone is reduced to predator and prey. Yet Xavier quickly grows disturbed at the necessity of taking human life and, as this disturbance grows, feels increasingly distant from his childhood friend, Elijah, who elevates himself through his intrepid skills as a sniper. Insisting that "there is nothing sacred anymore" (282), Elijah gives in to the insanity of war. In a strange re-enactment of history, Elijah begins scalping his victims, a practice encouraged by the French soldiers. Elijah's adoption of this behaviour reinforces the notion of the "savage Indian" and thus plays into racist expectations of him. Elijah further hopes that his war service will make him chief back home, underlining the collusion of patriarchal-colonial legislation and tribal governance at the time. Not only a disciplining institution, then, the military has the power to elevate Elijah to a "neo-tribal elite" (to use Brendan Hokowhitu's term), who can broker deals with the state (in McKegney, *Masculindians* 100). Like Frantz Fanon's discussion of the psychosocial dimensions of being colonized, these behaviours reveal the extent to which both Elijah and Xavier see themselves through the eyes of the White man. While Elijah's mimicry of White colonial masculinity mocks the authority of the military (one corporal tells him, "You do a better British accent than a Brit" [137]), Xavier notes how this act has ultimately eclipsed Elijah. "He couldn't speak in his old voice if he wanted to now," Xavier remarks of Elijah. "It's gone somewhere far away" (138). Seen through Xavier's eyes, Elijah's compulsive iteration of a British, hegemonic masculinity estranges him from his Cree language and identity. Richard Hill's discussion of the limits of decolonial mimicry bears a certain resemblance to Xavier's criticism of Elijah. Such acts of mimicry, Hill argues, may "pull in several directions at once as they strain under the descriptive inadequacy of the original binaries that they undermine" (21). Xavier criticizes Elijah's mimicry of White colonial masculinity with an awareness of how the performance ends up becoming the actor. Elijah's mockery of Xavier before their White superiors, moreover, reinforces the notion of the "backward Indian." In these ways, Elijah may not so much invert but maintain hierarchical categories of difference.

Elijah's power in this novel is largely symbolic. Straddling various categories – godlike and mortal, sane and insane, and trickster and windigo – Elijah is a fluid character who stands outside of what Steven Bruhm, discussing queer theory, calls a "stable material field" (29). Queering Elijah does not necessarily involve an interest in his sexuality (though his relationship with another soldier, Grey Eyes, is a constant preoccupation for Xavier, and Elijah's sexual identity would be germane to discussions of colonial power). My reading of Elijah as a queer figure stems from his subversive potential in the text as someone whose incoherence and slipperiness undermine categories of difference. Yet, for all the symbolic power that Elijah has in this narrative, and for all his subversive potential as a subaltern subject who upsets the authority of colonial discourse, Elijah is ultimately sacrificed in the narrative – killed by Xavier before Elijah has nearly killed himself with morphine. Such an environment makes each man turn on the other. Xavier eventually sees Elijah as lost – first to the act of colonial mimicry and then to the violence of war.

Xavier's and Elijah's reasons for joining the war effort are never fully revealed to the reader, but the novel suggests a warrior ethos as one of both of their motivations for enlisting. Warrior traditions – which have gained political ascendancy in recent activist movements and intellectual currency in the work of Indigenous writers like Taiaiake Alfred – figure in both Joseph Boyden's *Three Day Road* and Garry Gottfriedson's

"Forgotten Soldiers." The possibility of tribal warrior traditions translating in the First World War becomes undermined, however, throughout Boyden's novel. Xavier and Elijah's encounter with a character inspired by Francis Pegahmagabow serves to further undermine any hope of recalling a warrior identity from an earlier time. The historical Pegahmagabow was an Anishinaabek sniper from Wasauksing (Parry Sound, Ontario) who became a decorated war hero. Reflecting on their reasons for joining the war effort, Peggy dismissively remarks, "We all want to be warriors again" (286). Peggy's cynicism casts doubt on their war service offering them the opportunity to recover a pre-reserve male identity. Still, Peggy serves in the novel as one of the unique instances of an Indigenous soldier who maintains an ideological distance from the way war is done. Sniping on his own and thus refusing official corroboration of the many men he has killed, Peggy manages to maintain something of a sovereign space in the chaos of war. He tells Xavier and Elijah, "You know that the *wemistikoshiw* do not care to believe us when they hear about our kills in the field ... We do the nasty work for them and if we return home we will be treated like pieces of shit once more. But while we are here we might as well do what we are good at" (286–7). The real Francis Pegahmagabow became chief of Wasauksing First Nation at the age of thirty-three following his war service; during that time he attempted to reinvigorate traditional practices, re-acquire band lands, and organize other bands in the area to oppose the local Indian agent (Steckley and Cummins 41). Consistent with this record of him as a leader, Peggy's voice in this passage of *Three Day Road* is the most politically conscious, portentous articulation of what the Canadian nation will offer them after the war is over. Xavier attempts to emulate Peggy, preferring to work in isolation away from the men in his battalion and praying to atone for the killing he must do for his survival. However, Xavier is ultimately compromised by the violence of war to a point where his deteriorating mental state causes him to kill Elijah (224). In *Three Day Road*, the sacred is polluted by the savagery of an uncivilized war.

Three Day Road complicates this warrior ethos further by depicting competing interests that mobilize the warrior image to their own advantage. While Xavier and Elijah invoke a warrior ideal to justify their participation in the war, this image of the warrior is exploited by military officials who, rather than respecting Indigenous traditions, capitalize on Indigenous soldiers' readiness to become military fodder. As Al Carroll explains, Indigenous soldiers became "trapped within the natural warrior image by White attitudes" (112). Aboriginal men were thought to be "natural warriors, well prepared for soldiering by their racial attributes and wilderness skills" (Sheffield, "Indifference" 61). The image of the warrior became appropriated by military authorities who saw the value of these skills for combat but who failed to appreciate the many other dimensions of this warrior role. Today, the Canadian military continues to recruit youth from Indigenous communities in the form of its Bold Eagle and Raven programs that blend military training with "Aboriginal culture and customs" ("Bold Eagle"). The Canadian Forces now allows Indigenous members to wear their hair long ("Diversity in the CF"). Similarly, the US military actively attempts to attract volunteers from Indigenous communities, sending posters sprinkled with phrases like "in your warrior tradition." Lois Beardslee highlights the exploitation threading through this rhetoric:

> I have seen, more than I care to, military recruitment posters and signs addressed specifically to Native American youth. They misuse our ancient and cherished notions of warrior as a method of manipulation, to try to draw our youth into wars they have no business fighting, to fatten the pockets of the business elite who have traditionally been our enemies, those who have led to our socioeconomic lynching and emotional suicide. (257)

Beneath these attempts to appeal to Indigenous "traditions" is the unstated recognition of the youths' limited opportunities for upward social mobility. These recruitment efforts prey upon economically vulnerable groups who often face little alternative than to risk sacrificing their lives for economic survival.

Given these many unqualified uses of "warrior," then, it is necessary to ask what the term means. Beardslee wrests the notion of warrior from its misrepresentations:

> It never meant aggressor until the upheaval associated with land appropriation and the fur trade forced us into dysfunction. It meant protector. It is one of only five essential occupations of the Ojibwe: leader, teacher, healer, protector, and provider ... This notion of protector [*ogitchidaa*] is so sacred, so essential to our survival as a people, that we hurt ourselves by letting it be reinvented and abused by outside agitators. (258)

Neal McLeod likewise explains that the Cree word *okichitawak* roughly translates as "the providers." *Okichitawak* has often been narrowly translated as "warrior society," a translation that McLeod sees as representing "a very limited, superficial understanding of the term," since military protection is only one of the things this group provided. Taiaiake Alfred further fills in the contours of the "warrior":

> In most people's minds, the words "North American Indian warrior" invoke images of futile angry violence or of noble sacrifice in the face of the white march of triumph over this continent. To Euroamericans, the descendants and beneficiaries of conquest, "Indian warriors" are artefacts of the past; they are icons of colonization, that version of history in which the original people of this land have been defiant but defeated ... But history has not ended. There are still Onkwehonwe lands, souls, and minds that have not been conquered. For them, a warrior is what a warrior has always been: one who protects the people, who stands with dignity and courage in the face of danger. (97)

Being a warrior, as Alfred describes it in a recent context, involves a philosophical and correspondingly activist stance. In the past thirty years particularly, movements like the Mi'kmaq Warrior Society and Mohawk Warrior Society have formed in response to political and legal battles. The Mohawk Warrior Societies that emerged in the 1970s and 1980s, Alfred points out, bridged traditional teachings with a "contemporary movement ideology" (78). This re-conception of warrior, then, merges traditional philosophies, many of them spiritually based, with a contemporary model of political activism.

Like Xavier, the speaker of Garry Gottfriedson's poem struggles to maintain a sense of sacred duty as a warrior fighting a very different type of war. The poem begins, "Canada, my country, ... for you and for my Mother / through my duties, I will spin prayer" (80). This view of war service as a spiritual act deserves closer examination. James Dempsey writes that after the Canadian government prohibited warfare among Plains Indigenous groups[8] – a specific type of warfare that offered ritualized, codified ways of becoming a man – this warrior ethic became redirected to other forms of ritual, including spiritual ceremony. Dempsey

8 The signing of treaties in the 1870s and the introduction of a reserve system, Dempsey writes, increased the control that Indian agents and missionaries exercised over Plains Indigenous groups. After the Northwest Rebellion of 1885, the federal government tightened this control through even stricter regulations. See also Brian Titley's *A Narrow Vision*.

provides one way of understanding this proximity between war and spirituality. Gottfriedson also explains the spiritual motivations behind Indigenous men's decisions to enlist – an explanation, he qualifies, that is informed by his Secwepemc heritage and his discussions with his veteran father:

> Aboriginal men felt it was their duty to protect their communities in the event that a strong threat existed, so relying on cultural beliefs took them to the deepest level of spiritual sacrifice they knew, and that was simply to offer their lives in order to ensure that their women and children would be not only protected from a threat at hand, but believed that if they did nothing to try to protect the land and people then their people would suffer from a spiritual aspect ... that the spiritual world would induce more suffering if they didn't fulfill their cultural and spiritual duty. ("Re: Forgotten Soldiers")

"Thus it was their sacred duty to go to war," concludes Gottfriedson ("Re: Forgotten Soldiers"). Beyond the material reasons for enlisting, then, were spiritual and political factors that prompted the voluntary service of Aboriginal men. Tom Holm, writing about American Indigenous Vietnam veterans, observes that many men entered military service "for reasons wholly their own" (19). Holm follows: "They did not enter the military necessarily to better themselves in the eyes of the dominant society. The majority of them listed tribal and/or family traditions as having a significant impact on their decisions to enlist or accept conscription in the armed forces. They seemed to be taking their cues not from the larger society but from their own social and cultural environments" (19). Many Indigenous soldiers saw their war service in different terms than mainstream media reported at the time. Part of this motivation had to do with the spiritual responsibility of being or becoming a man, as Gottfriedson describes. Indigenous spiritual practices also became more visible and found new outlets during and after the First World War.[9] Thomas A. Britten writes that "many aspects of traditional Indian cultures gained renewed importance and vigor during World War I, allowing young people to witness, perhaps for the first time, aspects of their cultures about which they had only heard from elders" (149). This

9 The US military, as Holm points out, also revived tribal languages with its use of code talkers in the Second World War.

resurgence, Britten notes, consisted of elaborative going-away rituals, dances, feasts, death rituals, and cleansing rituals for those soldiers who returned. Some of these rituals had been banned for three decades. Yet the attempt to maintain spiritual integrity is ultimately undone for the speaker of Gottfriedson's poem, as it is for Xavier; descriptions of war trauma overwhelm the lines that follow:

> Canada, my country, I fight my own
> spirit; I throw rocks into rivers hoping to
> change the course of chronic war dreams
> Canada, my country, my mornings & my
> nights are always the same
> sharp edges like bayonets slicing off layers of musky skin (81)

The intrusion of these images into the poem points to the speaker's inability to achieve psychological distance from the violence that he has witnessed and in which he has participated. Scenes from the war multiply as the poem progresses:

> Canada, my country, I am jerked into the reality of
> war once again, piling junk sandbags
> piecing them together like broken
> pottery mending the mangled,
> motionless bodies: dead & scattered
> flowers blown
> apart by the force of air & stone (82)

The attempt at spiritual and psychic reintegration – here mirrored in the images of broken pottery and mangled bodies – produces little more than a sense of futility for the speaker, who remains stuck in a compulsive loop of traumatic memory. The sense of sacred duty that frames the speaker's understanding of his war sacrifice is frayed by the violence and trauma that engulf him.

Of course, the psychological disturbances that Xavier and the speaker of Gottfriedson's poem describe were widespread among those who had engaged in modern combat. Julia Emberley remarks that "the First World War provided a display of violence that in its techno-military superiority surpassed any previous modern comprehension" (112). The First World War did not only signal a massive transformation in technological or military powers but also conveyed a shift in war's relationship to individual identity and affect. Citing the work of Joanna Bourke and David Buchbinder, Emberley goes on to note that "the First World War ... represent[ed] a break with previous ideas about manliness and the emergence of a modern conception of 'masculinity'" (138). In Buchbinder's words, "World War I was a major blow to the traditional imagery of war as heroic, glorious and especially as befitting young men" (9). Undermining the ideal of the "military masculine," then, were the many men who returned emotionally and spiritually broken from the unimaginable effects of war. Xavier is addicted to morphine and missing one of his legs at the end of the novel, prompting his aunt Niska to wonder how he will survive in the bush. Today, Canada's Department of Defence is dealing with many men returning from Afghanistan with post-traumatic stress disorder, whose symptoms affect their ability to return home as husbands and fathers – symptoms, like addiction, that quite often result in their discharge. The First World War left a legacy of psychologically wounded men, a reality of war that the Canadian and American militaries are still reluctant to acknowledge. Twice as many Vietnam veterans are thought to have died from suicide as they did from war combat.[10]

Despite the more universal symptoms of war trauma that Gottfriedson's speaker describes, the poem develops his anger and sense of violation within a specific historical context of colonization. Boyden's novel, too, suggests that one cannot read the experiences of Indigenous soldiers apart from this history of colonialism; in its structure, his novel invites comparison between the trauma of the residential school and the trauma of war. "The barracks were just like the ones of the school of my childhood," Xavier remarks (221). With its military organization, the residential school created an almost seamless transition to the army. In the United States, boarding schools (the equivalent of residential schools in Canada) were used as enlistment stations during the First and Second World Wars (Holm 104). Berton Baptiste – who provides a first-person account in the Saskatchewan First Nations Veterans' Association's *"We Were There"* – also remarks that many young men from his residential school joined the military during the Second World War because of the cadet program run by the school. These vocational institutions created a pipeline to the front lines, a pipeline which not only targeted marginalized racial communities but also preyed upon the limited opportunities

10 This estimation of suicide rates of Vietnam veterans appears in *The Fifth Estate*'s documentary "Broken Heroes."

of the poor and working class in often isolated communities.[11] Thus, it is necessary to contextualize examples of Indigenous war service within the broader histories of colonization that frame them – a colonization that did not cease but rather continued with war's end. Gottfriedson looks to those Indigenous soldiers who, upon their return, became the charges of Indian Affairs – wards of the government or what R. Scott Sheffield calls the "Administrative Indian" (*"Red Man"* 12). "Canada, my country," Gottfriedson's speaker states, "my freedom is the entrapment / of your overlays of federal bureau files" (81). "Canada, my country," he continues, "your desire to liberate / concentration camps is your same desire / to imprison me on my return home" (83).

The alternative – enfranchisement – constituted a different type of betrayal and erosion of political autonomy. Many Indigenous men in Canada returned from war to learn that they had been involuntarily "enfranchised," which meant that they lost their status rights. In a 1947 brief, the Native Brotherhood of British Columbia addressed the violence done by enfranchisement: "Enfranchisement to us means that we must surrender everything that we have inherited from our ancestors. We must leave our homes and our people. We become strangers among strangers ... Once we are enfranchised, we become outcasts to our people, trespassers and a cause of discord ... if we seek our own friends and relatives on the reserves" (qtd. in Sheffield, *"Red Man"* 144). Evidently, the involvement of Indigenous soldiers in war was fraught with conflict, a conflict that grew rather than diminished upon their return. Even the war hero Francis Pegahmagabow found himself penniless. In some instances, those veterans who did receive land or remuneration were rejected by their communities.[12] While the speaker at the beginning of Gottfriedson's poem vows to forgive Canada's "black guilt in honour of my Mother & for my / people" (80), the mounting anger of this "forgotten soldier" dominates the remaining lines.

---

11 Militaries in Canada and the United States continue to prey on the limited opportunities of the poor and working class by promising educational opportunities in exchange for military service. In the United States, recruitment drives take place in economically depressed towns and in Black communities.

12 Two accounts in the Saskatchewan First Nations Veterans' Association's *"We Were There"* reveal the scrutiny that some veterans faced when they returned to their communities after having served in war. Marshall Brittain, who served in the Second World War, remarks, "Back on the reserve, people would hardly talk to us. We were treated like outsiders ... because we were in the war" (21).

Unlike the speaker of "Forgotten Soldiers" who returns home to find his life and future still buried in "overlays of federal bureau files" (81), Boyden's novel ends a mere three days after Xavier's return home, leaving him to wonder if his painful exploits abroad will change his place in the nation after the war's end. Xavier's time in the military allows him to experience a profound sense of fraternity with other Canadian men. Referring to the men in his battalion as his "brothers" (342), and grieving intensely for his fellow private and corporal killed in action, he remarks, "I realize I'd come to think of them as my relations" (317). War saw a forging of new kinships, a "brotherhood" as Xavier calls it, that extended across familiar cultural divisions. Yet while Xavier's time in the military draws him closer to those in his battalion, the novel questions the extent to which those bonds would translate in the formation of cross-cultural communities after the war. Would this sense of an extended national community remain intact when Indigenous soldiers returned to see reserve lands given to non-Indigenous veterans, when these same Indigenous veterans were denied land titles, loans, pensions, and allowances? Only enfranchised Indigenous veterans who gave up their rights to live on reserves were entitled to the same benefits as non-Indigenous veterans. In the United States, termination and relocation immediately followed the post-war period. The war service of Indigenous men, Holm and Britten argue, was used by the US government to promote assimilation. Recognizing the symbolic power of what they narrowly construed as Indigenous patriotism, the US and Canadian governments used these men's enlistment to "de-tribalize" and divide Indigenous communities.

Boyden's and Gottfriedson's works prompt consideration of the unique positioning of racial minority subjects in war. While Arif Dirlik emphasizes the decolonizing projects that emerged out of the world wars, arguing that "decolonization since World War II has restored the voices of the colonized and opened the way to recognition of the spatial and temporal copresence of those whom a Eurocentric modernization discourse had relegated to invisibility and backwardness" (1365), the conflicted position of Indigenous men serving in the world wars remains an underexamined and unresolved topic in discussions of global war geopolitics. Even the extension of citizenship to Indigenous veterans was too loaded with liberal intentions to count as a decolonizing gesture. The speaker of "Forgotten Soldiers" asserts,

> Canada, my country, you have
> forgotten: I can never surrender

my identity, even in the event of war
& your assimilation policies cannot turn me white. (83)

The type of masculinity that emerged with the Victorian period and endured in military cultures was part of a larger cultural sensibility tied to conquest and colonization. As Julia Emberley notes, it was a masculinity that secured national, military, and imperial dominance (141). The making of "White" masculinity was thus linked to the construction of racial and ethnic hierarchies that prompt consideration of the racialized inscription of savagery within this imaginary.

A more recent instance of the internal colonialism operating within the Canadian military emerged with Canada's peacekeeping mission in Somalia, when two Indigenous soldiers, Kyle Brown and Clayton Matchee, were seen as having taken "rough justice" too far and "outwhiting the white guys" in their torturing of Somali native Shidane Arone (qtd. in Razack 89). In her discussion of the Somalia affair, Sherene Razack partially rejects the argument that subordinate masculinities engage in acts of violence as a compensation for their marginalization.[13] "A compensatory argument," she insists, "takes the focus away from the structural conditions of what was in essence a colonial encounter" between the Canadian Forces and Somali civilians (112). Instead, Razack looks at the institutional culture of the military, or in this case, peacekeeping, as conditioning a racial violence towards those "dark threats" of the places they are called in to manage. All soldiers in the Canadian military, Razack suggests, are interpellated into this notion of White civility, even racial minorities. The military allows membership "in a white nation," but a membership in which "men of colour must forget about the racial violence that is done to them" (90). Yet, in the aftermath of the Somalia affair, Brown and Matchee were not seen as colourless. The civility of White peacekeeping against the savagery and lawlessness of Somalia was a logic that applied differently to Brown and Matchee during the

13 Razack argues that the military normalizes a violence in which all the soldiers – including White middle-class men – participate. In her discussion of Arone's torture, Razack emphasizes "how absolutely unremarkable the violence seemed to be to the men who enacted it, witnessed it, or simply heard it was happening" (115). Razack expressly attempts to avoid a tendency in much writing on race and masculinity to pathologize racial minority subjects. Instead, she urges consideration of the structural conditions that normalize such behaviours.

military trials, whose "race hung in the air," in contrast to the White soldiers who "remained unmarked" (89). "Dark threats," Razack argues, were found to be lurking within the peacekeeping mission, where the identities of Brown and Matchee, like those of Xavier and Elijah, were "overdetermined by race" (89). Contrary to Ed Borchert's claims of relative equality (which appear as an epigraph to this chapter), the experiences of Brown and Matchee point to an insistent racism operating within the Canadian military.

Boyden's and Gottfriedson's works call careful attention to the male identities created in cultures of war and to the subordinate masculinities that were less often represented in the military mythos. The histories and literature dealing with Indigenous soldiers point to the imbrication of gender and cultural identity. What happens to these characters' sense of themselves as Indigenous men in war? Did their enlistment mean a desire to be included in the nation of Canada, or did their participation mean something else that has been largely ignored in the chronicles of Canada's war involvement? Gottfriedson's poem ends, "I am a warrior/ & the land belongs to me" (84), suggesting the endurance of a sovereign identity and an insistent territorial claim to the land. Repeated throughout the poem is the speaker's address, "Canada, my country"; could this refrain suggest a conception of territory separate from Canada's operation as a nation-state? In making this address, could the speaker be reformulating the identity of this country as a place also claimed by others? In Loretta Todd's documentary film, *Forgotten Warriors*, one of the veterans states, "It was my duty. I even thought that it was more my duty than anybody else. I had just as much right – more right – to fight than anybody else because I was Indian. This is my country." Jonathan F. Vance's claim that "Native Canadians ... pointed to the war as the ultimate proof of their dedication to Canada and their right to equal treatment in the new nation" (245) needs to be reconsidered in light of this discussion. Some Indigenous soldiers did not view their service as proof of their dedication to "Canada" as a nation-state; rather, they saw their service as protecting a land against further imperialism – a land that they viewed as rightfully theirs.

Acknowledging the perpetuity and seeming universality of war, Srinivas Aravamudan asks if "the ubiquity of war across societies" results in "a shared structure of feeling" about war (1505). Even if war can be abstracted in such universal terms, Aravamudan answers, "a comprehensive approach ... would need to engage with war-related evidence from multiple histories" (1505). Examining the histories of Indigenous soldiers reveals that the experiences of servicemen, even within the same war, place, and time, were not symmetrical and not necessarily characterized by the same structures of feeling. The voluntary enlistment of Indigenous men did not indicate an unquestioning gesture of loyalty to Canada, nor was it necessarily an effort to prove themselves to mainstream society. Many Indigenous veterans saw their enlistment as entering into a political alliance – as a voluntary act of diplomacy.[14] The Report of the Royal Commission on Aboriginal Peoples (RCAP), in its section on Aboriginal veterans, acknowledges this sovereign notion of cooperation:

> Aboriginal communities approached military service with an eye to their history of relations with the Crown – very much as they had preserved the memory of their treaties and alliances among themselves. They wanted the government to understand that, as allies, they were free to offer their services to the Crown, each individual according to his own decision. Particularly during the Second World War, many Aboriginal nations initiated research into treaties and historical relationships so as to confirm their right to reject all forms of conscription in favour of voluntary enlistment. (Royal Commission)

Some of the most vocal and prominent Indigenous political groups emerged after the First World War: the League of Indians was established in 1918 by Fred Loft, a Mohawk lieutenant in the First World War. This political mobilization crested during the final years of the Second World War, a wave of organizing that saw the formation of such instrumental groups as the North American Indian Brotherhood, the Native Brotherhood of British Columbia, the Indian Association of Alberta, the Saskatchewan North American Indian Brotherhood, the Association of Saskatchewan Indians, the Protection Committee of the Indian Tribes in Québec, and the Grand General Indian Council of Cape Breton. The war service of Indigenous men, and the conditions that would follow in the post-war years – loss of lands, residential schools, uneven distribution of wealth, over-incarceration, and deepening structural racism

14 Several of the veterans interviewed in Todd's film, *Forgotten Warriors,* saw themselves as voluntarily choosing the side with which they would be allied. Similarly, in the United States, tribes like the Osage, Ponca, and Lakota declared war autonomously on the Axis (Holm 104).

– would give rise to another masculine identity: an activist stance formed out of specific national and racial protest. Indigenous groups would begin to engage in international diplomacy, seeking the support of international organizations like the League of Nations (Britten 168). Many Indigenous veterans would use their combat experience in various warrior societies as well as in one very instrumental organization of the twentieth century, the American Indian Movement (AIM).[15] Wars may be interesting experiences as long as you survive them, as Kelly asserts in his epigraph to this essay, but the war may never end psychologically and politically.

I close this chapter on a more recent moment of national remembrance and the misrecognition of Indigenous veterans within civic commemorative practices. On 11 November 2013, Davyn Calfchild was arrested at a Remembrance Day ceremony at Toronto City Hall while carrying a Haudenosaunee flag. Calfchild, a veteran who served five years as a peacekeeper in the former Yugoslavia, carried the flag to represent Indigenous soldiers who have served in the Canadian military. In previous years of attending the Toronto City Hall Remembrance Day ceremony, Calfchild had observed how Indigenous veterans were rendered invisible by the absence of Indigenous flags, cedar wreaths, tobacco ties, eagle feathers, or any other Indigenous cultural symbols (MacLellan). The Toronto police confiscated Calfchild's flag and arrested him, along with another Indigenous man carrying a Mohawk Warrior flag, for breaching the peace. Calfchild insists that he attended the event not to protest but to honour the contributions of Indigenous soldiers (MacLellan). This moment, which reveals contested spaces of remembrance and contested scripts for remembering (those wishing to lay a wreath or participate in the Remembrance Day ceremony must apply to the City of Toronto's protocol services in writing), points to a broader process of national commemoration that, a century after the First World War, continues to misrecognize the political and spiritual sovereignty of Indigenous soldiers.

15 A. LaVonne Brown Ruoff observes that many Indigenous servicemen in the United States "enlisted [in the First and Second World Wars] to get the combat experience necessary to join the warrior societies in their tribes." Tom Holm also points out that a number of AIM's leaders during its emergence in the late 1960s and early 1970s were Vietnam combat veterans (179).

WORKS CITED

Alfred, Taiaiake. *Wasáse: Indigenous Pathways of Action and Freedom.* Broadview, 2005.

Anderson, Karen. *Chain Her by One Foot: The Subjugation of Native Women in Seventeenth-century New France.* Routledge, 1991.

Anderson, Kim, Robert Alexander Innes, and John Swift. "Indigenous Masculinities: Carrying the Bones of the Ancestors." *Canadian Men and Masculinities: Historical and Contemporary Perspectives,* edited by Christopher J. Greig and Wayne J. Martino, Canadian Scholars' Press, 2012, pp. 266–84.

Aravamudan, Srinivas. "Introduction: Perpetual War." *PMLA,* vol. 124, no. 5, 2009, pp. 1505–14.

Bayers, Peter L. "Charles Alexander Eastman's *From the Deep Woods to Civilization* and the Shaping of Native Manhood." *Studies in American Indian Literatures,* vol. 20, no. 3, 2008, pp. 52–73.

Beardslee, Lois. "On Warriors, Living and Dead (in Respectful Memory of Charles J. Meyers)." *Not Far Away: The Real-life Adventures of Ima Pipiig,* AltaMira, 2007, pp. 257–9.

"Bold Eagle." Canada National Defence, 31 Aug. 2009. www.canada.ca/en/army/services/bold-eagle.html. Accessed 8 Jan. 2010.

Bourke, Joanna. *Dismembering the Male: Male Bodies, Britain and the Great War.* Reaktion, 1996.

Boyden, Joseph. *Three Day Road.* Penguin, 2005.

Britten, Thomas A. *American Indians in World War I.* U of New Mexico P, 1997.

"Broken Heroes." *The Fifth Estate,* CBC, 30 Oct. 2009. https://www.youtube.com/watch?v=8P-gjTHWUEA.

Bruhm, Steven. "Queer Today, Gone Tomorrow." *English Studies in Canada,* vol. 29, nos. 1–2, 2003, pp. 25–32.

Buchbinder, David. *Masculinities and Identities.* Melbourne UP, 1994.

Carroll, Al. *Medicine Bags and Dog Tags: American Indian Veterans from Colonial Times to the Second Iraq War.* U of Nebraska P, 2008.

Cook-Lynn, Elizabeth. "America's Iraq Attack and 'Back to the Indian Wars'!!" *Wicazo Sa,* vol. 11, no. 1, 1995, pp. 62–4.

Deloria, Philip J. "'I Am of the Body': My Grandfather, Culture and Sports." *Indians in Unexpected Places,* Kansas UP, 2004, pp. 109–35.

Dempsey, James. "Persistence of a Warrior Ethic among the Plains Indians." *Alberta History,* vol. 36, no. 1, 1988, pp. 1–10.

Dirlik, Arif. "Race Talk, Race, and Contemporary Racism." *PMLA,* vol. 123, no. 5, 2008, pp. 1363–79.

"Diversity in the CF." Canada National Defence, 6 May 2009. www.army.forces.gc.ca/boldeagle/diversity.asp. Accessed 26 Sept. 2010, no longer available.

Driskill, Qwo-Li. *Queer Indigenous Studies: Critical Interventions in Theory, Politics, and Literature.* U of Arizona P, 2011.

Emberley, Julia. *Defamiliarizing the Aboriginal: Cultural Practices and Decolonization in Canada.* U of Toronto P, 2007.

Fanon, Frantz. *Black Skin, White Masks.* 1952. Translated by Richard Philcox, Grove, 2008.

Finley, Chris. "Decolonizing the Queer Native Body (and Recovering the Native Bull-Dyke): Bringing 'Sexy Back' and Out of the Native Studies' Closet." *Queer Indigenous Studies*, edited by Qwo-Li Driskill et al., U of Arizona P, 2011, pp. 29–42.

Gilbert, Arthur N. "The American Indian and United States Diplomatic History." *History Teacher*, vol. 8, no. 2, 1975, pp. 229–41.

Gilroy, Paul. *Small Acts: Thoughts on the Politics of Black Cultures.* Serpent's Tail, 1993.

Gottfriedson, Garry. "Forgotten Soldiers." *Glass Tepee*, Thistledown, 2002, pp. 80–4.

– "Re: Forgotten Soldiers." Received by Deena Rymhs, 17 Nov. 2009.

Halberstam, Judith. *Female Masculinity.* Duke UP, 1998.

Hill, Richard. "Drag Racing: Dressing Up & (Messing Up) White in Contemporary First Nations Arts." *Fuse Magazine*, vol. 23, no. 4, 2001, pp. 18–27.

Hokowhitu, Brendan. "Tackling Māori Masculinity: A Colonial Genealogy of Savagery and Sport." *Contemporary Pacific*, vol. 16, no. 2, 2004, pp. 259–84.

Holm, Tom. *Strong Hearts, Wounded Souls: Native American Veterans of the Vietnam War.* U of Texas P, 1996.

Justice, Daniel Heath. "Notes Toward a Theory of Anomaly." Justice, Rifkin, and Schneider, pp. 207–42.

Justice, Daniel Heath, Mark Rifkin, and Bethany Schneider, editors. *Sexuality, Nationality, Indigeneity.* Spec. issue of *GLQ: A Journal of Lesbian and Gay Studies*, vol. 16, nos. 1–2, 2010.

Kitay, Pete. "Perfect Shot." Customer review, Amazon.ca, 17 Aug. 2007. www.amazon.ca/product-reviews/0143056956?pageNumber=3. Accessed 25 Sept. 2010.

Klopotek, Brian. "'I Guess Your Warrior Look Doesn't Work Every Time': Challenging Indian Masculinity in the Cinema." *Across the Great Divide: Cultures of Manhood in the American West*, edited by Matthew Basso, Laura McCall, and Dee Garceau, Routledge, 2001, pp. 251–73.

Lang, Anouk. "'A Book That All Canadians Should Be Proud to Read': Canada Reads and Joseph Boyden's *Three Day Road.*" *Canadian Literature*, vol. 215, 2012, pp. 120–36.

MacLellan, Stephanie. "First Nations Veteran Arrested at Remembrance Day Ceremony." *Toronto Star*, 12 Nov. 2013. www.thestar.com/news/gta/2013/11/12/first_nations_veteran_arrested_at_remembrance_day_ceremony.html. Accessed 1 May 2015.

McKegney, Sam, editor. *Masculindians: Conversations about Indigenous Manhood.* U of Manitoba P, 2014.

– "'pain, pleasure, shame. Shame': Masculine Embodiment, Kinship, and Indigenous Reterritorialization." *Canadian Literature*, vol. 216, 2013, pp. 12–33.

McLeod, Neal. "Re: Okichitawak." Received by Deena Rymhs, 9 Dec. 2009.

Morgensen, Scott Lauria. *Spaces between Us: Queer Settler Colonialism and Indigenous Decolonization.* Minnesota UP, 2011.

Osborne, Katherine M.B. "'I Am Going to Write to You': Nurturing Fathers and the Office of Indian Affairs on the Southern Ute Reservation, 1885–1934." *A Shared Experience: Men, Women, and the History of Gender*, edited by Laura McCall and Donald Yacovone, NYU P, 1998, pp. 245–70.

Razack, Sherene H. *Dark Threats and White Knights: The Somalia Affair, Peacekeeping, and the New Imperialism.* U of Toronto P, 2004.

Rifkin, Mark. *When Did Indians Become Straight? Kinship, the History of Sexuality, and Native Sovereignty.* Oxford UP, 2011.

Royal Commission on Aboriginal Peoples. *Report of the Royal Commission on Aboriginal Peoples.* 5 vols. Minister of Supply and Services, 1996. www.collectionscanada.gc.ca/webarchives/20071115053257/http://www.ainc-inac.gc.ca/ch/rcap/sg/sgmm_e.html.

Ruoff, A. LaVonne Brown. "Re: Indigenous Soldiers at War." Received by Deena Rymhs, 18 Nov. 2009.

Saskatchewan First Nations Veterans' Association. *"We Were There."* Federation of Saskatchewan Indian Nations, 1989.

Sheffield, R. Scott. "Indifference, Difference and Assimilation: Aboriginal People in Canadian Military Practice, 1900–45." *Aboriginal People and the Canadian Military: Historical Perspectives*, edited by Craig Mantle and Whitney Lackenbauer, CDI, 2007, pp. 57–71.

– *"The Red Man's on the Warpath": The Image of the "Indian" and the Second World War.* U of British Columbia P, 2004.

Smith, Andrea. *Conquest: Sexual Violence and American Indian Genocide.* South End, 2005.

Steckley, John, and Bryan Cummins. "Pegahmagabow of Parry Island: From Jenness Informant to Individual." *Canadian Journal of Native Studies*, vol. 25, no. 1, 2005, pp. 35–50.

Summerby, Janice. *Native Soldiers Foreign Battlefields*. Ministry of Supply and Services, 1993.

Tengan, Ty P. Kāwika. *Native Men Remade: Gender and Nation in Contemporary Hawai'i*. Duke UP, 2008.

Titley, Brian. *A Narrow Vision: Duncan Campbell Scott and the Administration of Indian Affairs in Canada*. U of British Columbia P, 1986.

Todd, Loretta, director. *Forgotten Warriors*. National Film Board, 1997.

Vance, Jonathan F. *Death So Noble: Memory, Meaning, and the First World War*. U of British Columbia P, 1997.

9 Reclaiming Indigenous Space through Testimonial Life Writing: An Antane Kapesh's *Je suis une maudite Sauvagesse* as Territorial Imperative

NATASHA DAGENAIS

The back jacket of *Je suis une maudite Sauvagesse* (1976) begins with a barbed question: "Of the two, the White man and the Indian, who can claim to be the most civilized?"[1] While no conclusive answer is given, it does echo the defiant tone used by An Antane Kapesh throughout her testimonial life narrative, which offers the following retort: "This is the disturbing monologue, the cry of an Indian who sees that her people have allowed themselves to be assimilated, and whose culture has been ruined due to the actions of the White man."[2] Kapesh expands on this retort deliberately and repeatedly in *Je suis une maudite Sauvagesse*, which reflects many of the issues associated with the *testimonio*, specifically what John Beverley calls its "urgency to communicate, a problem of ... subalternity" (32). This "urgency to communicate" for the Innu (or Montagnais)[3] life writer involves marginalization, oppression, poverty, and

I would like to thank Roxanne Rimstead for her collaboration on this version of the article.

1 Original French version (OFV): "Qui peut se prétendre le plus civilisé, du Blanc ou de l'Indien?" As this testimony was published in the mid-1970s, I have kept the word "Indian" to reflect word usage during this period.

2 OFV: "Monologue inquiétant, cri d'une Indienne qui voit son peuple se laisser assimiler et sa culture se détériorer sous l'action du Blanc."

3 French explorers called Kapesh's people "Montagnais" because they hunted game in the mountains (*montagnes* in French). In the original version of her testimonial narrative, An Antane Kapesh uses "innu" (meaning "human being") to refer to her people and culture, but in the French-language translation, the word primarily used is "Indien(s)." In this chapter I use the term "Innu" to refer to the people, language, and culture. Recent sources refer to the Innu language associated with Montagnais

struggle for survival within "the nation states which colonized them" because Indigenous peoples "still experience the consequences of past and continuing cultural racism" (Brown and Sant 3). In this chapter, I explore how testimony is used as a contested space for cultural survival, more precisely how Kapesh uses the written word to provide an alternate history of Indigenous identity, a counter-narrative that enables her to contest colonizers' distorted stories and fallacious re/presentations of indigeneity in Canada and the slow violence that continues to plague their lives long after colonial contact. The counter-narrative allows Kapesh to perform a symbolic reappropriation of the land, if not a remapping of both the land and her own people's past. Her testimony reclaims discursive territory and the space of memory[4] while it imaginatively contests the loss of material territory. Furthermore, Kapesh's insistence on putting her own Indigenous language on a par with the colonizers' language is an important means of contesting space in that it claims textual and symbolic space as a way of challenging the hierarchy of cultures that rationalized the appropriation of her people's lands. Testimony, on these representational levels, becomes a territorial imperative, an urgent taking back of space, and a construction of Indigenous space and collective identity in the shadow of colonial contact.

Published in a bilingual edition in which Innu and French appear side by side, Kapesh's testimony is as an act of resistance that serves not only to name her oppressors and denounce their unjust colonial systems but also to take back space. As an Innu woman forced into a White-dominant society and culture, Kapesh articulates her profound dissatisfaction and pain at the dispossession of her people. She testifies to the discontent, bitterness, and resilience of her people by confronting the various types of non-Aboriginals in positions of influence and authority: missionaries, politicians, teachers, gamekeepers, merchants, police officers, judges, journalists, and filmmakers, all of whom have played a

---

as Innu-aimun, giving a more precise title to this Innu dialect associated with Eastern Cree and spoken by about 10,000 Innu in Labrador and northern Québec and the James Bay area of Ontario and Québec (see www.innu-aimun.ca/).

4 The space of memory contested by Kapesh is national as well as local memory, and most importantly the colonial gaze infects both. For a more detailed discussion of the conflict between Indigenous and national memory, see Deena Rymhs's discussion of the containment and erasure of Indigenous soldiers in this collection.

pivotal and often detrimental role in Indigenous history. Kapesh constructs a counter-memory of colonization and posits it against the colonizing/colonizers' discourses that have stereotyped and dispossessed Indigenous peoples. The relation to the land represented in her testimony depicts Indigenous identity in close symbiosis with the land. Instead of an abstract discussion of territory or ownership, Kapesh remembers how her people dwelt in the land. As Robin Roth has argued in terms of alternative mapping by Indigenous subjects, abstract notions of the land fail to depict this close relationship; and thus a detailed knowledge of the land as a material and spiritual "dwelling space" needs to emerge in representations of Indigenous spatiality in order to see "more than abstract" (208–9).

For Kapesh, writing in Innu – her mother tongue – affirms categorically her Indigenous identity and the survival of Indigenous languages. She wrote her testimony, *Eukuan nin matshimanitu innu-iskueu*, in her mother tongue in order to encourage the preservation of Indigenous languages, to resist writing in the language of colonizers (even though it is the French translation, *Je suis une maudite Sauvagesse*, that enables her to reach a wide audience), and to emphasize how re/presentations of Indigenous peoples have contributed to their being objectified, in the aggregate, as "savages." Her testimony was translated by anthropologist José Mailhot with Anne-Marie André and André Mailhot, and my discussion is based on their French translation. It is important to specify here that *Je suis une maudite Sauvagesse* has never been translated into English. Although I have translated into English passages from the original French version in this chapter, I have opted to keep the original French title, which can be rendered in English as *I Am a Damned Savage*. All subsequent English passages from the work are my own translations.

As the testimony addresses non-Aboriginals directly, the French-language translation serves as the principal text but, as José Mailhot explains, "the original Innu version is there (on the left side of the page) especially to remind the French-language reader that this book was written by an Amerindian woman, in her own tongue" (my trans.; "L'écrit" 24).[5] Kapesh had to develop her own relationship with the written word

5 OFV: "la version innue [est] là (sur la page de gauche) surtout pour rappeler au lecteur francophone que ce livre a été écrit par une Amérindienne, dans sa propre langue."

considering that, as Chief Dan George remarks, "the spoken word is not enough" to illustrate "the true image / [of Native people]" (54–5). After all, George asserts, "everybody reads" (55). Here, George implies that Indigenous peoples who embrace the written word, by drawing on their traditional relationship with the spoken word, help to "tear down" colonialism because a community of readers witnesses "the act of writing [as] a political act that can encourage de-colonization" (Acoose 140). Although Janice Acoose here refers directly to Maria Campbell's landmark *Halfbreed* (1973), she suggests that testimonial writing by Indigenous peoples is based on resistance. For many Indigenous writers, therefore, testimonial writing is a necessary part of the decolonization process, in addition to being a strategy of cultural survival. Claiming space for her own language by keeping the original Innu beside the colonizer's language is a further discursive gesture towards decolonization, and one that echoes the contestation of material spaces, the subject of her testimony as territorial imperative.

In her preface, Kapesh confirms that while the act of writing is not a part of her traditional culture, it was nonetheless necessary for her to appropriate it in order to defend her culture, and her children's culture, with the purpose of, as Patience Elabor-Idemudia puts it, "transmitting Indigenous knowledge from one generation to the next" (102). Kapesh, who was fifty years old when *Je suis une maudite Sauvagesse* was published, speaks out as an adult who experienced a more traditional way of life than her children. She is a subaltern subject who writes out of resistance; yet perhaps more importantly, she speaks out as a mother aiming to correct misrepresentations of Indigenous peoples, thus reminding younger generations of Innu of the necessity of preserving their Indigenous ways, not as relics of the past but as living and changing. Indeed, Kapesh writes from an Indigenous mother's perspective that valorizes cultural knowledge and promotes resistance and survival. The autobiographical subject bears witness to a history of dispossession and "stolen lives" and strives to reclaim her indigeneity through shared knowledge of her language and culture, in particular for the empowerment of future generations of Innu. Kapesh's main purpose for writing draws a relationship between heritage and cultural memory, but more critically, it reflects, as Joseph Pugliese maintains, "a sense of futurity" (6) implied in preserving and sharing Indigenous knowledges with the next generation: "I want to write more. I want to write in order to defend my culture, in order for future generations of Innu to know that their people have lived elsewhere than on a reserve" (Kapesh qtd. in

Boudreau 11).[6] Testimonial writing as a strategy of cultural survival allows for the trauma survivor to preserve the past in order to foster "people's sense of belonging" (Pugliese 6). For Kapesh, therefore, testimonial life writing represents a recuperative strategy for cultural survival.

From the outset, Kapesh addresses her readers to demonstrate the depth of the destruction wielded by non-Aboriginal colonization and consumerism, not to mention the distortion of historical events or facts involving Aboriginals and non-Aboriginals. She elucidates, "But *we have had enough* of being, for a number of years, governed by Whites. *We have had enough* of being, for a number of years, mistreated by Whites, and *we have had enough* of being, for a number of years, disrespected by Whites" (*JSMS* 29, 31; emphasis added).[7] The repetition heightens the author's refusal to be silenced by the dominant society. Resistance, therefore, becomes an engaged survival strategy within the testimony because the "collective self [is] engaged in common struggle" (Gugelberger and Kearney qtd. in Mertus 150).

In her postscript, she summarizes the counter-narrative communicated in her testimony: "I am a damned Savage. I feel very proud when I am called Savage. When I hear the White man use this word, I know that he is constantly telling me that I am a real Indian and that I was the first to have lived in the forest. Well, everything that lives in the forest represents the best kind of life. May the White man always call me Savage" (*JSMS*, postface).[8] This reappropriation of the insult reflects her affirmation of and pride in her Indigenous identity as well as her claim that the Innu were first in the territory. It is also a sign of her resistance to being labelled inferior, to being assimilated into the dominant society. By appropriating the derogatory term "savage," used to marginalize her as an

---

6 OFV: "Je veux encore écrire, écrire pour défendre ma culture, pour que les Montagnais qui naîtront sachent que leur peuple a déjà vécu autrement que dans une réserve."

7 OFV: "Mais *nous en avons assez* d'être, depuis un certain nombre d'années, gouvernés par les Blancs. *Nous en avons assez* d'être, depuis un certain nombre d'années, malmenés par eux et *nous en avons assez* de les voir, depuis un certain nombre d'années, nous manquer de respect" (emphasis added). *Je suis une maudite Sauvagesse* is cited as *JSMS* in parenthetical references.

8 OFV: "Je suis une maudite Sauvagesse. Je suis très fière quand, aujourd'hui, je m'entends traiter de Sauvagesse. Quand j'entends le Blanc prononcer ce mot, je comprends qu'il me redit sans cesse que je suis une vraie Indienne et que c'est moi la première à avoir vécu dans le bois. Or toute chose qui vit dans le bois correspond à la vie la meilleure. Puisse le Blanc me toujours traiter de Sauvagesse."semble des Indiens [car] tous les Indiens ne sont qu'un."

Indigenous woman, she writes back against her oppressors, to contest hegemonic discourse and to set the record straight. The French title is, from the start, an attempt for the autobiographical subject to empower herself by appropriating this colonial idiom and reclaiming the pejorative "damned Savage" ("maudite Sauvagesse"), thus functioning as a basis from which to construct a counter-history. As Kateri Damm stresses, "colonizing governments have used language and the power of words ... to subjugate and control the Indigenous peoples of the land" (11). Kapesh uses her own language and, in turn, the language of the colonizer, through the French translation, to question the historical record and challenge the conventional descriptions of Indigenous peoples as articulated, for example, in many twentieth-century history books for primary- and secondary-school students. Kapesh contests the negative images of Indigenous peoples, as hostile, menacing, cruel, and bloodthirsty, still conveyed during the 1970s, when her testimony was published. These negative images, as well as derogatory names, are compounded with others that portray them as uncivilized, lazy, unclean, irresponsible, and unintelligent. According to Kapesh, this false representation of the Innu involves "Indians as a whole [because] they are one" (*JSMS* 175),[9] therefore indicating that this type of disparaging behaviour affects (and "infects" to varying degrees) all Indigenous peoples.

Still, the Innu author powerfully shows the effect of countering these multiple misrepresentations in her testimony with her own representations of non-Aboriginals, whose behaviour, she insists, contributed to the "miseducation" of Aboriginals: "I believe that *the White man* is *responsible* for all the bad things we, and our children, do today: *the White man is the one who changed our culture*" (159; emphasis added).[10] Indeed, Kapesh uses the written word to contest the prejudiced portrayal of the Innu as stupid, lazy, and inferior on television and in films. She names the consequential acts of non-Aboriginals and speaks uncompromisingly about non-Aboriginals needing to accept responsibility for the repercussions

9 OFV: "Je suis une maudite Sauvagesse. Je suis très fière quand, aujourd'hui, je m'entends traiter de Sauvagesse. Quand j'entends le Blanc prononcer ce mot, je comprends qu'il me redit sans cesse que je suis une vraie Indienne et que c'est moi la première à avoir vécu dans le bois. Or toute chose qui vit dans le bois correspond à la vie la meilleure. Puisse le Blanc me toujours traiter de Sauvagesse" (Postface).

10 OFV: "Moi j'estime que *c'est le Blanc* qui est *responsable* de toutes nos mauvaises actions d'aujourd'hui et de toutes celles de nos enfants: *c'est lui qui a changé notre culture*" (emphasis added).

of their colonial and racist policies/practices on Aboriginals. Kapesh outlines from the beginning the cultural as well as territorial invasion by using such words as *exploiter* ("exploit") and *détruire* ("destroy") to record their actions and aims in invading Indigenous territory and imposing their way of life on its people. She testifies to the different aspects of Indigenous life affected by colonizing institutions – for example, the loss of their land and natural resources, inadequate living accommodation, sedentary lifestyle, poor livelihood, and a non-Indigenous education for their children. Testimonial writing thus provides a textual space for Kapesh to tell the dominant society of the loss of customs and traditions, "the real story" (Ruffo 120).

Testimony allows Kapesh to counter abstract notions of the land, which are not as neutral as they so often appear in dominant versions of mapping (Roth). Abstract space and its mapping are "thoroughly bound up in the creation of nation-states and the expansion of capital" (209) and are thus thoroughly political, according to Roth, who argues for a greater understanding of Indigenous spatiality through a counter-narrative of land as dwelling space. Since maps tend to take into account surfaces to be occupied, rather than worlds to be inhabited, I propose here that testimonial life writing offers a detailed counter-narrative to this flattening of the land; it represents a journey into the Indigenous people's subjective relation to the land. Roth cites Henri Lefebvre and Tim Ingold in respect to the need to stop separating the material (physical) and the non-material (mental) in order to understand the production of space, especially Indigenous space (211). "Dwelling space is contingent on subjectivity," Roth writes, "produced in relation (to social, political, economic processes), and through interaction (with the physical environment and with other people), and is thus material, dynamic, and multiple" (211).

Je suis une maudite Sauvagesse is divided into nine chapters or episodes, ranging from the arrival of the White man on Innu land and the discovery of the iron ore in northern Québec to White education and White "prefabricated" houses. In the first chapter, entitled "The Arrival of the White Man on Our Land" ("L'arrivée du Blanc sur notre territoire"), Kapesh underscores the connectedness that binds Aboriginals to the land. This first chapter prepares its readers for the content and tone of the testimonial narrative with the opening affirmation: "When the White man wanted to exploit and destroy our land" (13).[11] By immediately

11 OFV: "Quand le Blanc a voulu exploiter et détruire notre territoire."

exposing collective reality in this opening chapter, more precisely how Aboriginals have been dispossessed of their lands, Kapesh illustrates the fundamental relationship between Aboriginals and the land that ties together community, culture, and spirituality. Her use of *le Blanc* ("the White man") is extensive. In fact, *Blanc*, employed either in the singular or plural form, is repeated more than fifty times in the first chapter alone (out of a total of eleven pages), again emphasizing every single damaging action and aim of Whites. In the original Innu version, *kauapishit*, corresponding in English to "White person," or literally "the one who is white," recurs almost as many times. She reproduces the voice of the non-Indigenous man, who utters frankly his intentions of duping, stealing, exploiting, and destroying all that is Aboriginal. "The White man never talked about this to Indians. '*I will exploit your land and destroy it. Today, you can see that it is still very clean ... In the future, I will waste your animals and dirty them, all of the Indian animals*'" (17, 19; emphasis in orig.).[12] This italicized passage, introduced by words conveying what the White man has not said but thought and printed as if the White man were speaking, is a further example of counter-narrative.

Every chapter in her testimonial is a story in itself because chronological order is not the main ordering principle: storytelling is. Kapesh writes in depth about the various historical and sociopolitical events that have played a significant role in her life as a member of the Innu nation. She recreates speeches by various non-Indigenous civil servants, blurring the line between reality and fiction, truth and lie, Indigenous and White. It must also be noted that the time frame is not strictly linear according to Western tradition. Rather, Kapesh incorporates history, oral tales, myths, speeches, opinions, beliefs, and advice not in sequence. She brings together "personal, tribal, and mythological history" by mirroring Aboriginal oral tradition in the construction of her testimonial (Petrone 114). Time moves fluidly between past and present to expose the Indigenous way of life before the arrival of non-Aboriginals compared to the impact of the dominating culture on the Innu after the arrival of non-Aboriginals. By using such words as "every Indian," "stories," and "telling,"[13] Kapesh

12 OFV: "Le Blanc n'a jamais parlé de cela aux Indiens. 'J'exploiterai votre territoire et je le détruirai. Aujourd'hui, vous voyez, il est encore très propre ... Plus tard, je gaspillerai et je salirai vos animaux, toutes les espèces d'animaux indiens'" (emphasis in orig.).

13 These words correspond to "*chaque Indien,*" "*histoires,*" and "*raconter*" respectively.

highlights this link between Aboriginals and orality. Furthermore, she introduces how memory functions intrinsically within orality, revolving around the act of remembering and sharing stories by word of mouth and passing them on from one generation to the next.

In addition to using history, oral tales, and speeches, Kapesh employs repetition as a tool to reclaim Indigenous discursive space. Repetition draws out the territorial imperative:

> *When the White man wanted to exploit and destroy our land,* he did not ask anyone's permission; he did not ask the Indians if they were in agreement. *When the White man wanted to exploit and destroy our land,* he did not give the Indians a document to sign indicating their consent that he *exploit* and *destroy* all of *our land,* in order for him alone to earn a living here forever. (*JSMS* 13; emphasis added)[14]

The author uses the all-important anaphora, a rhetorical technique consisting of the repetition of a word or a series of words at the beginning of successive lines common to Western rhetoric but also to Indigenous storytelling and orature. The repetition of the words "When the White man wanted to exploit and destroy our land" emphasizes the actions posed by the colonizers in juxtaposition with the repercussions these destructive actions have had on the Innu way of life. While repetition, as an integral element within the oral tradition, reminds the reader to pay close attention to Kapesh's rhetoric, the side-by-side Innu and French versions enable the author to persuade: 1) the Aboriginal reader/listener (text in Innu) that by writing in her mother tongue, Kapesh is ensuring its cultural survival; and 2) the non-Aboriginal reader/listener (text in French) that by providing a French translation of her testimony, Kapesh is taking a stand and talking back to the colonizer in his own language, by contesting the territorial and cultural invasion against the Innu, the slow violence,[15] and the symbolic and economic marginalization of a people who are effectively an "unimagined

---

14 OFV: "*Quand le Blanc a voulu exploiter et détruire notre territoire,* il n'a demandé de permission à personne, il n'a pas demandé aux Indiens s'ils étaient d'accord. *Quand le Blanc a voulu exploiter et détruire notre territoire,* il n'a fait signer aux Indiens aucun document disant qu'ils acceptaient qu'il *exploite* et qu'il *détruise* tout *notre territoire* afin que lui seul y gagne sa vie indéfiniment" (emphasis added).

community" within national imaginaries (Nixon 150). *Je suis une maudite Sauvagesse* is in fact an affirmation of the speaking subject in an urgent plea for recognition of a host of spatial wrongs in the distant past and in the present, represented here by Kapesh, who stands in to witness these wrongs as part of the whole.

Various chapters in Kapesh's testimonial narrative reflect elements of the oral tradition; for example, in the second chapter, "The Discovery of Ore in the North" ("La découverte du minerai dans le Nord"), which takes place in Schefferville, a northern town in Québec bordering Labrador, Kapesh tells a story her father told her of Tshishenish Pien, Father Babel, and Father Arnaud. During the nineteenth century, Fathers Babel (known as Kakushkuenitak, "The Serious One") and Arnaud (known as Kauashkamuesht, "The Clear Voice") were among the oblates sent to Christianize the Innu.[16] Their renaming by the Innu shows an insider's view of their reception and inverts the colonial renaming of Kapesh and her people. Atshapi Antane, Kapesh's husband's great-grandfather, is the Innu who guided Father Babel into Innu territory, while Tshishenish Pien is the Innu to have "found" ore in the North. By providing the information about the context, the Innu woman shows how well the Innu know this story, further illustrating the importance of shared knowledge in Indigenous culture. She begins, "This is the story of Tshishenish Pien, Father Babel, and Father Arnaud" (*JSMS* 37).[17] It is a story that cannot be found in books. It was passed on by word of mouth (Aboriginal culture) from generation to generation. The story of the iron ore takes on further oral qualities when Kapesh speaks from her father's point of view, as if he himself were in fact telling the story of Tshishenish Pien. Her father's version in the text is italicized (and takes up about half of the chapter in the French translation). The father's version is also italicized in the original Innu-language testimony. Printing

---

15 More than three decades after Kapesh's testimony appeared, Rob Nixon defined slow violence in respect to Indigenous peoples' and poor peoples' struggle for community, land, and survival by drawing attention to the environmental war that rages still in the wake of territorial wars. Nixon notes how activist-writers could wage a symbolic war by reimagining "unimagined communities" of Indigenous and poor people, communities that had been suppressed by national hegemony.

16 See José Mailhot's *Au pays des Innus* for more information on the various religious missions in northern Québec and Labrador.

17 OFV: "Ceci est l'histoire de Tshishenish Pien et des Pères Babel et Arnaud."

this story-within-a-story is a strategy to ensure its survival because her father told it to his daughter, and she, in turn, has shared it in print form for posterity.[18] "I was happy to listen to my father, at his age, today, tell me stories from the past. My father was not the only keeper of these stories; there were before him his father, his grandfather, and his great-grandfather" (45).[19] By relating in *Je suis une maudite Sauvagesse* the fact that her father, in his youth, had actually met Tshishenish Pien, who was then quite old, the teller lends greater credibility to this story.

Kapesh questions non-Indigenous interpretations of historical events or "facts." According to her account, Whites maintained that Father Babel "discovered" the iron ore, but how could he have been the one to have discovered the iron ore when it was the *Indien montagnais* who brought him inland, the Innu who showed him the way to the mine? As Kapesh points out, "it is also the Indian" ("c'est aussi l'Indien") who guided Father Arnaud deeper onto Indigenous land; "it is the Indian" who helped him weather living in a tent; "it is the Indian" who provided food for him by hunting various animals (39). Repeating the words "it is the Indian" reinforces the author's counter-history of the discovery of the iron ore. Kapesh also explains the context for telling the "real" story: the centenary celebrations of Schefferville in 1970, at which time she and other members of the Innu nation learned that these celebrations concerned the discovery of iron ore in the North by Father Babel. Kapesh uses irony to convey to the reader that the Innu had never heard the non-Indigenous version of a story that had been passed down from generation to generation in the Innu community. Again, the reader is exposed to two different versions of the same story, with the Indigenous version openly challenging the non-Indigenous one. Parenthetically, Kapesh mentions that Aboriginals were invited, at the Schefferville celebration of colonial history, to adorn themselves "in the Indian style of the past" (41),[20] thus evoking their playing "dress up" as if they were museum relics or artefacts of a discontinuous past. These generational counter-narratives enable Aboriginals to remember the past, the old ways

18 Kapesh specifies in her testimony that her father was ninety-one years old (likely at the time it was published in book form). See p. 45 for clarification.

19 OFV: "À l'âge qu'il a aujourd'hui, j'étais heureuse d'écouter mon père raconter les choses du passé. Il n'y a pas que mon père qui détienne des histoires, il y a aussi son père, son grand-père et son arrière-grand-père."

20 OFV: "à la manière indienne d'autrefois."

of their ancestors, and significant events that are representative of the Aboriginal way of life as an expression of the historical rootedness of the "live" versus the "dead Indian" (King). Remembering and telling stories (passed on in Kapesh's family) become important for continuity with the past: "That's the story my father was told by his parents, by his mother, by his grandmother, and by other Elders" (61).[21] By underlining this tradition of storytelling and its storytellers (father, grandparents, great-grandparents, and other elders) as repositories of Indigenous knowledge, Kapesh discloses the interconnection between the healing power of stories, Indigenous history, and cultural survival. The territorial imperative of the testimony is rooted not only in truth claims about the past but also in an ongoing process of community building and in healing. The maintenance of cultural spaces in the face of territorial dispossession is the route to negotiating new identities, which may include future land claims and reimagining an "unimagined community" (Nixon).

Another topic Kapesh broaches is formal education for the Innu and the resulting loss of elements of Aboriginal culture, including the changing of "Indian" names to French ones, in order to erase the identity of Aboriginal peoples. In *Au pays des Innus*, José Mailhot alludes to the Christian influence of name attribution or renaming: "Ever since they became Christians, the Innu have been given a European first name when they are baptized" (my trans.; 85).[22] Anne André, the Innu author's Christian name in French, equates to An Antane in her mother tongue. In her testimony, Kapesh points to the necessity of preserving Aboriginal names, as these constitute part of who the Innu are as a nation. Instead of being called Madame André, she would much rather others use her Innu name: "Today, I would be even prouder if others would call me AN KAPESH because it is my Indian name" (*JSMS* 91).[23] Formal education for Aboriginals engendered and provoked massive social, economic, and political changes in their way of life. In the following passage from the third chapter, titled simply "White Education" ("L'éducation blanche"), the anaphoric use of "it is true" ("il est vrai") produces an effect of

21 OFV: "Voilà l'histoire que mon père a entendue raconter par ses parents, par sa mère, par sa grand-mère et par d'autres Vieux."

22 OFV: "Depuis qu'ils sont chrétiens, tous les Innus ont un prénom de type européen, qui leur est attribué au moment du baptême."

23 OFV: "Aujourd'hui, je serais beaucoup plus fière qu'on m'appelle AN KAPESH car c'est mon nom indien."

forcefulness that persuades the reader/listener of how issues stand for Indigenous witnesses to colonialism:

> When the White man took our children away to put them in residential schools, *it is true* that he did not ask us for money. It did not cost us anything for our children to be clothed; the federal government paid for everything. And *it is true* that once the school was built, the inside looked like that of a store ... And *it is true* that the residential school was reserved for Indian children. (71; emphasis added)[24]

While Kapesh enumerates the good points of this residential school, built in 1953 in Sept-Îles, she quickly counters the previous passage with the ugly truth behind the artificial smiles and goodwill speeches by various officials within the Department of Indian Affairs. Their main objectives were to force the nomadic Innu into living a sedentary lifestyle (either in Sept-Îles or in Schefferville), to which they were completely unaccustomed, and to make them "disappear" through assimilation policies into mainstream society.

On the one hand, Kapesh discloses the remarks uttered by non-Aboriginals when explaining the "benefits" of education for the Innu; on the other hand, she responds by disproving them, by showing them to be lies, by revealing the "truth" from an Indigenous perspective. Initially she had hoped, as had others, that an education would provide a better future for the children of the community. Speaking again with the "we" that is used interchangeably with the first-person singular pronoun throughout her narrative, Kapesh affirms the following: "never could we have imagined that the school would be responsible for our losing our culture" (*JSMS* 67).[25] Indeed, she points to their belief in the benefits of the education proposed by civil servants within the walls of the newly built residential school, but the Innu had not predicted that this "prized" education would provoke considerable cultural loss. Once the children were put into this school, they essentially lost ties with their families and

---

24 OFV: "Quand on a pris nos enfants pour les garder au pensionnat indien, *il est vrai* qu'on ne leur a pas demandé d'argent, ils étaient habillés gratuitement, le gouvernement fédéral leur fournissait tout. *Et il est vrai* qu'une fois la construction de notre école terminée, l'intérieur avait l'aspect d'un magasin ... *Et il vrai* que le pensionnat était une école réservée aux enfants indiens" (emphasis added).

25 OFV: "jamais nous n'avons cru que cette école nous ferait perdre notre culture."

with the tight-knit social fabric of the Indigenous community in which they had an inherently central role. According to Kapesh, "When Indians lived according to their way of life, their culture prevented them from being separated from each one of their children" (73).[26] She compares the White man's false promises of formal education for Aboriginal children to the bleak reality of the collapse of Aboriginal families and communities due to the separation of children from parents. This also resulted in several generations of Aboriginal children, caught between two worlds, having to relearn their Indigenous language and culture. This next quote outlines how the Indigenous social structure began to disintegrate and transform Aboriginal culture: "priests, brothers, and nuns are the ones who took care of the Indian children" (71).[27] Consequently, a language/cultural barrier was erected between parents and children, as these "educated" children had not learned the traditional ways of the Innu as had their parents, including living in the woods, and had not learned to communicate in Innu. Kapesh reiterates this concept of cultural loss when she concludes, "Because of the White education they received, my children, today, do not know anything about their Indian culture; they are forgetting their Indian language" (83).[28]

Through repetition, Kapesh emphasizes how much was taken from the Innu and other Aboriginals: non-Aboriginals took away Aboriginal lands, hunting and fishing rights, cultural and linguistic traditions, and their children. This juxtaposition of past and present, of Aboriginal and non-Aboriginal, of the community and the individual, of respect for the land and profit from natural resources, embodies cultural differences, in particular their approach to the land. "Underlying every aspect of Innu culture is the belief that human beings should seek to understand and work with nature rather than trying to master or transform it" (Samson, Wilson, and Mazower 12). In her testimony Kapesh openly demonstrates the extent to which non-Aboriginals tried to transform Innu land in order to make a profit. Furthermore, when their children were transferred to a regular school, into an alien world, they then had to

26 OFV: "Quand l'Indien vivait sa vie à lui, sa culture ne lui permettait pas d'être séparé de chacun de ses enfants."

27 OFV: "ce sont les prêtres, les frères et les religieuses qui prenaient soin des enfants indiens."

28 OFV: "À cause de l'éducation blanche qu'ils ont reçue, aujourd'hui mes enfants ne connaissent rien de leur culture indienne, ils perdent leur langue indienne."

confront the prejudice of their non-Indigenous classmates and teachers. Yet Kapesh resists succumbing to colonization and internal colonialism by suggesting in *Je suis une maudite Sauvagesse* different strategies to foster cultural survival. For example, she wishes to see more books in Aboriginal languages made available on reserves and, pointedly, she highlights the need for Innu-language courses to begin earlier than grade 4, as was the case in the regular school at Schefferville (*JSMS* 87). She also encourages the reclamation of Innu names because of the powerful link between naming, identity, and culture. What becomes clear in this textual narrative is that Indigenous and non-Indigenous peoples need to collaborate to ensure the implementation of these and other cultural survival strategies.

In the fourth chapter, "The Gamekeeper" ("Le garde-chasse"), Kapesh explains how detrimental the roles played by such "authority" figures as politicians and gamekeepers were. These authorities prevented Aboriginals from following the ancient ways of their ancestors, namely, living in the woods and living on their catches from hunting and fishing expeditions. Past and present converge as she contrasts the Indigenous traditional lifestyle of "the past" ("autrefois") to the colonized way of life of "today" ("aujourd'hui"). To illustrate the visibly altered Indigenous lifestyle, Kapesh recounts how, at the time of publication, their ancestral lands had become overrun with non-Aboriginals (as in other settler countries, there are more non-Indigenous than Indigenous peoples living in the country that is now Canada). By remapping and remembering the uses of space that had been erased by Whites, Kapesh was able to critique the normalized use of colonial space, such as hunting clubs, resulting in less land and fewer animals for the Innu. She mentions how dams have also destroyed lands and various forms of life: "the land on which [my husband] used to hunt is now under water, with all of the Indian animals. I am referring to the Hamilton River where a dam was built – that is where we used to hunt ... our river, the Hamilton River, [which the White man has] blocked – all the hunting grounds are under water, and all the Indian animals are gone" (101, 103).[29] The author once more draws attention to the lack of respect for the land as displayed by certain non-Aboriginals who have wasted, or *gaspiller*, to

29 OFV: "le terrain où [mon mari] chassait se trouvait sous l'eau, avec tous ses animaux indiens. Je parle de la rivière Hamilton où on a construit un barrage, c'est là que se trouve notre terrain de chasse ... sur notre rivière, la rivière Hamilton, [que le Blanc]

borrow the term she repeats in her account, irreplaceable natural resources. Her testimony remaps the use of the land by showing how mining operations and the construction of hydroelectric dams have irrevocably transformed the traditional lands of the Innu.

Kapesh tells the story of her elderly father, a hunter since the age of eight, who was stopped in 1972 by gamekeepers and the RCMP when he returned from a fishing expedition. She explains that they confiscated the fish he had caught on the pretext that it was against the law (of non-Aboriginals) to catch certain types of fish, while in reality, she specifies, he was stopped on account of his Aboriginal status. Kapesh cites the uninformed gamekeepers and RCMP: "'We thought it was speckled trout,' they said. And they had seized lake trout" (113).[30] Here, as elsewhere, the testimony claims space for Indigenous subjective knowledge of dwelling in the land through several lines about the superiority of Indigenous knowledge of the land. This contests both the legal and proprietary claims of the Whites and their cultural memory of discovery. The passage begins on page 109 with the words "I will tell a story" ("Je vais raconter"), which she uses to introduce this story involving her father, giving the text again a teaching flavour of the storytelling tradition. Kapesh builds up reader/listener expectations by the repetition of words and symbols indicative of this tradition, but her repetition of truth claims also contests other versions and stories: "I believe that *there is nothing true* in what the newspapers publish about us and that *there is nothing true* in what you see about us on television or in films. As an Indian woman, I think that it is terrible and destructive to have the lifestyle we do now, the White man's" (173; emphasis added).[31] Repeating the keywords "I," "Indian," and "we" throughout this testimonial account reinforces the pride Kapesh manifests in her Innu identity. It serves to reinforce her staunch beliefs and

---

a barrée, les terrains de chasse des Indiens sont tous sous l'eau et tous les animaux indiens sont perdus." It should be noted that the name of the Hamilton River was changed to the Churchill River in 1965.

30 OFV: "'Nous pensions que c'était de la truite mouchetée,' ont-ils dit, et ils avaient saisi de la touladi." According to Fisheries and Oceans Canada, the touladi, a member of the salmon family, is also known across Canada as lake trout, grey trout, and salmon trout, among other names.

31 OFV: "Moi j'estime qu'aujourd'hui, quand on parle de nous dans les journaux, *il n'y a rien de vrai* là-dedans et quand vous nous voyez au cinéma et à la télévision, *il n'y a rien de vrai* là-dedans ... Moi, une Indienne, je trouve pénible et néfaste la vie que nous vivons maintenant qui est celle du Blanc" (emphasis added).

inclinations, manipulation of words, legitimization (in short) of the Innu nation, and reclamation of her Indigenous identity through testimony and memory space.

In chapters 5 and 6, Kapesh describes the discrimination and segregation the Innu experience at the hands of the hotelkeeper who introduced alcohol to Aboriginals and of the police officers and judges who condemned and imprisoned them without foundation. Interestingly, the translators of the French version add information concerning the Indian Act: "Passed in 1867, the Act included a clause prohibiting Indians from drinking alcohol. The clause was amended in 1963" (117).[32] Focusing on police brutality and the exploitation and abuse of her people, Kapesh enumerates the problems that have resulted from their exposure to alcohol, which she views as both the Innu's *disease* and a source of *unease*, and concludes that Whites had only given them an ill-adapted way of life based on non-Aboriginal values. In the short chapter "The Alcohol Merchant" ("Le marchand d'alcool"), she quotes Aboriginals who went to the hotel for drinks: "Alcohol is served to us Indians in glasses that are different" and "They open the windows when we Indians enter the hotel" (117).[33] The poor treatment of Aboriginals increased with the expansion of the hotel; segregation was more formally introduced, with a separate door for Aboriginals, far from the bar-salon "where only Whites were admitted" (119).[34] The hotelkeeper allowed the Innu only in "an unclean basement … very dirty and very dark" (119).[35] The author surmises that the hotelkeeper was interested more in money than in the health of Aboriginals, as underage Aboriginals, such as a couple of the author's children, were also served drinks, often until they had no more money to spend. According to Kapesh, the hotelkeeper would call the police once the inebriated Aboriginal customers had been "thrown out" as disposable objects. The French expression for "throw out," *jeter dehors*, is used ten times in a single paragraph to show the extent of contempt for Aboriginals (121, 123). It was at this point, according to Kapesh, after the hotelkeeper had called the police, that they, in turn,

32 OFV: "La Loi des Indiens, votée en 1867, comportait une clause qui interdisait aux Indiens la consommation de boissons alcoolisées. Cette clause fut amendée en 1963."

33 OFV: "Les verres dans lesquels on nous sert, nous les Indiens, sont différents"; "On ouvre les fenêtres quand les Indiens entrent à l'hôtel."

34 OFV: "où seuls les Blancs sont admis."

35 OFV: "une cave malpropre … très sale et très sombre."

would be able to "make some money off of the [Indians]" by arresting them (123).[36] Kapesh can only conclude, "These days, the alcohol merchant is very happy about mistreating and insulting Indians, and he shows no remorse in acting this way" (123).[37]

Je suis une maudite Sauvagesse includes the testimonies of abuse of others, thus demonstrating the frequency of the ill treatment of Aboriginals, whom the police do not serve and protect. In many instances, Kapesh contends, Aboriginals are reduced to silence because there is no justice in court (or on the streets) for them and no space to be heard. The Indigenous writer-activist contests elsewhere in her testimony stereotypes propagated by newspapers and films that have contributed to the negative images of Aboriginals. For example, one male Innu tells others of having witnessed one day the arrest of several Aboriginals just outside the hotel, with the derogatory words pronounced by the hotelkeeper: "Round those damned savages up too" (123).[38] Kapesh describes in greater detail how police officers treat "Indians" as brutes, savages, and subhumans by incorporating into her testimony recurrent lived experiences of abuse, and she cites as an example the beating and jailing in 1969 of one of her own sons, whose body bears physical traces of his arrest: "When he arrived at our home, his clothes were completely stained with blood; his face was swollen; his legs were full of bruises because he had been kicked by police officers; and his head was covered with swellings" (139).[39] Another male Innu talks about how he was beaten repeatedly by an officer after having asked for food (131).

Kapesh also questions the lies fabricated by White police officers who pretend to be hurt or wounded when in fact they are the ones to hurt and wound Indigenous peoples, who are intimidated, physically beaten, and verbally threatened. Her husband relates how a police officer answered his question about the whereabouts of his son (the one mentioned above who was severely beaten). The unveiled threat is unmistakable, and the tone blunt: "Your son's here. If he isn't quiet, we'll soon hang him" (139).[40] Kapesh demands to know why Indigenous

36 OFV: "faire de l'argent avec [eux]."

37 OFV: "De nos jours, le marchand d'alcool est très content de brutaliser et d'insulter l'Indien et il n'éprouve aucune honte à le faire."

38 OFV: "Ramassez-les eux autres aussi ces maudits sauvages-là."

39 OFV: "Quand il est arrivé chez nous, ses vêtements étaient tout tachés de sang, sa figure était tuméfiée, ses jambes remplies d'ecchymoses d'avoir reçu des coups de pied des policiers et sa tête couverte d'enflures."

peoples are the only ones being beaten up by police officers and, just as importantly, why there are so many Aboriginals filling the prisons: "Why are Indians the sole ones being beaten up by police officers when they are arrested? Why does the White man constantly fill his prisons with only Indians?" (151, 153).[41] Yet Kapesh does not expect an answer to these questions because, as she reiterates throughout her testimonial narrative, Indigenous peoples are considered inferior and savage, thus needing to be "civilized," by Whites.

Again, in Kapesh's own words: "As an Indian woman, I think that it is terrible and destructive to have the lifestyle we do now, the White man's" (173).[42] For the Indigenous woman, any discussion of Aboriginals by the media involves all Aboriginals collectively, in particular when non-Aboriginals criticize them for behaving badly after having forced their culture on them. She speaks unfalteringly and resolutely about the impact of alcohol on her people: "The White man is the one to have taught us to be constantly drunk" (175).[43] In the seventh chapter, entitled "Journalists and Filmmakers" ("Les journalistes et les cinéastes"), Kapesh questions these negative images of Aboriginals by the media, while in chapter 8 she explores the (enforced) relocation of her people in the 1950s. She points to a newspaper article that includes an uncomplimentary statement about Aboriginals being persistently inebriated. Kapesh indicates that journalists and filmmakers are not interested in preserving and presenting Aboriginal culture as it flourished before the arrival of Europeans. She maintains that the Innu culture she remembers having experienced no longer exists: "I know that it is very difficult today to show me my Indian lifestyle today because my culture no longer exists" (183).[44] Sylvie Vincent also alludes to the connection between Indigenous territory and cultural heritage: "the land also has a cultural foundation because Innu land is the place, it is said, where culture is rooted" (my trans.; 222).[45] Kapesh points out how the Innu were forced to buy and

---

40 OFV: "Ton fils est ici. S'il ne se tient pas tranquille, nous allons le pendre bientôt."

41 OFV: "Pour quelle raison n'y a-t-il que des Indiens qui soient blessés par les policiers lors de leur arrestation? Pour quelle raison n'y a-t-il qu'avec nous que le Blanc remplisse constamment ses prisons?"

42 OFV: "Moi, une Indienne, je trouve pénible et néfaste la vie que nous vivons maintenant qui est celle du Blanc."

43 OFV: "C'est le Blanc qui nous a appris à être constamment ivres."

44 OFV: "Je sais bien qu'aujourd'hui il est très difficile de me montrer ma vie d'Indienne parce que ma culture n'existe plus aujourd'hui."

live in shacks and to relocate several times due to the Department of Indian Affairs and the Iron Ore Company. Importantly, relocation and dislocation are symptoms of ongoing "slow violence," as discussed by Rob Nixon in terms of the colonization and exploitation of Indigenous lands for the extraction of resources. Kapesh quotes a federal civil servant representing the mining company: "*If you accept to relocate, the Iron Ore is telling you that, in exchange, the company will give you work. If you stay here near the town, the Iron Ore is telling you that you will be polluting the water*" (*JSMS* 191; emphasis in orig.).[46] Ironically, but perhaps not surprisingly, even after the Innu relocate back and forth from Sept-Îles to Schefferville (and non-Aboriginals begin, somewhat ironically, to sell them water), there are no promised jobs. First, the Iron Ore Company takes the best lands, providing Aboriginals with "rocky land" ("un terrain rocailleux") (197), where hunting is not as bountiful. After having lived several years in the Lake John area, Kapesh refuses, despite her family's erratic and uncertain standard of living, to move once again (this time to the city): "In 1967, I already knew that no one was going to drive me away from Lake John. Today, you and I both see that I am still in the Lake John area, but I must admit that things haven't worked out the way we wanted – for the houses to be built here first" (205).[47] One of the survival strategies Kapesh uses to resist this forced relocation is her involvement in the Association des Indiens du Québec and in the political association representing the Innu in her region, both advocating indigeneity and Indigenous rights. Yet the strategy of testimony is also a way to contest relocation in that it remembers and remaps the past and the present, as well as the Indigenous lands in the colonial present.

The title of the author's conclusion forms a question: "How will Whites see us from now on?" ("Comment le Blanc nous considérera-t-il à l'avenir?"). She reiterates, for the last time, the repercussions of non-Indigenous culture on Aboriginals, explicitly the impact of the break

45 OFV: "Le titre sur la terre a également un fondement culturel car le territoire montagnais est le lieu, dit-on, où s'enracine la culture."

46 OFV: "Si vous acceptez de déménager, l'Iron Ore vous dit qu'en retour elle vous donnera du travail. Si vous restez ici près de la ville, l'Iron Ore vous dit que vous allez polluer l'eau" (emphasis in orig.).

47 OFV: "Moi, déjà en 1967, je savais que personne ne me chasserait du lac John. Aujourd'hui, vous et moi le voyons, je suis au lac John mais je dois admettre que ça n'a pas marché pour qu'on construise des maisons ici d'abord."

from tradition, namely, on their once nomadic lifestyle. Here, Kapesh intervenes in the colonial construction of space-time. Kapesh herself would seem to agree, to a certain extent, that non-Aboriginals have been successful in fulfilling these objectives. However, time after time, she examines in her testimony the *resiliency* of the Indigenous way of life. In her conclusion, she recapitulates the objectives of White leaders of the time: 1) to destroy Innu culture, 2) to eradicate the Innu language, and 3) to steal Innu land. Kapesh also examines in this chapter and others the good points of the Indigenous way of life. In fact, the author restates how she refuses to abandon her struggle to reclaim and preserve her Innu identity. Kapesh has retained the knowledge that the old ways embody the "superiority" of Indigenous traditions, when "every Indian was his or her own government ... every father and mother were their children's teachers" (227).[48] Indigenous knowledge is particularly significant when taking into account how much so-called "civilized" non-Indigenous culture has marred Innu culture. Yet, as inferred by the Innu author, self-determination remains key to Indigenous cultural survival, as does advocacy for their right, as the Indigenous peoples of this land, to be here. Indeed, Indigenous testimonial life writing is an empowering response from communally lived experiences of space. Kapesh will no longer accept "the Native voice [being] stymied by the dominant society" (Ruffo 109). Life writing, therefore, enacts a strategy of survival by re-mapping the past in the present and in the future according to a territorial imperative. In this concluding chapter, Kapesh alludes to the feeling of imprisonment created by living continuously in one place: "as long as I live, I will never be able to escape this 'prison' where the White man has locked me in" (*JSMS* 223, 225).[49] This is not merely a lament for a lost way of life, the nomadic hunting culture displaced by settler society; it is also an expression of desire for a different way of knowing the land and being in the land – one not contained by borders and permits and deeds, nor by colonial representations of the land and the Innu. Kapesh draws attention as well to the damage colonizers have caused not only to Aboriginals but also to the land and its natural resources. Her way of

48 OFV: "chaque Indien était son propre gouvernement ... chaque père et chaque mère de famille agissaient comme professeurs pour tous leurs enfants."

49 OFV: "aussi longtemps que je vivrai, jamais je ne pourrai m'évader de l'enclos où le Blanc m'a enfermée."

delegitimizing the national and proprietary way of dividing up the land, relocating and containing Indigenous people on reserves, and exploiting the land is to tell the story of the Innu's subjective and objective relationship to their land. Furthermore, Kapesh's closing words evoke her resistance to being marginalized and misrecognized by claiming discursive space and territorial space over Whites: "And if the White man does not want to understand that he is the one who should be quiet, then he should go back to where he came from" (237).[50]

In *Je suis une maudite Sauvagesse*, Kapesh critiques and delegitimizes White-settler culture. She exposes the primary goal of non-Indigenous politicians, which involved colonizing and imposing dominant culture on Aboriginals in order to break down Aboriginal society and bury Aboriginal languages and customs through assimilation strategies. Kapesh also describes the symbolic and slow violence inflicted upon her people tagged as "savages" and placed into derogatory categories. The author thus provides a testimony that challenges and deconstructs defamatory stereotypes about Aboriginals by constructing their way of life from an Aboriginal perspective. In their resistance writing, Kapesh and other Indigenous activist-writers break down misconstrued stereotypes and misrepresentations about who they are and slowly rebuild their identities as a "decolonized" people (even though a number of Indigenous writers and critics claim that colonization has never stopped because neo-colonization continues to plague them). She employs repetition as a rhetorical tool of resistance to challenge, expose, and emphasize the lies uttered by non-Aboriginals: "As well as articulating a strong sense of personal and communal identity, many life narratives in the 1970s and 80s challenged white ignorance and apathy, revealing the hidden history of Native and Métis peoples" (Van Toorn 32). Following the oral tradition of her ancestors, Kapesh appropriates the power of the *word*, the oral tradition, and reappropriates the language of White-settler culture, *literature*. She combines these two traditions in such a way as to invoke the power of words to exorcise, heal, adapt, challenge, and, above all else, contest. For this all-important reason, *Je suis une maudite Sauvagesse* claims a contested space for remembering the past and for the collective Indigenous voice to be heard and read, a textual space for

50 OFV: "Et si le Blanc ne veut pas comprendre que c'est à lui de se tenir tranquille, c'est lui qui devrait retourner d'où il est venu."

Indigenous peoples to speak out and reclaim their space/place in Canadian society.

WORKS CITED

Acoose, Janice. "*Halfbreed*: A Revisiting of Maria Campbell's Text from an Indigenous Perspective." Armstrong, pp. 137–50.

Armstrong, Jeannette, editor. *Looking at the Words of Our People: First Nations Analysis of Literature.* Theytus, 1993.

Beverley, John. *Testimonio: On the Politics of Truth.* U of Minnesota P, 2004.

Boudreau, Diane. *Histoire de la littérature amérindienne au Québec: Oralité et écriture.* Hexagone, 1993.

Brown, James N., and Patricia M. Sant, editors. *Indigeneity: Construction and Re/Presentation.* Nova Science, 1999.

Damm, Kateri [Kateri Akiwenzie-Damm]. "Says Who: Colonialism, Identity and Defining Indigenous Literature." Armstrong, pp. 9–26.

Elabor-Idemudia, Patience. "The Retention of Knowledge of Folkways as a Basis for Resistance." *Indigenous Knowledges in Global Contexts: Multiple Readings of Our World,* edited by George J. Sefa Dei, Budd L. Hall, and Dorothy Goldin-Rosenberg, U of Toronto P, 2000, pp. 102–19.

George, Chief Dan. *My Heart Soars.* 1974. Hancock, 1996.

Kapesh, An Antane. *Eukuan nin matshimanitu innu-iskueu / Je suis une maudite Sauvagesse.* Translated by José Mailhot with Anne-Marie André and André Mailhot. Leméac, 1976.

King, Thomas. *The Inconvenient Indian: A Curious Account of Native People in North America.* Doubleday Canada, 2012.

Mailhot, José. *Au pays des Innus: Les gens de Sheshatshit.* Recherches amérindiennes au Québec, 1993.

– "L'écrit comme facteur d'épanouissement de la langue innue." *Recherches amérindiennes au Québec,* vol. 26, nos. 3–4, Winter 1996–7, pp. 21–7.

Mertus, Julie. "Truth in a Box: The Limits of Justice through Judicial Mechanisms." *The Politics of Memory: Truth, Healing and Social Justice,* edited by Ifi Amadiume and Abdullahi An-Na'im, Zed, 2000, pp. 142–61.

Nixon, Rob. *Slow Violence and the Environmentalism of the Poor.* Harvard UP, 2011.

Petrone, Penny. *Native Literature: From the Oral Tradition to the Present.* OUP, 1990.

Pugliese, Joseph. "Migrant Heritage in an Indigenous Context: For a Decolonising Migrant Historiography." *Journal of Intercultural Studies,* vol. 23, no. 1, 2002, pp. 5–18.

Roth, Robin. "The Challenges of Mapping Complex Indigenous Spatiality: From Abstract Space to Dwelling Space." *Cultural Geographies*, vol. 16, 2009, pp. 207–27.

Ruffo, Armand Garnet. "Why Native Literature?" *Native North America: Critical and Cultural Perspectives*, edited by Renée Hulan, ECW Press, 1999, pp. 109–21.

Samson, Colin, James Wilson, and Jonathan Mazower. *Canada's Tibet: The Killing of the Innu*. Survival, 1999.

Van Toorn, Penny. "Aboriginal Writing." *The Oxford Companion to Canadian Literature*, edited by Eva-Marie Kröller, Cambridge UP, 2004, pp. 22–48.

Vincent, Sylvie. "Terre québécoise, première nation et nation première: Notes sur le discours québécois francophone au cours de l'été 1990." *Discours et mythes de l'ethnicité*, edited by Nadia Khouri, ACFAS, 1992, pp. 215–31.

10 Norman Bethune and the Contested Spaces of Canadian Public Memory

CANDIDA RIFKIND

The Spanish Civil War, fought from 1936 to 1939, remains a touchstone for leftists everywhere as a moment when an anti-fascist victory seemed on the horizon and would herald new national and international formations of socialism. Almost 1,700 Canadians volunteered in Spain, the majority of whom fought with the International Brigades, eventually forming their own Mackenzie-Papineau Battalion (known as the Mac-Paps); 400 are presumed to have died on the battlefield. Despite Franco's victory over the Republican side, and the tainting of 1930s leftism more generally by the later revelations of Stalinism, the Spanish Civil War lingers in leftist cultural memory, and even appears in mainstream Canadian literature and culture, as an honourable, authentic, and worthy cause.[1] This is despite the Canadian government's official neutrality and the RCMP's attempts to arrest volunteers under the Foreign Enlistment Act, which forbids Canadians from joining overseas armies.[2] I am interested in how the anti-fascist struggles of the 1930s have been written into the field of Canadian literature but also in some more recent developments in Canadian print culture that have brought the memories of this and related 1930s overseas struggles back into prominence. These changing representations of Canadian leftists in the 1930s

1 For examples see Hugh Garner's *Cabbagetown* and Mordecai Richler's *Joshua Then and Now.*

2 See Victor Howard and Mac Reynolds's classic study, *The Mackenzie-Papineau Battalion.* Michael Petrou's *Renegades* is a more recent and complete history of Canadians who served in the International Brigades and elsewhere in Spain.

raise important questions about the contested spaces of commemoration and the politics of recovering a radical past to revise the national mythologies of the liberal capitalist state.

To focus my comments, and because we are now in another moment of the recovery and revision of Norman Bethune, I will explore the case of this Communist medical doctor who served in the Spanish Civil War and then died in 1939 fighting against the Japanese with Mao's troops in northern China. Since his rise to national prominence in the mid-1930s, Bethune has been a contested signifier and an unstable sign in both liberal and leftist Canadian culture. His significance remains an arena of struggle within both public and counter-public discourses in English Canada. This is due in large part to an active field of Bethune cultural production, spanning the last seventy-five years, that represents him variously as a selfless humanitarian, brilliant surgeon, committed Communist, and talented artist, but also as an arrogant renegade, egotistical doctor, relentless self-promoter, and reckless womanizer.[3] It is worth noting, moreover, that Bethune himself launched this minor industry in Canadian literature and culture. Not only did he circulate his own writing and art, but he also commissioned a documentary film about himself and the blood transfusion unit while serving in Spain in 1937. Called *Heart of Spain*, this documentary was screened to thousands of Canadian sympathizers later that year and accompanied Bethune on a national speaking tour.[4] Among his many other talents, Bethune was a powerful promoter of his causes but also of himself as a dynamic figure serving, in often prosaic and down-to-earth ways, the ideals of socialist international revolution. As Maurice McGregor (Bethune Exchange Professor at Peking Medical College in 1973) writes of his legacy, "most of all, Bethune had that critical heroic quality of a sense of drama" as he performed a "larger-than-life role" that swept away much of his audience (202). The transformation of the real man into a mythical character began with Bethune himself, then, and has continued since his untimely death in 1939, such that his name is relatively familiar in Canadian literature and culture. This accumulation of Bethune lore has yielded a figure best

3 I necessarily have to set aside Spanish and Chinese commemorations of Bethune in this chapter.

4 An article in the Communist newspaper *Daily Clarion* reports that *Heart of Spain* was seen by thousands in Vancouver at its premiere on 1 August 1937, and that it would accompany Bethune on his tour of Canada that autumn ("Dr. Bethune's Film").

defined by contradictions – most notably, between his aristocratic demeanour and love of the good life versus his revolutionary politics and pragmatic self-sacrifice – that contribute to his instability as a signifier. It has also generated a recent flurry of efforts to fix him as an icon in the service of contemporary state and institutional ideologies. Because this committed 1930s Communist fits uneasily within twentieth- and twenty-first-century mainstream neoliberal Canadian culture, he offers a keyhole perspective on the larger struggles for national self-representation between leftists and liberals, politicians and writers. As such, the many versions of Norman Bethune are a productive site through which to consider the work of public memorials and print culture in shaping public memory and counter-memory.

Norman Bethune's life story has been well documented on page, stage, and screen.[5] Briefly, he was born in northern Ontario in 1890 into a family with Scottish roots and long traditions of both medical service and Christian evangelism. Bethune went on to become a writer, painter, teacher, and medical doctor, a specialist in tuberculosis (with which he himself was infected) who pioneered public medicine in Montréal during the Depression and advocated the socialization of medicine across Canada. He was a renowned thoracic surgeon and invented instruments and procedures that are still referenced today. Increasingly concerned about the effect of poverty on health and the lack of government intervention during the Depression, Bethune travelled to the Soviet Union in

---

5 I explore some of the poems and novels about Bethune shortly, but it is worth noting the number of non-fictional versions of his life story. Some of the Bethune biographies in English are Ted Allan and Sydney Gordon's *The Scalpel, the Sword: The Story of Doctor Norman Bethune*; Wendell MacLeod, Libbie Campbell Park, and Stanley Ryerson's *Bethune: The Montréal Years*; Roderick Stewart's *Bethune* and *The Mind of Norman Bethune*; Wilson's *Norman Bethune: A Life of Passionate Conviction*; and the essays published in David A.E. Shephard and Andrée Lévesque's *Norman Bethune: His Times and His Legacy / Son époque et son message*. Biographies for young people include John Wilson's *Righting Wrongs: The Story of Norman Bethune* and Ann Corkett's *Norman Bethune: Doctor for the People*. There is also an ongoing visual record of Bethune, including the translation of a Chinese book titled in English as *Bethune: His Story in Pictures*. The 2008 to 2009 exhibit *Norman Bethune: Trail of Solidarity / La huella solidaria* at the McCord Museum of Canadian History in Montréal provided a photographic record of his time in Spain. Among English-language cinematic biographies, the best known are the NFB documentary *Bethune* directed by Donald Brittain and the feature film *Bethune: The Making of a Hero*, written by Ted Allan and starring Donald Sutherland and Helen Mirren.

1935 and came back impressed enough to join the Communist Party of Canada. In 1936, Bethune (along with public broadcasting pioneer Graham Spry) co-founded the Committee to Aid Spanish Democracy, a coalition of socialists, Communists, and progressive Christians to fund-raise for Spanish relief and educate Canadians about the distant struggle against Franco. Supported behind the scenes by the Communist Party of Canada, this committee raised the funds to send Bethune and others to offer help to the Republicans in Madrid in 1936. Before going, Bethune studied the latest developments in blood transfusion, which at that point was limited to hospitals far from the front, and so soldiers often arrived at medical stations too late to be saved. In Spain, Bethune and his Canadian and Spanish colleagues worked under the auspices of the Communist Party and in support of the International Brigades to develop a mobile blood transfusion unit, using ice to keep the donated blood cold on long and dangerous trips from hospitals to the front lines.

Before he left for Madrid, Bethune wrote his well-known poem "Red Moon" to compare peaceful Canada to war-torn Spain and vowed, in the final lines of the final version, "Comrades, who fought for freedom and the future world, / Who died for us, we will remember you" (103). In this expression of his desire to fight fascism overseas, Bethune imagines it as a memorial project to keep the spirit of the fallen comrades alive. He repeats, even if unwittingly, the rhetoric of First World War patriotic verse that promises, most famously in John McRae's "In Flanders Fields," to pass the torch from dead to living soldiers. As his poem illustrates, there is no mistaking the fact, however distasteful it may be to twenty-first-century leftist politics, that Bethune subscribed to a militaristic vision of overseas intervention as a necessary means to Communist revolution. He re-signifies the politics of First World War elegy when he substitutes the Communist collective for the Canadian one, but Bethune nevertheless uses his poem to mourn the war dead and vows to continue their battle with his characteristic zeal for action. According to an RCMP security bulletin of February 1937, Bethune lived up to his poetic promise in Madrid by managing to pull together an impressive medical unit with a staff of twenty-five specialists, nurses, technicians, and drivers to oversee all Spanish blood transfusion units and serve one hundred hospitals and front-line casualty units (Kealey and Whitaker 90).

Politically committed but personally volatile, Bethune only stayed in Spain for six months and, as access to the Comintern archives in Moscow reveals, left under a cloud of unfounded accusations by the Communist Party of immorality, theft, and spying. In his detailed discussion of

Bethune's time in Spain, Michael Petrou reproduces a 1937 party memo that itemizes the reasons Bethune was no longer welcome by the authorities in either a medical or a military capacity. These include "for being immoral" and too drunk to "lead a mission as delicate as blood transfusion"; for taking jewellery he claimed he would sell to raise funds but which then disappeared; for making a film about blood transfusion that he did not pass through the censors; and, most damning of all, for arousing suspicions that he was a fascist spy through his romantic connections to a mysterious Swedish woman who spent time with the blood transfusion unit (Petrou 164). As Petrou's research reveals, this woman was Kajsa Rothman, an attractive entertainer and dancer who volunteered as a reporter and nurse in Spain, and who was indeed Bethune's sexual partner. Petrou suggests that Rothman's confidence and independence challenged the gender norms of the time and place, and this may be one reason she came under suspicion (165). As numerous biographers note, however, the darkest accusation against Bethune was that he was observed on his blood delivery missions taking detailed notes about the state of roads and bridges and travel distance and times between specific points. Although Bethune was clearly trying to improve the speed and security of his mobile blood transfusion unit, party authorities interpreted his interest in road conditions as evidence he was a spy, an accusation Petrou dismisses as "implausible nonsense" (166) but which was powerful enough in a climate of heightened anti-spy and anti-foreigner suspicion to ensure that he was kept out of Spain by the party after April 1937. According to his most recent biographers, Bethune admitted to a friend that his unruly personal conduct was the reason for his recall (Stewart and Stewart 211). He then spent nearly a year on the Canadian lecture circuit fundraising and encouraging volunteers to go to Spain, but predictably the Communist press downplayed the real reasons for Bethune's departure from Madrid. On 26 July 1937, an article in the party's Toronto-based newspaper, *Daily Clarion*, boasted that $4,500 has been raised in western Canada by Bethune's lecture tour and that he read aloud on stage a grateful telegram from his Canadian colleagues in Madrid which concluded, "Salud to the Canadian people plus good luck to yourself" ("Canada" 1). Any rifts between Bethune and the Communist Party were quickly closed over in public upon his return and, indeed, kept secret until decades later.

Even while in Spain, Bethune had tried to bring the Japanese invasion of northern China to public attention, and it was not long before he volunteered to serve as a medical officer for the Chinese Communists fighting the Second Sino-Japanese War in Shaanxi Province. He died in China in November 1939, at the age of forty-nine, of blood poisoning due to a cut from a surgical procedure.[6] Bethune only met Mao Zedong once, but during the Cultural Revolution the Communist leader ensured that millions of Chinese people would commemorate Bethune by requiring children to memorize his essay, "In Memory of Norman Bethune." In this essay, Mao praises Bethune's embodiment of the Leninist principles of international solidarity among the proletariat and announces:

> I am deeply grieved over his death. Now we are all commemorating him, which shows how profoundly his spirit inspires everyone. We must all learn the spirit of absolute selflessness from him. With this spirit everyone can be very useful to the people. A man's ability may be great or small, but if he has this spirit, he is already noble-minded and pure, a man of moral integrity and above vulgar interests, a man who is of value to the people.

Mao's essay joined the official Chinese memorials to Bethune, for example, in statues and the naming of hospitals and schools, by adding the pedagogical and performative dimensions of mass memorization and recitation. Even if he were a state hero in Canada, official culture in this country reserves such collective public performances of nationalism for the commemoration of formative events rather than people (such as the Remembrance Day recitations of McRae's "In Flanders Fields" by children across the country). Following his trip to China in 1974, the doctor Maurice McGregor concluded that the Bethune legend "tells us more of modern China than of Bethune himself" (204); likewise, Bethune's less glorious memorialization in Canadian culture tells us a great deal about modern Canada and the Cold War effort to forget the influence of socialism and Communism on national politics and everyday life during the 1930s. Moreover, when Bethune's memory has been invoked by the Canadian government it has usually been for opportunistic reasons. In 1969, Prime Minister Pierre Trudeau sought to establish diplomatic relations with China, and so his ambassador in Stockholm screened the National Film Board of Canada film *Bethune* to Chinese diplomats. This

6 A sign of his international reputation at the time of his death is that the influential New York leftist magazine *New Masses* published pages from his diary posthumously in January 1940, explaining that they were setting the pages when news arrived of his death ("He Dies in China").

opened the door to the negotiations that led to the 1970 establishment of full diplomatic relations between Canada and China (Stewart and Stewart 373).

The Chinese government's commemoration of Bethune, particularly during the Cultural Revolution, has led to the often-repeated lament that this Canadian is better known in China than he is in Canada. There are three public memorials to Bethune in Canada that exemplify the complex position he holds in Canadian official memory, especially in the post–Cold War era. These memorials share an investment in constructing Bethune's life narrative as a public memory, but the specific interests they serve vary according to the sponsoring institutions. In his discussion of the differences between individual memory, collective memory, and public memory, Alan Gordon writes, "The events and individuals of public history often pass into lived experience by becoming an essential part of the public socialization of individuals as members of their society" (7). This public socialization is often manifested externally as monuments or public markers that perform the myth-history of the nation. Public monuments do the work of attaching individual members of the nation to its dominant myths and official history through the experiences of exemplary individuals. Similar to the traditional prose biography that narrates the life of the "great man" and makes claims to empirical knowledge of the subject, the public monument installs an official version of the individual's life story as the most authentic, verifiable, objective version. Public monuments are spaces of official memory that work to assert one version of the past, telescoped through an individual life, for use in the present.

Following Trudeau's use of *Bethune* to break the ice with Chinese diplomats, his government realized they needed to address the man's legacy at home. In 1972, the Historic Sites and Monuments Board of Canada recognized Norman Bethune as a figure of national importance, a decision that sparked some public debate (Stewart and Stewart 373). The announcement took place at what is now Bethune Memorial House National Historic Site of Canada. Located in what was the Bethune family home in the 1880s and 1890s, and where Bethune was born, this historical museum in Gravenhurst, Ontario, was acquired by Parks Canada in 1973. In 2013, they undertook extensive renovations to the visitor centre. The website invites visitors to "explore the restored 1890 birthplace and the new $2.5M Visitor Centre to uncover clues as to what led a small-town boy to become a renowned battle-front surgeon and how that story nurtured Canada's reputation as a society with a conscience" ("Bethune

Memorial House"). Even in this brief description, the myth-history of the liberal Canadian state is evident in the notion of a rural boy becoming famous for wartime heroism that repeats so many Canadian First World War narratives of individual and national coming-of-age. Indeed, the major exhibit for 2014 to 2015 marked the one hundredth anniversary of Bethune's enlistment in the Canadian Army Medical Corps and his service in the First World War. Deena Rymhs's discussion in this volume of Indigenous soldiers explains how the First World War inaugurated new understandings of masculinity and the mythos of White militarism. Her analysis of the racialized dynamic of this conflict is an important counterpoint to the dominant narratives of this war upheld at the Parks Canada site. The final part of the website statement ties Bethune to the myth-history of Canada as a "society with a conscience," which persists in contemporary discourses of Canada as a global human rights leader, despite domestic and international evidence to the contrary. The website also acknowledges that Bethune is better known in China: "Generations after his death, his story continues to be taught to millions of Chinese students" ("Bethune Memorial House"). Information at the website is posted in Chinese, tours are available to Chinese-speaking visitors, events at the site are trilingual, and guests may see many of the gifts donated to the site by Chinese visitors. Of the 15,000 annual visitors to the site, the majority are "mainland Chinese and recent immigrants" (Allemang).

At the same time that the Bethune Memorial House is a national memorial site that markets itself to Chinese tourists and Chinese Canadians familiar with the man's Communist allegiances, its public utterances perform a version of Bethune's life narrative that reconstructs his political commitments in the language of post–Cold War neoliberal capitalism. When the visitor centre reopened in 2013, the occasion was marked by the attendance of Tony Clement, Conservative Member of Parliament for the riding of Parry Sound–Muskoka and Treasury Board president. A *Globe and Mail* article notes the irony of this celebration of "an unlikely Conservative hero" but explains that Clement's support of the project derives from the "powerful bilateral connection" between Canada and China cemented by Prime Minister Stephen Harper's first trip to China in 2009 (Allemang). Clement's speech declared, "The thing about Dr. Bethune is that people see different things about him depending on their perspective ... I think we as Conservatives can be comfortable that there's a message here broader than just his communism, that goes to his humanism and entrepreneurship" (Allemang). In addition to recasting Bethune's invention of medical tools and development of blood transfusion procedures as "entrepreneurship," the Conservative government tapped into a post–Cold War phenomenon in China. According to experts quoted by John Allemang, Bethune's current popularity is part of a "Red nostalgia" for the early days of Communist Party leadership, and if this is useful for the current Chinese government then it is useful for the current Canadian government. This public memorial highlights how much global economic and political interests intersect with national ones when it comes to contemporary versions of myth-history. It externalizes Bethune's life narrative into a site of official memory that mines public memory in China to produce a useful public memory for Canada.[7]

A more recent public memorial to Norman Bethune is located at the University of Toronto Medical School. In 2014, on the seventy-fifth anniversary of his death, a statue of Norman Bethune by Toronto sculptor David Pelletier was erected on the grounds of the University of Toronto's Medical Sciences Building. Pelletier is better known for his Toronto ferry terminal sculpture of the late Jack Layton on the back seat of a tandem bicycle, which has been widely praised for humanizing the New Democratic Party of Canada leader. His sculpture of Bethune, who graduated from the university's medical school in 1916, likewise recasts a leftist icon as a personable individual. The sculpture is "part of the faculty's Bethune Legacy Celebration recognizing his international impact on health care and the university's associations with China" (Aschiek). The sculpture was funded by two Chinese businessmen and supported with the patronage of former governor general Adrienne Clarkson, whose biography of Bethune I discuss below. A slick forty-page program for the accompanying gala, *Boundless Inspiration: Celebrating the Legacy of Norman Bethune*, proclaims that "Norman Bethune is a potent symbol of the University of Toronto's historic ties with China." Testimonials from members of the Bethune family attest to their ongoing ties to China, and historical essays about Bethune conclude with information about other university medical staff with past or present ties to China. Bethune's service in the First World War and the Spanish Civil War is clearly less valuable to the

7 The Conservative Party's relationship to the history of Communism is further complicated by their proposal for a $5.5 million Memorial to the Victims of Communism to be erected near the Supreme Court in Ottawa. Both the idea and the design of the memorial have been met with opposition: a poll published on 25 May 2015 reports that only 23 per cent of Canadians support this memorial (Payne).

university's stated commitment to "intensifying its relationships with top research institutes in China" (24).

In a video of the making of the sculpture, bilingual (Chinese/English) subtitles explain how Pelletier's image of Bethune differs from "more strident" and heroic images of the man, implying that this Canadian memorial is distinct from the Communist Chinese ones in its emphasis on the subject's intellectual and inner life: "The life-sized, bronze seated sculpture of Bethune depicts him paused in a moment of contemplation, while writing in his journal during the Chinese campaign" (*Making*). The base of the sculpture quotes Bethune saying that he is most content when doing his work and feeling needed, and the film explains that the leafy green campus setting in which the sculpture has been placed evokes Bethune's pleasant student days between 1912 and 1916. It is worth noting that at least one biography describes Bethune's medical school days in a different light, as his studies were interrupted by military service from 1914 to 1915 and other students found him so odd that he "made no close friends" (Stewart and Stewart 28). Clearly, this is a Bethune memorial that constructs a public memory of its sponsoring institution as an idyllic training ground for humanitarian international medical work through an image of their infamous alumnus as likeable and introspective rather than arrogant and action-oriented. Both the Bethune Memorial House in Gravenhurst and the University of Toronto Medical School's Bethune sculpture manifest Brian S. Osborne's theory that Canada is "not a 'nation-state' or a 'state-nation,' but rather a 'nationalizing-state'" involved in ongoing projects of identity formation through arts and memorial heritage projects (149). Local memorial sites are "landmarks" or "*lieux de memoire*" in the senses proposed by Maurice Halbwachs and Pierre Nora respectively, but today they also have to accommodate the cultural hybridity produced by a diasporic population and "burgeoning transnationalist connections" (Osborne 149). These latter connections are at the forefront of these two official Bethune memorials that use his life story to produce an early figure of contemporary "civic cosmopolitanism," a moral consciousness attached to ideals of global community, that is the political rhetoric of neoliberal capitalism's trade agreements (166).

The third public memorial to Bethune I want to mention briefly is in Montréal, where he lived from 1928 to 1936 while working as a thoracic surgeon. This memorial differs from the previous two because it shows how official landmarks can become transformed into sites of counterpolitics. Place Norman Bethune (Norman Bethune Square) is a small triangular island in downtown Montréal. It is located at the intersection of Guy Street and De Maisonneuve Boulevard West, near Concordia University. In 1976, the City of Montréal named it Place Norman Bethune; in 1978, it installed a life-size, white stone sculpture of Bethune by Situ Jie that had been donated to the City of Montréal by the People's Republic of China ("Chronology"). This sculpture is a replica of the one in front of Norman Bethune International Peace Hospital in Shijiazhuang, China (Stewart and Stewart 374). The square fell into such disrepair that, by 2007, the urban affairs magazine *Spacing Montréal* described it as "ratty and weather-beaten," with the largest concentration of pigeons and their excrement in the city (DeWolf). This situation has since changed, however, thanks to a $3 million investment by the City of Montréal and Concordia University to restore the square as part of the 2008 "Homage to Bethune" seventieth anniversary events acknowledging Bethune's departure from Montréal to China. Before work started in 2005, the proposal for restoring Place Norman Bethune was part of the City of Montréal's Urban Development Mission to Shanghai led by Mayor Gérald Tremblay. As in Gravenhurst, the Montréal public memorial to Bethune depends upon official and unofficial Chinese support. However, in contrast to the Parks Canada site, there is relatively little didactic information and official discourse about Bethune in the park. Perhaps as a result of this diminished presence of official state history, and since its landscaping and the restoration of the sculpture in 2009, Place Norman Bethune has become a gathering place for political marches and protests, from Earth Day to May Day to anti-government rallies. In this sense, it has become a contested space of public memory rather than a commodified site of official history. Place Norman Bethune, unlike the Parks Canada site, socializes current individuals into a symbolic history of protest signified by the stone figure of Bethune in Maoist clothing. A humorous anecdote in the *Montréal Gazette* suggests that the local media recognize this confluence of past and present. During a 2012 protest in the square against the Canadian government's proposed Bill C-11, the Copyright Modernization Act, the statue's hand fell off when a protester used it to hang his placard. The protester was ticketed by police and informed that he would be billed by the City for the repair. The newspaper did not miss the opportunity to title the article "C-11 Protest Gets a Hand from Norman Bethune," ensuring that the current political uses of the public space are understood by readers to be in line with the past life it commemorates (Magder). Time will tell, but it seems that Place Norman Bethune has become the sort of "heterotopia of resistance" that Rita

Sakr writes about in her chapter on Rawi Hage's *Cockroach*. Much less a monumental space than one in which Montréalers meet to contest social and economic hierarchies, this memorial site to Bethune – perhaps because of its central urban location – has become the ground for new iterations of his radical politics.

Bethune's complex, contradictory personality and behaviour are obviously impossible to capture fully in any single sculpture. Likewise, biographical narratives at historical sites will inevitably privilege some events and subordinate others in the interests of coherent storytelling and nationalizing projects. What I find so fascinating about these Bethune memorials is not only that has his life narrative persisted into the present but that millions of dollars have been spent since the turn of the twenty-first century to insert Bethune into official memory through public spaces. Whether the product of a local tourism industry, a bilateral trade agreement, or urban renewal, these memorials to Bethune perform state, civic, and institutional utterances that repurpose a single life for collective politics. They reconstruct Bethune's life story, setting it figuratively and literally in stone, as a means for individual subjects of the state, city, or university to attach themselves to a larger ideology or objective. In some ways, the ideological drive of each of these public monuments is quite visible, especially when accompanied by heavy-handed marketing and public performances of the sponsoring institutions. The tradition of memorializing Norman Bethune in Canadian poetry and prose is no less ideological, but there are ways in which Canadian writers have had more freedom to play with the Bethune image and story.

Since his death, Canadian liberal and leftist writers have memorialized Bethune in a variety of ways that constitute a counter-public memory of him as a humanitarian and a doctor but also a Communist and a fighter. Here, I will focus on poetry and prose rather than on the numerous plays, operas, symphonies, and films that constitute a larger Bethune memorial performance culture.[8] The anthology *Sealed in Struggle: Canadian*

---

8 Of the English-language performances, the plays include Ken Mitchell's *Gone the Burning Sun* and Rod Langley's *Bethune: A Play*. In *Playwriting Women*, Cynthia Zimmerman mentions an unpublished play written and directed by Carol Bolt in 1976 titled "Norman Bethune: On Board the SS Empress of Asia," produced by the Muskoka Summer Theatre. I am grateful to Jody Mason for bringing this to my attention. Finally, composer Tim Brady's multimedia work for chamber orchestra, *Three Cities in the Life of Dr. Norman Bethune*, was performed in Montréal in 2003 and Toronto in 2005 and is available on CD.

Poetry and the Spanish Civil War, edited by Nicola Vulpe and Maha Albari, contains two sets of post-war elegies to heroic individuals. The first set of poems joins an international poetic chorus for the fallen Spanish poet and playwright Garcia Lorca, believed to have been killed by fascist forces at the beginning of the war; elegies to Lorca are an important tributary in the international flow of poems about Spain to which celebrated Canadian poets such as Dorothy Livesay, Louis Dudek, and George Woodcock contributed. A more Canadian contribution to the enormous international poetic output surrounding this conflict is the tradition of elegies to Bethune, which range from Raymond Souster's 1967 "The Good Doctor" to Robin Mathews's 1976 "Doctor Norman Bethune" to Milton Acorn's more irreverent 1977 "Drunk Thoughts of Bethune." However, an earlier sonnet by Acorn that was published before his first book, in a 1953 issue of the short-lived Canadian leftist magazine *New Frontiers*, takes the doctor more seriously and assumes the persona of one of Bethune's Chinese comrades. Titled simply "Norman Bethune, Died Nov. 13, 1939," the poem begins with the contradictory nature of Bethune's personality. The speaker describes himself as a child praying for Bethune's recovery, and the poem concludes with an image of Bethune's deathbed devotion to his cause as he exhorts his Chinese carer to keep working to "make improvements!" (40). Acorn's characteristic directness and abrupt ending of the poem are tempered by the deep sympathy, and even sentimentalism, of this elegy in sonnet form. This is a Bethune of "worn-out gentleness" (40), a paternal figure whose loss Acorn mourns much as Bethune himself grieved for fallen comrades on the Spanish battlefield in "Red Moon."

The apotheosis of this tradition of Bethune elegies, however, is Peter Stevens's 1974 collection *And the Dying Sky Like Blood: A Bethune Collage for Several Voices*. This collection combines poems with other texts, from newspaper clippings to telegrams, to produce a fragmented yet coherent long poem tracing Bethune's life in the context of national and global politics. It concludes with the announcement of his death on 12 November 1939 at 5:20 a.m., followed by short lines that lament the death of a man who "escaped many deaths" and yet who, despite his greatness, is memorialized by a "generation of indifference" with a "wreath of plastic flowers" (112). As these poems suggest, the late 1960s and 1970s marked a return to contemplations of Bethune. There is a solidarity expressed between the New and Old Lefts in these poems that lament their subject's passing but also the passing of an era in which the divides between right and wrong – schematized in the struggle between democracy and fascism – seemed much clearer than they did to the present generation. Stevens's closing lines both lament and chastise the forgetting of Bethune in the present, yet his final image of a "wreath of plastic flowers" points to the superficiality and artificiality of rituals of commemoration. As such, his collage insists that poetry, in particular the more radical experiments in the long poem that characterize his aesthetic moment in Canada, is a more authentic, complex form of commemoration than public rituals of wreath-laying.

In this and other ways there are elements in Stevens's collage of what Walter Benjamin calls "left-wing melancholy," an attitude of "left-wing radicalism … to which there is no longer, in general, any corresponding political action" (425); it takes concrete form in the text's moments of leftist hagiography. This is a Bethune who signifies a rugged Marxist masculinity of almost homoerotic proportions. In the poem "Blood Trip," one of Bethune's colleagues describes driving with him as they transport blood along a dangerous route outside of Madrid. The imagery is virile and primal, as the speaker imagines Bethune's blood, rage, and passion driving the truck forward and flowing through his own veins. The medical process of transfusion credited to Bethune becomes a metaphor for the transfer of political commitment from him to this doctor, who confesses that "his pulse converts me to a primitive/medicine man" (Stevens 82). While in these lines Bethune is a life force of elemental passions, later Stevens imagines him as a good shepherd for scared, war-torn people whom the speaker likens to a flock of miserable sheep (87).

The memory of Bethune as a Communist doctor who made enormous contributions in Spain and China, and as a nearly superhuman model of virile yet tender masculinity, was thus kept alive by male poets in the 1960s and 1970s. Even as these poems took shape within this era's formation of leftist nationalism in both federal politics and the field of English Canadian literature, changes in international politics lurked behind this flurry of Bethune elegies. The 1971 establishment of diplomatic relations between Canada and China that produced official recognition incited heated debate that once again highlights the contestation over Bethune as a signifier. According to Roderick Stewart, "for some, this belated tribute had been unpardonably delayed. For others, recognition of a Communist represented a shocking repudiation of traditional Canadian values. For still others, the question was not the fact of paying tribute to Bethune, but the motive" of increased trade with China (*Bethune* 167).

In the last decade, however, Bethune has emerged again in Canadian biography and fiction, but this revised figure is neither as hyper-masculine nor as politically dangerous; his commemoration seems to have sparked less controversy, but there is more to this than the cooling of heated debates with the passage of time. Instead, the signifier Norman Bethune has opened up to new sets of meanings shaped by changes in geopolitics, definitions of valuable citizenship, and understandings of the politics of memory. Bethune has been the subject of numerous prose biographies. The first was Ted Allan and Sydney Gordon's *The Scalpel, the Sword*,[9] published in 1952 and then in a revised edition in 1971 because of the authors' concerns that a flurry of books and films were misrepresentations. They call them "attempts to distort and falsify his image" (xiv) and imply the worst of these is the fictionalized Bethune in Hugh MacLennan's 1959 novel *The Watch that Ends the Night*, although MacLennan always denied that the character Jerome Martell is based on Bethune (xiv).[10] Another side of Bethune emerges in Larry Hannant's 1998 *The Politics of Passion: Norman Bethune's Writing and Art*, which gathers together all kinds of writing and art Bethune produced and which illustrates his energy and range of interests, from medical to aesthetic theory, poetry to painting. Perhaps the most comprehensive Bethune biography is Roderick Stewart and Sharon Stewart's *Phoenix: The Life of Norman Bethune*. Roderick Stewart is the author of multiple earlier biographies and has been researching Bethune for over forty years; however, this biography benefits from new research and unsealed archives as well as the co-authors' extensive travels and contacts with international Bethune scholars. It is a classic biography in that it covers the cradle-to-grave life story; draws extensively on archives, documentation, and interviews; and assumes an authoritative third-person narration with intimate knowledge of the subject's psychology. While the authors do not shy away from the difficult aspects of Bethune's personality – including his "rebellious nature and easily

9 Allan served with Bethune in Spain and would go on to fictionalize his experience in a novel, *This Time a Better Earth*, and in the screenplay for the Donald Sutherland film *Bethune*.

10 Allan and Gordon criticize MacLennan's novel, without naming it directly, because it presents Bethune as an "anti-Bethune" who is a "disillusioned idealist" and this is, to them, "not only a pitiful perversion of the truth – it is cynicism at its worst" (xiv). For a quite different reading of *The Watch that Ends the Night* which reads the portrayal of Bethune as MacLennan's "central indictment of conservative conformism in Canada, especially during the Cold War," see the dissertation by Zhongxiu He (89).

triggered temper" (12), as well as his alcohol abuse – they follow the convention in classic biography of establishing the childhood landscape as character-forming. The final paragraph of this thorough life narrative concludes that Bethune "remained quintessentially Canadian: his family roots, of which he was so proud, struck deep in the history of this country, and he was profoundly shaped by his love of the north woods and the rugged outdoor life he led as a young man" (Stewart and Stewart 378). This is a fine example of the tradition of Canadian "patriotic topography" that appeals to the northern Ontario landscape made famous by the Group of Seven painters and mythologized as the bedrock of a hardy, White, masculine Canadian identity (see Osborne 155). It is a common trope in Bethune biographies, and it works to reterritorialize his leftist internationalism through re-placing him in a mythologized nationalist landscape.

This trope also appears in the 2009 Bethune biography written by former governor general Adrienne Clarkson as part of Penguin Canada's Extraordinary Canadians series edited by her partner, John Ralston Saul.[11] While Clarkson's biography is neither as detailed nor as long as Stewart and Stewart's, her prominent public position means that her narrative reconstruction of Bethune's life extends into the official public life of the nation. Clarkson has long supported movements to recognize Bethune. She was the governor general who dedicated the monument to veterans of the Mackenzie-Papineau Battalion in Ottawa, funded by individual contributions rather than the government. She is also prominent in the publicity around the installation of Pelletier's sculpture at the University of Toronto Medical School. In her biography, Clarkson champions Bethune as an epic figure of the anti-fascist struggles of the 1930s but frames her advocacy for his public recognition in the contemporary discourse of global humanitarianism. Although she discusses his faults, failures, and frailties, Clarkson paints a portrait of an epic hero. These epic comparisons are both overt, for she likens Bethune to Ulysses in his

11 The Extraordinary Canadians series profiles twenty Canadians in biographies by eighteen writers (two of the biographies feature double subjects) and includes television documentaries to tie in to the books. In his introduction, Saul declares, "Each one of these people has changed you. In some cases you know this already. In others you will discover how through these portraits," and goes on to explain that "the authors I have chosen for each subject are not the obvious experts. They are imaginative, questioning minds from among our leading writers and activists. They have, each one of them, a powerful connection to their subject. And in their own lives, each is engaged in building what Canada is now becoming" (x–xi).

restlessness (*Norman Bethune* 4), and figurative, as she mythologizes his origins in the discourse of a topocentric nationalism that aligns the landscape with the character:

> Bethune lived his first few years in this southernmost part of the Canadian Shield ... You cannot see these rocks without wondering how they were formed, in what turbulence they were tossed in molten form until they oozed into place and hardened in the sinuous shapes found along the shores with water lapping implacably at their edges ... The Canadian Shield is the single greatest factor in creating the original wealth of our country ... Bethune, with his indomitable spirit, sprang right out of this granite, this hard land that made farming heartbreaking, virtually impossible. (24–5)

To bring Bethune back into public memory, Clarkson, like Stewart and Stewart, resorts to clichés that combine the spatial with the historical in an image of the hero as hardy survivor in an awe-inspiring and ancient sublime landscape.[12] Moreover, by rooting him firmly in Canadian soil, Clarkson repatriates the image of Bethune as individual national hero for Canadians rather than a collective national hero for the Chinese government.

As much as this biography picks up on the rugged masculinity of the earlier poems, Clarkson has the benefit of an accumulated set of texts on Bethune, from Communist biographies to literary fictions, to which she refers throughout, acknowledging from the outset that "everyone approaches Bethune with his or her own particular set of baggage" (14). Clarkson also corrects the most glaring gender gap in the predominantly

12 In her essay, "Notes from the Cultural Field," Barbara Godard works through the discourses of Canadian literature that have shaped it as an institution, using as her fulcrum Northrop Frye's famous 1965 question, "where is here?" One of the threads of Godard's argument is the topocentricism of Canadian literary criticism: Frye formulates his query about the very production of a national literature in spatial terms, a geographic investment that Godard contextualizes as a symptom of the Cold War period's "extreme anxiety over Canada's territorial boundaries." More recently, Godard observes, the dominance of spatial thinking in Canadian criticism has shifted such that "topocentricism remains an ordering figure but now 'Land [is] Sliding' when read as a trope operative in relations of power rather than as a static given available for naming and possessing" (249). My reading of Clarkson is that she resorts in this passage to the older form of topocentricism Godard diagnoses as a function of Cold War politics.

masculine tradition of Bethune stories by recognizing the role in his Chinese work played by a Canadian nurse, Jean Ewen, who had already spent five years working in China and who was both a medical colleague and interpreter upon whom Bethune depended. Ewen accompanied him on the first leg of his journey towards Shaanxi, until their professional relationship fell apart when she refused the traditional role he insisted upon of the nurse as handmaiden to the doctor. Clarkson notes that Ewen was present at the famous meeting between Bethune and Mao, and quotes generously from her account, but Clarkson does not comment on the fact that Ewen was literally left out of the picture, merely describing it as "one of the most famous propaganda posters of all time, showing Chairman Mao and Norman Bethune sitting at a table together" (167). Forty years after the meeting, Ewen wrote her own book, *China Nurse: 1932–39*. Clarkson is the first Bethune biographer I know of to quote from Ewen's version of life with Bethune, which was characterized by professional and ideological disagreements. By including Ewen's autobiography in her biography, Clarkson offers a fresh perspective on Bethune's experiences in China that also highlights how difficult it was for others to assist him in his medical missions, particularly female nurses who did not share his complete commitment to Marxism and the Communist Parties of both Canada and China.

On 24 April 2009, Clarkson reprinted part of her biography in a *Globe and Mail* article that calls for Bethune to be commemorated by the City of Toronto, as he has been at Gravenhurst and in Montréal ("Remember"). Even more disappointing to her, though, is the dedication of monuments, streets, and schools to him in China and Spain rather than in Canada. Clarkson repeats the complaint, uttered by Canadian Bethune supporters since at least the 1970s, that he is a hero in China who is largely unrecognized in his birth country. This lament overlooks official and institutional memorials to Bethune in Canada, including Bethune College at York University and Dr Norman Bethune Collegiate Institute in Scarborough, Ontario, as well as the 1990 commemorative stamps issued by Canada Post. Moreover, this refrain depends upon a mythology, perhaps even a stereotype, that all Chinese people know the story of Norman Bethune because Mao required schoolchildren to memorize his elegiac essay during the Cultural Revolution. Some of the 2009 web postings in response to Clarkson's article refute this stereotype, even suggesting that the era in which Bethune was a household name has passed and that many young people in China today, especially those under thirty, are as unfamiliar with him as are their Canadian counterparts. While

I have neither the space nor the expertise to pursue the complicated position Bethune now holds in official and unofficial Chinese culture, and the more recent emergence of "Red nostalgia" I alluded to earlier, I do want to flag the need to interrogate the persistence of this Canadian mythology about the official Chinese memorialization of Bethune which overlooks major generational and political shifts.[13] Just as the early 1970s witnessed an increased interest in Bethune due to the easing of Chinese-Canadian relations, so too has the twenty-first century produced ongoing transformations in post–Cold War geopolitics that suggest the waning of hard-line Communism in China has reshaped public memory in Canada. China's economic and political repositioning in relation to North America allows Bethune's 1930s and Cold War status as a Communist icon to be replaced by a new set of signs attached to his name, as we see in the public memorials. While she does not ignore his Communist affiliations, and indeed acknowledges that is largely why he has not received due recognition, Clarkson downplays Bethune's revolutionary ideology as an ancillary rather than core feature of his medical practice, constructing his political commitment as a peripheral dimension of the person rather than the organizing drive.[14]

Nowhere is this clearer than in John Ralston Saul's introduction to the biography: "Bethune carried an idea of the public good that cannot be

13 While Mao's essay is no longer memorized in schools, Bethune continues to be commemorated officially (on commemorative stamps, badges, medals, and coins, such as the ten yuan coin of 1998) and in popular culture (China Central Television's 2006 twenty-part miniseries, *Dr. Norman Bethune*, was the most expensive Chinese television series ever made). I am grateful to Helen Wang, curator of East Asian money at the British Museum, and Tina Chen, associate professor in the Department of History at the University of Manitoba, for this information. Chen also observes that Bethune has been mobilized by the Chinese state as part of the current remaking of Maoist culture, some of which taps into the nostalgia of an older generation and some of which is an attempt to provide heroes of the past who can be relevant to the future.

14 One of the more salacious aspects of Clarkson's biography is confirmation of the reciprocated romantic love between Bethune and Marion Scott, wife of poet and CCF (Co-operative Commonwealth Federation) activist F.R. Scott, and an important painter and contributor to Canadian modernist culture in her own right. Clarkson quotes from letters between them that eventually reveal a mutual renunciation of their love and the thwarting of any full-blown love affair (*Norman Bethune* 110). However, this biographical element has appeared in print before; Hannant's 1998 collection of Bethune's writing includes some of his love poems to Scott (nicknamed "Pony"). The Bethune-Scott relationship may also inform MacLennan's fictionalized Bethune in *The Watch that Ends the Night*.

limited to any particular movement or country. His life represents an unrelenting personal commitment to individual people in a way that gives meaning to internationalism" (xiii). Saul writes out Bethune's commitment to collective politics and to military intervention overseas, perhaps because the latter is now largely the cause of the political Right. In so doing, he liquidates Bethune's 1930s leftist commitments, some of which are at odds with contemporary liberal and leftist politics. Consequently, Saul hegemonizes the sign of Bethune in the service of the universal rather than the particular in order to re-signify 1930s militarized internationalism for twenty-first-century global humanitarianism. Yet another political transformation since Bethune's day has taken place at the national level through the legislation of multiculturalism and the construction of a national mythology of ethnic and racial inclusiveness performed at the highest level of office by the appointment of two governors general in a row who were non-White female refugees and immigrants to Canada. As the first of these appointments, Clarkson circulated widely her life story as a Chinese Canadian that begins in Hong Kong, with an early memory of hiding in the basement from the invading Japanese. Her public biography thus places her in geographical proximity to her subject, Bethune, authorizing both her knowledge and advocacy of his commemoration through a personal connection that is just as powerful as her political and cultural position.[15] Clarkson herself is a sign of the national mythology of Canada as a haven for refugees, a leader in international human rights, and a tolerant diversity of peoples and ideas. In his review of the Extraordinary Canadians series, Philip Marchand critiques Saul's choice of biographical subjects as part of an editorial campaign to shape Canadian history according to a liberal Protestant tradition of social reform and moral uplift; even Bethune the Communist, he notes, continued the Canadian Protestant interest in overseas work by becoming "the ultimate Chinese missionary" (Marchand).

15 Clarkson also has a long connection to the Canadian volunteers in Spain: when, as governor general in 2001, she unveiled the Mackenzie-Papineau Battalion Monument in Ottawa, she said that she first met some of the Brigadistas thirty years earlier and that ten years ago she had spent time with "the American nurse who helped Bethune with these transfusions [in Spain]. And her witness to history and to him stays with her." Her official speech on this occasion anticipates her more recent activities, as Clarkson points out that in 1996 the Spanish government "invited the surviving members [of the Mac-Paps] back to Spain, and honoured these Canadians with Spanish citizenship" (see Clarkson, "Speech").

Marchand points out that the selection of subjects for this series, those whom Saul identifies as the builders of today's Canada, either hinges on the individuals' actual Protestant pedigrees or on the biographers' beliefs "that the lives of their subjects were indeed successes, and they were successes in part because they became part of a progressive historical movement" understood as a form of liberal Christianity. Marchand's critique of the series in general is that it selects subjects whose lives fit with a model of nation-building as the project of progressive reformers, rather than acknowledging that the national history is also full of "Disappointed Extraordinary Canadians" – from Catholics to Theosophists to pessimists – whose religions, outlooks, and actions were against the grain of Anglophone Protestant Canada and its broader culture of individual and collective improvement.

Saul and Clarkson, then, write a narrative of Bethune embedded within a larger narrative of Canada as a nation built by self-reliant reformers of moderate Christian faith. They also re-signify Bethune in ways that register the changes in geopolitics and national politics since the earlier 1970s moment of his recovery. In his useful study of how official French culture has remembered the French Resistance, Nathan Bracher indicates how de Gaulle's epic narrative of the Resistance "transforms history into metaphysics" across two lines: "diachronically, the present is put in linear continuity with a glorious past from which it proceeds, while, synchronically, various constituencies of the nation are united under one banner" (48). Although de Gaulle's narrative of the Resistance, which became hegemonic, and Clarkson's narrative of Bethune, which seems on its way to hegemony, are clearly quite different, and the French Resistance was incorporated into post-war French national ideology while the Mac-Paps were largely written out of Canadian national memory, Bracher's reminder of the double axis of memorialization has an important bearing on this case study: Clarkson and Saul's project is a temporal and spatial one that seeks a return to the past in order to remember the space of the nation differently. It functions both diachronically, rewriting a historical moment of dissent to place it in linear continuity with the present moment's preoccupation with human rights and civic cosmopolitanism, and synchronically, using Bethune as a sign to unite the nation through the mythology of Canadian self-sacrifice overseas in struggles against tyranny. It is also worth noting that Clarkson's accumulation of social, cultural, and financial capital allowed her to promote the book in a variety of media so that it became, in the months following its release, the most widely publicized biography in the Extraordinary Canadians series.[16] Clarkson's media appearances in support of her book were as much a product of her own prominence as of any public interest in her subject. Indeed, the epilogue to her volume highlights her privileged biographical perspective by describing the important moments in her own recent biography connected to Bethune: her 2007 visit to Yan'an where she visited the simple room where Bethune and Mao famously met in April 1938, and her unveiling of the Mac-Paps monument in Ottawa in October 2001. The distinction she hopes to win for Bethune in Canadian public culture will be due, in no small part, to Clarkson's own position as a powerful Canadian and a potent symbol of liberal international humanitarianism, combined with her privilege in undertaking an ongoing recovery of Bethune into this ideology and practice.

My final example is a return to literature through a novel that, unlike MacLennan's, explicitly declares it is an imaginative reconstruction of Bethune. Dennis Bock's 2006 novel, *The Communist's Daughter*, is a fictionalized set of letters sent by Bethune to an imaginary daughter during his last days in China. In these letters, Bethune alternates between memories of his earlier life in Canada and Spain (where he met this daughter's mother, who is a fictionalization of the mysterious Swede, Kajsa Rothman) and documentary accounts of his present moment working in China. These are intimate letters in a confessional mode, through which Bock constructs the private life of a Bethune plagued by regrets and remorse, yet convinced of his special talents and driven by political commitment to serve the proletariat and fight fascism. The narrator's obsession with memory and setting the record straight for the next generation is thematized throughout as Bethune often blurs the past and present. For example, after performing a double amputation on a Chinese boy who stepped on a mine, Bethune recalls in a letter, "Today I considered what an obscenely apt metaphor a minefield is, and by that I mean its ability to surge up from the unknown, to grab hold and twist.

16 In addition to joining other biographers in this series on stage with Saul at several events in Ottawa and Montréal in April 2009, Clarkson spoke about Norman Bethune at Concordia University in Montréal on 15 April 2009, in conjunction with the City of Montréal and the Chinese consulate, and was interviewed on CBC Radio's *Q* on 18 May (Victoria Day) 2009.

Isn't this so much the case of our past, our hidden lives? Well, not always hidden, sometimes simply discarded or forgotten ... An honest man has no discarded memories, nothing worth dredging up" (63–4). This is a Bethune at his most paradoxically self-aware and self-delusional, affirming the strength of his ego by rejecting the very idea of a subconscious through which might break repressed memories of the past; heroism exists, in this statement, as a self-confrontation typical of Bethune's ideal of the fighting man of action. That this minefield metaphor leads Bethune, in the next section, to contemplate "a number of failures in my life. By which I mean my own failures that have affected people I've known" (64), suggests that Bock's choice of an epistolary first-person narrative has the benefit of allowing the character's personal reflections to take shape in a relational form. Although we only have his set of letters, rather than the more traditional exchange of letters of classic epistolary novels, the very idea of a set of confessional epistles that failed to reach their intended recipient thematizes the novel's concern with Bethune as a tragic figure, not of misdirected politics but of failed intimacies and blocked communications that can only be recognized as such once the possibility for their recovery is acknowledged as impossible. As reviewer Doug Brown notes, "opting for a quieter, less spectacular approach to Bethune's story means perhaps that the integrity and thoroughness of Bock's treatment becomes evident more gradually than would be the case had *The Communist's Daughter* been written as an epic historical novel" (5).

This novel's interest in the trials and tricks of memory itself is in part a refusal of the epic historical novel as a literary form that labours to fix the signs of the past, and this is most evident in its framing device. The letters are contained in envelopes rather than chapters because they are a set of papers found after Bethune's death that were presented, in 1939, to the Propaganda Department of the Central Committee of the Chinese Communist Party. The book opens and closes with correspondence from this committee, which concludes that the content of the envelopes is unsuitable for propaganda purposes because its personal nature undermines "Doctor Bethune's value as a symbol of the rightness of this struggle."[17] The committee concludes that these papers should be sealed because "only with significant editing and rewriting will

17 The letter from the committee is not paginated.

the Bethune memoir be suitable for translation and printing for wide-scale distribution"; therefore, "given the revolutionary and international importance of Doctor Bethune's life, a brief, more idealized biography or political eulogy" should be written to promote the present war effort. Bock thus concludes his novel by opposing the personal letters of Bethune to his public image and suggesting that Chairman Mao's essay on Bethune writes over a sealed archive of the man's true personality, feelings, and political commitments to which the public does not have access.

In this way, Bock fictionalizes the politics of public memory and illustrates that the archive is as much an institution of forgetting as remembering. As Jacques Derrida argues in *Archive Fever*, the "archiviolithic force [the drive to archive] leaves nothing of its own behind" (11), no trace of what it has erased, of the contestations over its formation. Bock's novel is self-conscious about the archiviolithic forces that circle around Bethune and uses its narrative structure to fantasize about the possibility of unsealing the archive of the private life of the man. But, of course, there is another Derridean dimension to this narrative structure that hinges on ideas of letters and their destinations. In his reading of Edgar Allan Poe's "The Purloined Letter," which he describes as a story "of a letter, of the theft and displacement of a signifier" ("Purveyor" 179), Derrida proposes that the send-and-receive circuit of the letter is always incomplete: "Not that the letter never arrives at its destination, but that it belongs to the structure of the letter to be capable, always, of not arriving" (187). As such, "a letter does *not always* arrive at its destination, and from the moment that this possibility belongs to its structure one can say that it never truly arrives, that when it does arrive its capacity not to arrive torments it with an internal drifting" (201). Jacques Lacan, in contrast, argues that the letter always arrives at its destination because the destination is wherever the letter arrives. He writes of Poe's characters as subjects whose roles are governed by their relationship to the letter as signifier: "Should they pass beneath its shadow, they become its reflection. Falling in possession of the letter – admirable ambiguity of language – its meaning possesses them" (44). *The Communist's Daughter* mediates between these two interpretations of the materiality of the signifier in the sense that both can be true: in this fiction, Bethune's letters did not reach their intended destination of his daughter, yet their penultimate destination before a Communist Party Committee lead to their ultimate destination in the archives and their unsealing for readers that is the conceit of the novel. The letters arrive before us, the readers, haunted by their capacity to never arrive at their destination, just as we become the proper place for the letters to land. Bock writes a version of Bethune into which he builds the dual individual and collective processes of fixing and revising memory on the one hand and sealing and unsealing the archive on the other.

As this avowedly limited survey of some of the memorial sites and print culture versions of Norman Bethune illustrates, what Bethune demands of us today is an analysis of the politics of public and counterpublic memory in Canada. His recent entry into public discourse creates an urgency for a critical analysis of why him, why now, and why in this way? To conclude, I will suggest one way to begin answering these questions, by sketching how Alison Landsberg's notion of "prosthetic memory" offers a framework through which to interpret the afterlives of Bethune. Landsberg defines "prosthetic memory" as a personal and deeply felt memory of a historical event experienced by someone who did not live through it and which shapes their subjectivity and politics. These prosthetic memories are a phenomenon of the contemporary era because, unlike the earlier transmission of memories through specific groups as part of their identity formation, prosthetic memories are transmitted by the commodified mass media so that no particular individual or group can lay a biological or natural claim to them (18). This memory is prosthetic, then, because the memory "originates outside a person's lived experience and yet [is] taken on and worn by that person" so that they emerge at the interface between individual and collective experience (19). Prosthetic memories "are privately felt public memories that develop after an encounter with a mass cultural representation of that past" (19). As Bock highlights and Clarkson asserts, there is no unmediated memory of Norman Bethune and, while I have focused on print culture, there is also a rich visual and performance culture of Bethune available in photographs, posters, and films (documentary as well as fictional) that contribute to his iconization. As much as Bethune is a contested sign, he is also a prosthetic memory for those today who remember him through the circulation of commodified images and connect that memory to themselves in a way that makes them feel part of a larger past, whether leftist or liberal, national or international. By paying attention to the print cultural production of Bethune, I hope to have shown not simply the form this prosthesis takes but also how it transforms the individual and collective bodies to which it is attached.

WORKS CITED

Acorn, Milton. "Drunk Thoughts of Bethune." 1977. Vulpe and Albari, p. 204.

– "Norman Bethune, Died Nov. 13, 1939." *New Frontiers*, Fall 1953, p. 40.

Allan, Ted. *This Time a Better Earth*. Heinemann, 1939.

Allan, Ted, and Sydney Gordon. *The Scalpel, the Sword: The Story of Doctor Norman Bethune*. 1952. McClelland and Stewart, 1974.

Allemang, John. "Tories Tweak Bethune Brand to Build Bridges with China." *Globe and Mail*, 11 July 2012. www.theglobeandmail.com/news/national/tories-tweak-bethune-brand-to-build-bridges-with-china/article4404789/. Accessed 12 May 2015.

Aschiek, Sharon. "New Sculpture Honours Norman Bethune's Legacy." *U of T Magazine*, Summer 2014. https://magazine.utoronto.ca/campus/history/new-sculpture-honours-norman-bethune%E2%80%99s-legacy-david-pelletier-sharon-aschaiek/.

Benjamin, Walter. "Left-Wing Melancholy." *Selected Writings Vol. 2, Part 2, 1931–34*, edited by Michael W. Jennings, Howard Eiland, and Gary Smith, Belknap, 1999, 423–7.

Bethune. Directed by Donald Brittain, National Film Board of Canada, 1964.

Bethune: His Story in Pictures. NC Press, 1975.

"Bethune Memorial House National Historic Site of Canada." *Parks Canada*, 29 Aug. 2012. www.pc.gc.ca/en/lhn-nhs/on/Bethune. Accessed 12 May 2015.

Bethune, Norman. "Red Moon." Vulpe and Albari, p. 103.

Borsos, Phillip, Ted Allan, Nicolas Clermont, Pieter Kroonenburg, Donald Sutherland, Helen Mirren, and Helen Shaver. *Bethune: The Making of a Hero*. Filmline International, 1990.

Bock, Dennis. *The Communist's Daughter*. HarperCollins, 2006.

Boundless Inspiration: Celebrating the Legacy of Norman Bethune. University of Toronto Faculty of Medicine, 2014. medicine.utoronto.ca/sites/default/files/Med_Bethune_Commemorative%20Brochure_May%2014%2C%202014_ENG_FINAL.pdf. Accessed 15 May 2015.

Bracher, Nathan. "Remembering the French Resistance: Ethics and Poetics of the Epic." *History and Memory*, vol. 19, no. 1, Spring 2007, pp. 39–68.

Brady, Tim. *Three Cities in the Life of Dr. Norman Bethune*. Ambiances magnétiques, 2005. CD.

Brown, Doug. "Cross-Sectioning Norman Bethune." Rev. of *The Communist's Daughter*, by Dennis Bock. *Books in Canada*, Nov. 2006, p. 5.

"Canada Rallies to Dr. Bethune." *Daily Clarion*, 26 July 1937, p. 1.

"Chronology of Place Norman Bethune and Sculpture." *Concordia University*. Media Relations, n.d. Accessed 12 May 2015.

Clarkson, Adrienne. *Norman Bethune*. Penguin, 2009. Extraordinary Canadians.
– "Remember Bethune? Apparently Not; He's Celebrated in China, Spain and Montréal. But Toronto—Forget It." *Globe and Mail*, 24 Apr. 2009, p. A15. www.theglobeandmail.com/opinion/remember-bethune-apparently-not/article785138/. Accessed 29 May 2009.
– "Speech on the Occasion of the Unveiling of the Mackenzie-Papineau Battalion Monument." *Working TV*, Canadian Union of Public Employees, BC Division, 20 Oct. 2001. archive.gg.ca/media/doc.asp?lang=e&DocID=1331. Accessed 25 Apr. 2009.
Corkett, Ann. *Norman Bethune: Doctor for the People*. G. Stevens Children's Books, 1990.
Derrida, Jacques. *Archive Fever: A Freudian Impression*. U of Chicago P, 1996.
– "The Purveyor of Truth." Translated by Alan Bass. Muller and Richardson, pp. 173–212.
DeWolf, Christopher. "Norman Bethune Square." *Spacing Montréal*, 15 Sept. 2007. spacing.ca/montreal/2007/09/15/norman-bethune-square/. Accessed 9 May 2015.
"Dr. Bethune's Film Has Coast Premiere." *Daily Clarion*, 10 Aug. 1937, p. 3.
Ewen, Jean. *China Nurse: 1932–39*. McClelland and Stewart, 1981.
Garner, Hugh. *Cabbagetown*. 1950. McGraw-Hill, 2002.
Godard, Barbara. "Notes from the Cultural Field: Canadian Literature from Identity to Commodity." 2000. *Canadian Literature at the Crossroads of Language and Culture*, edited by Smaro Kamboureli, NeWest, 2008, pp. 235–72.
Gordon, Alan. *Making Public Pasts: The Contested Terrain of Montréal's Public Memories, 1891–1930*. McGill-Queen's UP, 2001. ProQuest ebrary. www.jstor.org/stable/j.ctt7zzz3. Accessed 15 May 2015.
Halbwachs, Maurice. *On Collective Memory*. Edited and translated by Lewis A. Coser, U of Chicago P, 1992.
Hannant, Larry. *The Politics of Passion: Norman Bethune's Writing and Art*. U of Toronto P, 1998.
Heart of Spain. Directed by Herbert Kline, Frontier Films, 1937.
"He Dies in China." *New Masses*, 9 Jan. 1940, p. 19.
He, Zhongxiu. "The Prismatic Reality of Canada's Cold War Novels." Simon Fraser U, 2007. PhD dissertation.
Howard, Victor, and Mac Reynolds. *The Mackenzie-Papineau Battalion: The Canadian Contingent in the Spanish Civil War*. Carleton UP, 1986.
Kealey, Gregory S., and Reg Whitaker, editors. *R.C.M.P. Security Bulletins: The Depression Years, Part IV, 1937*. Canadian Committee on Labour History, 1997.

Lacan, Jacques. "Seminar on 'The Purloined Letter.'" Translated by Jeffrey Mehlman. Muller and Richardson, pp. 28–54.

Landsberg, Alison. *Prosthetic Memory: The Transformation of American Remembrance in the Age of Mass Culture*. Columbia UP, 2004.

Langley, Rod. *Bethune: A Play*. Talonbooks, 1975.

MacLennan, Hugh. *The Watch That Ends the Night*. 1959. McGill-Queen's UP, 2009.

MacLeod, Wendell, Libbie Campbell Park, and Stanley Ryerson. *Bethune: The Montréal Years*. Lorimer, 1978.

Magder, Jason. "C-11 Protest Gets a Hand from Norman Bethune." *Montréal Gazette*, 10 Feb. 2012. montrealgazette.com/technology/c-11-protest-gets-a-hand-from-normand-bethune. Accessed 15 May 2015.

Making of the Portrait Sculpture of Norman Bethune. Directed by Robert Adam King, *YouTube*, University of Toronto, 2014. www.youtube.com/watch?v=8u7jXf_DKzU. Accessed 15 May 2015.

Mao Zedong. "In Memory of Norman Bethune." 1939. *Selected Works of Mao Zedong*, Marxists.org, 2004. www.marxists.org/reference/archive/mao/selected-works/volume-2/mswv2_25.htm. Accessed 25 Apr. 2009.

Marchand, Philip. Rev. of "Extraordinary Canadians." *Walrus*, Apr. 2009. thewalrus.ca/2009-04-books/. Accessed 5 July 2009.

Mathews, Robin. "Doctor Norman Bethune." Vulpe and Albari, pp. 197–203.

McGregor, Maurice. "The Bethune Legend: Norman Bethune as Hero." Shephard and Lévesque, pp. 201–5.

Mitchell, Ken. *Gone the Burning Sun*. Playwrights, 1984.

Muller, John P., and William J. Richardson, editors. *The Purloined Poe: Lacan, Derrida, and Psychoanalytic Reading*. Johns Hopkins UP, 1988.

Nora, Pierre. *Les Lieux De Mémoire*. Éditions Gallimard, 1997.

Osborne, Brian S. "From Native Pines to Diasporic Geese: Placing Culture, Setting Our Sites, Locating Identity in a Transnational Canada." *Canadian Journal of Communication*, vol. 31, no. 1, 2006, pp. 147–75. www.cjc-online.ca/index.php/journal/article/view/1781/1905. Accessed 16 May 2015.

Payne, Elizabeth. "Most Canadians Oppose Communism Victims Memorial: Poll." *Ottawa Citizen*, 25 May 2015. ottawacitizen.com/news/local-news/most-canadians-oppose-communism-victims-memorial-poll. Accessed 25 May 2015.

Petrou, Michael. *Renegades: Canadians in the Spanish Civil War*. U of British Columbia P, 2008.

Richler, Mordecai. *Joshua Then and Now*. McClelland and Stewart, 1980.

Saul, John Ralston. Introduction. *Norman Bethune*, by Adrienne Clarkson. Penguin, 2009. Extraordinary Canadians, ix–xi.

Shephard, David A.E., and Andrée Lévesque, editors. *Norman Bethune: His Times and His Legacy / Son époque et son message.* Canadian Public Health Agency, 1982.

Souster, Raymond. "The Good Doctor." 1967. Vulpe and Albari, pp. 182–3.

Stevens, Peter. *And the Dying Sky Like Blood: A Bethune Collage for Several Voices.* Borealis, 1974.

Stewart, Roderick. *Bethune.* Paperjacks, 1973.

– *The Mind of Norman Bethune.* Fitzhenry and Whiteside, 1977.

Stewart, Roderick, and Sharon Stewart. *Phoenix: The Life of Norman Bethune.* McGill-Queen's UP, 2011.

Vulpe, Nicola, and Maha Albari, editors. *Sealed in Struggle: Canadian Poetry and the Spanish Civil War: An Anthology.* Center for Canadian Studies, Universidad de la Laguna, 1995.

Wilson, John. *Norman Bethune: A Life of Passionate Conviction.* XYZ, 1999.

– *Righting Wrongs: The Story of Norman Bethune.* Illustrated by Liz Milkau. Napoleon, 2001.

Zimmerman, Cynthia. *Playwriting Women: Female Voices in English Canada.* Simon and Pierre, 1994.

PART III

Culture from Below

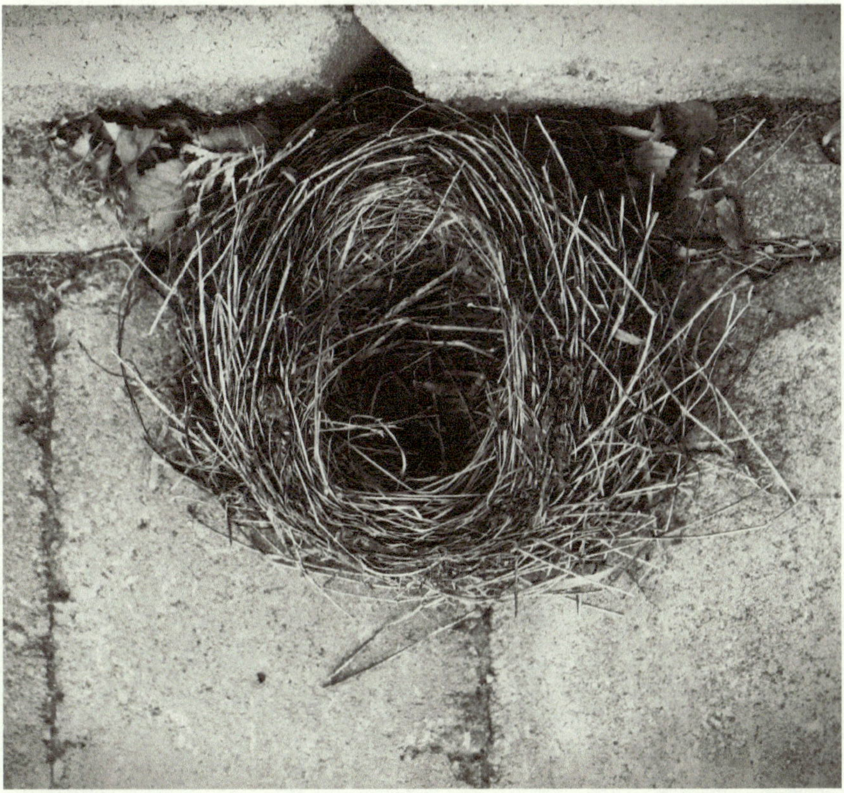

Urban bird nest, anonymous.

11 Knowing the Urban Other: Notes on the Ethics and Epistemology of Slumming in Novels and Reportage

ROXANNE RIMSTEAD

As a means of protest against Toronto's campaign to promote itself as a "world-class city" in 2005 (in conjunction with the world premiere of the film *Lord of the Rings*), a tenants' association took tourists and members of the media on a Lord-of-the-Slums bus tour to expose "world-class slums." In so doing, they appropriated the conventional performance of urban spectatorship begun in Victorian times, known as "slumming," and turned it into an indictment against all levels of government and uncaring slum landlords who draw profits from the neglect of these neighbourhoods. For a number of years, they continued to publicize the winner of the "Golden Cockroach Award" for the worst of the slum landlords and the "Golden Weasel Award" for the most unresponsive public officers (Parkdale, "Golden Cockroach"). In 2007, their interactive website (www.torontoslumtourism.com) declared itself the "official" site for slum tourism and, in addition to the bus tour, announced "Parkdale adventure getaway tours" for $900 a month, featuring "rat hunting in your own apartment, the Broken Elevator Workout," and so on (Parkdale, "Slums Unlimited").[1] The discourse used to describe the awards and the adventure tours shows that the activists are cognizant of a long tradition of slumming in that they invert the nightmare of descent in a world-upside-down cosmology that satirizes above and below:

1 The site www.torontoslumtourism.com no longer exists. Parts of it are reproduced or reported on the following sites: archives.truenorthperspective.com/July_10/July_16/parktales.html, www.toronto.com/news-story/58594-parkdale-tenants-association-selects-premier-for-golden-weasel-award/, and the official site of Parkdale Community Legal Services, www.parkdalelegal.org/index.php?option=com_content&view=article&id=55&Itemid=60.

> The Golden Cockroach is a tastefully decorated trophy much coveted by slum landlords and art exhibits. Mounted on an imitation marble and stainless steel stand, the illustration below the mounting bracket subtly hints at a crumbling apartment building, thus signifying the ever-present effort by slumlords to run their buildings into the ground at high rents. The stainless steel curves sweeping upwards towards the sky symbolize the ever-increasing rents which know no limit and the efforts by slumlords to charge sky-high rents. Finally, at its pinnacle, there is the Golden Cockroach itself, clad in all its gold and splendour, thus subtly denoting the filth and health hazards which these landlords aspire to create for their tenants. The gold also symbolizes the huge profits which slum landlords are making at the expense of their tenants. (Parkdale, "Golden Cockroach")

Through these countercultural performances, the tenants' association (supported by community legal services and cross-listed on the Osgoode Hall website for law students) goes beyond a merely comic inversion of the subject/object relation of traditional slumming whereby class tourists ogle the poor;[2] they appropriate and inhabit the spectacle of slumming as a way of constructing radical ways of seeing and knowing the Other in the city. The tenants talk back by externalizing blame, shaming those in power, and educating the media, the general public, and their own neighbours about systemic causes of poverty. In addition to the euphoria and catharsis created through irony and the carnivalesque, the website also passes on important information and ideas about possible social action by reporting on news and facts about the neighbourhood through a history of past activism, a list of what the city has done and should do, and advice to local tenants; for example, on how to "report a bad landlord ... get your building rated ... get help organizing your building." If the discourse of slumming can be so successfully read, inverted, and redeployed by those who inhabit the city from below, why have literary critics not paid more attention to the ethics and epistemology of slumming when reading literature about these urban spaces?

---

2 A similar, humorous inversion of class tourism is quoted by Patricia Smart elsewhere in this collection, when Denise Bombardier recounts a family car ride through rich and poor neighbourhoods in Montréal, while her father derided both classes as being too dumb to be elsewhere. However, the goal of the tenants' association's parody of class tourism quoted above is a more politically savvy, targeted counter-narrative that reappropriates space rather than entrenching hierarchical positions.

Writing and reading the so-called slums are forms of walking in the city, a tactic of knowing improper and proper places and inhabiting them from below (de Certeau). Textual practices of slumming may be as resistant as those of the tenants' association just discussed or as hegemonic as those of early Victorian practices that purported to rescue the poor while thrilling at the lowliness of their being. While slum novels and reportage are often ambivalent about class politics, they are easier to read when we take into account the tradition and discourse of slumming and its cultural politics. Penetrating city space to know the "unknowable" space of slums, whether by insiders or outsiders, has traditionally organized that space in terms of class hierarchy even by the very naming of a poor neighbourhood as a "slum." In some cases, the poor can be seen appropriating the tropes and hierarchical discourse of slumming to protest being fixed in this way as monstrous and voiceless subjects from below. In other words, poor subjects may internalize and reproduce the ideology of difference and the geography of exclusion by performing a "poor me" on the margins of the cityscape (Rimstead).[3] Likewise, contemporary reporters who venture into the slum to make public what is ostensibly hidden may ironically recycle the tropes and diction of Victorian slumming as a residual form (Williams, *Marxism*), which is neither wholly hegemonic nor resistant but as ambivalent as our nineteenth-century forerunners in terms of positioning the bourgeois self in respect

3 As Patricia Smart recounts (elsewhere in this collection), Denise Bombardier's memories of growing up poor in Park Extension include shame and multiple strategies of disguise; for example, by having well-to-do friends drop her off from diction classes in a better part of the neighbourhood so they would never see her true home. This memory echoes Florentine's similar disguise of a "poor me" in Gabrielle Roy's *Bonheur d'occasion* (1945) by having a friend drop her off far from home. Whereas denying the reality of being "at home" in the slum saves both women from shame and exposure, both instances of class shame represent the internalization of hegemonic space by "slum-dwellers." Smart also shows, however, how Lise Payette, another insider from Saint-Henri, despised the shame inspired by Roy's slum fiction because Payette felt as though she and her home were being seen through the eyes of an outsider. Initially devastated by being "known" in this way, she eventually denies this sort of distantiation as inauthentic and devotes a whole chapter of her autobiography to refuting the outsider's view of her home. Payette's writing back against Roy's novel, as described by Smart, represents a paradoxically anti-hegemonic representation of space, albeit one based on the hegemonic dream of social mobility. This counter-narrative of Saint-Henri constitutes the reappropriation, or the remapping, of both the representational space of the slum as lived space "from below" and the space of representation within the slum novel as projected space "from above."

to the poor Other. The more we know about the historical implications of slumming, the more we can understand our contemporary attraction and repugnance towards it, no matter how nuanced the cultural politics of these representations may be.

In the early stages of industrialization, "descending" into the slums of the city to see and know the inhabitants was a way to gain knowledge about an emergent urbanized culture. The market for these stories in daily newspapers and as bestselling books indicated a popular hunger for knowing the urban Other and, more specifically, for knowing the bourgeois self through contact with the class Other. A public discourse on slumming fixed the place of class subjects, the voyeur and the object of the gaze, in terms of distance, a distance that would preserve the privilege of one community and the abjectness of the other. But there was also a discourse of proximity attached to descent, one that was both overt and hidden. As Seth Koven observes in *Slumming: Sexual and Social Politics in Victorian England,* the paradoxical nature of "slumming," in terms of both class tourism and anthropological pursuits, was that it sent journalists and do-gooders into the slum apparently for the purpose of witnessing social injustice and righting it. While often an overtly engaged form of class contact, in many cases the "descent" itself also covertly signified a form of freedom for these bourgeois subjects, who then used the anonymity of the slum and the frequent practice of disguise to gain proximity to the poor in order to explore their own "deviant," or at least marginal, sexual appetites, often in taboo and exploitative forms of contact. Koven documents how the danger of this body knowledge in the context of Victorian London constituted a type of adventure that led to "frissons" or "thrills" that were communicated, even in the form of socially engaged reportage in the daily newspapers, with coded reference to sexual adventure and scandal beneath the surface discourse of philanthropy. For example, he documents how the repetition of scenes of nocturnal bathing in homeless shelters represented in newspaper accounts of slumming provided a voyeuristic function with homoerotic implications. It could be argued, however, that Koven's contemporary study of slumming itself markets the racier side of seeing and theorizing the class subject from below in the city. The subtitle of *Slumming – Sexual and Social Politics in Victorian England* – underscores sexuality, a more alluring topic than poverty alone would be, particularly in current times when the consensus for social reform and social welfare is crumbling in North America. Koven is not alone in this. There is a burgeoning traffic in books about the darker side of Victorian slums, with much less interest in current-day counterparts. Specialists in the field have also noted that Koven's evidence and strategies of decoding Victorian texts are more retrospective than properly belonging to the period (Gorham). For our purposes here, though, Koven's study is enlightening since it charts both the ethical ambivalence of slumming as a way of seeing the urban Other, in its early stages, and the complexity of the knowledge and collaborative relationships it produced.

However diverse the discourses of slumming may be, fairly constant is the image of descent into a space of culture from below, which testifies to a persistent hierarchization of the cityscape into those above and those below, a class-driven, residual social cosmology in the popular imagination that compels us to consider ascent and descent in the reading of urban fiction and reportage even in contemporary times. Interestingly enough, it is not only contemporary critics like Koven who have identified the murky politics of slumming, but also very early observers of the urban sport and of its literary counterpart, the writing of slum novels or reportage. As early as 1905, Gilbert K. Chesterton sensed the ethical risk of slumming and devoted a chapter titled "Slum Novelists and the Slums" to the issue in *Heretics*: "A great many hard things have been said about religious slumming and political or social slumming, but surely the most despicable of all is artistic slumming" (4). Castigating the short-sightedness of writers of slum fiction and reportage for making monsters of the poor for the mere thrill of voyeuristic sensationalism, Chesterton scowls at those who claim to know slum dwellers from a distance: "The missionary comes to tell the poor man that he is in the same condition with all men. The journalist comes to tell other people how different the poor man is from everybody else." In particular, Chesterton objected to authors attempting to capture the psychology of the poor as a species apart and in a sensational way that rendered them frozen in the moment, rather than showing them as part of the long history of humankind: "In short, these books are not a record of the psychology of poverty. They are a record of the psychology of wealth and culture when brought in contact with poverty. They are not a description of the state of the slums. They are only a very dark and dreadful description of the state of the slummers" (4). These early musings about how knowing the urban Other may be as revelatory of the bourgeois spectator as of the object observed anticipate Raymond Williams's observations over sixty years later in *The Country and the City* that literary attempts to know the Other in the city are as much about what the subject desires to know as they are about the knowable communities themselves. Yet despite a long tradition of savvy "slummers" in literature extending from the nineteenth to the twenty-first century, from Charles Dickens's Bildungsromans on street children to George Bernard Shaw's account of the elocutionary re-education of Eliza Doolittle, from George Orwell's *Down and Out in Paris and London* to other ambulatory works by Jack London, Jean Baudrillard, and Jack Kerouac; our critical acumen has lagged behind in recognizing the ideology of the various forms of literary slumming. The etymology of the term and its cultural history, on the other hand, reveal the ambivalence of slumming as a cultural practice.

The *Oxford English Dictionary* defines slumming as "the visitation of slums, esp. for charitable or philanthropic purposes" – noting the pejorative idiomatic use of the verb "to slum" for perhaps "discreditable purposes" or "immoral pursuits" as a voyeuristic pastime for adventure seekers and class tourists, as early as its origins in the 1860s ("Slumming" 2874). Yet, as Koven discusses in his cultural history, the surface pretext for slumming in Victorian times was very often social reform. Slumming was originally linked to moral intervention in a way that other closely related forms of walking in the city were not: for example, the bourgeois walking tour and the studied loitering of the flâneur. The bourgeois walking tour, of which slumming could be perceived a subcategory, was set up to make of the cityscape both a commodity for entertainment and a learning experience, but walking tours on the whole were less interventionist than slumming, since they included educational visits to monuments, parks, and bourgeois neighbourhoods as well as socially precarious spaces like slums. Taking an even more detached, if not ironic, stance towards walking in the city, the flâneur according to Baudelaire and Benjamin was the detached observer of the Paris arcades, closely linked to both consumerism and anti-consumerism and involved in a more solitary, maverick pursuit than organized walking tours. One was an icon of nonconformity while the other was firmly rooted in conservative values. As invested in spectacle and the gaze as class tourists, however, the flâneur was also involved in titillation and intrigue. However, neither walking tours nor the perambulations of the flâneur were deemed a site of rescue and social reform like the more engaged spectacle of slumming.

Although these genres of urban peripatetic movement and posturing emerged with industrialization and, not surprisingly, with the growth of the city, they ambled into modernity along different paths in respect to ethics and epistemology. Walking tours were civic-minded and bourgeois, but the flâneur was a maverick with little pretence to engaging socially, invested instead in detachment and consumption of the spectacle. Yet by the dawn of the twenty-first century, yuppie culture was using the term "slumming" to describe a chic form of authentic experience of culture from below, as in frequenting diners, bargain basements, and other "dives" as a reaction against the phoniness of upper-class culture. The most recent colloquial uses of the word reported online confirm both the denotation and the connotation of descent in terms of frequenting places or people considered to be "lower" than oneself, whether or not in respect to class hierarchy or for sexual liaisons ("Slumming," *Urban Dictionary*; "Slumming," *Wikipedia*). There is much evidence that slum tourism is growing internationally, but the goals of the activity can range from voyeurism to activism and solidarity (Frenzel et al.).

Koven's first case study of Victorian slumming is Dr Barnardo's forays into the streets of London to rescue orphans and relocate them eventually in foreign countries, Canada especially, where they would be adopted into farm families as a means of rescue, even though this too often meant being used as cheap child labour. In addition to the Barnardo orphans, Koven also discusses the social idealism of the slum sisters, the Salvation Army, reporters, and slum "settlements" – all social experiments of the period that made of slumming a site of urban rescue while simultaneously exploiting the lowliness of the class Other and the notions of descent, sensationalism, and titillation.

When the Barnardo scandal aired, it called into question the practice of slumming as philanthropy by charging the do-gooder with hidden forms of contact behind the public script of rescue: the misappropriation of funds, the hiring of sexually deviant assistants, the mistreatment of boys in his care, and his own moral waywardness in the hiring of prostitutes were all cited as evidence of his perverse interest in boys. Barnardo's fraudulent staging of "before-and-after" photos of the found boys was at the centre of the scandal; the ragged clothes in which they were "found" were later discovered to be provided by Barnardo's assistants when the boys' original clothing was not suitably ragged. In this way, Barnardo solicited public money based partly on pretence, but he also captured the "ragamuffins" as the iconic poor while claiming to discover them as they actually were. Note the original title of the photograph reprinted on the cover of Koven's book, "The Raw Material as We Find It" (Koven 107), which paralleled the title of a contemporary novel by Robert Michael Ballantyne about Barnardo orphans going to Canada, *Dusty Diamonds: Cut and Polished: A Tale of City-Arab Life and Adventure*

(1884). Both titles evoke the notion of found material from the slums, knowledge and lives that could be found, mined, controlled, polished, and turned into value (diamonds), especially labour power.

Decoding textual representations of the slums and the cultural politics of production, representation, and consumption is largely dependent on how much we know about the history of slumming as a cultural practice and how we apply this self-reflexivity to the reception of textual accounts as well as to the point of view or focalization within the texts themselves. With brief reference to two very different representations of poverty in the city – the Depression novel *Cabbagetown* by Hugh Garner and a recent series of newspaper articles by Jan Wong, called Maid for a Month, about working for a maid service in Toronto – I want to explore how urban fiction and reportage are alternative spaces through which we seek to know and remember, if not monumentalize and forget, the poor Other in the city.

In 2002, a web-published press release from McGraw-Hill Ryerson claimed it was an ideal time to reissue *Cabbagetown* some fifty years after its first appearance because "an entire generation of Canadians are unaware of this classic." In fact, the book was always, in both censured and full-length forms, a popular bestseller. Yet the publisher's self-acclaimed recovery of the book, like the repeated "discovery" of poverty itself, makes it seem as if *Cabbagetown* suddenly appeared on the literary scene, implying that this "reborn Canadian classic" is a natural phenomenon and effectively forgetting its neglect and silencing by literary gatekeepers. The publisher begins by claiming this slum novel as part of a burgeoning national literature, without mentioning its years of marginalization by the literati in Canada or the author's difficulty finding a publisher. Garner had to consent to radical cuts and changes in order to find a publisher who would finally agree to release the book, albeit at half its length, in 1950. (After strong sales, it would eventually be released in its full-length form in 1968.)[4] For example, Garner had to

4 The publishing history of the novel has been documented in biographical (Stuewe) and autobiographical works (*One Damn Thing*). More recently, Jody Mason has discussed the manuscript as artefact and how changes to the depiction of unemployment in the Depression novel related to market imperatives about popular fiction and state imperatives about post-war politics. However, Mason does not discuss the ongoing revival and popularity of the work in the context of urban renewal and local memory in the contested lived space of Cabbagetown. Few if any literary critics in Canada have perceived the work as slum fiction since the category itself is so seldom invoked.

omit a scene where a volunteer worker, a Big Brother, makes sexual advances towards the young male protagonist, Ken Tilling; and his first publisher asked him for a different ending in crime, a barroom brawl and stabbing versus the exit of the protagonist to fight in the Spanish Civil War. The original cover art on the 1950 paperback emphasizes the thrill of descent into the seedier side of culture from below by featuring a smoky barroom scene. These days, however, the novel is most often marketed as "social document" with a front cover that features the long-gone streets of brick row houses in Cabbagetown to selectively invoke and remember bygone days in Toronto, or, as McGraw-Hill Ryerson puts it, to respond to "a growth of interest in Canadian local history ... indicative in historical walking tours and community festivals across the country."

Garner's novel represents contested urban space in its marketing history as well as its testimony to life "in the largest Anglo-Saxon slum in North America," largely because of its ability to recall scenes of the neighbourhood that predated its almost complete destruction through an experiment in urban renewal. Beginning roughly ten years after the Depression, in which the novel was set, was the first and largest Canadian social experiment in public housing from 1948 to 1958. Working-class and poor inhabitants of Cabbagetown between Gerrard Street, the Don River, Parliament Street, and Queen Street were dispersed and relocated, their homes and streets razed to make room for large-scale public housing in impersonal high-rises that would be called Regent Park, a dehumanizing built environment to replace working-class brick row houses and neighbourhood culture. A spate of books came out in the sixties and seventies, and then later websites went up, to lament the dispersal of the neighbourhood, with many of them quoting copiously from Garner's novel as one strategy of recuperating cultural memory and putting a human face on the past. The strategy of slum clearance is by now recognized more as one of dispersal than improved housing for residents. Only 148 families of the original 638 in Cabbagetown were rehoused in Regent Park, and currently some 370 families are being relocated for a period of up to fifteen years to "regenerate" Regent Park as an eco-friendly, mixed condo/public housing space (Warden). Only a portion of the newly dislocated families will be able to return to the new "mixed" neighbourhood. Today, websites devoted to urban activism in Regent Park, protesting a second round of destruction and relocation of its inhabitants, invoke Garner's social realism as proof of a culture and a community lost.

The publisher's ad for the novel in 2002 not only naturalizes the notion of the division between the rich and the poor in the claim that "every city has had its own Cabbagetown," it also airbrushes over the class conflict in the history of urban renewal by exaggerating the recuperative power of the novel to reclaim what was lost: "Most of Cabbagetown was destroyed shortly after World War II, but the re-release includes several black and white pictures of the streets and times during its bleak period" (McGraw-Hill Ryerson). Notice that the "bleak period" refers to the original neighbourhood rather than the desolate, depersonalized, and crime-ridden landscape of Regent Park, now slated for more urban renewal (thus locating slums in the distant past). Moreover, the publisher's promotion co-opts the politics of slum organizing that have protested the dislocation and exile of the inhabitants of whom Garner wrote and their descendants through references to community festivals and a thriving market in nostalgia for the bygone days. This also glosses over the ongoing class conflict in the politics of urban renewal and gentrification that led to the razing of most of the working-class houses from the original neighbourhood. Thus the novel is made to function hegemonically as a textual site for visiting slums as part of the past, the novel being equated with "historical walking tours" (as opposed to politically incorrect "slumming"), a conventional and hegemonic positioning of the poor that locates them as part of the distant past rather than the continuous present (Bromley; Williams, *Country*; Rimstead).

However, the memory of Cabbagetown as lived space is as contentious as the function of the novel as cultural memory. The current city space is still highly contested even though it is also celebrated as a heterogeneous space where wealthy homeowners "mix" with people from subsidized housing or street people in public spaces. The politics of this "mixing" is clear, however; the gentrified Victorian houses that escaped destruction rise in value, which further empowers wealthy homeowners, while the working class and the poor renting space in low-cost high-rises are threatened with another forced eviction and displacement of their homes and neighbours. To add insult to injury, the high-end neighbourhood homeowners' associations currently use a shabby-chic Cabbagetown flag (green pop-art cabbage on black background between green borders, incidentally that replaces the red on white maple leaf and borders of the Canadian flag) to market their $600,000 to $900,000 "authentic" Victorian homes. Ironically, the flag in question features the icon of the cabbage, once grown on the front lawns by the working-class inhabitants as part of their economic struggle to eat rather than to beautify their urban space with flower gardens as mere adornment. This practice of flag-waving could just as easily signify class warfare since it symbolizes the struggle over local identity and cultural memory, between a gentrified yuppyish community of homeowners, their powerful homeowners' associations, and the city-state against a disposable, still vulnerable population of "wasted lives," a ghost of a working-class community. The homeowners of the gentrified houses underline their connectedness to the past by appropriating the icon of the cabbage for arty and nostalgic purposes but also to show how their investment in restoring historical homes to city code at great personal cost preserves the past and builds a new sense of community, that is, desirable versus undesirable community. They conduct their own walking tours oriented towards architecture to emphasize the cultural capital of their homes and to emphasize their contribution to the historically "authentic," restored architectural space, sprouting a remade neighbourhood of Cabbagetown in harmony with its ghostly past. Those in public housing refer to their development as Regent Park, not Cabbagetown, and are able to reunite under the flag of the cabbage (since they no longer have yards) only virtually on websites or at high school reunions – or through the reading experience of a novel such as *Cabbagetown*, reaching out to past tenants and occupants before they all die out. The contested space of the neighbourhood, or rather its ghost, converges around the reading of the novel to invoke cultural memory but for different performances of nostalgia: the book publishers and homeowners look to the novel to monumentalize the slum as part of a distant past that can be called up as part of the local history, charm, and value of the present space, while activist groups and survivors of relocation look to the novel to see the ghost of times past and a neighbourhood lost.

Since emergent groups of tenants' rights in Regent Park are more focused on the impending destruction of their high-rise homes and a new project of dispersal and relocation to be implemented by city planners, much of the local history on these activist websites is devoted to a history of forgetting, if not mourning. For example, there are a number of chilling testimonies to what the destruction of the old Cabbagetown was like, from the sounds of the bulldozers to the loss of friends, street culture, and a sense of home. The cultural politics of dispersing populations of the poor and workers in order to prevent organizing and resistance should by now be transparent to North American audiences. In short, it is in the interests of economic elites to construct poor neighbourhoods as slums which need to be eradicated or erased, as a sign of progress, and remembered only selectively through nostalgia (black-and-white photos, restored architecture, shabby-chic flags, social realist novels) rather than historically as spaces that need to be understood or remembered in their lived complexity.

As David Harvey and others have observed about North American cities, the doughnut shape of the dying inner-city slum surrounded by richer suburbs has been replaced by the checkerboard model (Harvey, *Justice* 405–6). As the wealthy move back into the centre of the city and construct walled communities and safe houses so that they can coexist in so-called "mixed" environments, the excess poor and working-class are dispersed to less valuable land sites in the now aging suburbs. Harvey stresses not only the dispossession of the poor at the centre of the city through gentrification, but also how the logic of capital determines what kind of social ties and spatial relations we live in our cities (Harvey, "Right"). In one of his early works, *Justice, Nature, and the Geography of Difference,* Harvey ends his analysis with a section called "Possible Urban Worlds," in which he explains that the shift in paradigms of urban development from the doughnut to the checkerboard meant that capital first abandoned the centre city and then moved back in order to gentrify the slums and thus set up multiple sites of difference heavily armed against each other. On one side were walled neighbourhoods and safe rooms and homeowners' associations; and on the other side were gangs and graffiti and co-ops. We are all, according to Harvey, "embroiled in a *global process of capitalist urbanization* or *uneven spatio-temporal development*" (emphasis in orig.) that we can see in two ways: as the forces of capital accumulation cutting up and speeding up, knocking down and rebuilding neighborhoods and cityscapes for the purposes of greater accumulation" (*Justice* 414). Or we can see these new spatial developments as offering spaces of hope where there can be a popular "seizure of the possibilities that capitalist technologies have created" (415). Migrancy, for example, can be seen as a space of resistance rather than an urban space of low-wage and informal and temporary working possibilities. One of the ways to seize these opportunities to recognize difference and to see the city differently is to engage in standpoint analysis and to see the city from below as well as from above, reading the city as a composite landscape, a layered palimpsest which shows us the contemporary city layered against previous cities. New urban forms cannot be constructed from a "tabula rasa" but on the collective memory of what came before, and the powerful symbolic meanings that entails (417). More importantly, when the city is read across space as well as across time, Harvey argues, we can expose how spaces are contested and how they serve the interests of capital, but also how they can, if we listen to other standpoints, serve as spaces of resistance. In keeping with this pattern of urban resettlement that has dismantled slums in contemporary times, my next illustration of slumming takes place throughout the city with no built environment as such associated with the poor Other. Instead, it is the job landscape of the working poor that constitutes the urban space in which a reporter goes slumming.

A series of feature articles by Jan Wong, which ran over several issues of the *Globe and Mail* (Canada's most prestigious English-language daily newspaper) in spring 2006, hinged on dressing up poor to investigate the life of domestic cleaners in Toronto. Using disguise and a discourse that re-inscribes the subject/object relation between the bourgeois writer and the poor and silent subjects, Wong reproduces many of the conventions of slum writing while failing to interrogate the hegemonic politics of ogling the class Other from a distance. The series brings Victorian practices into the context of yuppie culture, exposing little social evolution of attitudes, apart from a desire to unearth the facts and statistics of poor lives as a way of knowing the urban Other. From the outset, this tour into the underworld of domestic cleaners as a hidden strata of the city, not centred in any slum area but mobile and dispersed, cultivates ironic distance as a means of appearing self-reflexive. This makes it hard for many to fault the journalist on her classist attitudes since she seems not to take her own attitudes seriously, rather adopting instead a self-mocking tone during her descent into manual labour and poverty. The use of disguise, unquestioned derogatory discourse, and ample doses of yuppie irony and distantiation (a "here-but-not-here" form of detachment)[5] positions the slum reportage in a self-knowing rhetoric that attempts to mediate class distance, not through solidarity but through irony towards the descent. What Chesterton pointed out about slum fiction at the turn of the twentieth century holds true for Wong's reportage, that it is less about the psychology of the poor than about "the psychology of wealth and culture when brought in contact with poverty," less about "a description of the state of the slums" than "the state of the slummers." How does Wong get away with such a thin veneer of social caring, and why does the *Globe and Mail* expect people to consume these rather self-centred reports "from below" as informative

5 Thanks to Henry Sussman for his insightful comments on this aspect of my chapter and his suggestion to explore the "here, not here" positioning of the yuppie subject.

visits to the poor? What does this rather uncritical reception of slumming suggest about the way we consume slum novels and reportage in general in the here and now?

In one of the first articles of the series, Wong explains why she decides to take her sons along with her. It will be an educational experience, and they begin their education by referring to their low-cost apartment as "the hovel." Instead of correcting them on the insensitivity of these remarks, she takes up the slogan herself throughout the series to describe their temporary basement apartment in Scarborough, a suburb of Toronto. Her self-admitted concessions to their bourgeois past are to make sure her sons do not miss cello and hockey practices or miss private school while they are playing poor, and to go home herself every weekend to "[her] silk rugs and [her] potted orchid and the sun streaming through [her] windows" to play Handel and Mozart for two hours with friends (15 April 2006). Another important context for Wong's journalistic quest is that it comes out just five years after Barbara Ehrenreich's bestselling work on the same theme, *Nickled and Dimed: On (Not) Getting By in America* (2001), in which the author finds manual work and the struggles of the poor arduous and degrading. One of the main differences between their works is that Ehrenreich's focus is actually talking to fellow workers and recording the everyday reality of their lived experience while Wong divides her focus between her own culture shock (devoting much space to her dislike for slovenly and haughty clients) and a largely statistical overview or detailed and mundane reporting of the lives of the other maids versus qualitative interviews or oral history.[6] Some of Wong's remarks about the other maids are unabashedly condescending: "I think of my fellow maids. Poverty is also the absence of

6 Seeing workers and the poor is often synonymous with knowing them. There is, however, a fundamental difference between seeing and looking at the lives of workers, as Janet Zandy has noted in her prize-winning essay on worker photography in the United States, "Photography and Writing: A Pedagogy of Seeing." Zandy reflects of the ideology of workers' self-portraits and the way they have vied for dignity and visual space by seeing dirt differently, through pride in their physical labour, and through tools as extensions of their own body space. Examining how workers postured for the camera, often proudly with the tools of trade in hand to create a self-image that would honour their class identity, Zandy observes that new ways of seeing this photographic archive are necessary since "representations of workers in the history of photography were visually contained, kept to the periphery, occasionally elevated as pastoral or urban symbols of a generic, benign laboring class, but rarely seen as agents of their own representation with an alternate aesthetic." The "desire by

beauty. What is it like, when there's nothing in your life to look forward to except *Who Wants to Be a Millionaire?*" (15 April 2006). Maggie, her cleaning partner, is viewed from up close and with a modicum of empathy. But once again, in keeping with what Chesterton observed about the early days of slumming, "The journalist comes to tell other people how different the poor man is from everybody else," Wong stresses that the other maids do not know how to drive or fill out government forms. Considerable space is given to how the maids react to Wong and lighten her burden by giving her tips on work strategies, but Wong herself provides little empathic material on their everyday lives. On the whole, they are portrayed as passive, downtrodden, and unimaginative, incapable of change or even anger at their situation.

On the surface, this series of articles about dressing up poor inserts itself within an engaged form of journalism that, like George Orwell's descents into Paris and London, will garner knowledge and social criticism against the system, as well as knowledge about what it feels like to be positioned among the urban poor. Wong herself makes these connections between Dickens, Orwell, and Ehrenreich and her own writerly vision, but she concludes that bringing her children along changes the equation since she must worry about feeding others, implying her lot is more difficult. In the course of critiquing this series, I have heard spirited defences from acquaintances that Wong's series actually exposed how horrible it is to clean for the rich in Toronto. But Wong's focus is not on critiquing the system or empathizing with the poor, who are rarely heard speaking about their feelings in her seven-part series; rather it is a focus on describing the vertigo caused when people as cultured and knowledgeable as Wong and her sons end up dislocated by an adventure to live on minimum wage. From the titles, we can see that some of the instalments are focused almost entirely on her and her sons' experiences: "Sam's Story," "Ben's Story," and "Cinder Sam and Benderella"; and,

---

workers to be seen" can thus be interpreted within the larger social space of class relations, a visual space working to position them as peripheral figures, victims, or mere instruments of industry. It is not only the insider gaze that distinguishes workers' vision of their own lives from that of those who seek to know them by looking at them from the outside; it is also the ability to gaze back. Zandy argues that seeing beyond dirt when looking at workers entails a mutuality, an exchange of subjectivities that acknowledges the subjecthood of workers. This is precisely what is missing in Wong's reporting since she does not seem to really "see" the domestics or to picture them seeing themselves; she mostly looks at herself looking at them.

overall, she gives as much if not more space to her own feelings, their diet, and their culture shock than to the voices of the maids:

> For reasons that now escape me, I thought the best way to tell the story ... was to work – and live – at the bottom of the food chain. I would find a low-paying job, a low-rent apartment and, single-mom-like, take my boys with me for the month and see how we survived ... "Cool, what are we going to eat? KD?" said Sam, 12, who prizes Kraft Dinner because he's sick of triple crème French brie. His brother, Ben, 15, was the embodiment of teen irony. "So I'll have a urine-soaked mattress?" he said. "Is the floor going to be, like, concrete?" (1 April 2006)

In truth, the series reads more like an unintended exposé of yuppie insensitivity to poverty than it does as a probing investigation into poverty.[7] What surprises me is how quick otherwise discerning critics are to defend this type of posturing as well-meaning and informative, as if knowing the urban Other in this way in our place and time is the best we can hope for.[8]

In order to articulate more engaged strategies of reading slums in both lived and textual space, we need to reframe slumming as a historical discourse on class encounter and reframe the questions we ask of city space as represented in fiction and journalism. Instead of reading slums as landscape and poverty as descent, merely fixing difference and distance between class tourists and ragged subjects, radical reading strategies would interrogate and historicize the links and overlaps between class Other and urban tourist, novelist, or investigative journalist, including the ethical and epistemological dimensions of these imbrications. For example, such reading strategies might use the need for housing and clothing, class anger, dirt, and the critique of capitalism (examples

7 I would like to disassociate this critique of Wong's series, Maid for a Month, from the extensive controversy that occurred in September 2006 around her reporting of the Dawson shootings and her eventual firing by the *Globe and Mail.* My purpose, here, is not to target Wong personally for insensitive writing but to analyse the popular appeal of the hegemonic ideology of these representations in the larger context of spatial relations and knowing the urban Other. My point is that these views are more typical than atypical because they are a residual (Williams) form of classism that reinscribes difference and segregation within the "mixed" urban environment.

8 Wong was sued for her undercover work, but the media attention was on the ethics of how she had deceived employers and the cleaning company, not on how she represented the maids themselves.

of lived experience and knowledge from below) to question the cultural hegemony of a society that seeks to erase and naturalize the poor in the here and now while ogling them as Other as in times past.

WORKS CITED

Ballantyne, Robert Michael. *Dusty Diamonds: Cut and Polished: A Tale of City-Arab Life and Adventure.* James Nisbet and Co., 1884.

Baudelaire, Charles. *The Flowers of Evil.* 1857. Edited by Marthiel Mathews and Jackson Mathews and translated by C.F. MacIntyre, New Directions, 1989.

Benjamin, Walter. *The Arcades Project.* 1927–40. Translated by Howard Eiland and Kevin McLaughlin, Harvard UP, 1999.

– *Charles Baudelaire: A Lyric Poet in the Era of High Capitalism.* Verso, 1983.

Bromley, Roger. *Lost Narratives: Popular Fictions, Politics and Recent History.* Routledge, 1988.

Chesterton, Gilbert K. "Slum Novelists and the Slums." 1908. *Heretics.* Page by Page Books. www.pagebypagebooks.com/Gilbert_K_Chesterton/Heretics/Slum_Novelists_and_the_Slums_p5.html. Accessed 15 Dec. 2009.

de Certeau, Michel. *The Practice of Everyday Life.* U of California P, 1984. Translated by Steven Rendall as *L'invention du quotidien (1): Arts de faire,* new ed., Gallimard, 1980.

Ehrenreich, Barbara. *Nickled and Dimed: On (Not) Getting by in America.* Metropolitan Books, 2001.

Frenzel, F., K. Koens, and M. Steinbrink, editors. *Poverty, Power and Ethics in Global Slum Tourism.* Routledge, 2012.

Garner, Hugh. *Cabbagetown.* 1950. Ryerson Press, 1968.

– *One Damn Thing after Another.* McGraw-Hill, 1973.

Gorham, Deborah. Rev. of *Slumming: Sexual and Social Politics in Victorian England,* by Seth Koven. *Labour / Le travail* 57 (Spring 2006). www.jstor.org/stable/25149690?seq=1#page_scan_tab_contents. Accessed Nov. 2009.

Harvey, David. *Justice, Nature, and the Geography of Difference.* Blackwell, 1996.

– "The Right to the City." *New Left Review* 53, Sept.–Oct. 2008, pp. 23–53.

Koven, Seth. *Slumming: Sexual and Social Politics in Victorian England.* Princeton UP, 2004.

Mason, Jody. *Writing Unemployment: Worklessness, Mobility, and Citizenship in Twentieth-century Canadian Literature.* U of Toronto P, 2013.

McGraw-Hill Publishing Co. Cabbagetown. 2002. mcgraw-hillryerson.com/tpm/press+box/press+releases/_published/0070915520.php. Accessed 1 Sept. 2009, no longer available.

"Slumming" and "Slum." *Oxford English Dictionary*, pp. 247–8. Rpt. in *The Compact Edition of the Oxford English Dictionary*, Oxford UP, 1989, p. 2874.
Parkdale Tenants' Association. "Golden Cockroach Award." www.goldencockroach.org/. Accessed 2 Mar. 2009, no longer available.
– "Slums Unlimited: The Official Site of Slum Tourism Toronto." www.torontoslumtourism.com/. Accessed 24 Apr. 2009, no longer available.
Rimstead, Roxanne. *The Remnants of Nation: On Reading Poverty Narratives by Women.* U of Toronto P, 2001.
Stuewe, Paul. *The Storms Below: The Turbulent Life and Times of Hugh Garner.* Lorimer and Co., 1988.
Urban Dictionary. "Slumming." Aug. 2003–Mar. 2008. www.urbandictionary.com/define.php?term=slumming. Accessed 24 Nov. 2009.
Warden, Chris. "Cabbagetown History Pre-Regent Park and Early Development Period." *The Real Cabbagetown History.* chat.carleton.ca/~cwarden/projects/rp_history.pdf. Accessed Oct. 2009, no longer available.
Wikipedia. "Slumming." en.wikipedia.org/wiki/slumming. Accessed 15 Nov. 2009.
Williams, Raymond. *The Country and the City.* Hogarth Press, 1973.
– *Marxism and Literature.* Oxford UP, 1977.
Wong, Jan. "Coming Clean." Maid for a Month, *Globe and Mail*, 1 Apr. 2006. www.theglobeandmail.com/news/national/coming-clean/article705986/. Accessed 1 Apr. 2009.
– "Goodbye to All That." Maid for a Month, *Globe and Mail*, 29 Apr. 2006. www.theglobeandmail.com/news/national/maid-for-a-month-goodbye-to-all-that/article1099101/. Accessed 1 Apr. 2009.
– "Maggie and Me." Maid for a Month, *Globe and Mail*, 22 Apr. 2006. www.theglobeandmail.com/news/national/maggie-and-me/article18160985/. Accessed 1 Apr. 2009.
– "Modern Times." Maid for a Month, *Globe and Mail*, 8 Apr. 2006. www.theglobeandmail.com/news/national/modern-times/article4300632/. Accessed 1 Apr. 2009.
Zandy, Janet. "Photography and Writing: A Pedagogy of Seeing." *Exposure: The Journal of the Society for Photographic Education*, Spring 2008, pp. 26–32.

12 "You Should Think about It, Think What It Means": Working Girls in Canadian Women's Writing

PATRICIA DEMERS

An abandoned first wife in an Alice Munro story tries to explain the allure of her replacement with this stereotypical glimpse of the sex worker: "I think it was that she'd been on the streets. She was, you know. She lost her child and everything. She told him all about it. She got herself tattooed from top to bottom, that attracts customers" (Munro 73). Canadian women's fiction, memoirs, drama, and diaries in which actual sex workers play a prominent role are much more candid and capacious than Munro's story, as they incorporate elements of rebellion, disinhibition, and self-fashioning in their depiction and analysis of this subculture. The telling of these stories of racialized, classed, and sexualized violence and its connections to ideological frameworks, Shawna Ferris notes, "has the power to change or to reinforce cultural structures that produce and respond to extreme violence against marginalized women" (3).

Puncturing stereotypes, confounding boundaries, taking up a position on the fringes of respectability, the world of prostitution – the particular form of sex work which I intend to discuss – confronts the academic reader with a double perspective on the cultural imaginary of the sex industry. What are its ideological and cultural implications, and how might we undertake to analyse them? The "burgeoning interest in geographies of sexuality" (Hubbard 57) invites us to consider how the "city of fiction," as Sherry Simon's chapter in this collection analyses it, "is opening up to new territories" (p. 78). The prostitute presented in fiction and related in lived experience forces a "reconsideration of notions of freedom and responsibility" (Wyschogrod 54–5) as well as a "re-ordering of conventional, jurisprudential, and classed assumptions" (Demers 84). Challenging theories of victimization and complicity and spotlighting both critical intelligence and enacted, at times rationalized, naiveté, this multi-generic writing embraces a wide diversity of styles as it elicits a spectrum of responses. While exploring the feminist schism between seeing prostitution as work, "raced work, work originating in the conditions of capitalism and patriarchy, ... sexually freeing work," and as sexual violence, this writing complicates the issue of judging ability or inability in managing "transgressive 'whoring'" (Razack 342, 349). Demarcating a line between socially approved decency and degeneracy, prostitution "secures a bourgeois and white social order" (Razack 340). There is, too, the intricate moral obligation of the observer. Roxanne Rimstead alerts us, in this collection, to the "hegemonic politics of ogling the class Other from a distance" (p. 255). "An emblematic figure at the intersection of sexual and gender relationships," the prostitute as persistently stereotyped creates an image simultaneously "eroticized and demonized," constructed through "metaphors and metonyms of desire and disgust" (Hubbard 58, 61).

Canadian women's work on the experiences and the effects of prostitution subverts protocols of the "coherence," "crispness," and "pathfulness" of dirty realism (Wilson 81) in discourse comparable to Domenico A. Beneventi's reflections on bums, vagabonds, hoboes, and the homeless in this volume. It extends an understanding of the "continuous present" (Buss 162) and creates baroque dimensions for the Bildungsroman. But as the continual reports of unsolved cases of disappeared or murdered women testify, handling this job, leading this life, involves real dangers. Likening the anomalous zones of prostitution to the carnivalesque can be facile, William Ian Miller cautions, "Bakhtin's celebration of popular vulgarity remains strangely blind to the costs of 'authentic' people getting their rocks off" (1243). "The idea that there is a special ordering of how much we can care" (Razack 358) underpins the argument about the immoral spaces of prostitution and how the authentic personhood of the sex worker is perceived. Fiction, Shawna Ferris maintains, has the potential to "resist the current dehumanization of sex workers and other marginalized populations in Canada" (181).

The decision to concentrate on women writers is deliberate since women themselves, the subjects most intimately affected by heterosexual sex work, also supply the most acute commentary on its influence. As Laura Kipnis reminds us in her pertinent excavations of envy, sex, dirt, and vulnerability, "both femininity and feminism end up entangled in the same scenarios and repetitions"; in addition, when it comes to what women have and men want from them, "a detour through the subterranean, not-always-progressive recesses of the symbolic imagination" is called for (162–3). This project traces one selective route in "the myriad impasses of the female condition" (163).

Although almost four decades ago Margaret Atwood remarked on "a notable absence of Venuses" in Canadian writing (*Survival* 199), there has been in fact quite a steady stream of sex workers. Consider the registers of first-person voices – from Maria Campbell's *Halfbreed* (1973), Evelyn Lau's *Runaway* (1989), and Elisabeth Eaves's *Bare* (2002) to Nelly Arcan's *Putain* (2001; translated as *Whore*, 2005) and Catherine Hanrahan's *Lost Girls and Love Hotels* (2006). Moreover, the catalogue thickens with these mediated portraits: the pickpocketing Felicia and Lilly in Sheila Watson's *The Double Hook* (1959); the accommodating Phoebe Yeates and initiating Margie in Patricia Blondal's *A Candle to Light the Sun* (1960); Héloïse in Marie-Claire Blais's *Une saison dans la vie d'Emmanuel* (1965); the reproach and question of the eight-year-old Asha, the child prostitute in the "tea-shop cum brothel" whom Margaret Laurence befriends in *The Prophet's Camel Bell* (1963), and Ayesha in "The Rain Child" in *The Tomorrow-Tamer* (1963), "whose childhood lay beaten or lost somewhere in the shanties and brothels" (130), along with the life of Piquette Tonnerre weaving throughout Laurence's Manawaka novels (1964–74); Leah in Sharon Pollock's *Whiskey Six Cadenza* (first performed in 1983); and the Jezebels in Atwood's *The Handmaid's Tale* (1985). Dionne Brand's *At the Full and Change of the Moon* (1999) features a Black sex-worker protagonist who learns self-love, while with less meliorism and a focus on Vancouver's Downtown Eastside, Rebecca Godfrey's *The Torn Skirt* (2002) presents a poor street kid, and Maggie de Vries's *Missing Sarah* (2004) relates the biography of her sister who opted for life on the streets over a middle-class suburb. The benchmark figure for an exploration of the ironic, subversive, satiric, humorous, generous, arguably religious significance of the activity is Adele Wiseman's Hoda in *Crackpot* (1974). Concentrating on selected examples from this archive of direct and mediated narratives, I want to investigate their physical, social, and readerly locations. Does the prostitute's space relate to or reflect "the abject materials of a transgressive physicality," and how does it "violate the decorum of spatial boundaries" (Gilbert 111, 120)? In a context of "legal excorporation or social ostracizing," what is the role of desire in this sex work, and how does it "hover between state and event" (Bal 209, 196)? When we as readers encounter the choice and coercion, the semiotic and real violence of many of these lives, do we find ourselves engaged, responding to a *cri de coeur*, or as distanced from these sexual tunnellers as we might be from saints, "spiritual alpinists climbing high above the humdrum" (Duffy 31)?

Ostensibly the most direct accounts, the first-person narratives of *Halfbreed*, *Runaway*, and *Bare* convey unforgettable images of raw and rancid locales – "a filthy little hole in a basement" (Campbell 123), boarding houses in disrepair, and semen-sticky floors – on Vancouver's East Hastings for Campbell and Lau, and in Seattle's Lusty Lady Peep Show for Eaves. Despite large differences in class and privilege (Campbell is a road-allowance Métis;[1] Lau, a fourteen-year-old runaway; and Eaves, the child of professional parents, with an MA in international studies), one common feature is their refusal of the double standard that penalizes women and connives at their male customers. Another is the commentary each makes on the enclosure of her space. In a rhetorical gesture forecasting impasses in Beatrice Culleton Mosionier's *In Search of April Raintree* (1983), with its scenes of rape and suicide, and Jeannette Armstrong's *Slash* (1985), with the protagonist's anger about "empty words on paper that had no compassion for what is human on the land" (Armstrong 249), Campbell remarks that she feels "trapped within a certain kind of life" with no one to turn to, since "business and political leaders ... are involved in and perpetuate in private the very things that they condemn in public" (118). The sense of entrapment, coupled with rebellion, anger, and death wishes, is especially prominent in the writing of Aboriginal and ethnic-minority female subjects as prostitutes. A "smart" dropout who has "run away from home at fourteen and end[ed] up as a junkie whore" (Wong A11), Lau underscores victimization, acknowledging that her supposed protector, really her pimp, sees her as "no more than a fifteen-year-old foster kid he's having a fling with" (192). Yet with equal clear-sightedness and plangency she makes this declaration to her analyst:

> In prostitution, I mean, I can fulfill someone. Here, right now! Which I could never do with my parents ... I could never do [anything] with my parents. Does it matter if it's only a john? I mean it's somebody. I mean, at home I could never please them. I could get 95 or do 6 hours of housework

1 Road-allowance Métis lived on unused portions of government land, making their settlements on either side of the road in plots no wider than thirty feet. Campbell has translated *Stories of the Road Allowance People* (Theytus Books, 1995). Shawna Ferris includes an extensive analysis of *Halfbreed* in *Street Sex Work and Canadian Cities*, 144–57.

> and never go out. Always hoping for something, you know. Some sign of love. But nothing was ever good enough. (qtd. in Gunew 255–6)[2]

Rented rooms as well as the parental home can confine.[3] Self-possessed scholarship student Eaves, though not a runaway and not on the street, does analyse the peep-show box in which she performs for Pleasure Booth customers, in ways that extend her chosen epigraph from *Mansfield Park*, Edmund Bertram's advice to the shy but insightful Fanny Price: "you must really begin to harden yourself to the idea of being worth looking at" (Austen 133). Whether in hotel rooms or peep-show booths, the correlation between spatial containment and public vulnerability, perceived objectification and total exposure, is another salient feature. Eaves progresses from an initial fear – "as though I had to write an exam I wasn't prepared for" (44) – to an acute reflection on the commodity of the woman to be bought: "The naked, adoring, one-dimensional sex object ... creates the idea that women's appearance, behaviour and sexuality are for sale" (288). Recent criticism of Eaves for being "sensitive, well-educated, from a warm and supportive family," and of her observations on commodification as "hopelessly confused" and "drape[d] with women's studies jargon" (Roife 1, 3) overlooks the self-reflexive features of *Bare* and shortchanges Eaves's aperçus on the business of sexual stimulation and gratification.

For the transactional *is* uppermost, especially in *Putain* and *Lost Girls and Love Hotels.* These first-person narrators speak openly of the business of prostitution, thus illustrating what Pamela K. Gilbert labels the "new element" in the contemporary city, where "the woman seeks sex" and where "sex is that which both offers and defiles freedom and pleasure, with the doubling of the woman as subject ... and object" (116). Commenting on the first of her five novels, only the first two of which use the

2 Gunew is quoting from a 1993 CBC film, *The Diary of Evelyn Lau,* directed by Sturla Gunnarson. The scene recreated here is based on *Runaway* (86, 154, 225).

3 In his report on gifted children pushed by ambitious parents, Dave McGinn relates the story of Sufiah Yusof, admitted to Oxford at age thirteen to study math: "Having complained in 2001 that her father made her life a 'living hell' by making her follow his accelerated learning techniques, it was discovered last year that she was working as a prostitute in Britain" (L3).

genre of *l'autofiction*, Arcan views sex as a source of power: "There are no taboos acting as restraints. Women are conditioned by the profusion of images in advertising created to arouse desire" (qtd. in Ackerman 84). Although themes of the commodification of women are constant in Arcan's writing, she admitted to Chantal Guy on the occasion of the publication of her third novel, *À ciel ouvert*, that she was turning away from such self-exposure: "Je trouve que d'écrire sans le 'je,' c'est moins cher payé en exposition de soi-même" (Guy, "Portrait").[4] In *Putain*, Arcan, pseudonym of the late Isabelle Fortier, who held a master's degree, presents "une putain qui étudie" (32).[5] Her white-blonde narrator, "avec mes cheveux blonds, presque blancs à force d'être blonds" (23), operates from a suite with perpetually closed drapes in an innocuous-looking apartment building on Rue Dr Penfield watching over the intelligentsia "sur le coeur anglais de Montréal" (146).[6] Fees for her sexual services pay her tuition as a student of literature at the university and the bills of her psychoanalyst. The room itself is a stripped-down but dirty space; "le lit blanc en bois compressé au pied duquel s'accumulent les poils des clients" and weekly cleared trash bags "remplis de mouchoirs visqueux et de préservatifs" characterize its "saleté" (28, 128, 130).[7] Arcan belongs to a Montréal cohort of educated young female writers of autofiction for whom sex is primary material. Other subjectivities include the child savant in Heather O'Neill's *Lullabies for Little Criminals* (2006), the troubled childhood of the central character in Marie-Sissi Labrèche's *Borderline* (2000), the sexual fantasies of a rapist in Marie Hélène Poitras's *Soudain le Minotaure* (2002), and the incest-obsessed family in Irina Egli's *Terre salée* (2006). Alcoholic, drug-using, and promiscuous, Margaret, the "platinum blond" Torontonian narrator of *Lost Girls*, embodies the title in her desire to "sell [her] time and kill [her] body" in Tokyo – a wish almost fulfilled in this violent treatment of self-loathing (Hanrahan 6, 4).

4 As Arcan admitted in conversation with Chantal Guy, "I find that writing without the 'I' is less costly in exposing oneself" ("Nelly Arcan"). Born Isabelle Fortier in Lac-Mégantic, Québec, in 1975, Arcan died on 24 September 2009. Following *Putain*, her novels were *Folle* (2004), *À ciel ouvert* (2007), *L'enfant dans le miroir* (2007), and the soon-to-be-published posthumous work, *Paradis clés en main*.

5 "a whore who studies" (Arcan, *Whore* 25).

6 "with my blond hair, almost white because of its blondness"; intelligentsia at "the heart of English-speaking Montréal" (Arcan, *Whore* 17, 146).

7 "a white particleboard bed with the clients' body hairs accumulated around its foot"; trash bags "filled with sticky tissues and condoms" characterize its "filth" (Arcan, *Whore* 22, 116, 117).

Employed by the Air-Pro Stewardess Training Institute, which she nicknames "trolley-dolly boot camp" (7), Margaret also works in love hotels participating in the fantasies of anonymous sex while she shuts down "the smart [self], ... the [self she's] pushed farther and farther back into [her] head, the [self] that [she's] ignored, abused, neglected, subdued with pills, shushed with booze, violated" (52). With mock enthusiasm she even drafts passages for a proposed love hotel guidebook: "*What most people don't realize is that apart from the obvious sexual function, the love hotel can provide a refuge for the lost girl. A place to regroup*" (177; emphasis in orig.).

In both accounts by Arcan and Hanrahan, inflected with family backstories of abuse, rage, and the need to escape, the enactment of sexual desire is performative; the state of desire itself is negating, numbing, obliterative. Appropriating the name of a dead sister, abandoning her arthritic, bedridden mother, and fleeing the righteous father who "waits for the end of the world" as "he chases after whores" (Arcan, *Putain* 10, 28), Arcan's "Cynthia" resigns herself to trying "to reconcile what's happening in [her] head with what happens here in this apartment," to "calling out to life from death's side" (133, 172). The background of Hanrahan's Margaret involves parental infidelities, corrosive language, her mother's lesbianism, a gang rape, and an attempted murder at the hands of a psychotic brother; her sadomasochistic escape takes the form of "trolling the city" in search of "bad sex with worse men" (Hanrahan 47, 52). Her return to Toronto is "no happy ending" but rather "the sweet pain of home," where "*things are ragged and messy, ... torn apart by events*" (Hanrahan 208; emphasis in orig.).

Whether in Arcan's sinuous, conversational parataxis or Hanrahan's clipped, petulant staccato, these texts of abjection challenge the reader. Their narrators' nihilistic impulse provokes and competes with sympathy for such extreme vulnerability. Readers encounter another disjunction in recognizing the narrators' obsession and self-awareness, captured succinctly in this tossed-off remark from Hanrahan's Margaret: "Intimacy is a word with eight letters. A word with a sly hiss to it" (106). While slyness suggests a deliberate shock value, it coexists with a trenchant critique of what are shown to be the sham norms of fidelity and tenderness. This confrontational directness might also prompt us to consider the other sweep of the pendulum, in the potentially equally challenging directness of spiritual intimacy. Augustine explained the centre of his entire being in "the 'fleshy tablets of the heart,' not of the carnal mind," as "a living agent possessing sensation, in comparison with a stone, which is senseless."[8] "'With heart and voice and pen,'" Augustine was seeking "outer expression for his converted inner self, ... mediat[ing] his heart to others in writing" (Jager 7).

Instead of conversion, it seems that annihilation of the inner self is required in representations of prostitution in fiction by Canadian women writers. In contrast to the excavation of the psyche and probing of motivation in first-person reportage, fictional accounts resort to make-believe itself to numb the pain, blunt the edge of hypocrisy, and aestheticize or domesticate the undertaking. Madame Octavie Embonpoint's Public Rose Tavern, where Héloïse (the former postulant) services the town's worthies, and the club known as the Jezebels in the Republic of Gilead, where Offred and Moira have their last meeting, underscore the denial of expression. Amid the backdrop of the listless poverty of a family of sixteen children in an unnamed, pre–Quiet Revolution Québec village and the fundamentalist theocracy of a patriarchal dystopia, repression is the dominant mood. As Blais presents Héloïse, "elle avait mal aux dents, tout à coup sa mâchoire ouverte, cousue et recousue, et la denture de pierre enfoncée dans ces gencives encore saignantes" (*Saison* 151).[9] Anaesthetizing herself to the realities of the brothel, Héloïse fictionalizes the past – "ne cessant de comparer sa vie à l'Auberge avec le bien-être de la vie au couvent" – and, "rejetée sur un ravage stérile," imagines her role as maternal (145, 152).[10] "Elle voyait en l'homme qui piétinait sa jeunesse, sans égard pour la misère de son corps et la solitude de son désir, l'enfant, le gros enfant des premiers appétites suspendu à son sein" (151).[11] Not even a hint of the maternal is in evidence at the Jezebels, a club that "stimulates trade," tags women as "taken," and enforces the code of "blank, apathetic" faces (Atwood, *Handmaid* 223, 225). In this illicit club for officers, "Moira's subversive dress is merely an old misogynist uniform recycled and recontextualized: the playboy bunny outfit" (York 11). With a shrug that "might be resignation," Moira

8 *De spiritu et littera* 17.30, *Corpus Scriptorum Ecclessiasticorum Latinorum*, qtd. in Jager 5.

9 "How her teeth hurt suddenly, and her jaw where it had been split open, stitched up, and then restitched, and the stone teeth implanted in her still bleeding gums" (Blais, *Season* 118).

10 "never ceasing to compare life in the Tavern with her happy days spent in the convent"; "cast up on a sterile shore" (Blais, *Season* 113, 119).

11 "She saw the man now trampling on her youth with no regard for the misery he was inflicting on her body or the loneliness of her desire – saw him as a child, a big baby with primal appetites, suspended from her nipple" (Blais, *Season* 118–19).

confides, "nobody in here with viable ovaries either" (Atwood, *Handmaid* 234). With the possible exception of the now-widowed Phoebe Yeates, whose cohabitation with the town manager is belatedly accepted in Mouse Bluffs (Blondal), the fate of most fictionalized prostitutes is grim. Blais's Héloïse and Atwood's Moira endure confinement as sex objects. Laurence's Piquette perishes in a fire; Pollock's Leah, rumrunner Mr Big's "chosen daughter" (Pollock 208), is shot in the back of the head; Atwood's later figure of transient sex, Oryx in *Oryx and Crake*, has her throat cut.

How amazing and startling, then, is Wiseman's ebullient, strong-minded survivor, Hoda, whose larger-than-life presence in *Crackpot* both expands novelistic generic conventions and challenges the righteous inscription of the prostitute. Subject of abuse and ridicule since childhood, the butt of jokes who knows "they've been laughing at [her] all [her] life," Hoda strikes back with tart humour and exhilarating bravura, in the process becoming "something of a vested memory, ... somehow still unrepentantly out of pitch with the rest of humanity" (Wiseman 244, 286). As she "bloom[s] into a honeypot for all the bees" and feels "lighter than air" doing "cleaning jobs for bossy ladies," peddling baskets, and giving "private lessons" in her bedroom of the family's tumbledown North Winnipeg home, Hoda remains fiercely loyal to her blind father Danile, "a master of the aesthetics of ignorance," for whom she is the sole support (Wiseman 125, 117, 177). "Whore or no she was still a good daughter and took care of her father as well as any virgin might" (177). But as she caters for the abundant sexual needs of her community and experiences its retributive venom, Hoda adopts an instructive, bawdily satiric take on moral righteousness:

> Why did people always have to spoil things and try to make you feel dirty? Hoda didn't see why that woman [her grocer-client's wife] had to keep calling her all those names over and over again. Just because that was how she was making a living now didn't mean that was all she was ever going to be. Did that old dame think that all Hoda wanted to do for the rest of her life was pump old cripplecocks like her husband? ... If she felt like doing some charity work, on the side, she'd do it, like for that poor old guy for instance. With a wife like that he deserved a break sometimes. How was she so much better than Hoda anyway? (Wiseman 176)

Blending "the Lurianic story of creation and the messianic promise of redemption" (Kertzer 17), *Crackpot* is a novel preoccupied with brokenness and, sign of its remarkable power, with mending and wholeness. Its world is "full of shards of confusion and evil and sparks of divinity and beauty" (Mack 136), yet, as Francis Zichy sees it, "the very act by which mending is attempted can only be another act of breaking" (37). From the opening tale of Hoda's grandfather – the tinker, mender of broken pots – to the closing observation of the aware "fallen fat woman" who confronts and comforts "the horrible deformities of the human vessel" (Wiseman 285, 292), the narrative enacts Wiseman's interest "in describing people on the edge of society, people who are deformed either physically or psychologically" (Morisco 129), using the fracture between past and present to build new meanings. Illustrating Wiseman's own belief in stories as "potentially redeeming for the world" (Meyer and O'Riordan 156), Hoda admits and relaxes "her pride that nobody did know her, not really, not who she was underneath, not nearly as well as she knew them, even though they talked about her and laughed at her and looked down on her" (Wiseman 292). With Lazar, the Holocaust survivor, one of the "ma-kés, … the cursed ones" (Wiseman 301), and her own rich lore of origin, ridicule, and perseverance, the Winnipeg prostitute "in the ardour of her wisdom" foresees "stirring the muddy waters in the brimming pot together" (304).

As benchmark and question mark, Hoda, whose directive provides the title for this chapter, also engages in its most startling and provocative activity. The incestuous scene with Pipick is neither voyeuristic nor salacious; rather, it shows the breadth of her moral compass. In thinking about what "making love" means, she observes, "Sometimes all the love you get even though you're making like crazy is just a shiverful, a flash of feeling between you" (Wiseman 241). Expiating her sense of guilt for abandonment, she agrees to Pipick's sexual initiation after an acute, retrospective examination of right and wrong:

> Always she had wanted to do what was right. At first she had thought that what felt good was what must be right. Well, how was she to know? And how was she to know now that what felt just awful, what aroused in her a revulsion of loathing at the very thought, was wrong? If it wasn't right when it felt right, was it wrong because it felt wrong? … But knowing, … it was for a reason, and because she was a person, and she had a debt, an enormous, inerasable debt, and because it was the only thing she could think of that she could do, that maybe she was fit to do for him. (Wiseman 252)

Here the carnivalesque in all its ambivalent justifications and the grotesque confront and challenge the domain of moral rectitude. Hoda's still point of decision-making results in a generous act for which she feels uniquely qualified.

What determines fitness for this role, with its counter-aesthetic elements of transgression, abjection, and voyeurism of the self, we wonder. Charlotte Roche, author of the sensational, savage depiction of female anatomy and desire *Wetlands*, maintains that "the good thing about prostitutes is that you can get to the point straightaway; they're not shocked about anything you ask" (qtd. in Power 2). Heather O'Neill's approach is breezily entrepreneurial: as she observes, "If you're young and attractive, it's like having a walletful of money. It gets you things. You have a long time to exploit your beauty" (qtd. in Ackerman 85). Exploitative or exploiting, prostitution can be a release and a prelude. Maria Campbell, Evelyn Lau, and Elisabeth Eaves escape from or revolt against family conditions but emerge as writers about their period in the sex industry and beyond – Campbell as a memoirist, playwright, filmmaker, and Elder; Lau as a poet; and Eaves as a journalist. Writing itself can be both therapeutic and illuminating; as Lau notes, "Funny how in the process of writing I've straightened myself out" (212). Recasting, re-examining, they position themselves in a safe and now-critical distance. No such fortune is in the cards for Piquette, Leah, or Oryx.

And what about the range of reactions to this experience, "at the same time within and peripheral to" our society, and responses to the writing about it, with its provocative "blend of affiliation and dissidence" (Simon 119, 120)? In these autobiographical and fictionalized treatments of prostitution, the trenchant observations on both urban place and psychological space distinguish them, I suggest, from earlier, particularly Victorian, representations in writing and in life. The moralizing quality of Old World English portraits throws into relief the different, not necessarily amoral, perspective of judgment in contemporary writing, where the working girls themselves speak about their clientele, their choices, and their society. Judith Walkowitz has explored the "strong female subculture" in nineteenth-century prostitution, when "'outcast women' banded together" (25–6). Chronic poverty along with the stigmatization and public shaming of the Contagious Diseases Acts (1864–9) contributed to "the making of an outcast group" (Walkowitz 192). W.T. Stead's "prurient exposés" (Walkowitz 249) – "The Maiden Tribute of Modern Babylon," a four-part series which ran in the *Pall Mall Gazette* in 1885 – chronicled the lives of prostitutes, the deals made by procuresses, and the desires of upper-class paedophiles. When depicted by male writers, these earlier figures – necessary but often silent narrative elements – are presented as embodiments of both contagion and pathos, underclass objects of voyeuristic, occasionally reformative, interest. Phil Hubbard notes their symbolic importance in Victorian society as "the moral 'margin' crucial for defining the moral 'centre'" (58). Think of Nancy in *Oliver Twist*, or Dante Gabriel Rossetti's poetic characterization of Jenny, a country girl who becomes a dressy Haymarket prostitute in whose "desecrated mind ... all contagious currents meet" (lines 163–4), or his painting *Found* picturing another country girl "in her prostitute's finery groveling before her abandoned beau in his laborer's smock, as he discovers her in a visit to the city of London" (Gilbert 113). In the archive of Victorian biography, George Gissing's first marriage to seventeen-year-old alcoholic prostitute Nell (Marianne Helen Harrison) and his "hopes of making her respectable through contact with his own domestic requirements" failed (Bodenheimer 18), resulting in their separation and Nell's early death. Transgression as the controlled excursion into the periphery reveals that "what is excluded at the overt level of identity-formation is productive of new objects of desire" (Stallybrass and White 25); as in many figurations of the sex worker, and in all periods, desire and disgust are in constant fluctuation. Although alleged gender differences in the representation of the prostitute by Victorian writers can be riddled with inconsistencies, which themselves prove the difficulty of generalizations, some Victorian women writers' treatment of the "fallen woman" seems more attentive and nuanced. Think of Elizabeth Gaskell's characterization of Esther in *Mary Barton*, who uses her own history of abandonment and degradation to counsel her niece against a similar fate. Elizabeth Barrett Browning's epic poem *Aurora Leigh* demonstrates sympathy for Marian Erle, the working-class rejected fiancée who is raped in a brothel but ultimately refuses marriage to raise her child as the sole guardian.

Judging, diminishing, distancing prostitution, these Victorian cases emphasize its demi-monde aspects and objectification; they also expose how "excessive fears of pollution, disloyalty, and disorder" can yield feats of great self-control, "one of the hallmarks of middle-class gentility" (Davidoff 105). Such features are still prominent today, even though primarily women writers themselves are relating or creating the accounts and illuminating the deliberate choice of many of the principal actors in the process. One feature that links all narratives of prostitution is the commercial transaction. Even in the instructive example of the twice-widowed Canaanite Tamar – veiled as a temple prostitute to seduce and expose the patriarchal authority of her father-in-law Judah, who had to admit that "the woman hath been more righteous" (*King James Bible*,

Gen. 38.26) – Judah's transgression is revealed through the "pledge" (Gen. 38.18) of his signet, bracelets, and staff made to this supposed harlot. "The corporeal image of the prostitute soliciting for business in the public realm is thus a central motif in fixing the idea of commercial sex as immoral, for here the woman is adopting a masculine, predatory sexual role" (Hubbard 72).

What is the compelling reason we are drawn to these accounts? Is it the rawness of their disclosure of one of the most meaningful, potentially transformative, human activities? As Jerome J. McGann investigates the socio-historical conditions of textual development and mutation, he proposes that "the sexual event itself, ... a total body sensation almost mystical in its intensity[, is] ... one of the greatest scenes of textuality" (3). In the archive of Canadian women's writing under my study, this standard concerns Hoda alone; yet in light of the more common and less positive outcomes for the prostitute, some readers may find her rhapsodic delight an exercise in faux naiveté. Might academic readers imitate the movement and reflection of Alayna Munce's narrator in *When I Was Young and in My Prime,* as she encounters a working girl on the corner of King and Dowling in Toronto? "Passing her, giving her a wide berth so as not to disturb the charged ring she's conjuring around herself, I see for a second how hard the work is. Pouring oneself out into bottomless streets" (Munce 69). The work *is* tough, revealing, discomfiting – especially when it appears to have no exit. Whether in their own voices for Arcan and Hanrahan or through narrators' mediation for Héloïse and Moira, the status of sex object – the result of seeking or resignation – remains a troubling constant. It troubles because however much their confinement traces back to motivating factors, it also indicates a noncombative, willed acceptance. Although Hanrahan dedicates her text to her parents, Robert and Mary, Eaves thanks her clinical psychologist mother and mathematics professor father "for teaching [her] to explore, think, and work" (iii), and Arcan has insisted that her parents not read her writing in which she has "exposed some very deep wounds" (Ackerman 84), these parents remain silent – possibly helpless – observers of their daughters' real and fictionalized behaviour. Hoda, the substantial opponent of hypocrisy and righteousness, nevertheless opts for marriage and resignation from the street; her father, patronized as the wise fool who "probably knew, though he wouldn't admit it openly," is also the only parent to celebrate "God's grace in giving him a daughter who could spread her legs and let in the whole wide world" (Wiseman 177, 178). Hoda's understanding, born of stubbornness and pride, shrewdness and generosity, endures in an unparalleled, inimitable textuality. Unlike many of her co-workers, this survivor exults in her vocation while exemplifying agency in her willingness to engage in and determination to walk away from the streets. Against her triumphant indomitability we can measure and feel the carapace of neglect, vulnerability, and ostracism in the related and fictionalized world of prostitution in Canadian women's writing.

WORKS CITED

Ackerman, Marianne. "Femmes Fatales: Young Female Writers on the State of Sex in Québec." *The Walrus*, vol. 5, no. 4, May 2008, pp. 83–7.

Arcan, Nelly. *Putain.* Seuil, 2001.

– *Whore.* Translated by Bruce Benderson, Black Cat, 2005.

Armstrong, Jeannette. *Slash.* Theytus, 1985.

Atwood, Margaret. *Oryx and Crake: A Novel.* Nan A. Talese, 2003.

– *The Handmaid's Tale.* McClelland and Stewart, 1986.

– *Survival: A Thematic Guide to Canadian Literature.* Anansi, 1972.

Austen, Jane. *Mansfield Park.* Dover Publications, 2001.

Bal, Mieke. *Loving Yusuf: Conceptual Travels from Present to Past.* U of Chicago P, 2008.

Blais, Marie-Claire. *Une saison dans la vie d'Emmanuel.* Boréal, 1991.

– *A Season in the Life of Emmanuel.* Translated by Derek Coltman, Farrar, Strauss, and Giroux, 1976.

Blondal, Patricia. *A Candle to Light the Sun.* McClelland and Stewart, 1976.

Bodenheimer, Rosemarie. "Give Us a Break: Review of Paul Delany's *George Gissing: A Life.*" *London Review of Books*, 9 July 2009, pp. 18–20.

Brand, Dionne. *At the Full and Change of the Moon.* Alfred A. Knopf, 1999.

Browning, Elizabeth Barrett. *Aurora Leigh.* Edited by Kerry McSweeney, Oxford UP, 2008.

Buss, Helen. "Canadian Women's Autobiography: Some Critical Directions." *A Mazing Space: Writing Canadian Women Writing*, edited by Shirley Neuman and Smaro Kamboureli, Longspoon/NeWest, 1986, pp. 154–66.

Campbell, Maria. *Halfbreed.* McClelland and Stewart, 1973.

Davidoff, Leonore. *Worlds Between: Historical Perspectives on Gender and Class.* Routledge, 1995.

Demers, Patricia. "Working Girls in Print: A Growth Industry." *Topia*, vol. 12, 2004, pp. 83–98.

de Vries, Maggie. *Missing Sarah: A Vancouver Woman Remembers Her Vanished Sister.* Penguin, 2004.

Duffy, Eamon. "Conspiracy Theories: Review of Avied Kleinberg's *Flesh Made Word: Saints' Stories and the Western Imagination.*" *London Review of Books*, 29 Jan. 2009, pp. 31–3.

Eaves, Elisabeth. *Bare: On Women, Dancing, Sex, and Power.* Alfred A. Knopf, 2002.

Egli, Irina. *Terre salée.* Boréal, 2006.

Ferris, Shawna. *Street Sex Work and Canadian Cities: Resisting a Dangerous Order.* U of Alberta P, 2015.

Gaskell, Elizabeth C. *Mary Barton.* Edited by Shirley Foster, Oxford UP, 2006.

Gilbert, Pamela K. "Sex and the Modern City: English Studies and the Spatial Turn." *The Spatial Turn: Interdisciplinary Perspectives*, edited by Barney Warf and Santa Arias, Routledge, 2009, pp. 102–21.

Godfrey, Rebecca. *The Torn Skirt.* Harper Perennial, 2002.

Gunew, Sneja. "Operatic Karaoke and the Pitfalls of Identity Politics." *Literary Pluralities*, edited by Christl Verduyn, Broadview Press, 1998, pp. 254–62.

Guy, Chantal. "Nelly Arcan: L'amour au temps du collagène." *La Presse*, 26 Aug. 2007. www.lapresse.ca/arts/livres/entrevues/200909/25/01-905440-nelly-arcan-lamour-au-temps-du-collagene.php.

– "Portrait d'une comète littéraire." *La Presse*, 25 Sept. 2009. www.lapresse.ca/arts/dossiers/deces-de-nelly-arcan/200909/25/01-905745-portrait-dune-comete-litteraire.php.

Hanrahan, Catherine. *Lost Girls and Love Hotels.* Penguin Canada, 2006.

Hubbard, Phil. "Sexuality, Immorality and the City: Red-Light Districts and the Marginalization of Female Street Prostitutes." *Gender, Place and Culture*, vol. 5, no. 1, 1998, pp. 55–72.

Jager, Eric. "The Book of the Heart: Reading and Writing the Medieval Subject." *Speculum*, vol. 71, 1996, pp. 1–26.

Kertzer, J.M. "Beginnings and Endings: Adele Wiseman's *Crackpot.*" *Essays on Canadian Writing*, vol. 56, 1998, pp. 15–35.

King James Bible. Oxford UP, 1952.

Kipnis, Laura. *The Female Thing: Dirt, Sex, Envy, Vulnerability.* Pantheon Books, 2006.

Labrèche, Marie-Sissi. *Borderline.* Boréal, 2000.

Lau, Evelyn. *Runaway: Diary of a Street Kid.* HarperCollins, 1989.

Laurence, Margaret. *The Prophet's Camel Bell.* McClelland and Stewart, 1963.

– *The Tomorrow-Tamer and Other Stories.* McClelland and Stewart, 1963.

Mack, Marcia. "*The Sacrifice* and *Crackpot*: What a Woman Can Learn by Rewriting a Fairy Tale and Clarifying Its Meaning." *Essays on Canadian Writing*, vol. 68, 1999, pp. 134–58.

McGann, Jerome J. *The Textual Condition.* Princeton UP, 1991.

McGinn, Dave. "How To Raise a Two-Year-Old Genius." *Globe and Mail*, 5 May 2009, pp. L1–3.

Meyer, Bruce, and Brian O'Riordan. "The Permissible and the Possible: An Interview with Adele Wiseman." Panofsky, pp. 144–63.

Miller, William Ian. "Sanctuary, Red Light Districts, and Washington D.C.: Some Observations on Neuman's Anomalous Zones." *Stanford Law Review*, vol. 48, 1996, pp. 1235–43.

Mosionier, Beatrice Culleton. *In Search of April Raintree.* Edited by Cheryl Suzack, Portage and Main Press, 1999.

Morisco, Gabriella. "The Charm of an Unorthodox Feminism: An Interview with Adele Wiseman." *We Who Can Fly: Poems, Essays and Memories in Honour of Adele Wiseman*, edited by Elizabeth Greene, Cormorant, 1997, pp. 125–46.

Munce, Alayna. *When I Was Young and in My Prime.* Nightwood Editions, 2005.

Munro, Alice. "Fiction." *Harper's Magazine*, Aug. 2007, pp. 71–80.

O'Neill, Heather. *Lullabies for Little Criminals: A Novel.* Harper Perennial, 2006.

Panofsky, Ruth, editor. *Adele Wiseman: Essays on Her Works.* Guernica, 2001.

Poitras, Marie Hélène. *Soudain le Minotaure.* Éditions Triptyque, 2002.

Pollock, Sharon. *Whiskey Six Cadenza. NeWest Plays by Women*, edited by Diane Bessai and Don Kerr, NeWest, 1987, pp. 137–247.

Power, Nina. "The Dirty Girl." *Salon.com*, 4 Apr. 2009. www.salon.com/books/int/2009/04/04/charlotte_roche. Accessed 4 Apr. 2009.

Razack, Sherene. "Race, Space, and Prostitution: The Making of the Bourgeois Subject." *Canadian Journal of Women and the Law*, vol. 10, 1998, pp. 338–76.

Roife, Katie. "My Life in a G-String: A Round Up of Stripper Memoirs." *DoubleX*, 22 June 2009. www.morrissey-solo.com/threads/my-life-in-a-g-string-a-round-up-of-stripper-memoirs.101211/. Accessed 22 June 2009.

Rossetti, Dante Gabriel. *The Poetical Works.* Edited by W.M. Rossetti, Little, Brown, 1887. 2 vols.

Simon, Sherry. "The Language of Difference: Minority Writers in Québec." *Canadian Literature*, suppl. 1, May 1987, pp. 119–28.

Stallybrass, Peter, and Allon White. *The Politics and Poetics of Transgression.* Cornell UP, 1986.

Walkowitz, Judith. *Prostitution and Victorian Society: Women, Class, and the State.* Cambridge UP, 1980.

Watson, Sheila. *The Double Hook.* McClelland and Stewart, 2008.

Wilson, Robert R. "Diane Schoemperlen's Fiction: The Clean, Well-Lit Worlds of Dirty Realism." *Essays on Canadian Writing*, vol. 40, 1990, pp. 80–108.

Wiseman, Adele. *Crackpot.* McClelland and Stewart, 1978.

Wong, Jan. "Evelyn Lau Gets Perfect Grades in the School of Hard Knocks." *Globe and Mail*, 3 Apr. 1997, p. A11.

Wyschogrod, Edith. "Towards a Postmodern Ethics: Corporeality and Alterity." *The Ethical*, edited by E. Wyschogrod and G.P. McKenny, Blackwell, 2003, pp. 54–65.

York, Lorraine M. "The Habits of Language: Uniform(ity), Transgression and Margaret Atwood." *Canadian Literature*, vol. 126, 1990, pp. 6–19.

Zichy, Francis. "The Lurianic Background: Myths of Fragmentation and Wholeness in Adele Wiseman's *Crackpot*." Panofsky, pp. 31–54.

13 Border-Crossings and Alternative Social Spaces in Gabrielle Roy's *Bonheur d'occasion* / *The Tin Flute*

D.M.R. BENTLEY

While the contrast between the elevated dwellings of Montréal and Québec City and those beneath them both spatially and socially is a recurring feature of Canadian writing of the pre- and post-Confederation periods,[1] not until Gabrielle Roy's *Bonheur d'occasion* (1945) – *The Tin Flute*[2] – did it become a structuring device for a major work of Canadian literature. "Beyond [the Notre Dame Viaduct] ... the town of Westmount climbs in tiers toward the mountain's ridge in its stiff English luxury," observes the narrator near the beginning of the novel; "here poverty and superfluity will stare tirelessly at each other, as long as Westmount lasts, as long as St. Henri lies at its feet. Between the two the bell towers soar" (34). Of course, the most striking feature of this passage is the "geographical and social division" (Simon 175) that provides the backdrop against which Roy presents the movements and relationships – the

1 For two early examples, see Thomas Cary's *Abram's Plains* (1789), where the narrator looks across from Cape Diamond at the "villa" of Lord Dorchester (the Chateau Saint-Louis) and associates it with the health-giving "breeze" of the "plains" and down at the village of Lorette (now a suburb of Québec City) in which a contingent of Hurons "as villagers take up their resting place" (485–90, 412–15); and Cornwall Bayley's *Canada* (1806), where the City's Upper Town permits a comprehensive view of the Lower Town and the surrounding countryside (1–28 and later).

2 To date, Roy's novel has been twice translated into English as *The Tin Flute*: in 1947 by Hannah Josephson and in 1958 by Alan Brown. Although Brown's translation has not been without its critics, it has been used here because of its relative accessibility in the current New Canadian Library series of McClelland and Stewart, where it replaced Josephson's translation in 1988. Words and phrases from the original French text have occasionally been placed in parentheses after their English counterparts in Brown's translation for the purposes of clarification and resonance.

"rhomb[oids], ... triangles, [and] ... equations" (12) – of her predominantly French Canadian characters. Less striking, but also significant in the passage, are the possibilities of stasis and aspiration intimated by the "bell towers" of its closing sentence – architectural structures that are anchored in the ground where they were built and yet transcend the border or boundary between the poor *faubourg* of St Henri and the wealthy enclave of Westmount, and thus anticipate the border-crossings by the characters in the novel who literally or imaginatively climb Mount Royal.[3] Indeed, border-crossings and actual or contemplated escapes from the segmentations of the city are a recurring and important aspect of *The Tin Flute* that colours many facets of the novel, from the perception of the railway and canal that border St Henri[4] as avenues of escape by one of its male protagonists, Jean Lévesque (see 29–34, 82), to the creation of an alternative habitat in the city dump by a group of the city's poor in a "morbid ... astonishing" (307), and deeply resonant story that the other male protagonist, Emmanuel Létourneau, hears towards the end of the novel from a peripheral character named Alphonse Poirier.

In addition to providing structure and tension in Roy's novel, the contrast between the "great" and "rich" houses of the wealthy English Canadian inhabitants of Westmount and the much smaller and less salubrious dwellings of the French Canadian inhabitants of St Henri exerts a powerful, even formative, influence on a number of the novel's characters, most notably Jean and Emmanuel. For the former, "the mountain, whose lights you could mistake for a cluster of early stars,"[5] represents an

3 Running parallel to this line of ascent is Boulevard Saint-Laurent ("The Main"), which famously displays in its upward movement the waves of immigrants of different ethnicities whose port of arrival was Montréal. See also the chapter by Sherry Simon in this collection.

4 St Henri (Saint-Henri) is sandwiched between Westmount and Verdun, with the Canadian Pacific Railway tracks and St Catherine Street on its northerly side and what used to be the Grand Trunk Railway tracks and the Lachine Canal (which was closed in 1959 as a result of the construction of the St Lawrence Seaway) on its southerly side. For a discussion of poverty in Montréal as lived and described in autobiographical works by Lise Payette, Adèle Lauzon, Denise Bombardier, and France Théoret, see "Growing Up Poor and Female in Montréal, 1930–1960: Women's Autobiographies as Counter-Narratives" by Patricia Smart in the present collection.

5 The fact that many statements and passages in *The Tin Flute* blur or trouble the distinction between the narrator and the character in focus (in this instance Jean) may stem to some extent from Roy's well-known injection of her own experience of Montréal (and Winnipeg) into the novel, but it also stems from her use of a form

Olympian dream of financial and social ascent: "You know, beautiful," he tells the female protagonist, Florentine Lacasse, as he wheedles his way into her affections, "it won't be long before I have my foot on the first rung of the ladder ... and then good-bye to St. Henri" (80). For Emmanuel, Mount Royal is less a goal and a goad to upward mobility than the elevated side of an "abyss" between, on the one hand, the "mellow, impregnable calm," "English cosiness," and sense of "order" that emanates from its "warm stone houses, Georgian windows, lawns and honeysuckle bushes" and, on the other, the confused and unhappy thoughts that are a source first of "melancholy" and then of the existential alienation of an outsider – "it seemed to him that he was alone in the universe, ... holding in his hands ... the eternal human enigma" – a condition that the novel here associates with the sense of strangeness and alienation that can come with crossing from a familiar to an unfamiliar zone or neighbourhood in a spatially differentiated and segregated modern city (319–20).[6]

---

of the free indirect style whereby superficially objective descriptions by the narrator are coloured by the thoughts and emotions of a character. The presence of similar combinations of free and direct discourse can be observed in Duncan Campbell Scott's *In the Village of Viger* (1896) and M.G. Vassanji's *The In-Between World of Vikram Lall* (2005); and other works of fiction that treat distinct communities within Canada might suggest that such combinations reflect the need in these texts for narrators and a narrative perspective that are both a part of and apart from the communities being portrayed and thus able to represent them to themselves and to outsiders with a credible combination of detachment and empathy. For various essays by Roy about Manitoba and Montréal, see *Le Pays de Bonheur d'occasion* (Boréal, 2000), 11–62 and 81–100; and for a bibliography of the articles that she wrote in the early 1940s for *Le bulletin des agriculteurs*, including responses to St Henri that were incorporated into *The Tin Flute*, see François Ricard, *Gabrielle Roy, une vie*, 597–601.

6 Emmanuel chooses love as the solution to his dilemma, but the novel as a whole suggests that this is, at best, a delusive solution: the woman he loves – Florentine – is pregnant with Jean's child; the Second World War is imminent; and as he leaves St Henri with other soldiers from the suburb he glimpses "a tree in a backyard, its branches tortured among electric wires and clotheslines, its leaves dry and shrivelled before they were fully out" (383). In "Stranger and Afraid" (ca. 1945 and later), a novel that remained unfinished at his death, A.M. Klein also uses the ethnically differentiated and segregated zones and neighbourhoods of Montréal as a setting for the development of his Dostoyevskian protagonist (see Bentley, "New Styles" and, for Klein's possible debts to *Bonheur d'occasion* in *The Rocking Chair, and Other Poems* (1948), "Rummagings").

In her interactions with Emmanuel, Florentine is by turns "embarrass[ed]" and made "anxious" by his remarks (82), part of the reason being that, as is made clear when she is introduced in the novel's opening pages, her perspective on the world is more horizontal and fatalistic than vertical and ambitious. A waitress who works behind the "imitation marble counter" of a "restaurant at the back of ... [a] Five and Ten" cent store (7), she resembles the young woman who stares out at the viewer across the food- and drink-laden counter in Édouard Manet's *A Bar at the Folies-Bergère* (1882): in addition to being surrounded by objects and a mirror, she is both an observer and an object of observation in an environment dominated by glass that reflects and reveals a largely horizontal world: "a great mirror hangs on the wall of the restaurant"; Florentine "keep[s] an eye on the crowd entering the store through ... glass swing doors"; in her imagination she can see "the department store windows" of St Catherine Street, where "everything she desire[s], admire[s] and envie[s] float[s]" in a realm of "restaurants" with "gleaming bay windows" and "movie theatre[s]" with "cashier's glass cage[s]" and "tall, glittering mirrors" (7, 17). In their emphasis on glass windows and escapist fantasies, the descriptions of Florentine and her environment make her world a microcosm of what can now be seen as Benjaminian modernity, complete with a flâneur in the form of the somewhat dandified Jean, whose appeal to her rests partly on the nonchalance with which he wears "expensive things: the wrist-watch, whose glass flashed with his every move, the rich silk scarf slung casually around his neck, the fine leather gloves sticking out of his suit pocket" (17). In small, the flashing glass ("cadran miroitait" [*Bonheur* 18]) of Jean's wristwatch represents all that, in Florentine's eyes, lies outside and beyond St Henri and the cheap restaurant in which she works.

Despite the fact that, when Emmanuel ascends Mount Royal near the end of *The Tin Flute*, "the troubles and anguish of the lower town" and its "stink of poverty" seem to cling unshakably to him (319), his earlier perceptions and conceptions of St Henri are far from negative. In fact, for much of the novel, he views the suburb as "his village in the city," as a "neighbourhood" that more than any other part of Montréal has "kept its well-defined limits ... its special, narrow, characteristic village life" (284). In a passage that may well owe a debt to Stephen Leacock's celebration of small-town community in *Sunshine Sketches of a Little Town* (1912), Emmanuel arrives at the railway station in St Henri after a long absence and, aided by the "sights and smells" that he encounters, experiences a powerful feeling of belonging that Roy figures not merely as a counter to the cacophony of the city but also as an abolition of "partitions" that dissolves the boundaries between people and leaves in their place a feeling of the openness and interconnectedness of the local social fabric:

> Children were playing hopscotch near the station and their shouting pierced through the whistle ("s'entendaint à travers les sifflements" [*Bonheur* 252]) of the locomotive.
>
> All the windows were open, and the sounds of living, clattering dishes and conversation floated in the air as if the partitions of the world had been abolished and human life was on display in all its warmth and poverty ("en commun avec tous ses secrets" [*Bonheur* 253]) ...
>
> In the daytime there is the pitiless reality ("vie" [*Bonheur* 253]) of labour. But at night there is this village life, when chairs are pulled out to the sidewalk or people sit in door-sills and the talk passes from one threshold to the next.
>
> St. Henri: ant-heap village ("termitière villageoise" [*Bonheur* 253])!
>
> ... He saw St. Henri as he had never seen it, with its complex yet open weave ("sa vie complexe et pourtant sans secret" [*Bonheur* 253]). He liked it all the more, as we like our village after returning from some expedition, simply because everything is still in its familiar place, and everyone says hello! (284–5)

As perceived and conceived in these passages, St Henri resembles a "pedestrian pocket" of the sort for which new urbanists such as Peter Calthorpe, following in the footsteps of Jane Jacobs, yearn and advocate: "a mixed-use community within an average 2,000-foot walking distance of a transit stop and core commercial area that ... mix[es] residential, retail, office, open space, and public uses in a walkable environment, making it convenient for residents and employees to travel by transit, bicycle, foot, or car" (17, 56). As envisaged by Calthorpe, such "pedestrian pockets" or "transit-oriented developments" occur within or beside a suburban megacentre, but, of course, St Henri exists within such a centre and for that reason provides an even more accessible and appealing haven from the anonymity, monotony, and placelessness of modernity[7] – the sense of evanescence identified by Marx and the feeling of

7 In addition to Calthorpe's *The New American Metropolis*, see his and other essays in Doug Kelbaugh, ed., *The Pedestrian Pocket Book*.

anomie identified by Émile Durkheim.[8] With its "open" windows, "conversation in the air," and "talk pass[ing] from one threshold to the next," St Henri is a place in which distinctions between inside and outside and private and public space become fuzzy enough to permit members of the community to feel at home *in* the street.

Working-class suburb though it is, St Henri does not occupy the opposite pole from Westmount in *The Tin Flute*. That dismal distinction belongs to the (too) appropriately named Workman Street, along one side of which runs a "slum of grey brick … [that] forms a long wall with identical, equidistant doors and windows," some with "doors and shutters … walled up," others with "windows plugged with rags or oiled paper," and all carrying "a pitiful appeal to individuality" in the form of a number (97–8). As becomes especially apparent in this portion of the novel, Florentine and her family belong to the most insecure of the social strata, namely, the stratum on and around the border between the lower part of the middle class and the upper part of the lower class, a group that is always attempting to lodge itself securely in the middle class and fearful of descending permanently into the lower class. By arranging for Florentine's mother, Rose-Anna, to visit both Workman Street and Westmount, Roy makes the contrast between them painfully clear: in the slum, "children … play … on the sidewalk among the litter" and their "cries of misery come from the depths" of the houses; "women, thin and sad," either stand in "evil-smelling doorways" or stare "aimlessly" out of windows; on the mountain, "the air [is] … clear and pure" and the "private houses" are luxurious – phenomena that Rose-Anna fails to connect even as she recognizes that the children in the Mount Royal hospital in which her young son lies dying are "protected by the crystal air from the smoke, the soot and the foul breath of the factories which h[ang] around the low-lying houses like the breath of a monster straining at its work" (97–8, 217). Consonant with this contrast is Emmanuel's recollection that "it was not to commit any act of vandalism" that he and his friends went to Westmount when they were young (as Emmanuel recalls when he climbs Mount Royal later in the novel) "but to fill … [their] lungs with fresh air" (319). To Rose-Anna's mind, the removal

8 See Marshall Berman's *All That Is Solid Melts into Air* for a brilliantly illuminating discussion of modernity in the light of Marx's phrase (in the *Communist Manifesto*), which also has great explanatory value for such Canadian works as Archibald Lampman's "The City of the End of Things" (1900).

of her son from his family and familiar surroundings offsets any benefit to be derived from the "crystal air" of Mount Royal, but it was precisely that air, coupled with the "commanding prospect over the city" (Bouchette 1: 242), that commended it to the fur-trader Simon McTavish and his wealthy predecessors and successors of the Montréal elite who built houses there in the years when the city was the commercial capital of the Canadas.

In Roy's Montréal, excursions to the country also permit the less lofty to escape from the "breath of [the] monster," as does one of the most intriguing environments to be found in Canadian writing: the village in the city dump described to Emmanuel by Alphonse Poirier. "I knew a guy," Alphonse begins,

> he'd built up a little business at the dump. He picked up all the old pots and pans and he fixed them up and straightened them out and then he sold them ...
>
> He had a room in town. But there's thieves on the dump, just like any place else. So this guy built a summer cottage ("un petit chalet de plaisance" [*Bonheur* 274]) right on the dump, so he could keep an eye on his stuff. Those days there was a whole village in that place, a collection of shacks about the size of a dog kennel.[9] You didn't need a building permit and you didn't have to look far for boards ... You'd dig around there and pick whatever you needed, bits of pipe, four sheets of tin for the roof, and you chose a lot where it didn't stink too bad, right down by the water. You know, there's people ready to pay a thousand dollars to have a cottage and their Sunday visit down by the river. The guys at the dump, they had all that for nothin', except the Sunday visit. And the quiet! You gotta go a long way to find quiet like at the dump ... You left the city behind you, the city an' its relief cheques and ... tramps lining up for their bread tickets and all the

9 In "Playing House: A Brief Account of the Idea of the Shack," an essay written to accompany a 2002 exhibition of the work of the BC photographer and artist Liz Magor which focused on West Coast shacks, Lisa Robertson writes that "one sojourns, or starts out, rather than settles in a shack" and observes that "typically the shack reuses or regroups things with humour and frugality" and that "[a] shack describes the relation of the minimum to freedom" (175, 176, 178). Robertson's contextualization of Magor's shacks is a rich, imaginative, and informed discussion that draws upon and illuminates a variety of sources, including Marc-Antoine Laugier's famous narrative of the emergence of the primitive hut (see 176–7). "If architecture is writing," she suggests, then "the shack is speech. Like a folk song it stores a vernacular" (179).

> racket about God knows what, and the streetcars goin' clingety clang and the big cars spoutin' fumes at you as if you had the plague. An' you had no more smoke there, nothin', you were right at home. (307–8)

Consisting of male squatters and located on, if not beyond, the outer margin of society, the dump village is an enclave with its own architecture and amenities, a poor man's resort whose salient qualities – permanent escape from the noise and "fumes" of the city without cost – render it superior from Alphonse's perspective to the temporary escape provided by a city park like the one on Mount Royal[10] or the expensive and still only temporary escape provided by a summer cottage.

After an indeterminate number of years, the dump village is burned to the ground by "city health officers," ostensibly because "some poor devil was found dead all alone in his shack and the rats got at him," but surely also because its existence is a transgressive violation of (a) the boundary between cleanness (purity) and "uncleanness" (defilement) by which, as Mary Douglas has shown in *Purity and Danger*, societies seek to "create unity" and "order" in and for themselves (2–4); and (b) the contract between a city and its citizens that assumes one of its tangible forms in property and education taxes: "my ... friend ... ended up havin' a pretty nice life," observes Alphonse. "He didn't owe a cent to nobody, he didn't cost the city a cent. And he was bringin' up a kid in town, doin' pretty good by him" (308). In other words, the destruction of the dump village by the city authorities is an act of purification and an assertion of comprehensive power over a group within the city's borders who is perceived as taking from the community without giving anything back. It is also, according to Douglas's lights, a way for the officials and residents of the city proper to expiate their own anxieties about "dirt" by synecdochically attaching them to a poor space and community.

The destruction of the dump village proves to be only temporary, however, and when it rises from its ashes, it becomes even more utopian in Alphonse's eyes than it was before the fire:

10 See Frederick Law Olmsted's *Mount Royal, Montréal* (1881) for its designer's conception of Montréal's central park as "a prophylactic and therapeutic agent of vital value" for "the mass of people" in preventing and counteracting "the harmful influences of ordinary town life" (22).

> When you're used to country air you always come back. The guys built that damn village up again. Not one shack less, not one shack more. Just like before. Same chimneys as big as a flowerpot on the roofs. Same pots on the fire inside. And all th[e] thin cats ... came back when the people did, from all the places where they didn't get fed right – great big fightin' cats! And maybe you won't believe it, but flowers started growin' in front of the shacks. I suppose it was seeds that came on the wind. An' you can say what you like ... it's not such a bad life down in that country ("c'est une vie comme une autre dans ce pays" [*Bonheur* 276]) – an' it is another country ("autre pays")! It's not the same country at all! ... And ... if you ... miss people and that other country, why you just go into town and make the rounds of society. You pay a visit to the people of the other country! (308–9)

Both a part of and apart from the modern metropolis, the dump village is an ecological pocket where domestic cats revert to a state of nature and airborne (or bird-borne) seeds can thrive more successfully than in either the paved streets of St Henri or the manicured lawns of Westmount.[11] Its shacks are not the preliminary and temporary manifestations of civilization as were the tents, shanties, and log houses of earlier eras, but part of a development within that civilization that is both "spontaneous,"[12] in the sense that it derives from no official plan, and

---

11 Earlier in the novel, Roy provides a vivid picture of Montréal's vanishing natural history: "In other days ... St. Henri's last houses had stood ... facing waste fields, and an almost limpid, rustic air hung about their simple gables and tiny gardens. From those better days St. Ambroise [Street] now has no more than two or three great trees, their roots still digging in beneath the concrete of the sidewalk. Textile mills, grain elevators and warehouses had risen to face the frame houses, slowly, solidly, walling them in" (28–9). In *Cities and Natural Process*, Michael Hough points out that in "the forgotten places of the city" – "the landscape of industry, railways, public utilities, vacant lands, urban expressway interchanges, abandoned mining lands and waterfronts" – there frequently exists a more diverse flora and fauna than in lawns or city parks (6). Observing that "the reclamation of 'derelict' areas, or the creation of new development o[n] the city's edge where the native and cultural landscape is replaced by a cultivated one, involves reducing diversity, rather than enhancing it," Hough asks, "Which are the derelict sites of the city requiring rehabilitation? Those fortuitous and often ecologically diverse landscapes representing urban natural forces at work, or the formalized landscapes created by design?" (8).

12 See Elizabeth Wilson, *The Sphinx in the City*, for "shanty towns" within cities as "spontaneous settlements" – communities whose value and values, not least in combatting the "impersonal factors of urban life," have too often been overlooked (129–30).

deliberate, in the sense that it arises from the desire of a group of people to live on the periphery of society in a place and a manner that are distinct but adjacent – "another country" within "the other country."

In this way, the dump village in *The Tin Flute* hearkens back to both the hobo encampments of the Depression and the much-publicized encampments of the homeless that appeared in Montréal, Toronto, Calgary, Vancouver, and other Canadian cities in the years surrounding the millennium.[13] Composed largely of homeless people, the latter usually began as a small group of makeshift shelters on a vacant piece of private property or in an out-of-the-way public place; for example, the encampment in Montréal in 2002 comprised six men in makeshift shelters under an overpass; the one in Calgary in 2000 consisted of approximately twenty people who had built huts in a park; and the one that began in Toronto in 1998 and eventually contained more than a hundred people was located near the waterfront on the former site of an iron foundry.[14] In each case, the fact that the land was either privately owned or a public space provided a legal reason for the eventual eviction of the squatters by owners of the land or municipal authorities, who frequently bolstered the case for dismantling the encampment on the grounds that it constituted a fire or health hazard, an argument that raises a loud echo in Alphonse's narrative in *The Tin Flute.*

Nor is this the only echo that can be heard between Roy's dump village and the Toronto shantytown, for as Shaughnessy Bishop-Stall recalls in *Down to This,*[15] his memoir of the better part of a year spent in a shantytown, the "thieves and drug addicts, vagabonds and ex-cons" who lived there could

13 For valuable discussions of the closely related issue of homelessness and its spatial implications, see the chapters by Domenico Beneventi and Simon Harel in the present collection.

14 The information in this paragraph is drawn from numerous newspaper articles and television reports in the fall of 2002, when the Toronto encampment was a topic of much discussion and controversy, supplemented by John Bowman and Justin Thompson's "Tent City" backgrounder of 14 October 2002 (see also "Homeless Evicted from Toronto's Tent City," CBC News, 25 Sept. 2002, www.cbc.ca/news/canada/homeless-evicted-from-toronto-s-tent-city-1.339489).

15 For a discussion of homelessness in Bishop-Stall's novel, see Beneventi's "Exposed to the Elements."

> look around and realize that everything they've been hustling for ... [was] right [t]here: stereos and VCRs, room to move, a perfect hideout and waterfront property. They ... [weren't] way out in the lonesome countryside or the goddam suburbs or trapped in the same old city. In fact, the city look[ed] perfect from [t]here – the lake, the downtown high-rises, the sun setting beneath the tallest free-standing structure in the world – it ... [was] like a picture postcard. And best of all, [t]here ... [were] no cops – as long as they stay[ed] ... [in]side the fence.
>
> So they d[u]g into a corner of the rubble for something they ... [could] use to build. There's so much, they could [have] ma[d]e use of anything. But [at the beginning] they just thr[ew] together a few shelters using tarps and old office furniture. They b[ought] some beer, ... [lit] a fire ... The smoke ... [rose] for everyone to see, like a warning or an invitation." (2)

"I'll never be able to fully explain what it felt like in there," writes Bishop-Stall near the end of his memoir, in another passage that smacks of Alphonse's utopianism in *The Tin Flute*: "the wilderness and the city together, the breeze off the lake and the hum of the overpass, the fire barrels crackling and the moonlight on the water. The air felt both infinite and volatile, like we'd slipped from the edge of this world onto a whole other planet. And I will always miss that place" (474).

By the time the Toronto shantytown was evacuated in November 2001, it had attracted a huge amount of media attention both in Canada and in the United States and become a cause célèbre for the *Toronto Star*, the Ontario Coalition Against Poverty, Toronto city councillor Jack Layton, and other left-of-centre groups and individuals. It had also been dubbed "Tent City," a misnomer reminiscent of the "Tent City" that arose at Kent State University in 1977 to protest the university administration's plan to build a gymnasium annex on a site associated with the Kent State riots of 1970 in which thirteen students were killed. No doubt, the association of Toronto's "Tent City" with the American social protest movement of three decades earlier did much to solidify support for its residents and antagonism against their evictors (Home Depot), but it also obscured the identity of the shantytown as an episode and a site with profoundly significant resonances in the human and architectural history of this country. In nineteenth-century Canada, shanties and shantytowns were largely understood as a stage in an immigrant narrative that led from the tents of nomadic new arrivals to the stone houses of very successful settlers. En route to the Talbot Settlement on the north shore of Lake Erie, the immigrants of Adam Hood Burwell's *Talbot Road* (1818) pitch "nightly tent[s] ... [of] coarse design" in "rude encampments" where "wide arching" trees "supply / The place of roof" (169–70). Similarly, when the settlers arrive at their destination in Alexander McLachlan's *The Emigrant* (1861) they "spread" a "humble tent ... Such as wandering Arabs rear, / In their deserts lone and drear," a "temporary thing" that nevertheless makes their "hearts ... sing" because they recognize it as a transient stage in their advance towards permanence and prosperity; indeed, the tent is quickly followed in the poem by the erection of a "log cabin" in which "Hope" watches over the development of the settlement (4: 9–14; 5: 1, 23). At the other end of the spectrum of progress lies the "great ... house" with "stone walls" and "many windows looking everywhere" (3: 1–3) in Isabella Valancy Crawford's *Malcolm's Katie* (1884) – a panoptic structure that allows Katie's father, Malcolm Graem, to revel in his farm's prosperity. In the urban environment, the equivalents of the Graem house are the brick and stone mansions of areas such as Westmount, an early and never completed example of which was the house that Simon McTavish was in the process of building when he died in 1804: "a large handsome stone building ... at the foot of the mountain, in a very conspicuous situation" (Lambert 2: 68), with "wings of hewn stone" (Sansom 195).

In the narrative that flows between these extremes, shanties fall between tents and log cabins and were read by observers either as architectural signs of prosperity yet to come to their inhabitants or, in an eerie anticipation of attitudes to similarly constructed dwellings of the future, as signs of their inhabitants' flaws and failures. A "shanty is a primitive hut," observes Catharine Parr Traill in *The Backwoods of Canada* (1836) apropos a "squatters' ground" near Peterborough that in her estimation housed not only many "tidy folk" who would meet with success, but also some people who were merely unfortunate and others who were "indolent," deficient in "energy and courage," or "idle and profligate," who "spend the money they received ... [and] remain miserable squatters on the shanty ground" (82–3). In this light, the shanties and the poor of what became known as Toronto's "Tent City" should be remembered less as a continuation of the American protest movement of the sixties and seventies than as an eloquent testimonial to the deeply saddening persistence in Canada of the causes and conditions, human as well as social, from which the shanties of despair rather than hope are constructed. "Tent City is not a city and we ... [didn't] live in tents," Bishop-Stall recalls; "we live[d] in shacks and shanties on the edge of Canada's largest metropolis where the river meets the lake ... Junk Town would be a better name" (1, and see 11, 15, 18, 24, 65, and elsewhere). "Poverty and superfluity ... [still] stare tirelessly at each other."

WORKS CITED

Bayley, Cornwall. *Canada: A Descriptive Poem.* Edited by D.M.R. Bentley, Canadian Poetry Press, 1990.

Beneventi, Domenico A. "Exposed to the Elements: Homelessness in Recent Canadian Fiction." *Canada Exposed / Le Canada à découvert,* edited by P. Anctil, A. Loiselle, and C. Rolfe, Peter Lang Publishing, 2009, pp. 85–100.

Bentley, D.M.R. "'New Styles of Architecture, a Change of Heart'? The Architexts of A.M. Klein and F.R. Scott." *The Canadian Modernists Meet,* edited by Dean Irvine, U of Ottawa P, 2005, pp. 17–58. Reappraisals: Canadian Writers 29.

– "Rummagings 3: A.M. Klein's *The Rocking Chair, and Other Poems* and Gabrielle Roy's *Bonheur d'occasion.*" *Canadian Poetry: Studies, Documents, Reviews,* vol. 56, Spring–Summer 2005, pp. 5–8.

Berman, Marshall. *All That Is Solid Melts into Air: The Experience of Modernity.* Simon and Schuster, 1982.

Bishop-Stall, Shaughnessy. *Down to This: Squalor and Splendour in a Big-city Shantytown.* Random House Canada, 2004.

Bouchette, Joseph. *The British Dominions in North America; Topographical and Statistical Description of the Provinces of Lower and Upper Canada, New Brunswick, Nova Scotia, the Islands of Newfoundland, Prince Edward, and Cape Breton.* Henry Colburn and Richard Bentley, 1831. 2 vols.

Burwell, Adam Hood. *Talbot Road: A Poem.* Edited by Michael Williams, Canadian Poetry Press, 1991.

Calthorpe, Peter. *The New American Metropolis: Ecology, Community and the American Dream.* Princeton Architectural, 1993.

Cary, Thomas. *Abram's Plains: A Poem.* 1789. Edited by D.M.R. Bentley, Canadian Poetry Press, 1986.

Crawford, Isabella Valancy. *Malcolm's Katie: A Love Story.* Edited by D.M.R. Bentley, Canadian Poetry Press, 1987.

Douglas, Mary. *Purity and Danger: An Analysis of Concepts of Pollution and Taboo.* Praeger, 1966.

Hough, Michael. *Cities and Natural Process: A Basis for Sustainable Development.* Routledge, 2004.

Kelbaugh, Doug, editor. *The Pedestrian Pocket Book: A New Suburban Design Strategy.* Princeton Architectural / U of Washington P, 1989.

Lambert, John. *Travels through Canada, and the United States of North America, in the Years 1806, 1807, and 1808.* Baldwin, Cradock, and Joy, 1816. 2 vols.

McLachlan, Alexander. *The Emigrant.* Edited by D.M.R. Bentley, Canadian Poetry Press, 1991.

Olmsted, Frederick Law. *Mount Royal, Montréal.* G.P. Putnam's Sons, 1881.

Ricard, François. *Gabrielle Roy, Une Vie: Biographie.* Boréal, 2000.

Robertson, Lisa. *Occasional Work and Seven Walks from the Office for Soft Architecture.* Clear Cut, 2003.

Roy, Gabrielle. *Bonheur d'occasion: Roman.* Boréal, [1945] 2009.

– *The Tin Flute.* Translated by Alan Brown, McClelland and Stewart, 1989.

Sansom, Joseph. *Sketches of Lower Canada: Historical and Descriptive; with the Author's Recollections of the Soil, and Aspect; the Morals, Habits, and Religious Institutions, of that Isolated Country; during a Tour of Québec, in the month of July, 1817.* Kirk and Mercein, 1817.

Simon, Sherry. *Translating Montréal: Episodes in the Life of a Divided City.* McGill-Queen's UP, 2006.

Traill, Catharine Parr. *The Backwoods of Canada.* 1836. Edited by D.M.R. Bentley, McClelland and Stewart, 1989.

Wilson, Elizabeth. *The Sphinx in the City: Urban Life, the Control of Disorder, and Women.* Virago, 1991.

14 Growing Up Poor and Female in Montréal, 1930–1960: Women's Autobiographies as Counter-narratives

PATRICIA SMART

Since the appearance of Gabrielle Roy's iconic novel *Bonheur d'occasion* in 1945, readers and critics alike have regarded the book as a radical and compassionate work, one that gave voice for the first time in Québec literature to the poor and disenfranchised working-class population of the neighbourhood of Saint-Henri in Montréal and in particular to its women. And yet for the future television personality and Parti Québécois cabinet minister Lise Payette, then a fourteen-year-old girl growing up in Saint-Henri, reading *Bonheur d'occasion* was the first major blow to her confidence, a "cultural shock" that "almost killed" her and from which it took her a long time to recover (68). Payette states early in the first volume of her memoirs that she never forgave Gabrielle Roy for writing that novel, that she never attempted to interview Roy during her years as a television host, and that later, in her years living as a cabinet minister in Québec City, she was often tempted to go and knock on Roy's door and to explain to the author all the harm the novel had done to her.

What the novel *had* done to her, Payette writes, was to make her see her own experience from the outside and to confront her with the concept of the interminable and repetitive cycle of poverty:

> I saw my life and my world as if in a mirror through her characters … I looked around me with new eyes. I saw us as poor, insignificant, without ambition and without culture, "born to dine on breadcrumbs" and unable to get out of our situation, repeating from generation to generation the same gestures and the same errors. I was wounded to the quick. I saw us as lazy, satisfied with little and with no desire for change … I was ashamed. Ashamed to be what I was, ashamed to be from Saint-Henri, ashamed as well to have worn stockings with runs in them as her heroine,

with whom I identified, did. I felt like an animal caught in the headlights of a car. (67–8)[1]

By devoting an entire chapter of her autobiography to *Bonheur d'occasion* and its effect on her, Payette is clearly situating her own story in opposition to it and, more generally, to conventional bourgeois narratives of poverty which deny agency and individuality to "poor" subjects and envisage their situation as an inherited and unchangeable state of being. As her use of the well-known dictum "nés pour un petit pain" (born to dine on breadcrumbs) reminds us, the idea that poverty was the preordained destiny of French Canadians was communicated from the pulpit and passed on from generation to generation for almost a century before the Quiet Revolution of the 1960s. As D.M.R. Bentley demonstrates elsewhere in this volume, Roy's novel not only perpetuates this defeatist narrative but inscribes it spatially, contrasting the enclosed, tense, and chaotic space of Saint-Henri and its poverty with the elevation and spaciousness of Westmount and the mountain, associated with wealth, order, and Englishness.

In Payette's autobiography, the period of fragile self-esteem brought on by her reading of *Bonheur d'occasion* comes to an end when one of her teachers, a nun, explains to her that there is a difference between a novel and reality, and that she, unlike Roy's protagonist Florentine Lacasse, can do whatever she chooses to do with her life. The striking contrasts (and parallels) with *Bonheur d'occasion* in Payette's work indicate that she has fashioned this first volume of her autobiography (as well as the life that it recounts) as a response to and refutation of the novel. Unlike Roy's, Payette's Saint-Henri is a dynamic space where adolescent hopes and dreams are nurtured, and an expansive one, connected with a larger and stimulating culture outside its borders. Like Roy's protagonist

---

1 "J'ai vu ma vie et mon monde et je nous ai vus comme dans un miroir à travers ses personnages ... J'ai regardé autour de moi avec ses yeux. Je nous ai vus pauvres, insignifiants, sans ambition et sans culture, 'nés pour un petit pain' et incapables d'en sortir, répétant de génération en génération les mêmes gestes et les mêmes erreurs. Je fus blessée au cœur. Je nous ai vus paresseux, nous contentant de peu et ne désirant rien d'autre ... J'eus honte. Honte d'être ce que j'étais, honte d'être de Saint-Henri, honte aussi d'avoir porté des bas avec des échelles comme le faisait son héroïne à qui je m'identifiais. Je me sentais comme la bête traquée par les feux d'une voiture." (All page references in this chapter are to the French-language texts and all translations are mine.)

Florentine Lacasse, Lise works behind the soda counter at the Five and Ten, but, unlike Florentine, she does it on weekends, to help pay for her *cours classique.* Her reminiscences of the ritual battles in Selby Park between the boys of Saint-Henri and the anglophone boys from Westmount, which Lise attends in order to cheer on her friends, transform the spatial and social divide between Saint-Henri and Westmount into an occasion for pleasure and companionship. And, unlike the repetitive circle to which mother and daughter are condemned in *Bonheur d'occasion,* Payette's experience of poverty is a positive one, thanks largely to the attitudes instilled in her by her mother and maternal grandmother.

Payette's memories of the joy of being young; the discovery of classical music, theatre, and literature; the healthy and comfortable relationship between adolescent boys and girls; and the strong sense of pride, confidence, and family received from her mother and grandmother represent the interlocking spaces of family, school, and social life as a nurturing soil imparting a sense of community values and of individual possibility. "When the cupboards were empty we went to eat at the home of [our grandmother] Marie-Louise, where the door was always open to us" (23),[2] she writes. When bills cannot be paid and the electricity is cut off, her mother puts a candle on the table and serves her daughters pancakes with molasses or *pain doré,* "and for us those meals were transformed into feasts" (23).[3] Lise's mother, who had been an office worker before marriage, realizes she will have to return to the workforce to pay for her daughters' schooling and chooses, like her own mother before her, to work as a cleaning woman in the houses of Westmount so that she can be at home when her daughters return from school. But, like Lise's grandmother, she will only work for the francophone rich, believing that one can put up with taking orders in French if it's absolutely necessary, but never in English. Before the end of her high school years, Payette has become her school's representative in the progressive Jeunesses étudiantes catholiques, where she meets Gérard Pelletier, Jeanne Sauvé, and other future leaders of Québec and Canadian society. In all of these ways, her account of her adolescence opens and expands the space accorded to the poor and to women in Roy's narrative, allowing for the possibility of individual self-realization.

2 "Quand les armoires à nourriture étaient vides, nous allions manger chez [ma grand-mère] Marie-Louise, dont la porte était toujours ouverte."

3 "et pour nous ces repas se transformaient en repas de fête."

In *Remnants of Nation*, her study of Canadian women's poverty narratives, Roxanne Rimstead cites Paulo Freire's dictum that the poor "must find a way to value their own thoughts about the world" over and against cultural discourses imposed from above (3). Speaking of women, Farah Godrej similarly argues that their consciousness must be liberated from "its propensity to judge itself through the lens of the dominant group, to speak to itself and of itself in the voice of patriarchy" (112). The oppression of a patriarchal system is effective "precisely because the stories that dominant Others tell about us so easily and so often become the stories we tell about ourselves" (114), Godrej writes, and in order to construct an identity free of these internalized narratives of "humiliation, powerlessness, weakness and diminished status," women must find a space or a social milieu that offers them the possibility of counter-narratives. The four Québec women's autobiographies examined here are examples of such counter-narratives, contesting imposed ideologies and narratives of class, culture, and gender by their account of the authors' often difficult navigation through or around them towards a confident sense of self. Each provides a different description of the geographic and psychological landscapes of poverty as experienced by young girls growing up in Montréal in the 1930s, 1940s, and 1950s. Two of them – Lise Payette's already discussed *Des femmes d'honneur: Une vie privée 1931–1968* and Adèle Lauzon's *Pas si tranquille: Souvenirs* – are memoirs, while the other two – Denise Bombardier's *Une enfance à l'eau bénite* and France Théoret's *Une belle éducation* – are autobiographical novels.

Together, these works provide a map of the geographical spaces associated with poverty in pre–Quiet Revolution Montréal. Three of the four (those of Payette, Lauzon, and Théoret) are situated in whole or in part in Saint-Henri, and the stark contrasts in the way the quartier is represented owe more to differences in family background and attitude than to changes in Saint-Henri itself over the decades. Both Payette and Adèle Lauzon were born in Saint-Henri in 1931, but, unlike Payette, Lauzon left the quartier at the age of eight or nine when her parents, in a change of social status that dramatically illustrates the class mobility of the prewar period, moved to nearby Notre-Dame-de-Grâce (NDG) and enrolled their daughter in the upper-class convent school Villa Maria. Born in 1942 in the east end area of Hochelaga-Maisonneuve, Théoret moved to Saint-Henri in 1956 at the age of fourteen when her father, a corner-store grocer, decided that the poor of Saint-Henri, lacking mobility, would be more likely to shop at a corner store than a more affluent population would be. Unlike the other three writers, Denise Bombardier grew up in the multi-ethnic working-class area of Parc-Extension in the north of Montréal.

Sherry Simon's chapter in this volume refers to the well-known correspondence between geography and language in pre-1960s Montréal, with the immigrant and multi-ethnic Saint-Laurent Boulevard ("the Main") as the dividing line between the English-speaking west and the French-speaking east sections of the city. Even before the deconstruction of these divisions she identifies in contemporary literary texts, there were obvious exceptions to this mapping, such as the French-speaking areas of Outremont and Saint-Henri, both west of the Main. As well, as Denise Bombardier's hilarious account of an alcohol-fuelled drive around the city taken by her narrator's dysfunctional family illustrates, the socio-economic realities of the various geographical locations were at least as significant to members of the francophone working class as their associations with language and culture. As they ogle the houses of the anglophone *nouveaux riches* of Ville Mont-Royal with their picture windows and impeccably manicured lawns, the narrator's aunt observes, "They're rich but they look stupid" (118).[4] In Outremont, the young protagonist discovers that there are people of her "race" who are as rich as the English but is shocked by her aunt's gossip about their immorality. In Westmount, her father contemptuously explains that the owners of the mansions they are driving by also own all the forests, mines, and lakes of the province: "Duplessis, the Prime Minister, gives them the whole province and you, the 'Culbéquois,' keep electing him ... Keep on speaking 'culbéquois.' Keep on learning the catechism. The English are quite happy with things. You're playing their game" (120).[5] Finally, as they go down the mountain and cross the railway tracks into Saint-Henri, the father's derogatory comments reinforce all the negative stereotypes of the area and its poverty: "This is where you belong. This is what French-Canadians are like! Look at how happy they are on their balconies, with a cross around their neck and a dozen children in the house!" (120).[6]

4 "Ils sont riches mais ils ont l'air bête."

5 "Duplessis, le Premier ministre, leur donne toute la province et vous, les "Culbéquois", vous continuez de l'élire ... Continuez de parler 'culbéquois.' Continuez d'apprendre le catéchisme. Les Anglais sont bien contents. Vous faites leur jeu."

6 "Ici, vous êtes chez vous. C'est ça les Canadiens-français! Regardez-les sur les balcons comme ils ont l'air heureux: la croix dans le cou, puis la douzaine d'enfants dans la maison!"

Linked not only with particular geographic and psychological spaces but also with social class, poverty can be regarded with pride (Payette), with shame (Bombardier), as the motor for a struggle for social justice (Lauzon), or as a paralysing force for conformity (Théoret). In each case, the narratives of class and poverty are inseparable from the equally important ones of language and gender: being French Canadian and speaking French in a city where power and wealth are the prerogatives of the English ruling class, and being a girl in French Canadian culture, with its rigidly defined gender roles.

Among the works examined, the struggle for voice is most compellingly presented in France Théoret's *Une belle éducation*, whose very title evokes the education in conformity imposed both at home and in school during the 1950s in Québec – an education which systematically annihilates any possibility of a language of the self: "Impossible to speak of oneself. Those who speak of themselves are conceited, boastful, egoists, self-centred" (48).[7] In striking contrast to Lise Payette's cheerful and matter-of-fact way of dealing with poverty, Théoret's protagonist Évelyne, who lives in Saint-Henri and attends the same school as Payette had a decade earlier, experiences it as a deadening and stifling condition, passed on from generation to generation by those who, through destiny or choice, have become complicit in perpetuating its injustices. The novel is a stark and uncompromising evocation of the absolute desolation of poverty, paradoxically beautiful in the precision and unsentimentality with which it evokes the intolerable. The space of poverty is claustrophobic, silent, and paralysed, shot through with repressed rage and hostility: a moral and psychological prison that mirrors the oppressive ugliness of the material conditions in which the characters live. The tiny, dark, rat-infested house the family inhabits is bare of ornament and cut off from the community by the mother's decree that the front door be permanently locked and that there be no contact with the neighbours. When her daughters begin to develop friendships at school, their mother tells them they do not need friends, that all the teenagers of the quartier are juvenile delinquents who will end up in reform school, and that their proper role is to stay at home and obey their parents.

7 "Impossible de parler de soi. Ceux qui parlent d'eux-mêmes sont des orgueilleux, nécessairement des vantards, des égoïstes, centrés sur eux-mêmes."

In an earlier, more explicitly autobiographical work, *Journal pour mémoire*, Théoret talked about the intense need for beauty she felt as an adolescent and the painful, almost unbearable sense of deprivation caused by the lack of beauty in her surroundings. "I was caught up with beauty, had the cult of beauty ... I couldn't live without it. My need to love was so vast that reality appeared sad and painful to me ... Beauty was my portable shadow, my unattainable share of eternity, the image I fused with" (203).[8] A similar sense of constriction and unexpressed pain are present in the starkly realistic descriptions of *Une belle éducation*, beginning with the novel's first sentence, evoking the family's arrival in Saint-Henri: "As soon as we arrive I notice the nudity of the street and the absence of trees" (9).[9] The lodging consists of a basement and a main floor. The basement has a kitchen lit by a bare light bulb, where no daylight penetrates, and an area containing an oil furnace with pipes extending to the ceiling, which they transform into a living room by installing a television and a rickety sofa bed. The main floor contains the bedrooms, which lack doors, and a toilet. From the perspective of the hypersensitive protagonist Évelyne, we observe the lack of privacy when she uses the kitchen sink for all personal ablutions, her inability to escape from hearing her parents' constant arguments about money, the unpleasant odours, and the regular appearance of huge rats, which her younger brothers, in a rage and need for violence they will carry with them for life, catch and hurl against the brick wall in the asphalt courtyard behind the house. Évelyne's father, obese and constantly complaining, spends his time in front of the television set and never speaks to the children. His anger extends in particular to his eldest daughter Évelyne, whose intelligence and timidity he resents, and whom he constantly reproaches for her refusal to work in his store. Évelyne's mother is equally authoritarian, angry, and silent. She hates and resents the "dark, smelly, and cold" house she is forced to live in, and refuses to cook, clean the house, do washings, or put curtains on the windows.

In spite of her parents' middle-class aspirations, Évelyne's life as she enters her high school years is one of poverty and unremitting duty: returning home at lunchtime every day to heat up canned food for her

8 "J'étais éprise, j'avais le culte de la beauté ... Il m'était impossible de vivre sans elle. Ma propension à l'aimer était si vaste que la réalité m'apparaissait triste et pénible ... Elle fut mon ombre portée, ma part d'éternité invivable, l'image à laquelle je fusionnais."

9 "Dès notre arrivée, je remarque la nudité de la rue et l'absence d'arbres."

younger brothers, who have already learned to laugh at her and taunt her with the word "servant"; putting up with the unpleasant smells and filth of the house; grabbing a quick half-hour at the kitchen table to do her Latin homework; and (like Florentine Lacasse in *Bonheur d'occasion*) admiring the fashionable clothes she sees in the boutiques on rue Notre-Dame without any hope of acquiring them. All of this becomes "a habit, a way of existing. I never imagine that it could be any other way ... I learn not to desire anything that I can't have" (43).[10] Like Florentine Lacasse, although more consciously, she sees herself repeating the destiny of her mother: "My mother's voice penetrates my hearing, implants within me the idea of the unhappiness of living, of the inevitable submission of woman to the authority of her husband, of the dispossession of self in the service of others" (29).[11]

Against this education in submissiveness, strongly reinforced by the school system, Théoret proposes a counter-narrative tracing Évelyne's struggle to exist as an autonomous individual. Sensing that her only possibility of salvation lies in "knowledge," and in spite of the opposition of her family and a total lack of financial support, she embarks on the tenacious, step-by-step construction of a self – a fidelity to a vividly evoked "interior voice" which will eventually take her to university, where she hides the conditions of extreme poverty she lives in from her carefree middle-class fellow students. Never, however, is this poverty left behind her: she knows it defines her identity and, once she has embarked on her career as a writer, vows to be true to its reality and its devastating consequences in everything that she writes.

While Payette almost breezes through poverty, strengthened and supported by the pride in her gender and culture instilled in her by her mother, and while Théoret's character stubbornly drags herself out of the ignorance and prejudices she has been surrounded with at home and at school, Denise Bombardier's unnamed narrator (whom I'll choose to call "Denise") inhabits the space of poverty isolated by the bubble of her own self-regard and talent for performance. A "class traveller" saved only by the honesty with which she later recounts the snobbery and competitiveness that ruled her childhood and made her want to be

10 "une habitude, une façon d'exister. Je n'imagine pas qu'il puisse en être autrement ... J'apprends à ne vouloir rien d'autre que ce que j'ai."

11 "La voix de ma mère traverse mon oreille, creuse en moi l'idée du malheur de vivre, de l'inévitable soumission de la femme à l'autorité de son mari, de la dépossession de soi au service des autres."

a "winner" at all costs, she becomes an expert in hiding her class and economic background as she navigates into a more bourgeois milieu.

From as early as its first sentence – "I made my First Communion in a state of mortal sin" (9)[12] – *Une enfance à l'eau bénite* is propelled forward by the narrator's sense of being "unique, exceptional" (9). Like France Théoret's character, she will live her Catholic childhood and adolescence with a constant sense of guilt, but, in contrast, she claims to have experienced that guilt not as paralysing but as "stimulating": "If I am the greatest of sinners in the eyes of God, I have to be the best in the eyes of the adults who matter to me: my parents and my teachers. I will reach my goal by my scholarly triumphs" (9).[13] With two anglophone families living on her street, Denise quickly learns English and chooses to speak it with her mother in the elevators of the department stores downtown: "Above all, no-one must guess my origins" (10).[14] Filled with shame that her father does not go to church, she hides the fact from her teachers and classmates through a series of ever more elaborate lies.

With the complicity of her mother, Bombardier's narrator constructs a narrative which denies the reality of their poverty and gives her a false sense of assurance that will last until adolescence. By stealing money from her husband's pockets, her mother manages to sew dresses that make her daughter look like a little princess, attracting admiring glances from people on the streetcar each Sunday when they visit the maternal grandparents. Enrolled from the age of three onward in the *cours de diction* that were an important part of growing up in the 1930s, 1940s, and 1950s for many young Québécois, Denise soon comes to establish the connection between "speaking well, being educated, and being rich" (18).[15] At school, her piety and her perfect French make her the teacher's pet, and she is often hated by other pupils; in grade 5, her classmates go to the principal and complain about both her and the teacher: "We're sick of having our French corrected. Of being told to talk like the teacher's pet" (96–7).[16] At home, she prefers to play with the English kids

12 "J'ai fait ma première communion en état de péché mortel."

13 "Si je suis la première des pécheresses aux yeux de Dieu, il me faut être la meilleure face aux adultes qui m'importent: mes parents et mes maîtres. Par mes réussites scolaires, je parviendrai à mon but."

14 "Pour rien au monde, on ne doit deviner mon origine."

15 "bien parler, être instruite, et être riche."

16 "On est tannées de se faire corriger notre français. De se faire dire qu'y faut parler comme le chouchou."

rather than the French ones, because they do not make her feel uncomfortable about her *niveau de langue*, and by the age of eight or nine she has come to see the French language, even when spoken well, as "a language of lower-class people and inferiors" (18).[17]

The key element in the counter-narrative offered by Bombardier is her revelation of the ways in which the performer herself succumbs to the illusion created by her performance. Far from seeing herself as poor, Denise condescends to the even poorer: the unfortunate schoolmates referred to as *les queues*, who sit in the back of the class smelling of urine and are constantly humiliated by the nuns: "When they have an accident Sister of the Holy Martyrs makes them wash up their own mess and leaves them with wet underwear stuck to their behinds until the class is over" (37).[18] When Denise herself has a similar accident the teacher makes one of the poor girls clean up after her and takes her off to find a clean pair of bloomers. As she returns to her seat, Denise, humiliated about what has happened but happy at the treatment she has received, lacks the courage to exchange looks with the poor "*queue*" who's been forced to clean up after her. In the schoolyard, she refuses to participate in games if any of the "*queues*" are present:

> And as we, the ones who are first in the class, are popular, my companions agree without any objection to chasing them out of the group. And all this in full view of our teachers, who aren't the least bit bothered by it. When Mademoiselle Tremblay, preparing our souls for our bimonthly confession, asks us: "Have you loved your neighbour as yourself?" it never occurs to me to feel guilty for my odious attitude towards these poor "*queues*." My neighbours are my equals. They are my inferiors. (46)[19]

Before she reaches high school, Denise has perfected the art of passing for rich. She never invites friends to her house, getting the wealthy

17 "une langue de déclassés et d'inférieurs."

18 "Lorsqu'elles s'oublient dans leur culotte, sœur des Saints-Martyrs les oblige à laver leur mare et les laisse, jusqu'à la fin de la classe, avec des sous-vêtements collés aux fesses."

19 "Et comme nous, les premières de classe, sommes populaires, c'est sans objection que mes compagnes les chassent du groupe. Cela, au vu et au su de nos maîtresses qui ne s'en formalisent guère. Lorsque, en préparant nos âmes avant la confession bimensuelle, Mlle Tremblay nous demande: 'Avez-vous aimé votre prochain comme vous-même?' il ne me viendrait jamais à l'esprit de me sentir coupable de mon attitude odieuse à l'endroit de ces pauvres 'queues.' Le prochain, ce sont mes égaux. Elles sont mes inférieures."

parents of the young people who attend the *cours de diction* with her to drop her off a few blocks from home, in a "better" part of the neighbourhood. But, more and more frequently, she feels overcome by the falseness of her situation, isolated in a world in which she is ashamed of those she loves and cannot reveal the truth about herself to anyone: "I'm ashamed of the people I love, and, by placing me in a milieu that is above the one I come from, my mother, without meaning to, has condemned me to an oppressive solitude" (62).[20] To escape, she throws herself into a mystical and guilt-ridden Catholicism, and, far more importantly, she discovers books. Her comments on the mistrust of books and ideas in the culture around her echo similar observations by France Théoret regarding the hostility to ideas in her milieu: "The public library system was little developed. And I hardly knew anyone who owned any books. To read I needed to have a will stronger than the apathy of my surrounding milieu ... Those who had too much education weren't trusted. They frightened people" (64–5, 68).[21] Faced with her father's fury at the truncated Catholic version of history she's being taught in school, she begins to wonder if indeed the goal of being scalped by Indians for the glory of God is an ambition she shares. At the age of eleven, she asks her mother to withdraw her from the *cours de diction*, feeling that she cannot compete with the rich and confident others in her class (112). Bombardier's story is, finally, an account of how she frees herself not only from the prejudices and stupidities that permeated the education system of her time but also from the narrative she has constructed about herself and her class origins. As the book ends, the narrator reflects that she now feels closer to her father (whose attitudes towards religion and politics, she realizes in retrospect, were ahead of their time) than she had felt herself to be during her childhood.

Unlike the previous works, Adèle Lauzon's memoir, *Pas si tranquille: Souvenirs*, is a story of poverty left behind at an early age but permanently imprinted on the author's consciousness by the stigmatization she undergoes in the upper-class milieu into which she is propelled by her

20 "J'ai honte de ceux que j'aime, et, en me projetant dans un milieu supérieur au mien, ma mère, bien involontairement, m'enferme dans une solitude accablante."

21 "Le réseau de bibliothèques publiques était peu développé. Et je ne connaissais guère de gens qui possédaient des livres. Pour lire, il me fallait une volonté plus grande que l'apathie du milieu qui m'entourait ... On se méfiait des gens trop instruits. Ils faisaient peur."

father's rise in economic status. In it, poverty and Saint-Henri represent a geographic and psychological space from which the author is exiled, but which she carries within her as a burning desire for social justice. The book does, however, contain a portrait of Saint-Henri in the late 1930s and early 1940s, as background to the story of Lauzon's father, whose entrepreneurial instincts and skills led him to wealth, fame, and political influence, bringing to mind the 1945 observation made by Lise Payette's teacher that the people of Saint-Henri are free to make of themselves what they will. As in *Bonheur d'occasion*, Saint-Henri is depicted at a point of transition, retaining elements of its former existence as a French Canadian, Catholic village but poised on the verge of an era of individual economic opportunity.

The story of Lauzon's father's ascent from poverty and of the class snobbery that meant Adèle was shunned as a "*fille de garagiste*" (mechanic's daughter) for years after her father had moved up in the social world offers a rare glimpse into the class mobility that was possible for some in pre–Quiet Revolution Québec and into the negative and condescending attitudes to poverty of many of the *nouveaux riches* who had themselves clawed their way out of poverty in previous generations. Born in Saint-Henri, Lauzon was the son of a baker and the seventh of nine children. Educated by the Franciscans at their Collège Séraphique in Trois-Rivières with the idea that he would become a priest, he learned Latin and Greek and developed a love of literature (Adèle is named after the daughter of his favourite poet, Victor Hugo), as well as the ambition of becoming a lawyer. Forced to leave school at seventeen to support the family when his father lost his job and fell into a serious depression, he exhibited the first sign of his entrepreneurial brilliance by renting a space in Saint-Henri, opening a bakery, and hiring his father to bake the bread. Within a few years, Lauzon bread was being delivered to many Montréal homes. A few years later, after lending his car to a friend for a few days at a small cost, he decided to buy another car and rent it out, soon becoming the owner of the first car rental firm in Québec. By the 1940s, he had founded a driving school, publicized by a popular radio program on driving etiquette called "Les Lauzons de conduite," with himself as host.

More privileged culturally in many ways than the other three authors discussed here, Adèle Lauzon grew up in a house where there were plenty of books, where girls were considered the equals of boys, and where there was pride in Québec culture. As a young girl, she was taken by her father to hear Henri Bourassa speak, and she remembers performing her first "acte militant" at the age of eleven: inscribing the words "VOTEZ

NON" in chalk on the walls of her neighbourhood as part of the 1942 anti-conscription campaign. Her memories of shopping with her mother, who insisted on being served in French in the downtown department stores, recall those of Gabrielle Roy in her autobiography *La Détresse et l'enchantement*, and differ dramatically from the experience of Denise Bombardier and her mother, who would do all they could to pass for English while shopping in the same stores. Like Roy, Lauzon is embarrassed by her mother's stubbornness ("I thought she was brave but I was ashamed because she created scenes, which upset me because I was extremely timid"),[22] but the example of resistance and the insistence on the right to speak her own language remain with Lauzon for life. Her nationalism is further stoked by her tense relationship with her anglophone neighbours after the family's move to NDG: "I was ... humiliated by the feeling that the English were in charge everywhere and that we were only their much too obliging servants" (12).[23] At the same time, she and her classmates are attracted by American movie magazines and fashion, some of them even speaking English among themselves to demonstrate their sophistication: "English got us out of the stifling world of the good sisters, the Church, sin, and mediocrity. Using the English language transformed our grey landscape into a sparkling background" (18).[24]

Unlike the absent (Payette), oppressive (Théoret), or sarcastic (Bombardier) fathers in the other three autobiographical texts, Lauzon's father is supportive and open-minded. When Adèle becomes known for her radical articles in the Université de Montréal student newspaper *Le quartier latin* and for her support for the asbestos strikers in 1949, Duplessis advises her father – by then president of the prestigious Club Richelieu – that he should tell his daughter to "keep quiet," to which Lauzon *père* replies, "My daughter thinks what she wants and writes what she wants" (27).[25]

A lifelong radical, Lauzon claims that her passion for social justice grew out of the accident of listening to a radio version of Dostoevsky's

---

22 "Je la trouvais brave mais j'avais honte parce qu'elle provoquait des esclandres, ce qui m'affolait, car j'étais extrêmement timide."

23 "j'étais ... humiliée par ce sentiment que les Anglais étaient partout les maîtres et que nous n'étions que des serviteurs parfois trop complaisants."

24 "L'anglais nous sortait du monde étouffant des bonnes sœurs, de l'Église, du péché, de la médiocrité. L'usage de la langue anglaise transformait notre paysage gris en une scintillante toile de fond."

25 "Ma fille pense ce qu'elle veut et elle écrit ce qu'elle veut."

Crime and Punishment as a teenager, having been led by its title to expect a detective story. Afterwards, the task of finding a copy of the novel in wartime Montréal was not an easy one, but her father managed to do so with the help of bookseller Henri Tranquille, an important player in the liberalization of Québec culture in the Duplessis era. For her, Raskolnikov represented "a fantasy of power that compensated for my feeling of being weak, small, dependent, French-Canadian and, what made it all worse, a girl" (13).[26] She was radicalized as well by her experience at Villa Maria, where the *nouveaux riches* francophone parents of her Westmount classmates, still threatened by their closeness to their own class background, refused to allow their daughters to associate with her ("you invited *that* to the house?"[27] says one of the mothers when she sees Adèle in her living room). The effect of this rejection, she writes, was not to make her hate the rich or seek revenge for her humiliation, nor to feel ashamed of her parents, but rather

> an acute consciousness of my dignity and of that of my parents, as well as a particular sensitivity to humiliation that would later have an influence on my beliefs. What counted most from then on was respect. The respect that would be paid to me and my family. And that I would have for others. The respect for all who deserved it because of their intrinsic value and not because of their membership in a social class, a race, a religion, or an ethnic group. (16–17)[28]

This respect for the dignity of all human beings, regardless of their class, race, religion, or ethnicity, will lead her to gravitate towards the Communist Party as a student in France in the 1950s, and eventually to marry the young Communist Michel van Schendel, who returned with her to Montréal and later became an important Québécois poet.

26 "un phantasme de toute-puissance qui compensait mon sentiment d'être faible, petite, dépendante, canadienne-française et, ce qui aggravait le tout, d'être une fille."

27 "tu as invité *ça* dans la maison?"

28 "une conscience aigüe de ma dignité, de celle de mes parents aussi, une sensibilité particulière à l'humiliation, qui influença plus tard mes convictions. Ce qui compterait désormais, c'était le respect. Le respect qu'on me porterait à moi et aux miens. Que je porterais aux autres aussi. Le respect pour tous ceux qui l'imposaient par leur valeur intrinsèque et non pour leur appartenance à une classe sociale, à une race, à une religion, à une ethnie."

Is it possible to arrive at any generalizations about the experience of poverty based on the autobiographical accounts of these four Québec women? While the shared experience of growing up poor, francophone, Catholic, and female provides a number of recognizable tropes (the school uniform, the Catholic guilt, the envy of English wealth and confidence), one is equally struck by the differences in the lives and the perceptions of these young girls. That such differences owe as much, if not more, to individual temperament and family influence as to larger economic and social conditions is illustrated by the contrasting experiences of Lise Payette and France Théoret at the same school, run by the sisters of Sainte-Anne in Saint-Henri. While Payette remembers the encouragement provided by one of her teachers after her disastrous experience of reading *Bonheur d'occasion*, Théoret's narrator recalls an education in submissiveness typified by a painful session in which she is berated at length by the school principal on the dangers of pride when she receives a high score on a provincial IQ test. But in spite of the differences in their experience of the formal education system, the common thread in all these stories is the passion for learning and knowledge, seen by all of these young girls as a way out of poverty.

These four texts, with their complex interweaving of the individual, family, social, and economic factors that can shape one's response to poverty, offer counter-narratives that contest conventional discourses about the poor. As well, they open up a rich vein of cultural history, illuminating the various shades of light and darkness that coexisted in Québec in the years before the Quiet Revolution. In spite of their differences, each of the authors is true to her background, not obscuring it or turning it into an "individualized trajector[y] of upward mobility," as Roxanne Rimstead has suggested is often the case in such narratives (174). Finally, with their focus on the determination and the passion for knowledge and dignity of young women "growing up poor" in the period, these works demonstrate some of the conditions that finally allowed women's autobiographical voices to emerge in Québec after three centuries of silence.

WORKS CITED

Bombardier, Denise. *Une enfance à l'eau bénite.* Seuil, 1985.

Godrej, Farah. "Spaces for Counter-Narratives: The Phenomenology of Reclamation." *Frontiers: A Journal of Women's Studies*, vol. 32, no. 3, 2011, pp. 111–33. JSTOR, www.jstor.org/stable/10.5250/fronjwomestud.32.3.0111.

Lauzon, Adèle. *Pas si tranquille: Souvenirs.* Boréal, 2008.
Payette, Lise. *Des femmes d'honneur: Une vie privée 1931–1968.* Libre expression, 1997.
Rimstead, Roxanne. *Remnants of Nation: On Poverty Narratives by Women.* U of Toronto P, 2001.
Roy, Gabrielle. *Bonheur d'occasion.* Beauchemin, 1945.
– *La Détresse et l'enchantement.* Boréal express, 1984.
Théoret, France. *Journal pour mémoire.* L'Hexagone, 1993.
– *Une belle éducation.* Boréal, 2006.

15 Tramping across the Nation: Homeless Embodiment in Canadian Literature

DOMENICO A. BENEVENTI

The social and spatial exclusion of the poor and the homeless has always been achieved through the stigmatization of their homes and neighbourhoods, the dehumanization of their "messy" bodies made to conform to state regimentation in social service agencies, and through the accusatory language which attributes vice, sloth, and physical and moral destitution upon their bodies. Since the nineteenth century, the poor have been equated with the residues of industrial production, where the dirty environments in which they toiled tainted their bodies, their neighbourhoods, and their social status (Sibley). The desire to keep the poor at arm's length constitutes what Samira Kawash has described as the "geographies of containment," in which the abject poor and especially the homeless undergo violent processes of physical and symbolic exclusion that seek to control their bodies and movements in the city, ultimately effacing their very presence from the public sphere. The sight of the dishevelled, dirty bodies of homeless men and, increasingly, women, on the street is disturbing to the mainstream public for it not only evidences the ongoing economic disparity in our societies and our own roles in the maintenance of the status quo but also suggests that we, too, may one day fall victim to extreme destitution. For these reasons and others (public order, charity, security, etc.), the homeless body is subjected to the controlling hand of the state.

While homelessness may simply describe the condition of being unhomed – of not possessing continuous, secure, and adequate shelter – it also extends, by virtue of association, to a variety of social, spatial, and bodily practices and material conditions that have historically been marked as abject, irrational, undesirable – even criminal.[1] Amir Marvasti argues that "mental illness has been used as a method of social control for responding to poverty and vagrancy" (9), citing three periods in the history of psychiatry corresponding to three conceptions of the homeless subject: pauperism, institutionalization, and deinstitutionalization. Pauperism was the means by which the itinerant poor were identified in the pre-Enlightenment era, before notions of mental illness delineated between normality and abnormality. It became a catch-all term ascribed to the insane, the feeble-minded, the poor, and the unhomed – thus eliding distinct subjectivities, identities, and specificities of need and care. The disposal of undesirables was achieved through public manifestations of state power, while poor laws "actively discouraged undesirables from settling in places where they were not wanted" (11).

In the mid-nineteenth century, institutionalization became the principle response to homelessness and mental illness, as the increased medicalization of the subject enabled the state to legitimate more subtle distinctions between the insane and the merely poor. The number of hospitals and asylums increased, as did the elaborate systems of compliance and control of the unruly, as Foucault has shown in his analyses of the prison and the hospital. The increased specialization of the psychiatrist – from essentially being caretaker and moral administrator to scientist whose knowing gaze bears the weight of institutional legitimacy upon the body of the patient – made it such that the patient became increasingly reducible to a collection of facts, data, and courses of treatment.

The deinstitutionalization of the mentally ill, which began in the 1950s, saw a corresponding and dramatic rise in the number of homeless on the

1 While the many definitions of homelessness (legal, sociological, anthropological, statistical, and even cultural) are too numerous to list here, each suggests a fundamental difficulty in arriving at an adequate understanding of this catch-all term for various forms of socio-economic destitution. The United Nations includes a reference to homelessness in article 25 of its Declaration of Human Rights: "Everyone has the right to a standard of living adequate for the health and well-being of himself and of his family, including food, clothing, housing and medical care and necessary social services, and the right to security in the event of unemployment, sickness, disability, widowhood, old age or other lack of livelihood in circumstances beyond his control" (www.un.org/en/documents/udhr/). For other definitions of homelessness, see Christopher Jencks's *The Homeless*, Peter H. Rossi's *Down and Out in America*, and David Levinson's *Encyclopedia of Homelessness*.

streets. While it was thought that the emergence of the welfare state would provide for those in need, the explosion of the homeless population in the United States, Canada, and elsewhere proved otherwise. Some have argued that rather than right past wrongs, deinstitutionalization "simply marked the emergence of a new form of 'community-based social control' that operated under the auspices of the welfare state" (Marvasti 15). The treatment of the homeless problem has increasingly centred on repressive policies that constrain the homeless person's social, physical, and economic mobility; legislation and policing which criminalize strategies of survival; economic and housing policies which assure the continued presence of a disadvantaged underclass; architectural and urban design practices that make homelessness increasingly difficult and conspicuous; and an ensemble of social, cultural, and media discourses which depict the poor as transgressive, criminal, deranged, and abject.

The problem of homelessness has been discussed extensively in social work, urban studies, sociology, and psychology but remains rare in literary criticism in Canada.[2] While there is a tradition within Canadian criticism of describing national identity in spatial paradigms (landscapes, territories, regionalisms), it is only recently that critics have begun to deal with urban themes in Canadian literature, and the few studies of working-class literature and of "poverty narratives" (Rimstead) have not specifically addressed the literary representation of the homeless body in Canadian urban spaces. While a literary history of homelessness in Canada has yet to be written, many works have depicted tramping and homelessness in the streets of Canadian cities. Hugh Garner's *Cabbagetown* (1968), arguably Canada's first urban novel, depicts poverty and homelessness in Depression-era Toronto. J.B. Vaughn's *The Wandering Years* (1975) is a tramping memoir of the "dirty thirties" revealing the underclass of hoboes, loggers, and transient workers constantly on the move across the country in search of employment. More recently, Evelyn Lau's *Runaway: Diary of a Street Kid* (1989) provides a brutal account of life on the streets of Vancouver from the point of view of a young female prostitute – discussed by Patricia Demers in this volume – and Robert Majzels's *City of Forgetting* (1997), discussed by Simon Harel in this collection,

2 See for instance, Jody Mason's *Writing Unemployment*; Lianne Moyes's article "Homelessness, Cosmopolitanism and Citizenship"; and my chapter "Exposed to the Elements."

presents figures from history, mythology, and literature as homeless wanderers in an economically depressed and violent city of Montréal. Any history of homelessness in Canada must take into consideration the overrepresentation of Indigenous peoples and visible minorities among their number, as well as the changing demographics of the homeless population, which increasingly includes women, children, and entire families.

If the discourses of nationhood are enmeshed within the literary, social, and political inscription of bodies, then the historical disavowal of the poor and the spaces in which they dwell reveals the exclusionary practices that operate in the construction of a national spatial imaginary. In the following pages, I will discuss the tramp narratives of the 1930s in Canada, where hobo jungles, train yards, and boarding rooms are figured as spaces of transition, resistance, and refuge.[3] While these extreme habitats may physically transform homeless bodies, rendering them grotesque, monstrous, and even unrecognizable *as human*, they also constitute spaces of resistance, solidarity, and refuge from the elements, from urban violence, and from the social stigma that too often renders them obscene. This view of the homeless body as a source of danger to spatial order and to the social closure implied in the idea of the public sphere results in its being marked as a pollutant that must be contained:

> The public view of the homeless as "filth" marks the danger of this body *as body* to the homogeneity and wholeness of the public. The desire or ambition for such wholeness thus faces an obstacle that may be ideologically disavowed but that always returns as an irreducibly material challenge. The solution to this impasse appears as the ultimate aim of the "homeless wars": to exert such pressures against this body that will reduce it to nothing, to squeeze it until it is so small it disappears, such that the circle of the social will again appear closed. (Kawash 329)

This is seen both materially and symbolically in the repressive police violence against vagrants that seeks to banish the offending body, and in the regimentation of the poor and the charitable inspection of their needful bodies through the various agencies that seek to reform them. The homeless bodies in these texts highlight the extreme conditions to which the poor have been forced to live, but also their agency in

---

3 For an engaging discussion of the nineteenth-century shantytown and the present-day Tent City, see D.M.R. Bentley's contribution in this collection.

adapting to and appropriating these spaces for survival. If life on the street sometimes transforms the bodies of the unhomed into abject residues of the marketplace, such "recalcitrant bodies,"[4] to use Erin Manning's term, highlight the failures of the socio-economic system rather than some "monstrous" aspect of homeless embodiment and identity.

Hobo Jungles and the Great Depression

In attempting to piece together a literary history of homelessness in Canada, one may arguably begin with the hobo or tramp narratives of the 1930s and 1940s which depict the transient lives of the thousands of unemployed men who took to the road in search of work in the years after the stock market crash of 1929. While there is a sizeable body of tramp narratives, histories, and critical studies in the United States,[5] where the figure of the wandering hobo has achieved iconic status, in Canada very few vagabond narratives were written, and their critical reception is practically non-existent.

While the hobo jungles that emerged at the peripheries of Depression-era cities – and sometimes at their very centres – were places rife with danger, they also linked vagabond men in networks of solidarity, community, and mutual aid. In his groundbreaking discussion of the figure of the tramp in American social, political, and cultural history titled *Citizen Hobo: How a Century of Homelessness Shaped America*, Todd DePastino notes that hobo jungles were populated by "armies of migratory workers and migratory non-workers who came to rest, eat, wash up, and trade information ... virtually all accounts of jungle life include examples of

4 "The recalcitrant body is not a homogeneous dweller. The recalcitrant body emerges in the interstices of the state, the home, and the nation, residing at its limits, calling forth the necessity to rhetorize the political according to the bodies that remain outside the bounded limits of what is ordinarily thought of as 'politics' ... These are bodies that rewrite the political by accommodating themselves outside the normative structures of containment ... Such recalcitrant bodies provide us with an opportunity not only to theorize unhomed bodies and spaces, but also to engage critically with the discourse of security at the level of the body of the nation" (Manning 56).

5 For a seminal, early work on the sociology of homelessness, see Nels Anderson's *On Hobos and Homelessness* (first published in 1923). See also John Allen's *Homelessness in American Literature*, Todd DePastino's *Citizen Hobo*, and Kenneth L. Kusmer's *Down and Out, on the Road.*

both hearty camaraderie and the various dangers that threatened to disrupt the jungles' idyll" (71). Hobo jungles were more than just makeshift tent cities in which the unemployed and the down-and-out took refuge; they were complex homosocial spaces of racial, gender, and class conflicts and solidarities, engaged political radicalism, and subcultural forms of expression.

DePastino argues that the subculture of "hobohemia," as he describes it, constituted a serious challenge to a nation guided by reigning middle-class beliefs in private nuclear families, moderate domestic consumption, and steady work. Shifting constructions of poverty and vagrancy shaped and were shaped by larger debates around issues of domesticity, citizenship, and the welfare state, as well as race and gender status and expectations, particularly as they are defined and expressed in public space (xix). The roots of hobohemian subculture can be traced back to the late nineteenth century, when "a veritable army of homeless men" (xviii) spread out across the country in search of employment after the American Civil War in 1865. His analysis of a vast wealth of historical material produced by and about hobo communities reveals that homelessness was not simply the socio-economic condition of disempowerment and social marginality but also a position of agency, solidarity, concrete political action, and counter-discursive cultural practices. If the hobo way of life was "characterized by casual lodging, temporary labour, and frequent migration" (xviii), the vagabond populations had many means by which they contested social, political, and economic policies of the state. Through their pamphlets, newspapers, and songbooks, DePastino writes, "these organizations also disseminated a powerful set of hobo myths that enhanced group definition and celebrated hobohemia as a revolutionary vanguard" (xx). The figure of the vagabond as romantic outlaw thus embodied the emerging conflict between "nineteenth-century domestic ideals [and] the new realities of urban industrial life" (xviii), where public space was increasingly occupied by diverse types of bodies engaged in various types of activities.

If the figure of the vagabond has a certain measure of recognizable cultural currency in the United States, forming in fact a part of the romanticized mythology of unfettered freedom and movement westward, such a narrative is practically non-existent in Canada. This is not to suggest that hobo communities did not exist in this country, for while there were significant homeless communities throughout Canadian history, most discussions of homelessness have centred on its more recent incarnations since the 1980s, with emphasis placed on the urban transient and the visibly homeless on the streets. Earlier forms of homelessness – such as makeshift shantytowns and encampments during Canada's early period of settlement, immigrant and Native forms of homelessness, and the significant numbers of hobo villages and relief camps that popped up across the country during the Depression – have simply not entered into the spatial histories and imaginaries of Canada. As Todd McCallum points out, "Canada's homeless wanderers of rails and roads never gained the minor stardom afforded hobo writers in other countries ... the bulk of knowledge about Canadian Depression-era homeless men lies in government archives, [and] in documents produced within the framework of relief administration" (49).

In the following pages, I will examine the intersections of mobility, sexuality, and gender performances in the hobo or vagabond subcultures of the 1930s and 1940s, and attempt to show how these marginal spatial practices influenced and were influenced by discourses of national identity – particularly in terms of the desirable or undesirable citizen, in terms of state control over the type of activities permitted in public spaces, and in terms of the privileges and restrictions afforded to gendered and racially marked bodies. Through a close reading of Andrew Roddan's *Vancouver's Hoboes* (2004), first published in 1948 under the title *God of the Jungles*, J.B. Vaughn's *The Wandering Years*, published in 1975, and Jean-Jules Richard's *Journal d'un hobo*, published in 1965, I hope to uncover some of the marginalized spaces of hobo embodiment and interaction as counter-narratives of the mainstream spatial histories of Canada.[6] Where Roddan's testimonial of his years working among the homeless in Vancouver reveals the growing moral panic around the ever-increasing numbers of vagrants and vagabonds – inscribing onto their very bodies a symbology of dirt, sin, and moral and social corruption – Richard's novel celebrates the emancipatory possibilities of moving

6 It should be noted that the three texts under analysis in this chapter are fictionalized memoirs that look *back* to the Depression era for the material of their fictions. Each reveals particular ideological, political, and even aesthetic approaches to the experiences of homelessness; where in Roddan the language and tone is one of care and rehabilitation of the poor, we can see in Richard's *Journal d'un hobo* and Vaughn's *The Wandering Years* moments in which homelessness is presented as a romanticized experience of freedom and the open road, characteristic of the writing that emerges in the Beat and counterculture eras – seen, for instance, in Jack Kerouac's *On the Road* (1957).

along peripheral spaces and locations while exploring alternate sexual and gender identities.

Andrew Roddan provides one of the few rare glimpses into the hobo jungles in Depression-era Canada, where he describes his encounters with the homeless in his role as minister of the First United Church at the intersection of Gore and Hastings Streets, an area of Vancouver that to this day remains notorious for its homelessness and drug-addiction problems. As a form of memoir or engaged reportage, Roddan's essay is invaluable in that it reflects prevailing attitudes about poverty in general and the vagabond in particular at the historical cusp of Canada's industrialization and urbanization, which took place in the 1940s. While Roddan's charity work in the "absolute degradation" of the hobo jungles was "tempered by the Social Gospel," and by the conviction that the hardships of the vagabond men he witnessed were ultimately attributable to personal failings of morality, virtue, and character, he nevertheless acknowledges that the migrant workers who were once an "indispensible factor in the building of Canada" were summarily "cast aside when no longer needed" (ix).

Andrew Roddan describes the "dramatic growth of hobo jungles right in the heart of the city" (ii), which provided temporary shelter for as many as 200 individuals, most typically men. Todd McCallum points out that the hobo jungles were constructed for the most part by the homeless themselves, and order was established and maintained by them as well. "While far from harmonious," he writes, "jungle life was predicated on reciprocity in the distribution of food, drink, cigarettes and other goods ... jungles thus allowed the homeless to live a relatively autonomous existence, free from the prying eyes of social workers" (v). If these transients were a community that exhibited class solidarity, mutual aid, and even their own slang and forms of cultural expression distinct from that of the larger society, their increased visibility created moral panic that equated their dirty bodies with threats to the "peace, order, and good government" of an emerging nation. Roddan's text thus vacillates between moralizing criticism of the poor and a more humane understanding of and solidarity with the downtrodden. From his point of view of charity, the vagabond was seen as either an object of scorn or one of pity, a categorization which corresponds to notions of deserving and undeserving poor first introduced by Nels Anderson of the Chicago School in his studies of the homeless in the 1920s, and which are taken up here by Roddan. There are thus three types of vagabond: "the hobo who works and wanders, the tramp who dreams and wanders, and the bum who drinks and wanders" (Roddan iv). Each of these categories of vagrancy suggests different shades of social respectability, from hapless victim of market forces – the deserving poor – to drunken derelict unable to control his own appetites – the undeserving poor. This dual image of poverty opposes the desirable citizen from the undesirable one. Thus, if "robust men of grit and ability" who immigrated from far-off places such as Finland, Germany, and Scandinavia have been "indispensable in the building of Canada," they were, as a result of the Depression, "wasting their lives in idleness through no fault of their own" (Roddan 20). The more unsavoury types, the "human derelict ... rudderless and waterlogged" in contradistinction, are seen as "a menace to all who cross their paths" (26). Images of nation-building on the strong backs of manual labourers are set against those of the abject homeless who actively undermine social order – through their refusal to work, their moral failings, and the indulgence of their vices and appetites.

Roddan depicts the hobo jungle as a lawless state of nature residing at the limits of civilization, where "the light of the sun rarely penetrates": "the haunt of wild beasts and savage men" who may be found "in clumps of wild bushes or among the trees, on the side of a stream, by the side of the road, near the railroad tracks, or in a disused lumber camp or factory" (17). These spaces of transition (train stations, the edges of town, jungles), which tramps strategically occupy so as to avoid detection or more easily escape from if they are arrested, are negatively coded and morally suspect in the spatial imaginaries of nationhood – in contradistinction to the institutionalized spaces of economic privilege, familial domesticity, and state power. Their makeshift dwellings, composed of the refuse of respectable society, are read not as self-sufficiency but as symbols of their morally fallen condition: "old tins, boards, boxes, disused motorcars, anything and everything, gathered from the dump heap nearby and formed into a rough shelter into which crawl, not animals, but homeless men" (17).

Roddan's sympathy for the downtrodden and his genuine fascination with the vagabond subculture (their slang, their manner of vestment, their habits that flout social convention) are repeatedly undermined by a moralizing tone which ascribes all manner of degeneracy to the itinerant's character, body, and behaviour. But if Roddan sees in the salty slang of the vagabond evidence of their perverse natures, it is language faithful to the material realities of disenfranchisement, one given to resistance through linguistic subterfuge that excludes the privileged. The minister is both repulsed and fascinated by words such as moocher (for beggar), dummy (the art of playing dumb), blinker (blind beggar), canned heat artist (wood alcohol drinker), flopper (curbside beggar), peg (vagabond who lost a foot), or stick (one who lost both feet). This linguistic play suggests understanding and irony, subversion of and resistance to expected meanings, as well as a cutting criticism of the social and economic inequalities that have marked their bodies in sometimes brutal ways.

In spite of itself, Roddan's text subtly demonstrates that the vagabond community does in fact have agency, employing various strategies of resistance through shared knowledges, subversive communication, mutual aid, and group solidarity across vast networks of urban and rural spaces in order to circumvent social, economic, and physical harassment and exploitation.[7] By leaving signs in rail yards, train stations, and city buildings intended to tell other hoboes there is safe passage to be had, by sharing information about work opportunities or police repression across vast stretches of the continent, and by using slang inaccessible to the non-vagrant, the mobile vagabond communities of the 1930s and 1940s are "outlaw bodies" that "rewrite the political by accommodating themselves outside of the normative structures of containment" (Manning 56).

If the hobo jungles represent the dwellings of the abject poor on the peripheries of mainstream, institutionalized social spaces, the railway networks, train yards, and indeed the train itself represent sites of vagabond subterfuge, tenacity, and survival. Riding the rails encompassed the complex intersection of the material realities of class, subversive knowledges and practices, and constructions of the hobo as outlaw. As a historical reality and a narrative conceit, it brings together a dense symbology of dirt, the marginalized body in social space, the disciplinary discourses of civility and domesticity, but also the operations of gender, race, and class within the vagrant community itself.

In J.B. Vaughn's memoir *The Wandering Years*, the life of the vagabond is defined by the need to move into, through, and out of the spaces of poverty: boarding homes, unsafe factories, tenements, rail yards, work camps, and the open road. But "riding the rods," as Vaughn describes it, is the most constrictive space of poverty, involving, quite literally, laying in the compressed space of 2.5 feet between the spinning iron wheels of the train and its undercarriage. Thousands of men were injured or lost

7 In his chapter in this collection, D.M.R. Bentley shows that such political mobilization of the homeless has endured to the present day in his discussion of the media attention generated by Toronto's Tent City, which was eventually demolished in 2002.

their lives in this subversive form of travel born of economic necessity, which transforms the body of the vagrant through exposure to dirt and also through violence incurred from rail authorities or "yard bulls," RCMP officers, other vagrants, and the trains themselves: "When a man comes into the jungles after having been on the train for a week or two weeks, you would not know whether he was white or black. Dust begrimed he comes in, no questions are asked" (Roddan 20). Ken Tilling, the protagonist in Garner's *Cabbagetown*, is forced by poverty to ride the rails across a "hungry country ... his peaked cap was pulled down over his ears against the grit and smoke, and his face ... sunburned under its black bituminous coating" (171). Arriving in Jasper, the narrator of *The Wandering Years* remarks, "Soot and cinders had made me filthy; my eyes were sore and bloodshot. Young men, neat and lean, passed me with a disgusted casual glance. My humiliation was far less to be endured than the hardships of the road" (Vaughn 61).

The vagabond life demands specialized knowledges of survival and resistance, and as J.B. Vaughn makes clear, travelling this way "gets to be an art," for "it is essential that you know just where to catch the train, get to know the whistles, the lights, the flags on the engines and learn to distinguish between a red-ball freight and a local ... It also takes precise timing to grab the ladder on a boxcar to board a fast train. Many a man has been swept to his death under the wheels because he didn't judge correctly" (16). Just as the bodies of the working poor are transformed by poverty and subjected to violence by the industrial machinery of the work camp or the factory floor, here the vagabond's body is quite literally torn apart by the fierce and unstoppable power of the train. This image of the railway, as source of mortal danger to the disenfranchised, undoes the narrative of freedom, enterprise, and nation-building characteristic of mainstream constructions of the railway in Canada.

Hobosexualities

The hobo communities of the 1930s and 1940s were complex homosocial subcultures with networks of class solidarity and interdependence, yet they also contained racialized and gendered performances which both mirrored and contested those in the larger society. From the point of view of the mainstream observer, homelessness often effaces distinctions of race and gender, as Samira Kawash argues: "as a specific form of embodiment, the homeless body is not an identity but an emergent and contingent condition that occludes identity" (324). That is to say, particular social markers of age, ethnicity, and gender upon the body are blurred and, consequently, individuality and agency are reduced to the status of simply being unhomed. But from the point of view of the homeless person, nothing could be farther from the truth, as these distinctions will have profound effects upon the lived experience of homelessness, whether in terms of personal safety or in terms of the available networks of solidarity and aid. Vagabond communities were far from welcoming to all, for race and gender mediated the homosocial spaces of the hobo jungles and other areas in the city where transients congregated. From ethnic hierarchies within hobo jungles to the exploitation of women or the young among their number, "racialized and gendered meanings," DePastino writes, "shaped entitlements and exclusions of social citizenship" (xix).

DePastino's notion of "hobosexuality" offers up a context for thinking not only about the material conditions and social dynamic within which vagabonds moved across variegated landscapes of employment, need, and desire, but also about questions of gendered and classed performances and expectations that mediated those encounters. What were the assumptions of class, race, and gender, for instance, which entered into encounters between mobile transients or between those who were homeless and those who were not? How did they meet, and in what ways did these encounters constitute forms of outlaw embodiment within the larger mainstream understanding of the fixed nature of social cohesion and community defined by the distinction between public and private realms and identities? DePastino points out that the spaces in which and through which vagrants encountered each other grew out of the "cultural and neighbourhood associations of the working class, operating through networks of cafeterias, poolrooms, saloons, theatres, social clubs, parks, baths, and rooming and lodging houses" (85). Already negatively marked as the domains of the poor, these spaces were located outside of the disciplinary spheres of family and domesticity and thus enabled more "subversive" behaviours, including drinking, gambling, petty crime, and sexual encounters. Thus, homeless districts such as the Bowery in New York City provided "venues for highly visible modes of erotic interaction" (85). The romantic ideal of freedom on the road was often also an opportunity for unfettered sexual experimentation, whether with female prostitutes or with other transients, and hobo sexual practices must therefore be understood within the context of "general assumptions about sex and gender that pervaded working-class culture in the late nineteenth and early twentieth centuries" (DePastino 89). This did not necessarily emphasize the sex of one's partner but rather valuation of the gender "status" in terms of masculinist notions of personal freedom, autonomy, and independence from the constraints of family, domesticity, and social norms, laws, and conventions.

In his testimonial, Roddan reserves his harshest criticism of the vagabond for a section titled "The Sex Life of the Hoboes." Here, Roddan describes the lure of the big city for vagabonds, particularly for the "young and more attractive women who ply their trade"; when the hobo is "penniless and ragged," he associates with "the lowest of the low" (53). Hoboes spread venereal disease, thus becoming "a menace to all with whom he associates" (53). This "debauchery," Roddan suggests, is to be expected from such a population of men living "far removed from the influence of pure and true womanhood." Gender roles and expectations are imbricated in the spatial divisions of labour and capital; indeed, "true womanhood" remains in the private sphere of the home, where it does not challenge male economic power and privilege, while those who venture out are seen as fallen; similarly, males who are unable or refuse to be domesticated in their labour as in their sexuality are also seen as perverse.

Roddan worries that homosexuality has "come into vogue" among the homeless, for in their fear of infection by prostitutes, they turn to each other for sexual gratification; moral panic around homosexuality is thus described in both spatial and economic terms – the perversion of not working, of being idle, and of engaging in questionable activities in marginal locations is conjoined with the perversion of homosexual desire. A doubled image of the hobo – as homosexual predator upon the social and economic resources of the nation, and as sexual predator feasting upon its robust youth – falls in line with historical constructions of homosexuality as deviance. The tramp is "a real menace for the unwary youth," who is "immediately spotted by one of these old hardened rascals ('wolf'), who will worm himself into the good graces of the boy and keep him for his own unlawful use" (53). DePastino argues that such predatory relationships evidenced not only the homosexual undercurrent in hobo subcultures but also its "larger gender ideology that encouraged masculine domination. Coercing, cajoling or enticing punks [young initiates] into sex, jockers [older hoboes] offered in exchange protection, money, or general instruction in the skills of begging, freight hopping and securing food and shelter" (87). Sexuality among the hobo populations in many ways reflected larger gender roles and expectations, with the older male assuming the more dominant role over a more docile and even feminized younger man, who was often, ironically, seen as the more degenerate for seeming to be weaker and having a compromised masculinity. But DePastino also points out that not all homosexual practices among the vagabond were coercive and exploitative, and that there were in fact "more equitable homosexual relationships between hoboes" (90).

Worrying Gender

If, as Doreen Massey has argued, gender is in part constructed through its "intricate and profound connection to place and space," what are we to make of a vagabond figure who subverts not only the spatial practices and expectations of class but those of gender and sexual identities as well? If the spatial mobility of women has traditionally "pose[d] a threat to a settled patriarchal order" (11), how does a woman who is not quite one navigate the spatial interdictions and privileges accorded to each gender? The unnamed narrator of Jean-Jules Richard's *Journal d'un hobo* attempts to do just that; as a hermaphrodite who straddles both male and female identities, he/she escapes the "tyrannies de la famille" (16) in small-town New Brunswick in order to embark upon a journey across Canada, revelling in the sexually charged possibilities of being on the road as "un hors-la-loi et un apostat des conventions" (103). The dual identity of the "bardache," as he is so named by l'homme-sorcier, the Native elder to whom he is brought as a child by his mother, is expressed through the child's repetitive use of the self-reflexive "j'étions," "je savions" (16), and of the conjoined pronouns of IL/ELLE in moments of identitary crisis: "le balancier de ces deux présences en moi, ELLE et LUI, me donne le vertige" (39).

Ambiguities of gender and sexuality are explored in the marginalized spaces of transit of the vagabond: railcars, flophouses, and the open road, brothels, seedy taverns, and street corners where petty criminals congregate and where prostitutes ply their trade. As Victor-Laurent Tremblay suggests in the only published critical appraisal of this seemingly forgotten Québec novel, "la découverte de soi nécessitant un besoin d'espace et de liberté autant physique que psychique" (65).[8] Thus, in the contact with a variety of spatial configurations and body types, the androgyne undertakes various forms of passing – for male or female

8 "the discovery of self, necessitating a space of liberty that is both physical and psychic."

depending upon spatial environments and expectations – or passing between English and French in the translation of sexual encounters. A second order of translation is suggested in the narrator's attempt and, ultimately, inability to communicate his or her unique subjectivity as both male and female, most crucially at the end of the novel when his/her true gender status is revealed.

The figure of the androgyne, as Tremblay suggests, evokes the identitary crisis in Québec before, during, and after the Quiet Revolution, where sexual politics conjoined with identity politics, particularly in terms of colonialism figured as the transvestism or feminization of the francophone population in Québec: "Cette figure imaginaire, dont l'apparition dans l'histoire symbolise à la fois les moments de crise mais aussi l'espoir d'un renouveau, est née au Québec ... avec le roman de Richard, lors d'une période particulièrement fertile en contestation et en attente de toutes sortes" (84). The androgyne in this novel brings to mind Michel Tremblay's *Hosanna* (1973), staged during the same period in the early 1970s, where gender performances enact an inscription of identity politics on and through the body, and the revelation of one's true identity through a ritualized divestment is read as a symbolic act of decolonization. This same movement of revelation appears in Richard's novel, only it is a question of revealing not one's true gender but one's sexual status as both male and female and the ultimately untenable position of being in between: "Trahis par les deux êtres les plus chers de mon existence. C'est fini. Fini la vie généreuse, la prédestination de mes deux sexes en un seul corps" (Richard 284). The desire for escape from a constrictive and sexually repressed society pushes the androgyne to the open road, where the life of the vagabond becomes a revolutionary ideal: "si chaque vagabond avait le courage d'un seul acte de représailles par jour, on viendrait à bout de la voracité des riches et de leurs points d'appui: la police et la morale" (106). The protagonist organizes a "marche pour la faim" at the end of the cross-country journey, but that utopian vision is blemished by the material hardships and physical dangers of life on the road.

The various moments of passing which structure the novel point to the gendered marking of spaces and of the activities permitted within them. The indeterminate gender and sexuality of the protagonist offer up a variety of subject positions and expectations; from the sexually exploitable child observed by a priest in a confessional "avec appétit, comme un plat de petits oiseaux," to the transvestite sex worker on the streets of Montréal, to the androgynous rail-hopping "fillion" in the hyper-masculine subculture of the hoboes. When he/she enters a tavern in Montréal described as a "débit exclusif de bière ... pour hommes seulement," for instance, the narrator's androgynous appearance elicits the predatory gaze of men drinking in the bar: "j'évite des regards trop exactes braqués sur moi ... un homme dodu me montre le bout de la langue tandis que le trajet de ses yeux me désigne une piste vers la table" (77). When the little money he has is stolen by his own brother, he asks the bartender how one survives in the city alone: "Trois choses. Quêter, voler, ou bien vendre sa peau" (78). Wandering the streets, he is taken in by a sympathetic group of prostitutes, "les quatres dames en déshabillé ... la Comtesse, la Marquise, Lady Melba, Alice Récamier, Maria Chapdelaine" (79), only to discover that they too are passing, for they are in fact transvestite prostitutes (80) who offer him a room to stay in in exchange for working in the brothel.

Leaving the city, the narrator is confronted with the same dangers more commonly associated with women in public spaces – including potentially sexually exploitive encounters with other vagabonds – and must therefore hide his/her gender status. The railway is described as "une pieuvre, [qui] s'étend dans toutes les directions," and the men hidden within the train cars are described not as shifting, shuffling scavengers but rather as hidden adventurers stepping lightly across a vast terrain that is otherwise hostile to them: "abouchés les uns aux autres, de mystérieux pouvoirs les font circuler. Ils glissent dans la nuit ... on dirait des danseuses de ballet en grandes robes" (95). This conjunction of bodies on the train makes for a space of camaraderie and, sometimes, recognition, a "tangle of humanity" which suggests erotic possibility, as in one scene in which the narrator comes across a sleeping vagabond in a boxcar: "J'éteins le mégot et je m'assimile lentement au corps du dormeur. Sentant la chaleur, il s'ajuste à mon orbite et nous embarquons sur la même étoile filante. Une main glissée sous son bras rencontre un coeur qui se niche volontiers entre mes doigts" (120).

But close physical contact and opportunities for erotic interaction did not, as DePastino points out, "explain desire or performance. Indeed, while close quarters and shared beds may have facilitated sex between hoboes, they also generated taboos against homosexual behaviour," and hobo communities "raised strict prohibitions against eroticizing their relationships" through "the protocol of circumspection and reciprocal guardedness" (87). The figure of Le Moustachu, for instance, who pursues the androgynous narrator throughout the novel, embodies this aggressive masculinity and questions his/her ambiguous gender through threats and coercion: "On te présente comme une fille, on le croit, et quand on réussit à t'approcher, on se demande si c'est vrai. Fais voir. N'essaie pas de déguerpir, je te pousse en bas du train" (192). The hardships of living on the road – in close, cramped conditions in boxcars, flophouses, and homeless shelters – brought men into close physical contact, and this proximity was sometimes played out through the extremes of violent aggression. This is the case when the narrator's performative masculinity is discovered by the other vagabonds on the train: "La nouvelle circule vite, comme le feu dans l'essence ... Lui! Celui de la manche courte, c'est ... c'est une fille" (182). What follows is a scene of gang rape and violence that brutally re-enacts the gendered coding of the spatial and the assumption that women in public space are by definition sexually exploitable.

Both Roddan's *Vancouver's Hoboes* and Jean-Jules Richard's *Journal d'un hobo* reveal the construction of the hobo in the Depression era as perverse menace to the emerging middle class, since their peripatetic lives challenged the status of the home as "a central place of being and building block of social order ... [and thus] rejecting the range of manners, morals, and habits associated with middle-class domesticity" (DePastino xx–xviii). This often resulted in moral panic around the figure of the transient and, as evidenced in Roddan's text, their portrayal as a perverse threat constantly lingering on the peripheries of the nation. Richard's novel goes even further in questioning the gendering of the spatial through the transgressive possibilities of bodily performance and passing. Indeed, the common images of bodily transformation in vagabond travel narratives is doubled by the gender transformations of the narrator. Thus, along with the usual images of "vêtements poussiéreux, pantalons tordus autour des jambes. Figure masquée de crasse" (99), we find the striking adjacency of male and female corporality which conjoins the gendered performativity of the streetwalker or prostitute with the slow shuffle of the haggard homeless: "Je marche la tête de côté pour me voir passer dans toutes les vitrines et je passe bien quand même. Mais je ne suis pas moi. Je suis une petite bonne femme masculine attirant la curiosité ... Moi, flâneuse, n'ayant même pas de sac à main. Où est-ce que je le mets, mon fric? Dans le corsage? Et la poudrette, le rouge à lèvres?" (223). As Judith Butler makes clear in *Undoing Gender*, "the body has its invariably public dimension; constituted as a social phenomenon in the public sphere, my body is and is not mine. Given over from the start to the world of others, bearing their imprint, formed within the crucible of social life, the body is only later, and with some uncertainty, that to which I lay claim as my own" (21).

Discourses around the homeless, particularly in terms of the representation of their bodies and their scandalously peripatetic lives detached from the disciplinary institutions of home, domesticity, and civility, demonstrate the moral panic of a society attempting to rein in its messy collective body and defining its national character, its economic structures, and its spatial borders. The anxiety elicited by the recalcitrant bodies of the dispossessed speaks volumes about national mythologies and collective memories that depend upon the control of its physical spaces and the bodies that move upon them. Bums, vagabonds, hoboes, the homeless – all are interpellated by state power, but each may use physical spaces strategically in order to subvert that power and, in so doing, create alternate mappings of the national imaginary.

WORKS CITED

Allen, John. *Homelessness in American Literature: Romanticism, Realism, and Testimony*. Routledge, 2004.

Anderson, Nels. *On Hobos and Homelessness*. U of Chicago P, 1998.

Beneventi, Domenico. "Exposed to the Elements: Homelessness in Recent Canadian Fiction." *Canada Exposed / Le Canada à découvert*, edited by P. Anctil, A. Loiselle, and C. Rolfe, Peter Lang Publishing, 2009, pp. 85–100.

Butler, Judith. *Undoing Gender*. Routledge, 2004.

DePastino, Todd. *Citizen Hobo: How a Century of Homelessness Shaped America*. U of Chicago P, 2003.

Foucault, Michel. *Naissance De La Clinique*. Presses Universitaires de France, 1988.

– *Surveiller Et Punir: Naissance De La Prison*. Gallimard, 1975.

Garner, Hugh. *Cabbagetown*. Ryerson Press, 2002.

Jencks, Christopher. *The Homeless*. Harvard UP, 1995.

Kawash, Samira. "The Homeless Body." *Public Culture*, vol. 10, no. 2, 1998, pp. 319–39.

Kusmer, Kenneth L. *Down and Out, on the Road: The Homeless in American History*. Oxford UP, 2001.

Lau, Evelyn. *Runaway: Diary of a Street Kid*. HarperCollins, 1989.

Levinson, David, editor. *Encyclopedia of Homelessness*. SAGE, 2004.

Majzels, Robert. *City of Forgetting*. Mercury Press, 1997.

Manning, Erin. *Ephemeral Territories: Representing Nation, Home, and Identity in Canada*. U of Minnesota P, 2003.

Marvasti, Amir. *Being Homeless: Textual and Narrative Constructions*. Lexington Books, 2003.

Mason, Jody. *Writing Unemployment: Worklessness, Mobility, and Citizenship in Twentieth-century Canadian Literatures.* U of Toronto P, 2013.

Massey, Doreen. *Space, Place, and Gender.* U of Minnesota P, 1994.

McCallum, Todd. "*Vancouver through the Eyes of a Hobo*: Experience, Identity, and Value in the Writing of Canada's Depression-era Tramps." *Labour / Le travail*, vol. 59, Spring 2007, pp. 43–68. journals.lib.unb.ca/index.php/LLT/article/view/5842/6847.

Moyes, Lianne. "Homelessness, Cosmopolitanism and Citizenship: Robert Majzels' *City of Forgetting.*" *Canadian Studies*, vol. 64, 2008, pp. 123–38.

Richard, Jean-Jules. *Journal d'un hobo.* Parti pris, 1965.

Rimstead, Roxanne. *Remnants of Nation: On Poverty Narratives by Women.* U of Toronto P, 2001.

Roddan, Andrew. *Vancouver's Hoboes.* Subway Books, 2004.

Rossi, Peter H. *Down and Out in America: The Origins of Homelessness.* U of Chicago P, 1989.

Sibley, David. *Geographies of Exclusion.* Routledge, 1995.

Tremblay, Michel. *Hosanna suivi de La duchesse de Langeais.* Leméac, 1984.

Tremblay, Victor-Laurent. "L'Androgyne dans *Journal d'un Hobo* de Jean-Jules Richard." *Studies in Canadian Literature / Études en littérature canadienne*, vol. 21, no. 2, 1996, pp. 62–88.

Vaughn, J.B. *The Wandering Years.* Hancock House, 1975.

Afterword

ROXANNE RIMSTEAD AND DOMENICO A. BENEVENTI

If there were ever any doubt that contestation over space has the power to protest and destabilize as well as explain the relation between the "haves" and "have-nots," two events that took place during the compiling of these chapters testified to a globalized movement from below and a growing concentration of wealth and privilege from above: the Occupy Wall Street (OWS) movement of 2011, which originated with the Canadian anti-consumerist magazine *Adbusters*,[1] and the Québec student movement of 2012, the largest mobilization of youth ever in North America. It took a deep consciousness of the growing rift between the rich and the poor, the monied and propertied elites versus the disenfranchised and disposable youth, to get people out into the streets to protest in such great numbers in a largely apathetic and unevenly affluent Western country like Canada. These emergent struggles over the practice of owning and controlling space within unregulated capitalism – including virtual control in the increasingly rapid exchange and speculation over capital, or concrete control in the policing of public spaces – remind us, as did ancient bread riots and sixties sit-ins, that contestation is so often spatialized as a performance because it defies the power of elites over lived space. Contestation also often seeks to block the fluid networks of exchange by which capital is moved physically and virtually. A case in point is the red square as icon of the student demonstrations in Québec in 2012: this contestation was over cultural space and cultural access in the sense that tuition-fee hikes spelled the financial and cultural exclusion

1 Martin Kaste, "Exploring Occupy Wall Street's 'Adbuster' Origins," NPR, 20 Oct. 2011, www.npr.org/2011/10/20/141526467/exploring-occupy-wall-streets-adbuster-origins.

of large portions of Generation Y by limiting access to higher education for a group who could already see joblessness on their horizon. As David Camfield surmised in *New Socialist*, the contestation over cultural and financial space soon occupied concrete space and spilled over into the possibility of solidarity and dissent, as well as concerted movements to take back the public space of the streets: "The movement's symbol, a red square (first used in 2005, because higher tuition would put students 'squarely in the red'), was soon being worn by tens of thousands of people and made visible in other ways on the streets and online."[2] The viral symbol of the red square went global (even Mick Jagger and Arcade Fire sported a red shirt and red felt square with safety pin, respectively), thus spatializing the conflict in terms of its allusion to concrete space and alternative futures and national spaces, newly imaginable to disenfranchised youth. Solidarity and dissent from capitalism evoked the Red Square in Moscow and the unthinkable notions of anti-capitalism, coupled with the countercultural reverberations of "Classe," the name of one of the most militant student organizations in Québec. Social justice is often won through contestation and the struggle over symbolic territory, which usually mark, in some fundamental way, disputes over material space (land use, public space, institutional space), cultural space, discursive space, embodied space, or transformable and mobile space (flows, marches, etc.).

How is conflict represented as spatiality in literary texts and popular cultural performances? In what ways do marginalized individuals and communities represent, contest, or appropriate spaces as counter-discourses or as expressions of culture from below? And how does spatiality shape conflict, counter-memory, and culture from below? These are some of the questions we have confronted in this volume on contested spaces. We have focused on contestation over harmony and consensus in order to disturb idealist constructions of space and to carry literary analysis and cultural studies into spaces often undetected and unforeseen, although they figure prominently in the literature itself. Instead of a neoliberal and modernist focus on mobility, flows, and liquid rapidity, we have brought sustained attention towards the increasing control of spaces from above, the systemic entrapment and enclosure of subjects from below, as well as their fantasies of escape, and the management of

2 David Camfield, "Quebec's 'Red Square' Movement: The Story So Far," *New Socialist Review*, 5 Aug. 2012, newsocialist.org/quebec-sredsquaremovement.

voices, bodies, and memories in public space along with the transgressions made possible through counter-narratives. Currently in cultural and literary studies in Canada, we are more likely to valorize papers on the contestation of skateboarding in urban space than on the sensation of entrapment in inner-city public housing projects because the fantasy of individual liberty is more popular than materialist approaches to conflict over lived space. This collection has attempted to show that multiple approaches to contestation and transgression are needed to expose the power interests behind the complex production of space.

We have revisited iconic spaces in Canadian and Québécois literatures and cultures in order to refigure the city, to rewrite the unclean, and to expose the exclusions of urban and national space and the hidden order of monumentalized space. But we have also tried to find the possibility and hope that exist in spaces of community and solidarity, new or old, and the purposeful optimism of social movements as well as the more directionless meanderings and journeys of walking and riding through lived space. It is not only the narratives themselves that test and contest space in these ways but also the (re)readings of these narratives that contest old and new meanings. Crosstown journeys, slumming, tramping, and streetwalking are not, however, merely peripatetic meanderings but practices of space that trace a social logic often tied to beliefs and assumptions about above and below, inclusion and exclusion, being and non-being. Furthermore, Labour Day parades, protest demonstrations, border-crossings, and other transgressions may dramatize spatial conflict in terms of collective spectatorship or suppress its story in terms of secret and subterranean movements. Contestation occurs on a continuum of visibility, with the oppressed often adopting hidden transcripts to challenge space, while elites dominate space more openly through visual, legal, memorial, and military means, with a sense of entitlement that makes their claims to space seem normative, familiar, and orderly. As we claimed in the introduction to this collection, "Contestation does not always announce itself as such, nor is it always what it announces itself to be."

Contributors

Domenico A. Beneventi is an associate professor of English and comparative literature at Université de Sherbrooke. His research interests and publications focus on Canadian and Québécois literatures, urban writing, gender and queer studies, and representations of marginality in the city. He is co-editor (with Roxanne Rimstead and Simon Harel) of *La lutte pour l'espace: Ville, performance, et culture d'en bas* (Laval UP, 2017), co-editor (with Lianne Moyes and Licia Canton) of *Adjacencies: Minority Writing in Canada* (Guernica, 2004), and guest editor of a special issue of *Canadian Literature* called *Queer Frontiers* (2015). He is the director of the VersUS research centre at Université de Sherbrooke. In 2017, he was Visiting Professor of Canadian Studies at the Christian-Albrechts-Universität in Kiel, Germany.

D.M.R. Bentley is recognized as a leading authority on Canadian and Victorian literary and cultural studies. Particularly interested in the long cultural continuity that exists in Canadian literature, Bentley's studies span the country's history, pre-dating Confederation and continuing to contemporary works. His scholarship on pre-Confederation poetry is widely credited with defining and even creating the area of study. Bentley, who recently received the first Premier's Discovery Award for the Arts & Humanities, is also renowned for pioneering work in Canadian ecocriticism and on cultural and social memory in Canada. He is a member of the Royal Society and a Distinguished Professor at University of Western Ontario. Among his publications are *The Confederation Group of Canadian Poets, 1880–1897* (U of Toronto P, 2004); *The Gay[Grey Moose: Essays on the Ecologies and Mythologies of Canadian Poetry 1690–1990* (U of Ottawa

P, 1992); numerous critical editions of early Canadian works; and the journal he founded, *Canadian Poetry*.

Amaryll Chanady is a professor of comparative literature at the Université de Montréal and chair of the Département de littératures et langues du monde. Her main areas of specialization are inter-American studies, Latin American literature and culture, collective identity, hybridity, and postcolonialism. Among her publications are *Entre inclusion et exclusion: La symbolisation de l'autre dans les Amériques* (Honoré Champion, 1999), *Latin American Identity and Constructions of Difference* (editor; U of Minnesota P, 1994), and *America's Worlds and the World's Americas* (co-editor; U of Ottawa P, 2006).

Natasha Dagenais obtained her PhD in comparative Canadian literature at the Université de Sherbrooke, where she lectures in English literature and translation. The title of her dissertation is *Testimonial Life Writing as Cultural Survival: Indigenous Voices from Canada and West Africa*, an intercultural study of life writing by Indigenous subjects as a site of testimony to personal and collective survival. Her research interests include Canadian literature, Indigenous writing from Canada and Africa, testimony, prison narratives, poetry, and literary translation. For the ongoing Culture from Below project, she did research on radical autobiography and testimony, as well as on domestics and prisoners. In addition, she co-edited the online bibliography on Culture from Below at culture-from-below.recherche.usherbrooke.ca.

Patricia Demers, FRSC, is a cross-appointed professor in the Department of English and Film Studies and the interdisciplinary program in comparative literature at the University of Alberta. She researches and teaches in the areas of early modern literature, women's writing, children's literature, and contemporary Canadian women's writing. Recent publications include *Women's Writing in English: Early Modern England* (U of Toronto P, 2005), Hannah More's *Coelebs in Search of a Wife* (editor; Broadview Press, 2007), and *From Instruction to Delight: An Anthology of Children's Literature to 1850* (editor; OUP, 2008). *The Beginning of Print Culture in Athabasca Country – A Facsimile Edition and Translation of a Prayer Book in Cree Syllabics* appeared in 2010 from University of Alberta Press. Other publications are *Travels and Tales of Miriam Green Ellis: Pioneer Journalist of the Canadian West* (editor, U of Alberta P, 2013) and an annotated edition of Lady Anne Bacon's translation of Bishop John Jewel's "Apologia Ecclesiae

Anglicanae": *An Apology or Answer in Defence of the Church of England* (Modern Humanities Research Association, 2016), along with essays on early modern writers Lady Margaret Beaufort, Lady Anne Cooke Bacon, and An Collins, and Canadian novelists Patricia Blondal and Grace Irwin. She chaired the Royal Society expert panel and its subsequent report on the status and future of Canada's libraries and archives, *The Future Now: Canada's Libraries, Archives, and Public Memory* (2014).

Jeff Derksen is an associate professor of English at Simon Fraser University and dean and associate provost of Graduate and Postdoctoral Studies working with an interdisciplinary view of culture and globalization in the twentieth century. His areas of special interest are national cultures and the role of the state in the era of globalization; cultural imperialism and the politics of aesthetics; the poetry and poetics of globalized cities; the emergent global cultural front (in a general cultural context and in avant-gardes); culture and gentrification in global-urban spaces; architecture and urbanism; and cultural poetics, cultural studies, and cultural geography.

Alan Filewod is a professor of theatre studies at the University of Guelph. His books include *Committing Theatre: Theatre Radicalism and Political Intervention in Canada* (Between the Lines, 2011; winner of the Ann Saddlemyer Award, Canadian Association for Theatre Research; and shortlisted for the Gabrielle Roy Prize, Association for Canadian and Québec Literatures); *Collective Encounters: Documentary Theatre in English Canada* (U of Toronto P, 1987); *Performing "Canada": The Nation Enacted in the Imagined Theatre* (Textual Studies in Canada, 2002); and, with David Watt, *Workers' Playtime: Theatre and the Labour Movement Since 1970* (Currency Press, 2001). He is the editor of several anthologies. His current research centres on the history of radical political theatre in Canada. He is a past president of the Canadian Association for Theatre Research and of the Association for Canadian and Québec Literatures / Association des littératures canadiennes et québécoises and is a former editor of *Canadian Theatre Review.*

Mary Jean Green is a professor emerita of French at Dartmouth College in New Hampshire. She has published on women writers of the francophone world, including *Women and Narrative Identity: Rewriting the Québec National Text* (McGill-Queen's UP, 2001). She is currently completing a book on women and the writing of history, which will include discussions of Régine Robin, Maryse Condé, and Assia Djebar.

Simon Harel is a professor in the Département de littératures et de langues du monde at the Université de Montréal and was previously director of the Département de littérature comparée for a number of years. Trudeau laureate from 2009 to 2012, he is also a member of the Royal Society of Canada. Over the last twenty-five years he undertook an innovative field of research in literary and cultural studies and was one of the first academics to discuss migration in Québec society. *Voleur de parcours* (XYZ), published in 1989, is considered one of the most significant contributions of the 1980s and 1990s in the field of cultural studies in Québec. He has written and edited over thirty publications and has been interested in questions of interculturalism, the status of the Other in society, and the question of precarity. Recent publications include *Les passages obligés de l'écriture migrante* (XYZ, 2005), *Braconnages identitaires: Un Québec palimpseste* (XYZ, 2006), *Espaces en perdition I: Les lieux précaires de la vie quotidienne* (Laval UP, 2007), *Espaces en perdition II: Humanités jetables* (Laval UP, 2008), and *Été 1965: Fictions du Hobo* (Nota Bene, 2017; finalist for the Gabrielle Roy Prize). He is co-editor (with Domenico Beneventi and Roxanne Rimstead) of *La lutte pour l'espace: Ville, performance, et culture d'en bas* (Laval UP, 2017).

Candida Rifkind earned her PhD in English from York University. She is presently associate professor in the Department of English at the University of Winnipeg. Rifkind specializes in modernism and anti-modernism in Canada, popular and leftist writing, and graphic narratives. Her book *Comrades and Critics: Women, Literature, and the Left in 1930s Canada* was published by the University of Toronto Press in 2009. She has published articles in numerous journals and in the critical anthologies *The Canadian Modernists Meet* (U of Ottawa P, 2005), *Wider Boundaries of Daring: The Modernist Impulse in Canadian Women's Poetry* (Wilfred Laurier UP, 2009), *Canadian Literature and Cultural Memory* (Oxford UP, 2014), and *Material Cultures* (Wilfred Laurier UP, 2015). Rifkind is currently working on a manuscript titled "The Continuing Adventures of Canadian Modernism: Serial Fiction from Pulp to Prestige." Her essay "When Mounties Were Modern Kitsch: The Serial Seductions of Renfrew of the Mounted" won the F.E.L. Priestly Prize (ACCUTE) for 2013. In 2016, she co-edited with Linda Warley *Canadian Graphic: Picturing Life Narratives* (Wilfrid Laurier UP), which won the Gabrielle Roy Prize for Canadian Criticism.

Roxanne Rimstead has published internationally on cultural studies, feminist criticism, textual resistance, working-class culture, poverty and literature, oral histories, and Canadian literature(s). Her book *Remnants of Nation: On Poverty Narratives by Women* appeared in 2001 (U of Toronto P) and won the Gabrielle Roy Prize. She is co-editor (with Domenico Beneventi and Simon Harel) of *La lutte pour l'espace: Ville, performance, et culture d'en bas* (Laval UP, 2017). An early essay on Emily Carr's *Klee Wyck* won the Don D. Walker Award (Western Literature Association). In 2003, she guest-edited a special issue of *Essays on Canadian Writing* called *Cultural Memory and Social Identity*, and more recently a special issue of *Canadian Literature* with Deena Rymhs on prison writing/writing prison. A professor at the Université de Sherbrooke, Rimstead teaches comparative Canadian literature/littérature canadienne comparée and English and intercultural studies. She has been member of the editorial boards of *Canadian Literature, Tulsa Studies in Women's Literature*, and *Race, Gender & Class: An Interdisciplinary and Multicultural Journal* (SUNO). Her current research is on culture from below as a concept to be reworked within cultural studies (see culture-from-below.recherche.usherbrooke.ca/). In 2017, she received the title of honorary professor from Universidad de Holguin, Cuba.

Deena Rymhs is an associate professor in the Department of English at UBC. Her research examines narratives of incarceration with a particular focus on Indigenous writers. She is the author of *From the Iron House: Imprisonment in First Nations Literature* (Wilfred Laurier UP, 2008). Deena is currently working on her next SSHRC-funded book, *Directing Traffic: Roads, Mobility, and Violence in Indigenous Literature.* This project explores racialized and gendered experiences of mobility and provides a larger audit of mobility, risk, land use, territory disputes, and the social and cultural impacts of industry on First Nations communities.

Rita Sakr is a lecturer in world literature at Goldsmiths, University of London. She is the author of *Monumental Space in the Post-Imperial Novel: An Interdisciplinary Study* (Continuum, 2012; Bloomsbury, 2013), and of *"Anticipating" the 2011 Arab Uprisings: Revolutionary Literatures and Political Geographies* (Palgrave Macmillan, 2013). With Caroline Rooney, she is co-editor of *The Ethics of Representation in Literature, Art and Journalism: Transnational Responses to the Siege of Beirut* (Routledge, 2013) and co-director and co-producer of the Research Councils UK–funded documentary on Beirut, *White Flags* (2014). With Finn Fordham, she co-edited *James Joyce and the Nineteenth-century French Novel* (Rodopi, 2011).

Sherry Simon is a professor in the French Department at Concordia University. She was co-editor of the Québec cultural review *Spirale* for ten years and directed the interdisciplinary PhD in humanities program at Concordia University from 1995 to 2000. Among her publications are *Fictions de l'identitaire au Québec* (in collaboration; XYZ, 1989); *Le trafic des langues* (Boréal, 1994); *Gender in Translation* (Routledge, 1996); *Culture in Transit* (editor; Véhicule, 1996); *Hybridité culturelle* (Éditions Île de la tortue, 1999); *Translating Montréal: Episodes in the Life of a Divided City* (McGill-Queen's UP, 2006; Gabrielle Roy Prize winner), which appeared in French translation in 2008 as *Traverser Montréal: Une histoire culturelle par la traduction*; and *Cities in Translation: Intersections of Language and Memory* (Routledge, 2011), which appeared in translation in 2013 as *Villes en traduction: Calcutta, Trieste, Barcelone et Montréal.* She is the co-editor, with Paul St-Pierre, of *Changing the Terms: Translating in the Postcolonial Era* (U of Ottawa P, 2000) and, with Pierre Anctil and Norman Ravvin, of *New Readings of Yiddish Montréal – Traduire le Montréal Yiddish* (U of Ottawa P, 2007). She is a member of the Royal Society of Canada and a Killam Research Fellow (2009 to 2011).

Patricia Smart is Distinguished Research Professor and Chancellor's Professor Emerita in the Department of French at Carleton University. She was the recipient of the Governor General's Award for *Écrire dans la maison du père* (Québec/Amérique, 1988), and her own translation of the work, *Writing in the Father's House* (U of Toronto P, 1991), received the ACQL Gabrielle Roy Prize. Her monograph *Les femmes du Refus global* (Boréal, 1998) was a finalist for the Governor General's Award. She is also the author of *Hubert Aquin, agent double* (PUM, 1973) and of a critical edition of the autobiography of Claire Martin, *Dans un gant de fer* (PUM, 2005). Her critical history of women's autobiography in Québec, *De Marie de l'Incarnation à Nelly Arcan* (Boréal, 2014), won the Gabrielle Roy Prize in 2014 and the Jean-Éthier-Blais Prize in 2015 and was a Trillium Award and a Governor General's Award finalist for 2015. She self-translated this book for McGill-Queen's University Press and it appeared as *Writing Herself Into Being* in 2017. Pat Smart is a member of the Royal Society of Canada and received the Order of Canada in 2004.

Index

www.ingramcontent.com/pod-product-compliance
Lightning Source LLC
LaVergne TN
LVHW041112090826
844660LV00061B/719/J

* 9 7 8 1 4 4 2 6 2 9 9 0 5 *